P+P   Nn 1985   No 109

p. 44.

PEASANTS AND LORDS IN MODERN GERMANY

Recent Studies in Agricultural History

Edited by

ROBERT G. MOELLER
Columbia University

Boston
ALLEN & UNWIN
London   Sydney

Allen & Unwin, Inc.,
8 Winchester Place, Winchester, Mass. 01890, USA

George Allen & Unwin (Publishers) Ltd,
40 Museum Street, London WC1A 1LU, UK

George Allen & Unwin (Publishers) Ltd,
Park Lane, Hemel Hempstead, Herts HP2 4TE, UK

George Allen & Unwin Australia Pty Ltd,
8 Napier Street, North Sydney, NSW 2060, Australia

First published in 1986

Library of Congress Cataloging in Publication Data

  Peasants and lords in modern Germany.
Includes index.
1. Peasantry – Germany – History – Addresses, essays, lectures.
2. Peasant uprisings – Germany – History – Addresses, essays, lectures.
3. Farm tenancy – Germany – History – Addresses, essays, lectures.
4. Agriculture and state – Germany – History – Addresses, essays,
lectures. I. Moeller, Robert G.
HD655.P34 1985 305.5′63 85–6113
ISBN 0–04–943037–8 (alk. paper)

British Library Cataloguing in Publication data

  Peasants and Lords in modern Germany: recent studies in agricultural
history.
1. Peasantry – Germany – History 2. Germany – Rural conditions
3. Land use, Rural – Germany – History 4. Germany – Rural conditions
I. Moeller, Robert G.
305.5′63 H1339.G4
ISBN 0–04–943037–8

Set in 10 on 12 point Bembo by Computape (Pickering) Ltd, N. Yorkshire
and printed in Great Britain by Mackays of Chatham

Contents

For Hans Rosenberg

Acknowledgements

This book grew out of my discussions with Jonathan Osmond, Hanna Schissler, Josef Mooser and other friends who share a common interest in modern German agrarian history. I took on the task of co-ordinating the project, but without the co-operation, support, patience and enthusiasm of my co-contributors, I could never have seen it through to the end. To them I owe particular appreciation and thanks. David Blackbourn read through a preliminary version of the completed manuscript and offered excellent suggestions for revision. A grant from the National Endowment for the Humanities provided funding for translations from the German of the articles by Schissler, Mooser and Hans-Jürgen Puhle. Lynn Mally took time from her research on the Russian Revolution and proletarian culture to do the difficult work of translation, and her efforts deserve particular recognition.

The contributors to this volume along with all other students of modern German agrarian history have learned an enormous amount from the writings of Hans Rosenberg. His pioneering studies of the Junkers and his work in nineteenth-century agrarian history are models of social historical scholarship. It is to him that this book is dedicated.

Introduction: Locating Peasants and Lords in Modern German Historiography

ROBERT G. MOELLER

Historians of modern Germany generally agree that peasants and lords were among those 'pre-industrial' groups most resistant to political and economic change in the nineteenth and twentieth centuries.[1] In particular, conservative agrarians are identified as important and vigorous opponents of Germany's advance towards democratic, parliamentary government. In the English-language literature, the culpability of conservative agrarians has, however, more often been asserted than analysed and explained. A comparison of the range of recent studies in German agrarian history with the treatment of other countries highlights the extent of this relative neglect. For example, the rich literature which permitted Eugen Weber to describe the process by which peasants were made into Frenchmen finds no equivalent in the historiography of modern Germany.[2] There is no study comparable to F. M. L. Thompson's *English Landed Society in the Nineteenth Century*,[3] nor does Teodor Shanin's provocative sociological analysis of the Russian peasantry, *The Awkward Class*,[4] find a ready counterpart in the German literature. The rich cross-fertilization of French agrarian history by historical sociologists like Charles Tilly[5] or political scientists with a keen sense of historical development like Suzanne Berger[6] similarly is without parallel in the English-language literature on Germany.

The basic outlines of agricultural development which emerge from any general treatment of modern German history can be summarized briefly. Agricultural producers appear in the historical literature to make their contribution of food and surplus labour to early industrialization, and peasants struggle with land-hungry nobles in the wake of the Stein-Hardenberg reforms at the beginning of the nineteenth century. Some peasants join the forces of revolution in 1848, protesting the last vestiges of the feudal order, while others ally with lords to play a major supporting role in the conservative reaction to the revolution. Both peasants and lords are crucial elements in the conservative foundation of Bismarck's Reich and sworn enemies of Weimar democracy, and both are infamous

1

as particularly zealous and overrepresented supporters of National Socialism.[7]

To be sure, some German historians have undertaken serious attempts to fill in these outlines. Moving beyond a narrow concentration on technological change, crop rotations and modification of legal property ownership relations, historians in the Federal Republic of Germany have re-examined the agricultural revolution of the eighteenth century, revising the standard view that the agricultural sector was static before the Stein-Hardenberg reforms.[8] This work has confirmed and amplified the findings of Wilhelm Abel, whose innovative study *Agrarkrisen und Agrarkonjunkturen* first appeared in 1935.[9] Abel's concentration on the inter-relationship among demographic movements, production, prices and wages anticipated in many ways the primary concerns of subsequent generations of social and economic historians, but like those who have followed his lead, his studies end in the first part of the nineteenth century.

Studies of the nineteenth and twentieth centuries by German authors have frequently moved away from prices and changes in production to politics. Particularly important in this regard were the studies of Hans Rosenberg whose work described the evolution of the east Elbian elite as a social, economic and political ruling class from the sixteenth to the nineteenth century.[10] Strongly influenced by Rosenberg, Hans-Jürgen Puhle's research focused on the institutional and ideological forms which the Junkers created to pursue their anti-democratic objectives in the late nineteenth century. His study of the Agrarian League (*Bund der Landwirte*) provided not only a detailed investigation of the adaption of east Elbian estate-owners to the realities of mass politics during the Wilhelmine period, but also established an important model for investigations of other pressure groups.[11] The outlines of Puhle's study, revised almost twenty years after its initial publication, appear in English for the first time in this volume.

Politics, particularly as practised by conservative, east Elbian estate-owners, remained primary as well in Jens Flemming's treatment of the National Rural League (*Reichslandbund*), the successor in Weimar to the Agrarian League. Flemming skilfully picked up the story of the Junkers where Puhle left off, tracing the history of these conservative, aristocratic agrarians through the First World War and into the Weimar Republic.[12] The agricultural policies of the national government and the major political parties in the same period have been discussed in the comprehensive study of Martin Schumacher,[13] and Dieter Gessner has pursued this topic into the last years of Weimar.[14] Rudolf Heberle's 1932 analysis of the origins of peasant support for National Socialism in Schleswig-Holstein still stands out as a model study of that topic,[15] and this micro picture has been complemented by the discussion of National Socialist electoral tactics and programme in the work of Horst Gies and others.[16]

These efforts by German historians in West Germany have been complemented by the work of their colleagues in the German Democratic Republic. Working within a Marxist–Leninist framework, they have also devoted considerable attention to agriculture's eighteenth-century contribution to economic development, particularly the nature of technological change which preceded and in some senses necessitated the political reforms from above in the early nineteenth century. In addition, their work on this period has illuminated the patterns of rural class formation brought about by the agrarian reforms.[17] East German historians have also attempted to confirm Lenin's thesis of the 'Prussian path' to economic development according to which the future of agrarian change in Germany was irreversibly shaped by a reform from above, not a popular revolution from below. The preservation of large estates and large capitalist peasant holdings by the Stein-Hardenberg reforms permanently anchored the political power of the estate-owning class, the Junkers.[18] The central importance of this structure of landownership determined the social relations between estate-owners and agricultural labourers, and the terms of 'class' conflict between these two groups has defined another major area of East German research.[19] A preoccupation with the Junkers is further evident in GDR research into the role of the agrarian elite in the collapse of Weimar.[20]

These contributions to a history of the agricultural sector and agrarian politics in modern Germany are far from negligible, but they remain scattered villages in a landscape of social and economic history dominated by factories, cities and the workers and industrialists who populated them. Moreover, as this brief review makes clear, what literature exists has been written almost exclusively by Germans, a sharp contrast with the agrarian histories of other European countries which have drawn investigators from outside their own borders.

Why have English-language historians shown so little interest in the agrarian history of an industrial Germany? This neglect cannot be explained by the disappearance of peasants and lords from the historical scene. Table 1.1 tells the story of agriculture's *relative* decline, but it is worth emphasizing that in absolute terms the agricultural sector continued to hold its own long after industrialization was a fact of life in Germany. Nor were peasants and lords to be found only east of the Elbe or in a heavily agrarian Bavaria. Even in the proximity of important industrial centres in Germany like the Ruhr and Saxony, peasants continued to survive and even prosper in the surrounding countryside. Industrial concentration in some areas led to the 'agriculturalization' of others.[21] Moreover, although agriculture employed only a quarter of all Germans in 1939, this was an impressive share compared to the 1940 figure for the United States, 17·6 per cent, or the figures for Belgium

Table 1.1 *Contribution to Gross National Product (Percentages)*

	Agriculture	Industry and Mining
1848–54	45·2	21·2
1870–4	37·9	31·7
1895–9	30·8	38·6
1910–13	23·4	44·6
1930–4	20·5	41·8
1955–9	8.2	59.9
Share of active employed labour force		
1849–58	54·6	25·2
1878–9	49·1	29·1
1895–9	40·0	35·7
1910–13	35·1	37·9
1933	33·9	32·6
1939	27·4	40·8
1955–9	16·5	46·8
Absolute numbers employed (000s)		
1849	8,298	3,491
1871	8,541	5,017
1900	9,754	9,525
1913	10,701	11,720
1925	9,778	12,451
1933	9,034	8,713
1939	10,855	16,227
1955	4,527	10,902

Source: Walther G. Hoffmann, *Das Wachstum der deutschen Wirtschaft seit der Mitte des 19. Jahrhunderts* (Heidelberg and Berlin, 1965), 33, 35, 204–6.

(17·3 per cent) and the United Kingdom (6·0 per cent) for 1930 and 1931 respectively.[22]

In Germany, and for that matter in many other Western European industrial countries as well, the absolute numbers of those employed in agriculture did not decline dramatically until after 1945 as mechanization of production increased significantly. Even in post-Second World War Europe, small-scale family farming has continued to survive. The division of Germany and the collectivization of large estates in the east finally eliminated the large landholding estate-owners, but in the west agrarian interests continue to wield considerable social and political influence. Anyone who forgets this need only think of the headaches which the agricultural sector continues to give economic planners in the European Common Market.[23]

The dearth of studies of peasants and lords is thus not explained by the

4

dwindling numbers of those earning their livelihoods from work in the agricultural sector. Neither is it a reflection of a general indifference to social and economic history among those who study modern Germany. Indeed, these areas have been veritable growth industries since the 1960s. In the process, a historiography, once restricted by the narrow confines of a Rankean framework in which the decisions of great men and the clash of great nation states determined the course of history, has been substantially rewritten. The project has involved not only German historians but also many British and American historians of modern Germany. Measured on any scale, the output of these social and economic historians has been extremely impressive. In particular, they have devoted substantial attention to the history of the working-class movement, the economic interest groups which dominated German political life and the economic trends which shaped social and political phenomena. By comparison, the dimensions of agricultural development and agrarian politics remain poorly illuminated.[24]

Not surprisingly, those who see themselves as part of this continuing attempt to recast the outlines of German social, economic and political history and are drawn to the study of agriculture have reflected on the reasons for their relative isolation. Ian Farr, in the introduction to his contribution in this volume, offers some suggestive thoughts. He notes the limited degree to which local and regional history, particularly appropriate for the study of rural society, have been practised in Germany, and the conceptual and theoretical short-sightedness of many of those local studies which *do* exist. He also identifies the reluctance of German historians to employ the methods of social anthropology, family history and demography, disciplines still burdened by unpleasant associations with Nazi racialism, but none the less particularly well suited for the investigation of peasant life and culture.[25]

Building on Farr's insights, we can add another plausible explanation for the relative neglect of the countryside in the recent contributions to German social and economic history. The generation of historians which has undertaken the task of re-evaluating modern German history has in many instances shared an implicitly socially critical perspective, often strongly informed by Marxist theory.[26] The understandable concern with establishing the historical development of a progressive political tradition in Germany – or explaining its absence – has led, one might argue, to a corresponding fascination with the successes and failures of the most 'progressive' historical force, the working class, or with its most immediate oppressors, the entrepreneurial elite. Rural social relations fit much less readily than those created by industrial capitalism into the categories of class analysis which many of these historians often implicitly or explicitly employ. This is hardly surprising given that Marx himself had

5

no particular interest in or sympathy for the countryside and the 'idiocy of rural life'.[27] Engels was no less outspoken in his contempt for peasants whom he discarded in the 1890s as 'completely beyond redemption' and 'vestigial survivals from a bygone method of production'.[28]

Perhaps Marxists and neo-Marxist historians share their mentors' contempt for rural society. Certainly the Social Democratic Party programme of 1891, the famous Erfurt Programme, which long described the attitude of most German socialists to the peasantry, predicted the peasantry's eventual disappearance as the laws of the concentration of capital went to work in the countryside, destroying 'petty commodity producers'. Although the Erfurt Programme was subsequently modified, the attitude of many socialist-minded German historians often seems to have changed very little. The peasantry's reluctance to fulfill Marxist predictions is taken as an index of its failure to accept the realities of an industrial society.[29] Like Social Democratic politicians of the 1890s, socially critical historians seem to have written off the agricultural sector, leaving it to be organized by their conservative colleagues.[30]

This disdain for the 'idiocy of rural life' also resounds in analyses of peasant political attitudes. For Marxist and many liberal historians, the economic backwardness of peasants is matched only by their consistent rejection of progressive politics. Indeed, in much of the literature, proclivities toward one seem to accompany the other, and an implicit equation is made between economic backwardness and susceptibility to reactionary political appeals. The apparent consequence is that the political behaviour of agricultural producers seems to hold few surprises and to deserve no lengthy examination.

One extremely clear statement of this alleged interrelation of rural economic and political backwardness can be found in Alexander Gerschenkron's *Bread and Democracy in Germany*. Indeed, since its appearance over forty years ago, perhaps no English-language work on German agriculture has been so widely cited and has exercised such a significant influence.[31] According to Gerschenkron, by the last quarter of the nineteenth century German peasants, threatened by and unable to cope with rapid socio-economic change, sought privilege and protection in the form of an alliance with the pre-industrial elite par excellence, the Junkers. The Junkers' connections to the civil service, the military and the court allowed them an influence on government policy far out of proportion to their numbers or economic significance. The peasantry, confronted by declining prices for grains in the 1870s, refused to pursue the rational alternative of shifting their production to high-quality dairy and other livestock products by importing inexpensive feeds and abandoning unprofitable production of grains. Instead, they sought protection for grains and won it by accepting the myth of the unity of all agricultural producers behind the leadership of the politically powerful Junkers who were able to win Bismarck for their cause.

Apparently unwilling and unable to form their own political beliefs, in the analysis of Gerschenkron and those who have followed his lead, peasants retreated behind the political leadership of the Junkers just as they hid behind tariff walls. Peasants thus won protection for their out-dated modes of production, while Junkers won crucial recruits for their protofascistic, anti-democratic, anti-socialist campaigns and permanently blocked any potential movement by peasants in a leftward political direction. The continued political influence of the Junkers, of course, had regrettable consequences for the chances of true democratization in Germany. Their position of dominance shaped the 'feudalization' of the bourgeoisie and constituted a major bulwark against parliamentary reform.[32]

The characterization of a peasantry readily accepting the direction of a conservative elite was not new with Gerschenkron. It was also widely held by turn-of-the-century agrarian ideologues.[33] Of course, a pecu-liarly German virtue for conservative defenders of the status quo became a peculiarly German vice for authors like Gerschenkron and others as diverse as Barrington Moore, Jr., Hans-Ulrich Wehler and Nicos Pou-lantzas.[34] Conservatives praised the stable bases of a unified rural society in the Kaiserreich. Critics of Imperial Germany sought the nineteenth-century origins of German fascism and an adequate description of the conservative agrarian march from Kaiserreich to Third Reich. Invariably viewing the peasantry from the vantage-point of 1933, their investi-gations sketch out at least three different routes: either the Junkers lead their peasant followers into the National Socialist fold in a last-ditch attempt to preserve their position and eliminate the threat to their social status presented by parliamentary rule;[35] or the peasantry, finally disillu-sioned by its leaders' inability to provide solutions to the agrarian crisis of the late 1920s, turns to the Nazis, pulling their former conservative leaders behind them;[36] or peasants and lords, estranged from one another by the late 1920s, arrive independently at the decision to support National Socialism as the only way out of the crisis of the Weimar system.[37]

Whatever their differences in emphasis, most scenarios depict peasants as following the political lead of others, whether traditional elites or those espousing the populist rhetoric of *Blut und Boden*. Moreover, in all cases the lines of continuity from the late nineteenth century to 1933 are crystal clear. Thus, for example, Barrington Moore, in his major comparative work, *Social Origins of Dictatorship and Democracy*, contends that 'the effort to establish a massive conservative base in the countryside long antedates the Nazis'. Leaning explicitly on Gerschenkron, he continues: 'the basic elements of Nazi doctrine appear quite distinctly in the Junkers' generally successful efforts, by means of the Agrarian League established in 1894 [*sic*!], to win the support of the peasants in non-Junker areas of smaller farms. *Führer* worship, the idea of a corporative state, militarism, anti-Semitism, in a setting closely related to the Nazi distinction between "predatory" and "productive" capital, were devices used to appeal to anti-capitalist sentiments among the peasantry.'[38] From the agrarian crisis of the late nineteenth century and rural support for the Agrarian League it is thus a straight path to the agrarian crisis of the late 1920s and rural support for National Socialism.

New Perspectives on Peasants and Lords

This volume offers a new and in some cases quite different and explicitly revisionist perspective on the history of peasants and lords in the nineteenth and twentieth centuries. It brings together the work of three British and two American students of modern German agrarian history. We are joined by three German colleagues whose important work has up until now not been available in English. Our shared project is the elevation of the study of agrarian economic development and rural politics to the level long since reached by our colleagues who study industrialization, urbanization and the working-class movement. The essays move away from an exclusive concern with *either* rural politics *or* rural economic development and attempt to suggest some of the points at which those two spheres intersect. These concerns unite essays which differ in temporal focus, regional emphasis and scope. They define a community of interests, drawing together the authors whose work is represented in this volume.

The lords, most frequently the focus of studies in modern German rural history, appear here in a new light. In her wide-ranging treatment of the Junkers as a social, political and economic force in nineteenth-century Germany, Hanna Schissler describes a group characterized less by its resistance to change than by its resilience, flexibility and adaptability. In a highly suggestive comparison of the Junkers and the nineteenth-century English landed elite, moreover, she argues that within a comparative framework, it becomes necessary to re-evaluate interpretations which emphasize the inherently conservative nature of the east Elbian estate-owning class and the Junkers' significance in defining a German *Sonderweg*. Schissler thus joins others who have argued recently that the peculiarity of German development was in some sense not so peculiar at all.[39]

In Hans-Jürgen Puhle's discussion of the emergence of the Agrarian League in the late nineteenth century, lords figure prominently as well. Building on his major study of the Agrarian League, he discusses the new forms of conservative agrarian politics created in the 1890s and the integration of peasant constituents, both east and west of the Elbe, into an institutional framework dominated by the interests of grain-growing estate-owners. The success of the Agrarian League restricted the space in which competitors might have arisen to capture the discontent of peasants in the 1890s. In his account, a 'traditional' elite was thus able to maintain itself by exploiting extremely non-traditional tactics and appeals.

The peasants who appear only in the background of the analyses of Schissler and Puhle move to the forefront in the other essays in the volume. The move from top to bottom of the social hierarchy is, moreover, accompanied by a move from national politics to regional analysis. Such provincial and local perspectives yield a rich detail obscured at the national level, and in addition, reveal clearly the outlines of important regional, confessional and political differences dividing peasants from peasants within Germany.

Mooser's study of eastern Westphalia in the years from the agrarian reform until the revolution of 1848 is a model for the social historical investigation of the countryside. Rural class formation, he shows, must be measured not only in terms of land-holding and capital accumulation, but also in terms of changing conceptions of property, criminality and state authority. This theme is sensitively developed in a careful examination of patterns of rural criminality in two neighbouring regions, one dominated by proto-industrialization, the other characterized by intensified agricultural production.

In Farr's investigation of the Bavarian Peasants' League in the 1890s, it becomes obvious that lords were not alone in organizing new ways to express their discontent over the economic impact of the agrarian crisis of the early 1890s. Indeed, as Farr's analysis reveals, a Catholic peasantry in Bavaria vehemently criticized not only the state but also the east Elbians who headed the Agrarian League. The populist strains of peasant radicalism in the 1890s provoked a response both from the state and from the Centre Party, fearful that agrarian discontent tinged with anti-clericalism might bring defections from political Catholicism.[40] Farr's case study does much to illuminate the complex interaction of leaders and those they sought to lead.

Together, Jonathan Osmond and I concentrate on peasant experience in the First World War, the revolutionary conjuncture of 1918–19 and the postwar inflation. Drawing on research for a regional study of the Rhineland and Westphalia, my essay outlines the economic dimensions of peasant protest in the decade of war and inflation. Sustained shortages of food, a deep rift between city and countryside, and state regulation of the agricultural sector defined important elements of continuity, unifying the years 1914–23. It was against this background that the profound political ruptures of defeat in war, revolution and the introduction of parliamentary government rocked a conservative countryside. Concentrating on southern and western Germany, Osmond analyses the forms of rural collective action which emerged in response to these elements of continuity and change. Often beyond the control or direction of pre-1914 interest group leaders, peasant protest emerged in new organizational forms and with a rhetoric even more radical than that of the 1890s. Osmond's essay thus allows ready comparisons with the forms of protest which Farr describes. Osmond also looks ahead to the later years of Weimar when the postwar proliferation of interest group organizations reappeared in the agrarian splinter parties which contributed significantly to the disintegration of the Weimar political system.

These splinter parties constitute the focus of Larry Jones's contribution. Jones's analysis is an important corrective to the widespread view that peasants, dissatisfied with existing political parties and interest group organizations, raced headlong into the open arms of National Socialists.[41] As Jones argues, agrarian radicalism of the late 1920s did not translate automatically into support for National Socialism.

In other parts of Germany not treated by Jones, of course, the Nazis did effectively establish themselves. How well the Nazis, once in power, rewarded those so crucial to their political success and to Weimar's demise is studied by J. E. Farquharson in this volume's final essay. Farquharson's useful overview of National Socialist agrarian policy reveals that visions of *Blut und Boden*, ubiquitous in Nazi propaganda before and after 1933, translated into policies often opposed by those who worked the soil. Moreover, as Germany prepared for war and Hitler openly conceded the abandonment of autarkic fantasies, the gap widened between rhetorical promises to elevate the 'Peasant Estate' and the realities of Nazi policy. The agricultural sector found its interests subordinated to the demands of rearmament.

This far-ranging survey brings together much of the best of recent research into the agrarian history of modern Germany. It is not, however, intended as a comprehensive treatment of that vast subject, and it reflects the particular concerns of each author. None the less, read together, the essays emphasize several common elements and themes which offer a decidedly new perspective on the history of the German agricultural sector in the nineteenth and twentieth centuries.

Certainly, one central argument advanced by Gerschenkron and echoed by many others fares very poorly in this volume. A theme running through virtually all of the essays presented here is that neither peasants nor lords are properly characterized as economically backward or unaware of the workings of the market. Even in Mooser's case study

10

of the first half of the nineteenth century, it is obvious that peasant reaction to the elimination of feudal rights reflected their understanding of changing class relations in the countryside under the influence of industrial growth and an expanding capitalist market. Peasant response to these developments should not be seen as reactive or regressive, but rather, more properly, as adaptive. It reflected an adjustment to, if not acceptance of, the changed social relations which accompanied changed relations of production and ownership. As Schissler emphasizes, it is also clear that large estate-owners were anything but unaware of changing market structures and patterns of demand.[42] Indeed, serfdom itself, established east of the Elbe only in the sixteenth century, represented an attempt to secure a labour force for the production of grains for export to Western and Southern Europe. In the early nineteenth century the Junkers were, moreover, also able to turn the abolition of serfdom to their advantage by consolidating their holdings and introducing modern agrarian techniques, which allowed them to play a major role in providing food for England's industrial revolution. When English landlords succeeded in imposing tariffs on east Elbian grains, estate-owners shifted to production of the wool demanded by the expanding English textile industry. With the suspension of the Corn Laws in 1846, the Junkers could once again concentrate on production of grains for export. By mid-century they had successfully completed the transition from a feudal estate, legally defined by birth, to an economic class, determined by its ability to function within a capitalist world market.

Shearer Davis Bowman, a student of the comparison between antebellum southern planters and *Vormärz* Junkers, has recently offered a definition of capitalism as 'an economic system that rests predominantly on private property and private disposition over capital and that facilitates production of commodities for the purpose of profit'. According to these criteria, there can be little doubt that the Junkers were agrarian capitalists.[43] Indeed, 'feudal' and 'precapitalist' are terms decidedly inapplicable to the economic behaviour of these east Elbian estate-owners in the nineteenth century, and in underscoring these themes, Schissler confirms and builds on the pioneering work of Hans Rosenberg. On the contrary, the ability of the Junkers to respond effectively to the ebb and flow of the world market economy was a key ingredient in their ability to provide a firm basis for their claims to political power and prestige.[44]

The essays of Farr, Jones, Farquharson and my own contribution indicate that peasants also adjusted to the realities of a capitalist market economy in the period after 1848. Farr's explanation of Bavarian peasant protest in the 1890s emphasizes the importance of the economic crisis in the first half of that decade in motivating peasant producers to act collectively. The economic problems prompting peasant mobilization included the threat of competition from foreign grain-producers, high labour costs pushed up by competition from a growing industrial sector, the absence of adequate credit facilities, and unproductive indebtedness dating back to the inflation of land prices in the 1860s. These were the difficulties of a peasantry fully integrated into the market, not one which held that market at arm's length or produced only to cover its subsistence needs.[45] In my research on peasant producers in the Rhineland and Westphalia, the situation was no different. Unlike east Elbian estate-owners, agricultural producers in these regions produced primarily for nearby urban, not foreign export markets. By the 1890s they had adjusted their production quite successfully to the changing nature of demand from urban centres in the Ruhr and other nearby areas of industrial concentration. I argue as well that the sensitivity of agricultural producers to price changes seriously undermined attempts to regulate agricultural production with a system of maximum prices during the First World War and in the postwar inflation.

In the late 1920s, as Jones makes clear, it was not economically 'backward' peasants, but those most directly affected by the market's impact, who showed the greatest susceptibility to radical appeals.[46] The responsiveness of peasant producers to the demands of the market economy is evident as well in Farquharson's analysis of peasant resistance to the Nazi law of Hereditary Farm Entailment (*Erbhofgesetz*). Opposition to the law was based at least in part on the fact that it made it impossible for peasants to assume mortgage debt beyond a set limit, thus cutting off a source of investment capital for productive improvements, while doing nothing to increase agricultural efficiency. In addition, Farquharson demonstrates that although the price-setting functions of the Nazi Reich Food Estate (*Reichsnährstand*) were welcome in the first years of the regime when agriculture was still recovering from years of insecurity and agricultural crisis, those policies were decidedly less well received in the second half of the decade since they maintained prices below levels which would have been achieved in a free market.

In short, it is a central contention of several of the essays in this volume that German agricultural producers clearly understood the economic circumstances confronting them and adjusted their production accordingly, often with great success. Their mobilization in political organizations and interest groups was closely related to their economic concerns, and reflected not the search for a lost world but rather the attempt to control and regulate the market into which they were so completely integrated.

Although the contributions in this volume thus shake one central pillar of standard accounts – the assertion of German agriculture's economic backwardness – they do not topple the other – the historical fact of the political conservatism of German agrarians. They do make it clear, however, that the acceptance of the market in a capitalist society and acceptance of political democratization and parliamentary institutions need not go hand-in-hand. None the less, a language of 'anti-modernism' seems ill advised even for describing the political behaviour of the Junkers, and as Schissler and Puhle argue, aristocratic landowners were unusually innovative and flexible in discovering new methods to assert and defend their political position. Indeed, unlike the liberal politicians of the Kaiserreich, who after the 1890s continued to rely on a system of notable representation, established networks of influence and assumptions of the deferential behaviour of subaltern classes (*Honorationen-politik*),[47] the east Elbian elite learned to sing the harmonies of 'politics in a new key'.[48] 'Pseudodemocratization', as Hans Rosenberg has called it, is perhaps the best way to describe Junker political behaviour, and the conclusion that can be abstracted from the work of Puhle and Schissler is that from the late nineteenth century on, conservative agrarians used highly effective 'modern' means to pursue anti-parliamentary, anti-democratic ends.[49]

At the same time, the contributions in this volume also make clear that the longevity of the east Elbian conservative elite was not simply a function of its success as a manipulator of an unwitting peasant constituency. The other side of the aristocratic-peasant conservative agrarian alliance is described fully in the work of Farr, Osmond and Jones, and touched on in the contributions of Farquharson and in my own work as well. The sources and forms of peasant activism which we identify indicate that an aristocratic elite followed their constituents as often as they were in the lead; the dynamic of rural politics was determined by the complex interaction of pressure from below and direction from above. To be sure, peasants alone had difficulty generating, let along sustaining self-defined organizations and articulating political programmes. Some form of leadership, often by non-peasants, was a constant characteristic of the rural interest group organizations described in these essays.[50] However, the mobilization of the peasantry outside and sometimes against established organizations, particularly around pressing economic concerns, could force major political parties, agricultural interest groups, established elites and the state to adjust their policies and priorities. Thus, the survival of 'traditional' agrarian elites represented not only their understanding of the changing contours of national politics but also their responsiveness to pressure from below.

Read together, these essays also question interpretations which stress unbroken lines of political and economic continuity linking the nineteenth and twentieth centuries. The emphasis by Gerschenkron and others on a defensive Junker-peasant alliance, in place from 1878–9 and ultimately integrated into the Nazi regime, neglects important discontinuities in modern German history. Even for Puhle, whose contribution underscores lines of continuity from Kaiserreich to Third Reich, the 1890s represent an important watershed. Conservative agrarians, once reliable supporters of the state, moved when necessary into open opposition to the Kaiser and his ministers. For Farr also, the 1890s mark the emergence of new forms of protest and agrarian radicalism which prompted new forms of accommodation from the Catholic Centre Party.[51] In my work, the period of the First World War and the inflation represents another clear discontinuity, characterized by the suspension of a normally functioning market, continued state intervention into the agricultural sector, and as Osmond stresses, new forms of peasant radicalism in the wake of a lost war and an accelerated advance towards democratic government. The late 1920s confronted agricultural producers with entirely unfamiliar circumstances once again, and although renewed agrarian demands for tariff protection sounded like a hypochondriac's cry for even greater doses of the same old medicine, the sickness was in fact entirely new. The agrarian crisis of the late nineteenth century, created by the combination of secular price declines, increased foreign competition and improvements in international transportation networks, was overcome by the end of the 1890s. For most of the two decades before 1914, the German agricultural sector faced a market which absorbed virtually everything it could produce. The agricultural crisis which climaxed with the Great Depression of the 1920s was one of worldwide overproduction and falling prices for all primary producers, both at home and abroad. Thus, the route of German agricultural producers from Kaiserreich to Weimar, from Weimar to Third Reich and from Third Reich to a divided Germany is a zigzag course in which elements of change are at least as crucial as those of continuity.

These are some of the most important findings that emerge from the collection of essays which follows. On the firm foundation they provide, it will be possible to pursue questions which they raise but cannot fully answer. These essays offer not only the beginning of a revised account of the agricultural sector in an industrial Germany; in addition, they suggest a research agenda and point to a number of key areas where additional work is essential:

(1) Underrepresented in current research and thus in this volume is a careful consideration of demographic change in the countryside and patterns of urban–rural migration.[52] Investigations of these dimensions of rural life could reveal much about the process of proto-industrialization in Germany and the experience of peasants on the way to becoming industrial workers. They could also illuminate the agricultural sector's contribution to the creation of 'human capital' in the process of industrial development. Careful comparisons of the exchange between city and

14

countryside could provide an objective background to the ideological battle over *Agrar-* v. *Industriestaat* which dominated the Kaiserreich and re-emerged in the Nazi rhetoric of the late 1920s. Demographic dimensions of the agricultural sector and the gender composition of the labour force over time could also offer sharper comparisons of the differences between family life among the classes of rural society and between similar classes in urban and rural society.[53] At present, city and countryside are studied too much in isolation. The points of their intersection and the forms of their exchange deserve careful investigation.

(2) Although the collection effectively spans two centuries, one striking temporal gap is the period of the nineteenth-century 'Great Depression' (1873–96). This reflects no arbitrary editorial decision, but rather the lack of recent research on this period, and little has been done to fill in the provocative outlines sketched by Rosenberg more than forty years ago.[54] Farr and I both emphasize that these years are inadequately characterized as ones of agrarian stagnation or retreat, but our studies begin as the 'Great Depression' ends. Additional work is essential not only to illuminate the dimensions of rural economic change, but also to describe the dimensions of rural radicalism at the local and regional level which predated the height of the agrarian crisis in the 1890s. Recent studies which stress the 'political conjuncture' of the early 1890s may well overstate the novel character of the peasant radicalism which erupted into the national political arena in the first half of that decade.

(3) Schissler and Puhle do much to illuminate the response of the east Elbian elite to economic policy and state decision-making at the level of national politics, but such analyses must be deepened with investigations of the forms of aristocratic influence at the local level and the day-to-day exercise of hegemony by the Junkers and landed elites elsewhere in Germany. Surely, the interaction of peasants and lords at this level shaped the political priorities advanced in Berlin, the nature of conservative agrarian politics and the political conceptions of the conservative elite. Heinz Reif's extensive work on the Westphalian aristocracy in the nineteenth century indicates that forms of elite control and the process of elite recruitment are not easily reduced to simple formulae. They must be differentiated by region and the structure of land-holdings, as well as political traditions and confession.[55] Nothing comparable to the rich studies of the 'world the slaveholders made' exists in the German literature, but such models make clear how much we can learn from investigations of this sort.[56]

(4) The 'political culture' of lords is thus open to more nuanced and detailed treatment and so too is that of peasants. The work of Farr and Osmond and my own research shows the usefulness of the region as a framework for analysis, but a more detailed and complete picture of peasant culture and society will require digging at least one layer deeper.

Indeed, a full understanding of peasant politics will involve research into all facets of rural associational life, co-operative marketing, purchasing and credit networks as economic, social *and* political institutions, organizations of women and youth within agricultural interest groups, patterns of authority at the local level and within the peasant family, and peasant culture, broadly defined to include religion and popular festivals.[57] The analysis of peasant politics has remained largely at the level of national and provincial interest group representatives and political parties. Looking below this level can allow us to expand our understanding of peasant politics, and also to examine the ways in which ostensibly apolitical institutions profoundly influenced rural political attitudes.[58] Studies of working-class life on the shop floor, in the home and in the community reveal clearly how important these dimensions can be for a full understanding of the forms of political authority at the local level, the relationship between local politics and politics at the national level, and the varieties of politics which engaged contemporary actors.[59]

(5) Yet another important aspect of rural social relations – relations between capitalist agricultural producers and agricultural wage-earners – also deserves more attention. Research in this area is not altogether lacking,[60] but there is still much more to be done. In particular, we still know very little of agricultural labour relations in areas outside the east Elbian provinces.[61] Wage labour did not disappear on many large peasant family farms, but relations between a limited number of contractually bound workers and their peasant employers were obviously different from those which prevailed on large east Elbian estates. As Mooser's contribution indicates, an analysis of those differences can tell us much about the nature and forms of rural social conflict in different parts of Germany.

(6) For the years after 1933, Farquharson has done much to outline National Socialist agricultural policy, but again, it would be useful to push below the national level to an analysis of the meaning of fascism for rural society, and the political and economic response to fascism by agricultural producers at the regional and village levels. Such works as William Sheridan Allen's *The Nazi Seizure of Power*[62] and the documentation efforts of the research team of the Institute for Contemporary History in Munich[63] provide excellent models for research of this sort, and indicate how much can be gained for the understanding of German fascism from this viewpoint.

(7) Finally, although these essays end in 1945, the history of the agricultural sector in an industrial Germany does not. Studies of the post-1945 period, comparisons of the forms of agricultural reform in the two Germanies, lines of continuity and change in the agricultural sector in the transition from National Socialism to a divided Germany – these

are essential and as yet inadequately told parts of any attempt to reconstruct this most recent chapter of Germany history.[64]

This collection thus represents not a culmination but an exciting introduction to the 'state of the art' in modern German agrarian history. In the methodological, conceptual and thematic range which they encompass, the essays brought together here indicate that the 'art' is thriving. The English-language literature on German agriculture will not catch up with one step to the rich literature already available on other aspects of modern German social and economic history but these essays move significantly closer to that goal. The collection challenges accepted interpretations, suggests some alternatives and at the same time offers a context in which new questions can be posed and answers can be sought.

Notes: Introduction

1 A summer grant from Columbia University's Council for Research in the Social Sciences provided me the time to write this introduction. My thanks to David Blackbourn, Geoff Eley, Gerald D. Feldman and, in particular, Lynn Mally, for their useful critical comments on earlier versions. References are offered as one, by no means exhaustive, guide to further reading.

2 Eugen Weber, *Peasants into Frenchmen: The Modernization of Rural France 1870–1914* (Stanford, Calif., 1976).

3 F. M. L. Thompson, *English Landed Society in the Nineteenth Century* (London, 1963).

4 Teodor Shanin, *The Awkward Class: Political Sociology of the Peasantry in a Developing Society: Russia 1910–1925* (Oxford, 1972).

5 Charles Tilly, *The Vendée* (Cambridge, Mass., 1964).

6 Suzanne Berger, *Peasants against Politics: Rural Organization in Brittany, 1911–1967* (Cambridge, Mass., 1972).

→ 7 See the textbook study of Hans-Ulrich Wehler, *Das deutsche Kaiserreich 1871–1918* (Göttingen, 1973), 19–24, 53–6 and passim; Gordon Craig, *Germany 1866–1945* (New York, 1978), 98–100, 549–50; Martin Kitchen, *The Political Economy of Germany 1815–1914* (London, 1978), 165–6, 168, 248–9; Helmut Böhme, *An Introduction to the Social and Economic History of Germany: Politics and Economic Change in the Nineteenth and Twentieth Centuries*, trans. W. R. Lee (New York, 1978), 17–32, 67–86.

8 See especially Friedrich-Wilhelm Henning, *Dienste und Abgaben der Bauern im 18. Jahrhundert* (Stuttgart, 1969); idem, *Bauernwirtschaft und Bauerneinkommen im Fürstentum Paderborn im 18. Jahrhundert* (Berlin, 1970); Harald Winkel, *Die Ablösungskapitalien aus der Bauernbefreiung in West- und Süddeutschland: Höhe und Verwendung bei Standes- und Grundherrn* (Stuttgart, 1968); Friedrich Lütge *Geschichte der deutschen Agrarverfassung vom frühen Mittelalter bis zum 19. Jahrhundert* (Stuttgart, 1963); and Wilhelm Abel, *Geschichte der deutschen Landwirtschaft vom frühen Mittelalter bis zum 19. Jahrhundert*, 2nd ed. (Stuttgart, 1978). A useful English summary of some of the central arguments in this literature which discusses the impact of the reforms on agricultural productivity is provided by Robert A. Dickler, 'Organization and change in productivity in Eastern Prussia', in *European Peasants and their Markets: Essays in Agrarian Economic History*, ed. William N. Parker and Eric L. Jones (Princeton, N.J., 1975), 269–92.

9 Wilhelm Abel, *Agrarkrisen und Agrarkonjunkturen: Eine Geschichte der Land- und Ernährungswirtschaft Mitteleuropas seit dem hohen Mittelalter* (Hamburg, 1978) (first published in 1935).

10 See in particular, Hans Rosenberg, 'Die Pseudodemokratisierung der Rittergutsbesit-

zerklasse', in *Machteliten und Wirtschaftskonjunkturen: Studien zur neueren deutschen Sozial- und Wirtschaftsgeschichte* (Göttingen, 1978), 83–101 (first published in 1958).

11 Hans-Jürgen Puhle, *Agrarische Interessenpolitik und preussischer Konservatismus im Wilhelminischen Reich (1893–1914): Ein Beitrag zur Analyse des Nationalismus in Deutschland am Beispiel des Bundes der Landwirte und der Deutsch-Konservativen Partei*, 2nd ed. (Bonn-Bad Godesberg, 1975); and idem, *Politische Agrarbewegungen in kapitalistischen Industriegesellschaften: Deutschland, USA, und Frankreich im 20. Jahrhundert* (Göttingen, 1975).

12 Jens Flemming, *Landwirtschaftliche Interessen und Demokratie: Ländliche Gesellschaft, Agrarverbände und Staat 1890–1925* (Bonn, 1978).

13 Martin Schumacher, *Land und Politik: Eine Untersuchung über politische Parteien und agrarische Interessen 1914–1923* (Düsseldorf, 1978).

14 Dieter Gessner, *Agrarverbände in der Weimarer Republik: Wirtschaftliche und soziale Voraussetzungen agrarkonservativer Politik vor 1933* (Düsseldorf, 1976); idem, 'The dilemma of German agriculture during the Weimar Republic', in *Social Change and Political Development in Weimar Germany*, ed. Richard Bessel and E. J. Feuchtwanger (London, 1981), 134–54; and idem, 'Agrarian protectionism in the Weimar Republic', *Journal of Contemporary History* 12 (1977): 759–78.

15 Rudolf Heberle, *Landbevölkerung und Nationalsozialismus: Eine soziologische Untersuchung der politischen Willensbildung in Schleswig-Holstein 1918–1932* (Stuttgart, 1963). A much abridged English version appeared as *From Democracy to Nazism: A Regional Case Study on Political Parties in Germany* (Baton Rouge, 1945).

16 Horst Gies, 'NSDAP und landwirtschaftliche Organisationen in der Endphase der Weimarer Republik', *Vierteljahrshefte für Zeitgeschichte* 15 (1967): 341–76; idem, 'The NSDAP and the agrarian organizations in the final phase of the Weimar Republic', in *Nazism and the Third Reich*, ed. Henry A. Turner (New York, 1972), 45–88; idem, 'Der Reichsnährstand – Organ berufsständischer Selbstverwaltung oder Instrument staatlicher Wirtschaftslenkung?', *Zeitschrift für Agrargeschichte und Agrarsoziologie* 21 (1973): 216–33; idem, 'Revolution oder Kontinuität – Die personelle Struktur des Reichsnährstandes', in *Bauernschaft und Bauernstand 1500–1970*, ed. Günther Franz (Limburg/Lahn, 1975), 323–30.

17 See, e.g., the contributions in *Probleme des Feudalismus und des Kapitalismus* (Tagungsmaterial vom September 1976), Parts VII and IX (Wilhelm-Pieck-Universität Rostock, Sektion Geschichte, 1977), and the numerous contributions to this discussion since the early 1960s in the G.D.R.'s chief journal for economic history, *Jahrbuch für Wirtschaftsgeschichte*, particularly the work of Hans-Heinrich Müller, Hartmut Harnisch and Rudolf Berthold. See in particular, Rudolf Berthold, 'Zur Herausbildung des kapitalistischen Klassenschichtung des Dorfes in Preussen', *Zeitschrift für Geschichtswissenschaft* 20 (1977): 556–74; Hartmut Harnisch, 'Die kapitalistische Agrarreform: Ihre Bedeutung für die Herausbildung des inneren Marktes und die industrielle Revolution in den östlichen Provinzen Preussens in der ersten Hälfte des 19. Jahrhunderts', in *Preussische Reformen 1807–1820*, ed. Barbara Vogel (Königstein/Ts., 1980), 111–31; and, for the later part of the nineteenth century, Ilona Ballwanz, 'Bauernschaft und soziale Schichten des Dorfes im Kapitalismus', *Jahrbuch für Wirtschaftsgeschichte*, Part III (1980): 9–24; Sigrid Dillwitz, 'Die Struktur der Bauernschaft von 1871 bis 1914: Dargestellt auf der Grundlage der deutschen Reichsstatistik', *Jahrbuch für Geschichte* 9 (1973): 47–127; and Jan Sølta, *Die Bauern der Lausitz: Eine Untersuchung des Differenzierungsprozesses der Bauernschaft im Kapitalismus* (Bautzen, 1976).

18 For a review of the literature on the 'Prussian path', see Gerhard Heitz, 'Varianten des preussischen Weges', *Jahrbuch für Wirtschaftsgeschichte*, Part III (1969): 99–109; Georg Moll, 'Zum "preussischen Weg" der Entwicklung des Kapitalismus in der deutschen Landwirtschaft', *Zeitschrift für Geschichtswissenschaft* 26 (1978): 52–62; and the excellent treatment of agriculture in the imperial period in Dieter Baudis and Helga Nussbaum (eds.), *Wirtschaft und Staat in Deutschland vom Ende des 19. Jahrhunderts bis 1918/19* (Vaduz/Liechtenstein, 1978), 177–248. Lenin's original discussion can be found in 'The agrarian programme of social-democracy in the first Russian Revolution 1905–1907', in *Collected Works*, Vol. 13, 'June 1907–April 1908' (Moscow, 1962), 238–42; see also the lucid discussion by Judith Ennew, Paul Hirst and Keith Tribe, '"Peasantry" as an economic category', *Journal of Peasant Studies* 4 (1977): 295–322.

18

19 On the struggles between capitalist estate-owners and agricultural wage-earners, see Johannes Nichtweiss, *Die ausländischen Saisonarbeiter in der Landwirtschaft der östlichen und mittleren Gebiete des Deutschen Reiches: Ein Beitrag zur Geschichte des preussisch-deutschen Politik von 1890 bis 1914* (Berlin, 1959).

20 See, e.g., Bruno Buchta, *Die Junker in der Weimarer Republik* (Berlin and Leipzig, 1959).

21 Frank B. Tipton, *Regional Variations in the Economic Development of Germany during the Nineteenth Century* (Middletown, Conn., 1976), 47, 65, 89–91.

22 Figures for the United States are from Puhle, *Politische Agrarbewegungen*, 248, and for Belgium and the United Kingdom, from B. R. Mitchell, *European Historical Statistics 1750–1970* (New York, 1978), 51, 61.

23 See, e.g., Ulf Renborg, 'Tendencies towards concentration and specialization in agriculture', in *Economic Problems of Agriculture in Industrial Societies*, ed. Ugo Papi and Charles Nunn (London, Melbourne, Toronto and New York, 1969), 209–33; H. Priebe, 'The modern family farm and its problems: with particular reference to the Federal German Republic', in *Economic Problems*, 251–63; Friedrich-Wilhelm Henning, *Landwirtschaft und ländliche Gesellschaft in Deutschland*, Vol. 2 (Paderborn, 1978), 228–85; Onno-Hans Poppinga, *Bauern und Politik* (Frankfurt and Cologne, 1975).

24 To take one rough index, Hans-Ulrich Wehler's *Bibliography zur modernen deutschen Sozialgeschichte (18.–20. Jahrhundert)* (Göttingen, 1976) offers six pages of entries on peasants, agricultural wage-earners and aristocrats, and thirty-five on the bourgeoisie, salaried white-collar workers, artisans, workers and the workers' movement. The years since the appearance of Wehler's bibliographies have seen no changes in these tendencies.

25 See below, p. 111.

26 This is obviously a generalization, but none the less seems a fair characterization of the work of Hans-Ulrich Wehler, Jürgen Kocka and also such students of working-class politics as Klaus Saul and Erhard Lucas.

27 The reference is from the 'Manifesto of the Communist Party'. See the version in Robert C. Tucker (ed.), *The Marx-Engels Reader*, 2nd ed. (New York and London, 1978), 477. Marx's other most familiar comments on peasant political attitudes come from *The Eighteenth Brumaire of Louis Bonaparte* (New York, 1963), where he describes the 'great mass of the French nation', 'formed by simple addition of homologous magnitudes, much as potatoes in a sack form a sack of potatoes'. He continues: 'In so far as millions of families live under economic conditions of existence that separate their mode of life, their interests and their culture from those of the other classes, and put them in hostile opposition to the latter, they form a class. In so far as there is merely a local interconnection among these smallholding peasants, and the identity of their interests begets no community, no national bond and no political organization among them, they do not form a class. They are consequently incapable of enforcing their class interest in their own name, whether through a parliament or through a convention. They cannot represent themselves, they must be represented' (*Eighteenth Brumaire*, 124).

28 Cited in William Harvey Maehl, 'German Social Democratic agrarian policy, 1890–1895, reconsidered', *Central European History* 13 (1980): 126. See also Hans Georg Lehmann, *Die Agrarfrage in der Theorie und Praxis der deutschen und internationalen Sozialdemokratie: Vom Marxismus zum Revisionismus und Bolschewismus* (Tübingen, 1970), 61, 129.

29 In general, see Maehl, 'German Social Democratic agrarian policy'; Lehmann, *Die Agrarfrage*; and Athar Hussain and Keith Tribe, *Marxism and the Agrarian Question* (Highlands, N.J., 1981), Vol. 1, *German Social Democracy and the Peasantry 1890–1907* (written by Hussain).

30 See, e.g., Heinz Haushofer, *Die deutsche Landwirtschaft im technischen Zeitalter*, 2nd ed. (Stuttgart, 1972), and the excellent critique by Hans Rosenberg, 'Deutsche Agrargeschichte in alter und neuer Sicht', in *Probleme der deutschen Sozialgeschichte* (Frankfurt M., 1969), 109–23. More recent treatments, e.g. Ernst Klein, *Geschichte der deutschen Landwirtschaft im Industriezeitalter* (Wiesbaden, 1973), and Henning, *Landwirtschaft und ländliche Gesellschaft*, are an improvement over Haushofer, but remain strictly within the confines of economic history, narrowly defined, and seldom venture into the areas

of rural social relations or political behaviour, or the relation of the agricultural sector to the larger society.

31 Alexander Gerschenkron, *Bread and Democracy in Germany* (Berkeley and Los Angeles, 1943) (virtually unaltered in a second edition in 1966). Gerschenkron's influence is clear in the works cited above in note 7, and for other examples see Charles P. Kindleberger, 'Group behavior and international trade', in *Economic Response: Comparative Studies in Trade, Finance and Growth* (Cambridge, Mass., and London, 1978), 22–3, 34; Derek W. Urwin, *From Ploughshare to Ballotbox: The Politics of Agrarian Defense in Europe* (Oslo, Bergen and Tromsø, 1980), 96–7; Werner T. Angress, 'The political role of the peasantry in the Weimar Republic', *Review of Politics* 21 (1959): 530–2; Peter Alexis Gourevitch, 'International trade, domestic coalitions, and liberty: comparative responses to the crisis of 1873–1896', *Journal of Interdisciplinary History* 8 (1977): 185–94; and Barrington Moore, Jr., *Social Origins of Dictatorship and Democracy: Lord and Peasant in the Making of the Modern World* (Boston, Mass., 1966), 448–50.

32 The general critique of the Junkers as integrally linked to German 'backwardness' and Germany's 'flawed' development can be located as early as Max Weber's professorial inaugural address in 1895. See 'Der Nationalstaat und die Volkswirtschaftspolitik', in *Gesammelte politische Schriften* (Munich, 1921), esp. 24–5; and 'National character and the Junkers', in *From Max Weber: Essays in Sociology*, ed. H. H. Gerth and C. Wright Mills (New York, 1958), 386–95.

33 See Klaus Bergmann, *Agrarromantik und Grossstadtfeindschaft* (Meisenheim, 1970); Kenneth D. Barkin, *The Controversy over German Industrialization 1890–1902* (Chicago and London, 1970); Hermann Lebovics, '"Agrarians" versus "Industrializers" – social conservative resistance to industrialism and capitalism in late nineteenth century Germany', *International Review of Social History* 12 (1967): 31–65; and on the early nineteenth century background, John G. Gagliardo, *From Pariah to Patriot: The Changing Image of the German Peasant 1770–1840* (Lexington, Ky., 1969). As David Blackbourn suggests, the liberal and conservative perception of the *Mittelstand* in general converged on this point. See his 'The *Mittelstand* in German society and politics, 1871–1914', *Social History* no. 4 (1977): 409–33. A similar perspective is offered by James C. Hunt, 'Peasants, grain tariffs, and meat quotas: imperial German protectionism reexamined', *Central European History* 7 (1973): 311–31.

34 See the references to Wehler above in note 7, Moore, above in note 31, and Nicos Poulantzas, *Fascism and Dictatorship: The Third International and the Problem of Fascism* (London, 1979), 279–80, 286–7.

35 This position is stated most clearly by Gerschenkron.

36 The significance of radicalization at the grass-roots level is emphasized particularly by Heberle, *Landbevölkerung und Nationalsozialismus*.

37 See, e.g., David Abraham, *The Collapse of the Weimar Republic: Political Economy and Crisis* (Princeton, N.J., 1981), 53–115, esp. 111–12.

38 Moore, *Social Origins*, 448.

39 See in particular the controversial discussion by David Blackbourn and Geoff Eley, *Mythen deutscher Geschichtsschreibung: Die gescheiterte bürgerliche Revolution von 1848* (Frankfurt/M., Berlin and Vienna, 1980); and for a critical review of this position, Robert G. Moeller, 'Die Besonderheiten der Deutschen? Neue Beiträge zur Sonderwegsdiskussion', *Internationale Schulbuchforschung* 4 (1982): 71–80; and idem, 'The Kaiserreich recast? Continuity and change in modern German historiography', *Journal of Social History* 17 (1984): 655–83.

40 See also Ian Farr, 'From anti-Catholicism to anticlericalism: Catholic politics and the peasantry in Bavaria, 1890–1900', *European Studies Review* 13 (1983): 249–69.

41 For only one example, see Craig, *Germany 1866–1945*, who asserts that 'farmers', who comprised 14 per cent of NSDAP membership in 1930, were 'greatly in excess of . . . their percentage of the national population' (549–50).

42 In this context, see also the important work of Hans Rosenberg, 'Die Ausprägung der Junkerherrschaft in Brandenburg-Preussen 1410–1618', in *Machteliten und Wirtschaftskonjunkturen*, 24–82.

43 Shearer Davis Bowman, 'Antebellum planters and *Vormärz* Junkers in comparative perspective', *American Historical Review* 85 (1980): 783. Bowman adopts this definition

from Jürgen Kocka, *Klassengesellschaft im Krieg: Deutsche Sozialgeschichte, 1914–1918* (Göttingen, 1973), 149 n. 14. In general, Bowman's discussion of agrarian capitalism and its relationship to the constitution of conservative elites is particularly illuminating. See also Rosenberg, 'Pseudoemokratisierung'; James J. Sheehan, 'Conflicts and cohesion among German elites in the nineteenth century', in *Imperial Germany*, ed. idem (New York and London, 1976), 62–92, esp. 65; and on the integration of the Junkers into the world capitalist market long before the nineteenth century, Immanuel Wallerstein, *The Modern World-System: Capitalist Agriculture and the Origins of the European World Economy in the Sixteenth Century* (New York, 1974), 88–91, 99–100.

44 On the development of agriculture under protection in the late nineteenth century see Steven B. Webb, 'Agricultural protection in Wilhelmine Germany: forging an empire with pork and rye', *Journal of Economic History* 42 (1982): 309–26; idem, 'Tariff protection for the iron industry, cotton textiles and agriculture in Germany, 1879–1914', *Jahrbücher für Nationalökonomie und Statistik* 192 (1977): 336–57; and J. A. Perkins, 'The agricultural revolution in Germany 1850–1914', *Journal of European Economic History* 10 (1981): 71–118.

45 See the comparative perspective offered by Gavin Lewis, 'The peasantry, rural change and conservative agrarianism: Lower Austria at the turn of the century', *Past and Present* 81 (1978): 119–43.

46 On this see Heberle's perceptive analysis. See also the interesting comparative perspective offered by Anthony L. Cardoza, *Agrarian Elites and Italian Fascism: The Province of Bologna 1901–1926* (Princeton, N.J., 1982); and Frank M. Snowden, 'From sharecropper to proletarian: the background to fascism in rural Tuscany, 1880–1920', *Gramsci and Italy's Passive Revolution*, ed. John A. Davis (London, 1979), 136–71.

47 See the lucid discussion of this by Geoff Eley, *Reshaping the German Right: Radical Nationalism and Political Change after Bismarck* (New Haven and London, 1980), 29–40.

48 The phrase is taken from Carl E. Schorske, 'Politics in a new key: Schönerer', in *The Responsibility of Power: Historical Essays in Honor of Hajo Holborn*, ed. Leonard Krieger and Fritz Stern (Garden City, N.Y., 1969), 251–70.

49 Rosenberg, 'Pseudodemokratisierung'. See also the useful discussion by Hartmut Harnisch, 'Probleme junkerlicher Agrarpolitik im 19. Jahrhundert', *Wissenschaftliche Zeitschrift der Universität Rostock, Gesellschafts- und Sprachwissenschaftliche Reihe* 21 (1972): 99–117; and Frank B. Tipton, 'Farm labor and power politics: Germany 1850–1914', *Journal of Economic History* 34 (1974): 951–79.

50 See the useful theoretical introduction to this problem in Boguslaw Galeski, *Basic Concepts of Rural Sociology*, ed. Teodor Shanin and Peter Worsley (Manchester, 1972); and the stimulating historical treatments by Berger, *Peasants against Politics*; Shanin, *The Awkward Class*; and Tony Judt, *Socialism in Provence: A Study of the Origins of the Modern French Left* (Cambridge, London, New York and Melbourne, 1979).

51 This emphasis parallels the recent arguments of Eley, *Reshaping*, and also David Blackbourn, *Class, Religion and Local Politics in Wilhelmine Germany: The Centre Party in Württemberg before 1914* (New Haven, Conn., and London, 1980); and idem, 'Peasants and politics in Germany, 1871–1914', *European Studies Quarterly* 14 (1984): 47–75.

52 For some attempts in this direction, see Josef Mooser, 'Soziale Mobilität und familiale Plazierung bei Bauern und Unterschichten: Aspekte der Sozialstruktur der ländlichen Gesellschaft im 19. Jahrhundert am Beispiel des Kirchspiels Quernheim im östlichen Westfalen', in *Familie zwischen Tradition und Moderne: Studien zur Geschichte der Familie in Deutschland und Frankreich vom 16. bis zum 20. Jahrhundert*, ed. Neithard Bulst et al. (Göttingen, 1981), 182–201; and Gerhard Wilke and Kurt Wagner, 'Family and household: social structures in a German village between the two World Wars', in *The German Family: Essays on the Social History of the Family in Nineteenth- and Twentieth-Century Germany*, ed. Richard J. Evans and W. R. Lee (London, 1981), 120–47; and Karl Ditt, *Industrialisierung, Arbeiterschaft und Arbeiterbewegung in Bielefeld 1850–1914* (Dortmund, 1982), 9–39.

53 See, e.g., Arthur E. Imhof, 'Women, family and death in four communities in nineteenth-century Germany', in *The German Family*, 148–74; John E. Knodel, *The Decline of Fertility in Germany, 1871–1939* (Princeton, N.J., 1974), 88ff.; and idem, 'Town and

country in nineteenth-century Germany: a review of urban-rural differentials in demographic behavior', *Social Science History* 1 (1977): 356–82.

54 See in particular, Rosenberg, 'Political and social consequences of the Great Depression of 1873–1896 in Central Europe', in *Machteliten und Wirtschaftskonjunkturen*, 161–72; and idem, *Grosse Depression und Bismarckzeit: Wirtschaftsablauf, Gesellschaft und Politik in Mitteleuropa* (Berlin, 1967).

55 Heinz Reif, *Westfälischer Adel 1770–1860: Vom Herrschaftsstand zur regionalen Elite* (Göttingen, 1979).

56 See, e.g., Eugene D. Genovese, *The World the Slaveholders Made: Two Essays in Interpretation* (New York, 1969); idem, *Roll, Jordan, Roll: The World the Slaves Made* (New York, 1976); and most recently, James Oakes, *The Ruling Race: A History of American Slaveholders* (New York, 1982).

57 A forthcoming study by Renate Bridenthal, *Their Own Drummer: Women who Marched toward Hitler*, on women's organizations in the Weimar Republic will provide extremely valuable information on the forms of association among women in the countryside.

58 On this, see the useful model provided by Rudy Koshar, 'Two "Nazisms": the social context of Nazi mobilization in Marburg and Tübingen', *Social History* 7 (1982): 27–42. Another extremely promising model is offered by Steven Hahn, *The Roots of Southern Populism: Yeoman Farmers and the Transformation of the Georgia Upcountry, 1850–1890* (New York, 1983).

59 See, e.g., Gerhard A. Ritter, 'Workers' culture in imperial Germany: problems and points of departure', *Journal of Contemporary History* 13 (1978): 165–89, and the other articles in this special issue of that journal; also, Richard J. Evans (ed.), *The German Working Class: The Politics of Everyday Life* (London, 1982); Evans, *The German Family*; Werner Conze and Ulrich Engelhardt (eds.), *Arbeiter im Industrialisierungsprozess: Herkunft, Lage und Verhalten* (Stuttgart, 1979); Jürgen Reulecke and Wolfhard Weber (eds.), *Fabrik – Familie – Feierabend: Beiträge zur Sozialgeschichte des Alltags im Industriezeitalter* (Wuppertal, 1978); and the articles in *Archiv für Sozialgeschichte* 16 (1976), an issue devoted substantially to working-class history and the history of working-class culture. For attempts to pursue similar lines of research for rural society, see the works cited above in note 52 and also the articles in the special issue of *Archiv für Sozialgeschichte* 19 (1979).

60 See, e.g., Klaus Saul, 'Der Kampf um das Landproletariat: Sozialistische Landagitation, Grossgrundbesitz und preussische Staatsverwaltung 1890 bis 1903', *Archiv für Sozialgeschichte* 15 (1975): 162–208; Jens Flemming, 'Landarbeiter zwischen Gewerkschaften und "Werksgemeinschaft": Zum Verhältnis von Agrarunternehmertum und Landarbeiterbewegung im Übergang vom Kaiserreich zur Weimarer Republik', *Archiv für Sozialgeschichte* 14 (1974): 351–418; Frieda Wunderlich, *Farm Labor in Germany 1810–1945* (Princeton, N.J., 1961); and from an East German perspective, in addition to the work cited in note 19, Martin Polzin, 'Junkerherrschaft – Militarismus – Landarbeiterfrage (Zum Kampf um die Einbeziehung des mecklenburgischen Landproletariats in die revolutionäre deutsche Arbeiterbewegung)', Part 1, *Wissenschaftliche Zeitschrift der Universität Rostock, Gesellschafts- und Sprachwissenschaftliche Reihe* 11 (1962): 209–52, as well as the articles in the special issue of the same journal, 'Von der Novemberrevolution zur demokratischen Bodenreform in Deutschland: Beiträge zur deutschen Agrargeschichte von 1917 bis 1945', vol. 17 (1968).

61 For interesting exceptions, see the collection, Dietmar Sauermann (ed.), *Knechte und Mägde in Westfalen um 1900* (Münster, 1972); and Regina Schulte, 'Bauernmädge in Bayern am Ende des 19. Jahrhunderts', in *Frauen suchen ihre Geschichte: Historische Studien zum 19. und 20. Jahrhundert*, ed. Karin Hausen (Munich, 1983), 110–27.

62 William Sheridan Allen, *The Nazi Seizure of Power: The Experience of a Single German Town 1930–1935* (Chicago, 1965).

63 Martin Broszat, Elke Fröhlich and Falk Wiesemann (eds.), *Bayern in der NS-Zeit: Soziale Lage und politisches Verhalten der Bevölkerung im Spiegel vertraulicher Berichte* (Munich and Vienna, 1977), esp. 327–68. Also interesting in this respect are Falk Wiesemann, 'Arbeitskonflikte in der Landwirtschaft während der NS-Zeit in Bayern 1933–1938', *Vierteljahrshefte für Zeitgeschichte* 25 (1977): 573–90; idem, 'Juden auf dem

Lande: Die wirtschaftliche Ausgrenzung der jüdischen Viehhändler in Bayern', in *Die Reihen fast geschlossen: Beiträge zur Geschichte des Alltags unterm Nationalsozialismus*, ed. Detlev Peukert and Jürgen Reulecke (Wuppertal, 1981), 381–96; and the suggestive outlines in Adelheid von Saldern, *Mittelstand im 'Dritten Reich': Handwerker – Einzelhändler – Bauern* (Frankfurt and New York, 1979).
64 Poppinga, *Bauern und Politik*, and other references above in note 23.

1 The Junkers: Notes on the Social and Historical Significance of the Agrarian Elite in Prussia

HANNA SCHISSLER

The Prussian Junkers were a ruling class for centuries – economically successful, politically powerful and socially dominant in equal measures.[1] No one questions their influence on the history of Prussian Germany well into the twentieth century, an influence which is just as often the topic of historical idealization as of historical critique. It has frequently been noted that the Junkers were able not only to survive under changing circumstances but also to maintain their influence and power in an authoritative way, even when the currents were against them, as for example in the first years of the Prussian reforms or at the end of the nineteenth century. They are given credit for the rise of Prussian Germany and are also made to bear a large part of the responsibility for the destruction of the German Reich. It is a 'fascination with historically momentous events' which draws us to their collective history, the history of their successes and failures.[2]

When one attempts to determine the 'historical significance' of the Junkers, a multitude of questions present themselves. How did they successfully maintain their ruling position into the twentieth century? What factors determined their place in the social structure? What relationship did they have to other classes and social groups? How great was their ability to adapt to altered economic circumstances and conditions which threatened their position politically or economically? How, and through what means, were they able to maintain their estate-standing and social exclusivity? Industrialization and revolutions in the eighteenth and nineteenth centuries shook the economic basis of all European pre-industrial elites and threatened their claims to power and dominance. In what way and with what consequences, counter-strategies and attempts at consolidation did this process unfold for the Junkers? How did the Junkers as a social class experience and digest the rise and fall of their economic power? What role did the Junkers play in Germany's often cited 'Sonderweg', its divergence from the model of Western democracy? Were the Junkers an inherently conservative force? Can one specify the ways in which the Junkers can be held responsible for the failed attempts to democratize German society?

In order to reduce the complexity of the many problems presented here and to make them manageable in the context of this essay, the subject will be approached from two different perspectives. In the first section, basic aspects of the Junkers' objective material conditions will be outlined. This will include a discussion of the preconditions and circumstances of their economic success and political dominance beginning in the sixteenth century. It will also investigate their reactions to attacks against that dominance through the Prussian reforms and the endangerment of their economic status beginning in the last third of the nineteenth century. The second section will attempt a comparison with the English aristocracy in order to illuminate and articulate the importance of the Junkers in Prusso-German history. In addition, it will critically approach certain basic frameworks which assume both the paradigmatic quality of English development and the peculiarity of Germany's historical path.[3]

I

The success of the Junkers as a landed elite before the nineteenth century rests on a variety of factors, which can only be briefly noted here. They include the commercialization of east Elbian grain-based agriculture which, in the wake of economic differentiation between Eastern and Western Europe, had facilitated the expansion of noble enterprise since the fifteenth and sixteenth centuries; the combination of political and economic power in the system of *Gutsherrschaft*[4] and *Gutswirtschaft*; and finally, the way in which the nobility was domesticated by Prussian absolutism and the place it assumed in the social fabric of the eighteenth century.[5]

In the course of the development of international trade relations, product specialization and the evolution of separate yet mutually intertwined and dependent economic zones in the sixteenth century, the countries of Eastern Europe became the principal grain-producers for the commercially and industrially more advanced regions of the West, especially England and Flanders.[6] In the east Elbian regions, a specifically agrarian kind of growth was thus induced which depended on the world market, or more concretely, on the development of demand and on price fluctuations in Western European centres. The surge of commercialization had strong repercussions on the internal social structure of the eastern area which produced and exported grain. During this process of commercialization, a class of estate-owning entrepreneurs emerged which was oriented towards profits and based on export markets. At the same time, the peasant labour force was increasingly tied to the estates. Step by step, formerly free peasants lost their rights, were bound to the soil and were burdened with labour services and dues. In short, there developed what G.D.R. historians refer to as 'the second serfdom'.[7]

Without a doubt, the thrust towards commercialization in the sixteenth century[8] was the strongest force resulting in the confrontation between Junker estate-owners and a peasantry which was deprived of all rights, dependent and bound to the land. An explanation of this process, however, requires consideration of additional factors as well. The late medieval agrarian depression, poor harvests, famines and epidemics had brought about a decline in population, and with it an expansion of unused land.[9] Manorial income decreased sharply, an indirect result of the agrarian depression and a direct result of population decline, falling prices for agricultural products, loss of purchasing power and a general depreciation. In comparison to the time around 1300, the nobles in Lausitz, for example, had lost four-fifths of their rental income by the sixteenth century.[10] The result was a compelling drive to find new revenues. The historical response to this challenge was the replacement of property management based on rent (*Rentengrundherrschaft*)[11] with direct control (*Gutsherrschaft*), and the creation of new sources of income by strengthening personal direction and replacing peasant rent with labour services and dues. The sixteenth century was, to use Hans Rosenberg's words, 'the era of consolidation of Junker power'.[12] In this period, the expansion of the manorial economy took place in full force. What followed was 'the repressive solidification of social control mechanisms' as, so to speak, 'the social costs of production gains in a market economy'.[13] The main characteristic of the Junker's *Gutsherrschaft* was the instrumentalization of sovereign rights for economic purposes. This also was behind the particular harshness of noble–peasant power relations and the ambiguity of these relations in the Age of Enlightenment, economic liberalism and citizen emancipation.[14] Until well into the eighteenth century, the state authority did not impede the Junkers from expanding their estates. On the contrary, in East Prussia the state itself was a motivating force in this process.[15] In addition, the rulers continually sanctioned the Junkers' noble privileges, and in particular never interfered with seigneurial rights on their estates. This is part of what one could call 'chronic political horse trading'.[16] It served to domesticate the nobility which was made responsible for giving the expanding state financial backing. The state, thus assured of necessary financial support, gave the nobility a free hand on their estates in return.[17]

It was only in the eighteenth century, however, that the *Gutsherrschaft* and the Junkers' power entered their true 'classical age'. Although the Junkers' battle with the peasantry in the sixteenth century was, for the most part, victorious, and the peasants were successfully forced into submission, a struggle with Prussian absolutism was still to come.[18] From the Junkers' perspective, this altercation was characterized by a struggle against any encroachment on their estate-based power and against the expanding state system. From the perspective of the prince and later the Prussian king, the struggle was to attain a general peace within the state, to pacify the feuding nobility and the robber knights, and later to finance and personally recruit a viable standing army. Friedrich Wilhelm I could still utter his famous sentence, 'I will ruin the Junkers' authority and establish my sovereignty like a rock of bronze',[19] when the East Prussian nobility opposed the introduction of a general military tax. But under Friedrich II, the relationship between the nobility and the absolute monarchy changed in a truly dramatic fashion.

In the course of the eighteenth century, the aggressive, rebellious nobility became the mainstay of the Prussian state. The transformation, which was hardly a victory on all fronts for absolutism, contained all the elements of a compromise. The nobility made concessions on the issue of estate-based taxation, which made the development of the Prussian army financially possible. After decades of opposition, it let itself be integrated into the officer corps of the king's army. In the process, the nobility gave up its spirit of estate-based separatism and developed its own form of loyalty to the state, or rather to the king as the supreme military commander. The list of concessions and privileges which the absolute monarchy offered the nobility as its part of this compromise is a long one. It granted the nobility preferential treatment in the state bureaucracy and military. It allowed it to further expand the *Gutsherrschaft* (with the exception of the state's own laws protecting the peasantry).[20] Finally, it gave the nobility secure control of their property, which guaranteed their monopoly over estate ownership, offered them a chance to transform their land into entailed estates and provided them with exclusive credit institutions backed by state subsidies, the *Landschaften*.

Slightly altering the language of the modern 'military industrial complex', one might best describe the conditions of Junker power in the eighteenth century as a 'military agrarian complex'. This reciprocal relationship, so brilliantly analysed and described by Otto Büsch,[21] manifested itself on two levels. In society, monarchical absolutism gave the nobles free rein to expand their estates, or at least it did not stand in their way. In return, the Junkers agreed to let themselves be integrated into the absolutist state through military and bureaucratic service. Or as Büsch summarized the compromise agreement between Prussian absolutism and the Junkers, 'During the eighteenth century, it became evident that the only way to make the Junkers fulfill their military duties without friction was for the state to give them power in their social sphere'.[22] At a local level, the Junker developed a double role as both military commander and as a holder of local power on his estate.[23] This resulted in the development of a unique collective mentality for the Junkers, characterized by a special familiarity with power at all levels of social, military and political life. It also meant a militarization of civil rule.[24] The Junkers had undoubtedly been strengthened by their struggle with absolutism.[25] In the last decades of the eighteenth and throughout the nineteenth century, their magic bastions of power and influence were the landed estate, the officer corps and the state bureaucracy.

The favourable agricultural cycle in the last third of the eighteenth century, the expansion of the domestic market fuelled by demands from a growing army and the rapidly increasing demand for grain from an industrializing England combined to stimulate the expansion of the agricultural sector in an unprecedented fashion and assured the Junkers high revenues and profits.[26] At the end of the eighteenth century the Junkers' situation was characterized by material expansion, exclusive privileges in the state and society, and a unique, almost constitutional guarantee of the nobility's privileged position written into the Prussian Legal Code (*Allgemeines Landrecht*) of 1794.[27] And yet at the close of the century a number of crisis symptoms took shape which, at first in a latent and imperceptible way, changed the situation of the landed nobility and undermined their monopoly in Prussian society. The full scale of the crisis was not apparent until after 1806–7, when the Junkers felt its consequences in full force. Its origins lay in the growing indebtedness of Junker estates, the numerical growth of the nobility and finally in the failure of absolutist policies intended to conserve the estate system, in particular those measures aimed at guaranteeing the material security of the landed nobility. All three factors were closely intertwined.

According to recent research, the expansion of estates, in which, to be sure, the Junkers took part, was none the less carried out to a great degree by non-nobles. Working as tenant farmers, landowners (even before 1807, 10 per cent of the estates were in the hands of bourgeois owners) and managers or leasers of so-called 'private estates', they implemented innovative and financially successful agricultural practices.[28] Bourgeois owners and leasers earned great fortunes in agriculture in the last third of the eighteenth century.[29] Buyers from the bourgeoisie stepped forward to purchase noble estates, even though formally this could only take place with the king's special permission before 1807. Private holders of mortgages made their appearance as well.[30] The mortgage debt held by the *Landschaften* reached a level of 54 million Talers compared to 307 million Talers of mortgage indebtedness in private hands.[31] The property transfer that took place in the first decade of the nineteenth century served primarily to clear away the mountains of debts which noble estate-holders had accumulated.[32]

Neither their legal monopoly on land nor the opportunity given to them to entail their holdings, and certainly not the noble credit institutions, the *Landschaften*, were sufficient to maintain the Junkers as a special estate, although this had been the political goal especially under Friedrich II. The Junkers also frequently circumvented their legal property monopoly without difficulty, and the possibility to entail estates was seldom taken before 1803. Entailments took place in two waves which in both instances were first precipitated by bourgeois capital directly endangering Junker property. The first wave started after 1807 and the second after 1850, when one-half of all entailments existing in 1878 were started.[33] The *Landschaften* had been established after the Seven Years' War explicitly for the purpose of preserving the needy nobility. Yet over time, they proved themselves to be one of the strongest, if not the stongest, means of breaking the Junkers' property monopoly. The possibility of obtaining cheap credit certainly also contributed to an improvement and expansion of production. However, its weighty economic and social consequences were without a doubt the unimpeded encouragement of speculation and an artificial boom in the product market. The collapse of the boom was painful for those involved, but in the final analysis it had been caused by the Junkers themselves.[34]

Another factor contributing to the precarious condition of the Junkers at the end of the century was the numerical expansion of the nobility, caused by the immigration of Polish and French nobles, by the generous policies of ennoblement, especially during Friedrich II's reign, and finally by the natural expansion of well-established families. The Prussian nobility had always been an 'open' estate in the sense that it assimilated immigrants and newly created nobles quickly and efficiently.[35] The consequence was that by 1800 the nobility constituted a social problem. Evidence for this is found in the existence of numerous impoverished nobles and in the penetration of the nobility into all offices of the state service, even that of postmaster, because there were no other ways to earn a living. There were noble peasants and even nobles who were beggars and vagabonds.[36] The discrepancies in property-holdings within the nobility were enormous. There were the latifundia of magnates in Silesia, and to a lesser degree in East Prussia, which had been formed during the days of mercenary armies. There were 'well-to-do' nobles who usually held several estates and villages and who constituted almost a quarter of the nobility, according to the informed estimates of G. Czybulka. There were the 'middle' nobles who possessed one or two estates and villages which Czybulka estimated to be almost half of the nobility. And finally

29

there were the 'poor' nobles, the last quarter who possessed only a small estate or only part of an estate. This petty nobility led an impoverished existence and was often difficult to distinguish from the surrounding peasantry.[37]

The agrarian expansion during the last years of the eighteenth century was for many estate-owners only an illusion because of uncontrolled speculation. None the less, it did cause hidden and actual property transfers due to sales (some forced) and debts. It also had a very ambivalent effect on estate labour relations and therefore on the rural social structure as well. For some, more rational and effective estate management started a trend towards the emancipation of labour. Liberal economic policies and practical experience had shown that one could manage better with free labour than with the unwilling labour dues of peasants. For others, however, exactly the same conditions, namely favourable prospects for profit leading to efforts to rationalize estate management, had exactly the opposite results. In some cases, labour dues were increased to six days a week in order to squeeze the last drop from the peasants. The extensive use of an *available* labour reserve was of course much cheaper and more immediately profitable than using a more costly free labour force. The increase of freed labour power, as well as the intensified exploitation of peasant dues, both undermined the social order in the countryside, exacerbated existing tensions and heightened readiness for conflict.[38]

The nobility's position at the end of the eighteenth century had declined socially and economically. As a result of the French Revolution, which drew all of Europe in its wake, and especially after Prussia's military defeat by Napoleon in 1806–7, their political position became precarious as well. The reforms which began in Prussia in 1807 had, so to speak, a 'purging' effect on the Junkers. The agrarian reforms widened the social basis of the Junkers and consolidated their economic position by officially opening up noble estates (*Rittergüter*) to non-nobles.[39] The nobles' property monopoly was eliminated, as was that estate-based exclusivity guaranteeing certain rights and privileges to them alone. One observer felt that the reforms were the only way for the Prussian Junkers to survive; otherwise they would have inevitably been driven to economic destruction.[40] Even when one does not go this far, there is no doubt that the reforms broadened the legal basis for an expansion of large land-holdings.[41] It was only in the nineteenth century that east Elbian estates experienced an expansion in territory.

The Junkers themselves, or at least a good number of them, were afraid that they would be eradicated as a privileged estate by the 'gang of homeless fellows lost in theories', as the Frondist von der Marwitz from Mark Brandenburg called the highest levels of state officials.[42] For the most part, the Prussian nobility reacted to the revolution and the reforms with fearful fantasies of social decline. The Prussian reaction was not at all atypical. In England as well, the revolutionary wars were accompanied by a wave of aristocratic reaction.[43] To those most affected, the reforms must have often seemed like a frontal attack on their place in state and society. A more careful perusal, however, revealed that the reforms were not at all the deadly blow against the aristocracy described so passionately by von der Marwitz.

Many landowners, especially those in East Prussia, recognized early on the advantages to be gained from the reforms of agrarian conditions and the property structure, which seemed to be both politically and economically imperative.[44] The Junkers perceived the intervention into their controls over peasant labourers as restrictive. They also resented the unimpeded flood of bourgeois and peasant estate-owners. However, these measures not only legalized social-economic processes which were already under way; for the most part they also served to support those people who quite unjustifiably feared their destruction as a privileged estate and a special property-owning class. Moreover, the transformation of the nobility from an estate into a property-owning ruling class no longer defined exclusively by noble birth, the legal emancipation of labourers and the transformation of peasant land into private property were all undertaken in such a way as to make the hardships of transition easier for the landowners. In addition to this, a number of indirect and direct measures which supported property-owners accompanied the reforms. The comprehensive protection of indebted nobles from their (bourgeois) creditors through credit moratoria, which lasted for decades in some provinces, was only the most obvious example.

The Junkers were able to boycott reforms of the state's political constitution almost entirely. They succeeded in delaying and defusing those reforms which touched upon their material interests as landowners or tax-payers. To some extent, the Junkers were able to force the bureaucracy to rescind in practice laws which had already been passed. This was the case in 1816 when the authorization for small peasants to take possession of their land was retroactively denied.[45] Still intact were the rights of political rule which had proved themselves to be both practical and effective in dealing with the rural population over the centuries. They were, so to speak, only 'democratized', since they were made open to everyone, even to the large number of new owners who took control of estates.[46]

The lasting, immutable result of the social, economic and agrarian reforms was to open up the Junkers as an advantaged propertied class and to transform it into a new class of noble estate entrepreneurs composed of both noble and bourgeois property-holders.[47] This new class certainly remained sufficiently privileged and indeed was equipped with additional

31

rights. This not only guaranteed its survival; it also assured the new prop-ertied classes, fused together in the course of a few decades, excellent opportunities for a start in the age of agrarian capitalism.[48] Koselleck described the effects of the reforms on the landed nobility in the follow-ing way: 'Precisely because it had been placed on equal economic footing with the bourgeoisie, the nobility could salvage more privileges during the 19th century than would have been possible otherwise. Thus adap-tation took place on both sides, and the nobility remained the winner in the end.'[49] The nobility could defeat or neutralize political attacks on its predominance at all levels, as for example in the dispute over laws governing rural police or in the struggle over provincial constitutions.[50] Attempts were made to limit the political effects of the 'embour-geoisement' of noble landowners in a number of ways. Along with the economic measures protecting noble holdings, there was in addition a kind of personal estate mentality which was to some degree grafted on to the possession of a noble estate.[51]

Eckart Kehr characterized the altercations between the nobility and the bureaucracy during the reform years in the following, somewhat cryptic way: 'From 1807 to 1812, the foundations were laid, then shaken, then stabilized for a situation which must be described as a firm alliance against everyone not involved and a bitter struggle between the allies on every possible point where their interests intersected.'[52] The somewhat drama-tic formulation describes the 'reversed fronts' which characterized noble resistance to the reforms. It describes the completely fabricated suspicions of an ancient, oppositional nobility, which feared that the bureaucracy intended to do away with it.[53] In the struggle against the reforms and against the replacement of monarchical absolutism with bureaucratic rule, which was perhaps even more important, the alliance between the monarchy and the nobility was renewed.[54] This alliance had dominated politics and the structure of society since the eighteenth century, especially in its second half. Then, however, there were no competing claims to power from the bureaucracy and there was not the same degree of pressure on the nobility's economic position from the bourgeoisie. This struggle for power and reform, or for the 'regeneration of the Prussian state' as it was called in the elevated language of the reformers themselves, took place between different parts of the ruling elite.[55] In the process, the enemies very quickly saw eye to eye. As has been stated in a somewhat more pointed way, by 1822 at the latest, 'the bureaucratic monarchy [found itself] in league with Junker class interests'.[56]

A number of factors were decisive for the collective history of the Junkers in the first decades of the nineteenth century:

The opening of the Junkers as a privileged estate and its transformation into a 'mobile economic class'[57] was accomplished with encumbering property transfers, especially in the 1820s, and in part through a painful process of accommodation.[58]

The landed nobility assimilated the *homines novi* within a few decades, in the second or third generation at the latest. However, its power of integration only went far enough to retain the nobles' dominance within the newly constituted estate-owning class.[59]

The bourgeoisie pushed to take part in existing economic opportunities and rewards. Politically, however, it hardly made any demands. At least in the reform years and during the wars of liberation, it was not an important factor in the struggle for positions of power and influence.[60]

The bureaucracy needed an ally in order to make a breakthrough and secure its own power, but the bourgeoisie was not available. The bureaucracy's claims to power meant essentially the continuation, modernization and rationalization of monarchical absolutism. Potential bourgeois demands, for example for the parliamentarization of political rule or for the state to give up its regulation of political and social processes, could hardly have supported the bureaucracy in an effective way. This situation, along with the prevailing power relations and the fact that Prussia's high officials came mainly from the landed nobility, necessarily put the bureaucracy into contact with the Junkers, placing both groups into the same camp.[61] The Bonapartist alternative of a coalition with the urban and rural lower classes against the Junkers and the monarchy was not a realistic option at this moment in history.

The peasants had become accustomed to their lack of rights and to Junker rule over the centuries. They acquiesced to the conditions created for them by the reforms almost without protest, accepting the Junkers' political control in daily life and at most petitioning for the removal of particularly crass injustices. In competition with the economically superior Junkers, who were well endowed with privileges and power, they found their legal position on the free market to be much weaker.[62] The Junkers and both the central and local administrations thought that 'the natural relationship' of protection, supervision and dependence between larger and more cultured landowners and the small peasants was as useful to the small landowners as it was to the state.[63] The peasants accepted this situation in the *Vormärz* period, although enough social resentments and seeds of discontent had accumulated over the years.

The Junkers were the real winners in the agrarian reforms. They were also the privileged beneficiaries and participants in a new distribution of political power during the reform years. Expanded by the addition of a capital-rich bourgeoisie, they faced a deep economic crisis in the 1820s which was a difficult test for their economic stability.[64] During these years, when most of the property transfers took place through forced auctions, the most viable and economically successful estates emerged.

Agile agrarian entrepreneurs who saw an opportunity in the European market and took advantage of it in time were saved from bankruptcy by switching to sheepraising when grain prices were at their lowest.[65] The first decades of the nineteenth century were a time of difficult economic consolidation for the landowning class. These years were marked by a struggle for economic survival, adjustment to new agricultural methods using free labour[66] and a significant general increase in the value of commodities.[67]

In the 1850s and 1860s the Junkers attained the historical peak of their economic power. On the supply side, factors contributing to their economic power were extremely low wage levels and an abundance of agrarian labourers, both resulting from population expansion and pauperism.[68] On the demand side, the suspension of the English Corn Laws in 1846 and the development of an internal market played a determining role. The economic significance of the east Elbian Junkers would never be greater. Through its exports, the agrarian sector contributed substantially to general economic growth and also indirectly to industrialization. Junker ties to international trading networks transmitted English demand on to the German market. In addition, the Junkers were virtually the sole suppliers of agrarian products for the domestic market.[69]

There could hardly have been a worse time to try to take away the Junkers' power than the revolution of 1848. Given the great economic importance of east Elbian agriculture, which lasted into the 1870s, a coalition against the Junker elite was of necessity unstable, weak and fragile. It is easier for a class to maintain its social and political dominance when it has legitimized itself through economic success. For the Junkers, this was the case in the 1850s in contrast to the years of defensive reaction in the reform era. Kehr described the same development in a positive fashion: 'Conservatism remained active because it was part of a large, modern, agrarian class, not because it was feudal.'[70]

Since they were accustomed to economic success, the Junkers were understandably poorly prepared for a conjunctural change starting in the mid-1870s, the effects of which were most directly felt at the high point of the agrarian depression in 1893–94. The break was sharp. The previous increase in prices did not continue during the European-wide 'Great Depression'. At times, grain prices even fell.[71] Old debts and new ones incurred to improve production or to speculate in land had been easier to bear during the years of agricultural expansion, rising prices, available markets and high profits. By the end of the century, however, they were a heavy burden for east Elbian landowners.[72] Faced with these secular trends, the grain-exporting east Elbian Junkers also met with overseas competition, especially from America, as a result of the transport revolution and low shipping rates.[73]

This situation, already very difficult for the export-oriented, exclusively grain-producing Junkers, was aggravated by two internal economic factors. In all industrializing countries, agriculture has always been the long-term loser in economic development. Growth rates in agriculture stayed behind those of industry, as did agrarian profitability, productivity, profit margins and volume. The percentage of agricultural workers in the labour force declined in general. The east Elbian Junkers were confronted with precisely these structural problems in the years of acute agricultural crisis.[74] Finally there was yet another imminently momentous economic and social problem – the mass exodus of agrarian labourers to the industrial centres in the west. This was above all the result of a demand for industrial labour, encouraged and accelerated by the low wages and poor working conditions prevalent in agriculture. This flight from the land was, therefore, also a postponed consequence of the social problems left over from the agrarian reforms.[75] The cut went deep and the Junkers found it especially painful.

Instead of trying to adapt economically to the changed market conditions, the Junkers called for state aid. In keeping with their economic interests, the Junkers had always been traditional free traders before 1879. This was at the root of the East Prussian noble liberalism in the *Vormärz* period.[76] From the middle of the 1870s onwards, the Junkers demanded and received protective tariffs. Protectionism was costly for both the state and for society, and was carried to such an extreme that by 1931 German grain prices were 300 per cent over the world market level.[77] For consumers and tax-payers, in particular for the mass of workers, but also for small agrarian producers dependent on cheap imported fodders, the economic and social consequences of these protectionist policies were only too obvious.[78] The preservation of the now unprofitable agrarian structure of East Prussia resulted in an intensification of distribution struggles and increasing political legitimation problems. According to Puhle, this 'not only [presented] an economic problem with implications for power in the state, the province and local government, it was also a class problem'.[79]

The Junkers compensated for their loss of economic significance by exercising forced political influence, and the political constellation of Imperial Germany offered excellent chances of success. With the founding of the Agrarian League (*Bund der Landwirte*) in 1893, the landowners created an unusually effective mass organization, an instrument through which they could not only achieve economic and political success, but which would also help to popularize right-wing radicalism.[80] The economic demands of the east Elbian Junkers (and the readiness of the state rulers to meet them) finally culminated in the 'emancipation of the agrarian sector from the free market' at the end of the Weimar Republic.

It also resulted in 'the complete nationalization of the market, of distribution and price formation and the complete reduction of entrepreneurial risk with the National Socialist *Reichsnährstand* (Reich Food Estate)'.[81] By fighting for their economic and political survival, the Junkers made an unfortunate contribution to the destruction of Weimar democracy and to the advent of National Socialism, a process fully described by Puhle and Rosenberg. The Junkers, 'unwilling to come to personal terms with the humiliating realities of their shattered ruling position',[82] perished as a social class together with the Third Reich.

II

Historians agree that the Junkers represented a great political, economic and social burden for Prusso-German history. The bill for preserving the Junkers as a social class was also presented during twelve years of National Socialist dictatorship and two World Wars and finally paid off through defeat and destruction. A catalogue of critical assessments can be compiled with ease. For example, Hans–Ulrich Wehler's judgement,

> Much testifies to the fact that precisely in Germany important economic, social and political decisions were made in the interests of ruling agrarian social elites after 1866–71 which influenced the development of Imperial German industrial society in the most profound way. Indeed, a good portion of the obvious 'discrepancies' and 'exceptional qualities' of this society can certainly be attributed to this.

For Wehler, the 'long list of heavy historical burdens' begins with 'the influence of pre-industrial leadership groups, norms and ideals', and 'the superimposition of estate gradations and class differences'.[83]

In the actions of the Agrarian League, which was dominated by east Elbian landowners, 'along with neo-estatist tendencies . . . and the resistance to democracy and parliamentarization', Puhle sees 'a definite structural characteristic of something which can be called German proto-fascism. This mirrors a society without a minimal democratic consensus which apparently only preceding revolutions can accomplish.'[84] The harshest assessment in Western historiography is to be found in Rosenberg's work:[85]

> Even in their destruction, for which they themselves were to blame, the old ruling groups [*with the Junkers in the most important position, H.S.*] played significant, if also mainly catastrophic roles. In the

Weimar Republic they were essentially the co-directors in the destruction of parliamentary democracy, the restoration of authoritarian forms of government and the sanctioning of dictatorship.

And in another place:

In Imperial Germany and the Weimar Republic, with the exception of a few renegade loners, political democratization of the rejuvenated landed aristocracy was limited to the donning of a democratic mask and the exploitation of democratic methods for undemocratic goals with antidemocratic convictions.[86]

A list of similar opinions can be extended indefinitely. Despite many differences in details, there are two common points which unify these critical judgements. The first is an awareness of the difficult problem of continuity in German history, including a sense of the 'burdens' which pre-industrial elites and value systems can create for industrial societies. The second is a more or less latent image of the prototypical nature of the Western, and especially the Anglo-Saxon, democratic and parliamentary path of development. The first point and its implications for critical historiography will not be examined. That would overstep the boundaries of this essay. The second point, however, deserves some critical consideration in the context of this discussion. In the following point-by-point comparison, which in no way claims to be systematic, similarities and differences in the history of the German Junkers and the English landed aristocracy will be explored. Although it can only be done in a fragmented and suggestive way, the persuasive power of the 'Anglo-Saxon model' will be questioned here. This model is frequently only implicit, but its prototypical nature shapes opinions in this and other areas.

While the role of the Junkers in German history is generally judged harshly, and surely not without justification, positive tones prevail in assessments of the English aristocracy. Here are just three brief examples. Spring calls the English model of development that 'extraordinary misture of democracy and aristocracy to be found nowhere else in Europe'.[87] Kluxen credits the English aristocracy with 'that political sense which places freedom above truth and compromise above intransigence in the interests of human understanding',[88] an extremely euphemistic way to describe the English upper class's ability to exert itself in politics in the eighteenth century through influence, patronage, bribery and corruption. Finally, Moore determines that the English aristocracy knew how to leave the historical stage at the right time, to hand over its power to the bourgeoisie and 'commit decorous suicide'.[89] In this stereotypical vision, a cosmopolitan, politically shrewd, socially mobile and flexible English aristocracy, helping to facilitate economic advance in both agriculture and industry, is contrasted with the ignorant, socially narrow-minded Junkers clinging to their privileges and pursuing reactionary political goals. Surely this is a crude simplification which distorts the historical role of both ruling elites.[90]

The English nobility and the Prussian Junkers were both *agrarian* elites. The roots of their political power, the source of their prestige and the basis of their fortune and income all lay in the possession of land.[91] As landed aristocrats they distinguished themselves from the French and especially the Russian nobility. Since the reign of Louis XIV the former were mainly court nobles and the latter were service nobles.[92] Although the Prussian Junkers had considerable land at their disposal in the nineteenth century, the English aristocracy none the less had direct control over more land. Estate-holders in Prussia owned approximately 40 per cent of the land, although in the 'typical' Junker provinces they had direct control of around 60 per cent (in Pomerania it was 62 per cent, in Posen 55 per cent). In England, the nobility owned 55 per cent of the land, and when judged by the size classifications of Western Europe, even 69 per cent. In contrast, the French nobility only possessed about 20 per cent of the land at the beginning of the nineteenth century and the nobles in European Russia only 14 per cent.[93]

The nobility dominated the army and administration in both England and Prussia. In England this was accomplished through patronage and in Prussia through custom and the legally guaranteed 'privileged right of the nobility to hold favourable positions in the state'.[94] For centuries, both the English nobility and the Prussian Junkers constituted a 'ruling class'. However, the collective state powers of the English aristocracy were much more clearly apparent.[95] The parliamentarization of political rule primarily insured the nobility's power until well into the nineteenth century, when democratization took place step by step through a series of voting reforms. The long century after 1688 was the 'classical period of the nobility' and of noble parliamentary rule.[96] And even in the nineteenth century it has been said that there were practically no tensions between the bureaucracy and the nobility 'because the English landowners were the country's ruling class'.[97]

In contrast, the Prussian Junkers in the eighteenth and nineteenth centuries were only *part* of the ruling elite coalition. They shared their claims to power with an absolute monarchy for which there were no parallels in English history and only vague attempts at emulation under George III (1760–83), and with the bureaucracy, which was a stronger and more independent factor in Prussian German history.[98] In Prussia and Germany, the 'ruling consensus' had to be renegotiated from time to time between different sectors of the ruling elite which occasionally opposed one another, or else it had to be secured against advancing social forces like the bourgeoisie and organized labour. This took place during the reign of Friedrich Wilhelm I, in the reform period of 1806–7, during the conflict over the constitution until the Empire was formed under Bismarck and of course also after the German Revolution of 1918–19. For the English upper classes, the introduction of a parliamentary system took place over centuries and was a means of preserving their interests, achieving their rule and effectively regulating and avoiding internal conflict. In Prussian Germany, this process took place in the nineteenth century under completely different historical conditions and functional factors.[99] The parliament never became a sovereign, manageable instrument of rule for the Prussian Junkers in the way that it was for the English aristocracy. Although the parliament in Prussia did in fact decisively secure the political influence of the nobility and estate-owners through its upper house and three-tiered voting system,[100] the Reichstag with its democratic voting system had the primary function of securing and popularizing the influence of the government and the bureaucracy.

Both the English and Prussian nobilities were 'open' social classes. Both were ready and willing to accommodate social climbers and newcomers, and for both, this generally took from two to three generations. In both cases, the predominance of noble value systems and behavioural patterns were none the less retained.[101] The social appeal of land-ownership as a measure of prestige, not rational economic power, was also the same in both cases.[102] In both countries, there were legal reforms which contradicted liberal economic policies. These reforms, in Prussia the entailment laws and in England the 'strict family settlement', aimed to secure noble property and to keep land out of bourgeois hands.[103]

It is illuminating to compare the methods employed to maintain noble estates in both cases. In England, an optimum of flexibility was sought, since the 'strict family settlement' was only good for a limited period of time and was usually renegotiated between the father and the eldest son in every generation. In this way, indebtedness or sale of property could be undertaken at periodic intervals should they become necessary so that the financial situation of the property could be adjusted to economic conditions. The Prussian entailment was decidedly less flexible. Once it was established with the king's permission, it existed in perpetuity and could only be revoked with royal sanction or through a court decision.[104]

Both the Junkers and the gentry were economically active elites long before the nineteenth century; both played a decisive role in the commercialization and capitalization of agriculture. However, the two patterns of development differed greatly in the way in which commercialization and capitalization were carried out and in the social processes which they unleashed.[105] The gentry leased out their land and became capitalist rentiers. The central position which sheepraising had in English agriculture resulted, among other things, in a gradual release of labour power. In east Elbia, on the other hand, the expansion of grain-growing which was stimulated by export opportunities played the decisive role in agrarian progress and partially expanded and intensified what Moore has called a repressive labour system using labour dues and serfdom. In contrast to England, in addition to their income from land-leasing, the Junkers' personal economic control played an important role.

The untimely dominance of the nobility and of an aristocratic value system in an industrialized society is often given as the decisive factor of Germany's special developmental path. However, in this respect Prussian Germany is not fundamentally different from England. The statement that 'the agriculturalists were able to keep their political position so much longer than their economic role warranted' sounds like a stereotypical description of the burdens bequeathed to German history during the imperial period, yet it was recently formulated in reference to England.[106]

Along with the many similarities which the Junkers share with the English landed aristocracy, there are a number of differences which are crucial for the comparison. In contrast to the position of all other continental European nobilities, there was no legally guaranteed personal estate standing for a noble in England. Only the ownership of property brought with it political rights. There were no personal privileges which belonged to the nobility per se.[107] One consequence of this was that the open character of the aristocracy took on a special character which differed decisively from the situation in Prussia. In England, the nobility found itself in a lively interchange with the bourgeoisie. Social mobility was, for the most part, not caused by the advance of the bourgeoisie. In this respect the English aristocracy was no more open and no less exclusive than the Prussian Junkers, and certainly no less exclusive than any other continental aristocracy.[108] Instead, the distinctive feature of exchanges between the nobility and the bourgeoisie was the extensive downward mobility among the aristocracy's younger children. As a result or by-product of this, social barriers and limits on communication between the nobility and the bourgeoisie were much less important. Financial and industrial occupations were also more viable socially, while not lessening the prestige of landownership.[109]

In Prussia, the nobility and bourgeoisie were legally fixed estates and until the October Edict of 1806, nobles were not allowed to pursue 'bourgeois' professions. During the nineteenth century the abstinence of the Junkers from industrial activities was quite noticeable. Mortgage bonds and state papers were preferred as investments.[110] In comparison, the

English aristocracy participated in industrial development. It directly promoted the transport revolution and took part in industrial ventures, and indirectly it provided capital and licences, for example in coal production and iron-smelting.[111] Access to property ownership was always open in England, at least as long as the market made it possible. State prohibitions and statutes regarding property and the practice of professions, like those in Prussia, never existed in England. However, in Prussia too the divisive and monopolistic intentions advanced by the state before 1806 proved increasingly ineffective; after the reforms they were officially abandoned.

One of the most important differences between the English nobility and the Prussian Junkers was surely the ability of the English aristocratic elite to integrate rising economically strengthened groups *politically* (and a central part of this was also the ability to neutralize them).[112] They gave up positions of political power when these could no longer be defended. The history of the English suffrage reforms in the nineteenth century provides many examples for this. This 'political sagacity' is generally regarded as the most typical characteristic of the English aristocracy, along with its economic openness. It cannot really be compared with the reactions of *any* continental aristocracy because nowhere else besides England was the aristocratic elite in such an unequivocal position of power.

'Political sagacity', however, did not imply abandonment of claims to social status and influence. The tendencies towards a 'refeudalization' of society in Imperial Germany, which found their most significant and exaggerated expression in the institution of the Reserve Officer Corps,[113] completely corresponded with the successful efforts of the English elite to inculcate advancing social groups with aristocratic values. One need only refer to the key role of elite 'public schools' and the consciously elitist selections of Cambridge and Oxford, not to mention the effectiveness of social images like that of the ideal gentleman, who was a dilettantish yet universally educated aristocrat.[114]

The English aristocracy identified itself with the state as its 'ruling class' and was willing (and able) to take on enormous taxation burdens during the Napoleonic Wars. The Junkers only identified themselves with the state in so far as it allowed and guaranteed them a privileged position in society. This was the essential prerequisite for their 'pro-state' attitudes and the basis of their compromise with monarchical absolutism in the eighteenth century and with the bureaucracy in the nineteenth century. They vehemently protested against the intentions of the reform bureaucracy to take away their traditional taxation privileges.

Of course, this schematic comparison raises more questions than it can answer. In areas of political and social integration, why were peaceful solutions almost always found in England, and why were the Prusso-German developments characterized by extreme social tensions and political ruptures? Why was the English aristocracy a forerunner of parliamentarization? Although it slowed the process of democratization – especially during the violent struggles around the suffrage reform in 1832 – why did it not block expansion of the suffrage altogether? Why were the Junkers not supporters of parliament? Why were they committed enemies of democracy? Or to put these questions more generally, why is the historical judgement of the English aristocracy so much more positive than that of the Prussian Junkers?

Only provisional answers can be offered here:

(1) Like its English counterpart, Prussian liberalism had its roots in free trade.[115] In Prussia, however, the economic basis for support of free trade evaporated after 1870 with the change in the economic situation for agricultural producers and the massive threat of overseas competition. Without wanting to exaggerate the significance of East Prussian noble liberalism, surely the English landed gentry was not *eo ipso* liberal nor were the Prussian Junkers reactionary. The reactions and struggles of the English agrarian upper class from 1790 to 1850, an important phase in English social history, testify eloquently against this.[116] Both the aristocratic reaction in the Prussian *Vormärz* period and the Junkers' struggle for economic survival after the late 1870s in Germany, with all their political ramifications, are not without their English parallels. The decades of the Corn Laws, 1816–46, called forth class tensions and reactionary coalitions which posed a 'potentially centrifugal opposition'.[117] The class struggles in England in this period ended with the electoral reforms in 1832 and the suspension of the Corn Laws in 1846.

The ability to find a 'peaceful solution' to social conflicts still remains the most obvious characteristic of English development. In contrast, one of the most characteristic traits of Imperial Germany was to repress inner tensions, to impose a stigma of illegitimacy on them, to create scapegoats responsible for them and, finally, to channel inner conflicts outwards by militarizing society.[118] Pollard emphasizes that the peaceful solutions of class conflict in England, especially during the time of the Corn Laws, had very much to do with the 'special position of England within the European industrialization process'. It was a forerunner not only in the economic field, but also in the search for original solutions to social conflicts. The political prowess of the agrarian ruling class in defusing very explosive class tensions in the first half of the nineteenth century must be seen in this context. Agrarian growth definitely mitigated agriculture's losing battle against industry. This encouraged and facilitated the rural ruling elite's readiness for political concessions and compromise.[119]

(2) In England, the aristocracy secured its rule through parliament.

After 1688 it was successively able to hem in and control monarchical rule with the parliament. In Prussia and later in the German Empire, the Junkers were part of a ruling elite coalition, outlined above. Their power was exercised directly in *Grundherrschaft* and at the local and provincial level; it was exercised indirectly by their personal participation in the institutions of the military and the bureaucracy. As it was introduced into Prussian Germany in the nineteenth century, parliamentarization could no longer be adapted into a more or less sovereign operational instrument to serve the inclinations and interests of the agrarian ruling elite. Parliamentarization in Germany was demanded by the propertied and educated bourgeoisie. The Junkers had more chances of success when they challenged these claims from within their traditional bastions of power and through established channels of influence. Parliaments were institutionalized in Germany at a time when the agrarian elite only had more to lose politically and economically in the foreseeable future. In England, on the other hand, the drive for parliamentary reform found the aristocracy at its historical peak and its power was still undisputed by the bourgeoisie. Historically, the parliament turned out to be a far more appropriate instrument for regulating internal conflict and social strife than bureaucratic rule. Indeed, in Prussia the bureaucracy had already exhausted its power to ease tensions and solve social conflict after the *Vormärz* period and its position 'above parties' was increasingly in question in the last half of the century.[120] The rules of the game for the English aristocracy, learned in a long historical process, consisted of making their political influence felt in parliament while also accepting the loser's position in parliamentary affairs. In contrast, the Junkers' traditional playing rules dictated the exercise of influence over the state's instruments of power and, in a practice conditioned since the sixteenth century, in the compensation for political concessions with economic opportunities. By the end of the nineteenth century, under different circumstances, this led to tariff protection which was entirely in keeping with the state's guarantee to secure the economic existence of the Junkers; during the Weimar Republic, it led to massive subsidies for east Elbian agriculture, long since unprofitable.

England is an exceptional case in almost every respect – in its role as an economic pioneer, its geographic position, its original solutions to social conflicts and its regulation of political problems.[121] Still for many reasons it is tempting to compare the English and German developmental paths and to come to the conclusion that German history followed a 'special' course. A pioneer sets the standards of measurement by which the followers must measure themselves. A critical assessment of the problems, burdens and catastrophes of one's own history necessarily leads to comparisons with the 'costs' of other developmental paths. However,

43

distortions of historical judgement very often lie precisely in the problem of weighing 'historical burdens' in German development and in the comparison with England as a model. Reinhard Bendix gives the following apt characterization:

> It will not do to contrast these liabilities of the German transformation with the positive results of the English and French revolutions. The consequences of German autocracy and the weakness of German liberalism should be compared rather with the costs of economic individualism in the industrial development of England or France as well as the cost of 'free trade' imperialism in colonial empires of both countries. As a general rule, comparison requires a consideration of assets and liabilities, rather than contrasts between the liabilities of the one country and the assets of another.[122]

This is not to deny the existence of German historical burdens, to rationalize or still less to glorify the rule and the significance of the Junkers in its historical development. Rather the thoughts offered here only demonstrate that the mandate for historical 'justice' and systematic precision both dictate that the levels of comparability be specified and that judgements resting on comparisons be carefully tested. This essay cannot fill such a demanding agenda, but it can suggest that pursuing it rigorously offers an extremely effective strategy for challenging well-worn prejudices.[123]

Notes: Chapter 1

1   This is a revised and shortened version of Hanna Schissler, 'Die Junker. Zur Sozialgeschichte und historischen Bedeutung der agrarischen Elite in Preussen', in H.-J. Puhle and H.-U. Wehler (eds.), *Preussen im Rückblick*, Sonderheft 6, *Geschichte und Gesellschaft* (Göttingen, 1980), 89–122. Some of the references have been shortened for this version. It appears here with permission of the publisher. The translation was provided by Lynn Mally.

2   G. Schultz, 'Deutschland und der preussische Osten. Heterologie und Hegemonie', in H.-U. Wehler (ed.), *Sozialgeschichte heute. Festschrift für H. Rosenberg* (Göttingen, 1974), 87. A polemical or pejorative tone is frequently implicit in the word Junker or *Junkertum*, as for example in the expressions *Krautjunker* (country bumpkins) or *Junkerparlament* (country backbenchers). The word was freely associated with the collective qualities of stubbornness, self-interest, egotism, ignorance, boorishness, provinciality, lack of education and narrow-mindedness. However, the word Junker was as commonly used as a term of self-definition and, as in the case of Bismarck, was a proud form of identification. In the following, both the negative and positive connotations of the words Junker and *Junkertum* will be avoided. The terms landed nobility, landed elite, knight's estate-owner (*Rittergutsbesitzer*) and Junker will be used more or less interchangeably. One will be given preference to another only to highlight certain characteristics. For the semantics of the term 'Junker', see H. Rosenberg, 'Die Ausprägung der Junkerherrschaft in Brandenburg-Preussen 1410–1648', in his *Machteliten und Wirtschaftskonjunkturen* (Göttingen, 1978), 24–6.

3   The decision to treat such a global question as the role and function of the Junkers in Prussian history in this way stems largely from personal interests which can, of course, be explained objectively. Two limitations of this essay should be made clear from the outset. The first part concentrates on the global characteristics of the development of the Junkers' collective history. Relationships with other social groups and classes will be excluded or treated only in a tangential way. In the second half, I will concentrate on the West German historiography, occasionally referring to American authors. I will thus avoid a confrontation with East German authors (for example, H. Harnisch, R. Berthold, H. H. Müller and others) whose contributions to the field of Prussian social, economic and agrarian history have been very productive. This limitation is made largely for practical reasons. On this issue see J. Kocka, 'Preussischer Staat und Modernisierung im Vormärz. Marxistisch-leninistische Interpretationen und ihre Probleme', in *Sozialgeschichte heute*, 211–27.

4   *Gutswirtschaft*, economic control of an estate, was the system which predominated in the Prussian provinces east of the Elbe. It involved the lord's direct control not only over property but also over the peasant labour force which worked the estate. *Gutsherrschaft*, also associated with ownership of a large, landed estate, refers to the lord's extensive political powers, including rights of patrimonial justice and police authority over the peasants on the estate, as well as legally established control over the local government. The system of *Gutsherrschaft* is typically contrasted with that of *Rentengrundherrschaft* which was characteristic of southern and western Germany. Under this system, the feudal lord maintained legal control over landed property, but not over the peasants who farmed it. Indeed, in the areas of western, north-western and southern Germany where this system prevailed, peasants often enjoyed tenant rights which were hereditary, and in other cases, estates were legally divided among peasants in return for payment and monetary compensation for the lord's residual feudal rights. In virtually no cases did peasant dependency take the form of personal services to the feudal lord, as was the case in areas of *Gutsherrschaft* east of the Elbe. See Werner Conze, 'The effects of nineteenth-century liberal agrarian reforms on social structures in Central Europe', in F. Crouzet, W. H. Chaloner and W. M. Stern (eds.), *Essays in European Economic History 1789–1914* (New York, 1969). [Ed.]

5   H. Rosenberg has presented a comprehensive social history of the Junkers in a number of works. See his article cited in note 2 and relevant passages in *Bureaucracy, Aristocracy and Autocracy. The Prussian Experience 1660–1815* (Cambridge, Mass., 1958). His essays 'Die Pseudodemokratisierung der Rittergutsbesitzerklasse' and 'Zur sozialen Funktion der Agrarpolitik im Zweiten Reich' have recently been reprinted in his book, *Machteliten*. Both of these essays are cited here using the 1969 Frankfurt edition. Unfortunately, Rosenberg has not brought his writings on the social history of the Junkers together into a comprehensive synthesis. On what follows, see especially 'Junkerherrschaft'.

6   Rosenberg, 'Junkerherrschaft', 68, 71; I. Wallerstein *The Modern World System*, vol. 1, *Capitalist Agriculture and the Origins of the European World Economy in the 16th Century* (London, 1974).

7   F. L. Carsten, *The Origins of Prussia* (Oxford, 1954), esp. chs. 8 and 11.

8   Grain trade with the West was carried out as early as the fourteenth century by German knights. However, in the following centuries it declined again. Carsten 96; Rosenberg, 'Junkerherrschaft', 68.

9   On the late medieval agrarian depression and its consequences for population decline and the spread of unused land, see W. Abel, *Agrarkrisen und Agrarkonjunktur* (Hamburg, 1966), 55–96, and idem *Die Wüstungen des ausgehenden Mittelalters* (Stuttgart, 1976).

10 W. A. Boelcke, 'Die Einkünfte Lausitzer Adelsherrschaft im Mittelalter und Neuzeit', in *Festschrift für F. Lütge* (Stuttgart 1966), 183–205; see also Rosenberg, 'Junkerherrschaft', 65f.

11 See the discussion above, note 4.

12 Rosenberg, 'Junkerherrschaft', 63.

13 ibid., 69, 71. An important outcome of this process was also to subvert the role of urban merchants and therefore gradually to undermine the importance of cities. Rosenberg, 'Junkerherrschaft', 76ff.; Carsten, 117–35.

14 On this topic, see F.-W. Henning, *Herrschaft und Bauernuntertänigkeit. Beiträge zur Geschichte der Herrschaftsverhältnisse in den ländlichen Bereichen Ostpreussens und des Fürstentums Paderborn vor 1800* (Würzburg, 1964), and H. Wunder 'Peasant organization and class conflict in east and west Germany', *Past and Present* 78 (1978): 47–55.

15 Carsten, 104f.

16 Rosenberg, 'Junkerherrschaft', 74.

17 loc. cit.; Carsten, 155–7; G. Czybulka, *Die Lage der ländlichen Klassen Ostdeutschlands im 18. Jahrhundert* (Braunschweig, 1949), 14–18.

18 For a general introduction, see O. Hintze, 'Geist und Epochen der preussischen Geschichte' and 'Die Hohenzollern und der Adel', in his *Regierung und Verwaltung* (Gesammelte Abhandlungen, Vol. 3) (Göttingen, 1967), 1–29 and 30–55.

19 Cited in Hintze, 'Hohenzollern', 41.

20 The peasant protection laws, introduced in the eighteenth century, limited the ability of estate-holders to extend their property-holdings at the expense of peasant holders. The laws were aimed primarily at assuring the state a steady source of revenues from independent peasant farms, not subject to the same exemptions as the Junkers, and also at guaranteeing the state a pool of army recruits, outside the Junkers' control. The laws thus ran counter to the attempts by the Junkers to extend their economic and social control over landed society and represented a key element in the conflict between the Prussian state and the Junkers which intensified throughout the eighteenth century. [Ed.] The state's peasant protection laws were only intended to hinder further expansion of estates, and in no way infringed upon the existing *Gutswirtschaft* and *Gutsherrschaft*. Moreover, their effectiveness was limited. Evidence for this can be found in the numerous repetitions of edicts protecting the peasantry during the eighteenth century and in the fact that peasant protection in eastern Prussia, for example, was not realized at all.

21 Otto Büsch, *Militärsystem und Sozialleben im alten Preussen 1713–1807* (Berlin, 1962).

22 ibid., 135.

23 In this context, the functioning of the canton system, that is, the way in which peasants were recruited for the regiment, was just as instructive since the intended purpose of the peasant protection laws was to protect the peasant soldier, ibid., 11–20, 56–61.

24 ibid., 163. See also 97.

25 ibid., 138.

26 On the material conditions of the landed nobility in the last third of the eighteenth century in general, see H. Schissler, *Preussische Agrargesellschaft im Wandel* (Göttingen, 1978), 59 ff., esp. 78–87; on the agrarian conjuncture, Abel, *Agrarkrisen*, 182–204; on the development of the domestic market through military demand, see Büsch, 111f.

27 The General Prussian Legal Code, completed in 1794, was part of the attempt in the late eighteenth century by the Prussian civil service to avoid revolutionary change from below by introducing reform from above, while at the same time striking a compromise with the Junkers. The Code established certain fundamental civil rights, guaranteed the independence of the judiciary, subjected the interests of legally defined estates to the 'common objectives of the state' and sketched out the legal basis for a future bourgeois society which would replace the feudal order. [Ed.] On the position of the nobility in the Prussian legal code, see the brilliant and nuanced interpretation of R. Koselleck which portrays the complex ambiguities and the progressive and conservative elements of this code, *Preussen zwischen Reform und Revolution* (Stuttgart, 1975), 78–115; see also G. Birtsch, 'Zur sozialen und politischen Rolle des deutschen vornehmlich presusischen Adels am Ende des 18. Jahrhunderts', in R. Vierhaus (ed.), *Der Adel vor der Revolution* (Göttingen, 1971), 82–7.

28 Especially the work of H.-H. Müller has made this point in an impressive and convincing fashion. See his *Märkische Landwirtschaft vor den Agrarreformen von 1807* (Postdam, 1967), and the comprehensive review of this book by Otto Büsch in which Müller took the opportunity to expand his thesis, 'Bauern, Pächter und Adel im alten Preussen', *Jahrbuch für Wirtschaftsgeschichte*, Part I (1966): 259–77.

29 Müller, *Landwirtschaft*, 116ff.; Czybulka, 34–7; Schissler, *Agrargesellschaft*, 87–9.

30 There are countless examples of this in Müller and in F. Martiny's *Die Adelsfrage in Preussen vor 1806 als politisches und soziales Problem* (Stuttgart, 1938), 34ff.

31   Schissler, *Agrargesellschaft*, 84; see also Koselleck, 83, and Martiny, 30f. See also A. Goodwin, 'Prussia', in his *The European Nobility in the Eighteenth Century* (New York, 1967), 96f.

32   On the extent of property transfers, see Koselleck, 82f.

33   Martiny, 29; J. Conrad, 'Die Fideikommisse in den östlichen Provinzen Preussens', in *Festschrift für G. Hanssen* (Tübingen, 1889), 259–300.

34   On speculation in goods and the *Landschaften*, see M. Weyermann, *Zur Geschichte des Immobiliarkreditwesens in Preussen* (Karlsruhe, 1918); H. Mauer, *Das landschaftliche Kreditwesen in Preussen* (Strasburg, 1907); Koselleck, 86f.; Schissler, *Agrargesellschaft*, 81–93. There are many examples of the speculative agrarian boom in R. Stein, *Die Umwandlung der Agrarverfassung Ostpreussens durch die Reformen des 19. Jahrhunderts*, Vol. 1 (Jena, 1918), and in J. Ziekursch, *Hundert Jahre schlesischer Agrargeschichte vom Hubertusburger Frieden bis zum Abschluss der Bauernbefreiung*, 2d ed. (Breslau, 1927).

35   Czybulka, 63f. In comparison to the Prussian nobility, the nobility in Westphalia was much more concerned with preserving its exclusivity through family arrangements, restrictions in marriages, and so on. See H. Reif, *Westfälischer Adel 1770–1860* (Göttingen, 1979).

36   On this, see Martiny, 65ff., esp 71; Birtsch, 88f. Koselleck, 80ff.; Goodwin, 99f.

37   For a perceptive analysis, see Czybulka, 65–9.

38   On the ambivalent effects of the attempts to rationalize noble holdings, see Koselleck, 85f.; Schissler, *Agrargesellschaft*, 71; idem, '"Bauernbefreiung" oder Entwicklung zur agrarkapitalistischen Gesellschaft?', *Sozialwissenschaftliche Informationen für Unterricht und Studium* 8 (1979): 138.

39   On the Prussian reforms in general, see B. Vogel, *Allgemeine Gewerbefreiheit. Die Reformpolitik des preussischen Staatskanzlers Hardenberg (1810–1820)* (Göttingen, 1983); idem (ed.), *Preussische Reformen 1807–1820* (Königstein, 1980). On the agrarian reforms in particular, see Koselleck, 487ff. and Schissler, *Agrargesellschaft* 105–44.

40   Goodwin, 83.

41   Rosenberg, *Bureaucracy*, 218; see also Schissler, *Agrargesellschaft*, 106–15.

42   Cited in ibid., 123.

43   See the discussion below; and R. Stadelmann, 'Deutschland und die westeuropäischen Revolutionen', in his *Deutschland und Westeuropa* (Laupheim, 1948), 22.

44   Koselleck, 519 ff.

45   On the declaration of 1816 and the development of the agrarian laws in general, see what is still the standard work, G. F. Knapp, *Die Bauernbefreiung und der Ursprung der Landarbeiter in den älteren Teilen Preussens*, 2 vols., 2d ed. (Leipzig, 1927).

46   Rosenberg, 'Pseudodemokratisierung', 16; idem, *Bureaucracy*, 217–19; Schissler, *Agrargesellschaft*, 164f.

47   It is not always easy to determine the estate-based and class-based social characteristics of the Junkers, since both groups of characteristics, each with specific combinations, were introduced historically beginning in the sixteenth century. Koselleck uses the terms 'new class', 'estate', 'occupational estate', 'propertied class' and 'entrepreneurial class based on the *Gutsherrschaft*' to describe the Junkers at the beginning of the nineteenth century, at a point when their social characteristics as a class finally superseded those as an estate. Koselleck, 487f. and 507. Rosenberg calls the nineteenth-century Junkers a 'mobile economic class' and an 'exclusive feudal occupational estate'. 'Pseudodemokratisierung', 16f. See also the useful discussion in J. Kocka, 'Stand-Klasse-Organisation. Strukturen sozialer Ungleichheit in Deutschland vom späten 18. bis zum frühen 19. Jahrhundert', in H.-U. Wehler (ed.), *Klassen in der europäischen Sozialgeschichte* (Göttingen, 1979), 138–41; see also Wehler's introduction to the book, 'Vorüberlegungen zur historischen Analyse sozialer Ungleichheit', ibid., 9–32.

48   Compare, for example, the many competitive advantages which the landed elite had over the peasants and the unequal opportunities for landowners and agricultural labourers on the labour market when pauperism was prevalent in the *Vormärz* period. The large numbers of people seeking work caused wages to fall and forced labourers to accept almost all labour conditions. Schissler, *Agrargesellschaft*, 168–85. On the fusing of the landowning class and the assimilation of bourgeois owners, see Rosenberg, 'Pseudodemokratisierung', 26f.; and H. Heffter, *Die deutsche Selbstverwaltung im 19.*

Jahrhundert (Stuttgart, 1969), 221f.; J. R. Gillis, 'Aristocracy and bureaucracy in nineteenth century Prussia', *Past and Present* 41 (1968): 115; R. Stein, *Die Umwandlung der Agrarverfassung Ostpreussens durch die Reformen des 19. Jahrhunderts*, Vol. 3 (Königsberg, 1934), 514f.

49 Koselleck 85, and similarly, 508.

50 ibid., 499ff.; H. Obernaus, 'Finanzkrise und Verfassungsgebung', in G. A. Ritter (ed.), *Gesellschaft, Parlament und Regierung* (Düsseldorf, 1974), 57–75.

51 Koselleck, 516–23. The *Rittergut* property was thus graded into many different categories and given different political and economic privileges. There were the lords of the 'old and established *Rittergut* property', 'properties of limited *Rittergut* quality' and properties which allowed one to take part in local assemblies (*Kreistagsfähige Rittergüter*). Schulz, 92.

52 Eckart Kehr, 'Zur Genesis der preussischen Bürokratie und des Rechtsstaats', in H.-U. Wehler (ed.), *Der Primat der Innenpolitik* (Berlin, 1976), 39.

53 On the dialectic of conflict and compromise in the confrontations of the bureaucracy and landed estate-owners, see Schissler, *Agrargesellschaft*, 123–35.

54 This is how Rosenberg interprets the reform period. *Bureaucracy*, 202–8.

55 ibid., 204.

56 Heffter, 207. This formulation is certainly somewhat too extreme. Of course the bureaucracy did not coincide with the 'Junkers' class interests', but rather differentiated itself from those on many points. In other places, Heffter himself stresses this, for example when he calls the *Vormärz* period 'the classic age of the bureaucracy, which was characterized by incorruptibility, high education, carefulness and dependability in its day-to-day affairs'. ibid., 210.

57 Rosenberg, 'Pseudodemokratisierung', 16.

58 On the property transfer, see Koselleck, 511 f.; Gillis, 113.

59 Koselleck, 515.

60 In this context it is enough to mention what negative consequences the political abstinence of the bourgeoisie had for the development of its 'political power', when combined with the assimilation of bourgeois owners by the Junkers. See Koselleck, 514f.; Rosenberg, 'Pseudodemokratisierung', 28; and Kehr, 'Genesis', 43 for a judgement on the entire nineteenth century.

61 Rosenberg interprets the alliance of the bureaucracy and the Junkers as a condition for the bureaucracy's victory over the absolute monarchy. *Bureaucracy*, 22.

62 Koselleck describes the peasants' position as a 'transition state between economic freedom and political semi-dependence' (p. 556). On the peasants' situation see Koselleck, 500–3; Schissler, *Agrargesellschaft*, 168–73; E. Jordan, *Die Entstehung der konservativen Partei und die preussischen Agrarverhältnisse von 1848* (Munich, 1914), 38–54.

63 Rumpf, cited in Koselleck, 524.

64 There is a large economic historical literature on the agrarian crisis. See, for example, Abel, *Agrarkrisen*, 205–25. For its effects on the landowning class, see Jordan 17–82, and Koselleck, 507–25.

65 Schissler, *Agrargesellschaft*, 152.

66 In this context, the development of a kind of semi-feudal sharecropping system (*Instenverhältnis*) is especially interesting. Freely contracted labourers were paid both in kind and with part of the profits. See M. Weber, *Die Verhältnisse der Landarbeiter im ostelbischen Deutschland* (Leipzig, 1892); Schissler, *Agrargesellschaft*, 173–85.

67 Running parallel to this trend were measures to write off the indebtedness of property. The mortgage debt did grow absolutely from 53 million Taler in 1805 to 124 million in 1855. However, Jordan (pp. 23f.) feels that there was a substantial change in the character of the debt during these decades, and movement from speculative debts to production credits. In his opinion the picture would look much better if one could bring debts and property assets into relation with one another. Puhle has a much more negative view of the tendency towards indebtedness. H.-J. Puhle, *Agrarbewegungen in kapitalistischen Industriegesellschaften* (Göttingen, 1975), 44. On the indebtedness of large estates in the second half of the nineteenth century, see also Schulz, 96–101.

68 On the secular trend, see Abel, *Agrarkrisen*, 226–42; on the effects on the relationship betweeen agricultural employers and workers, Jordan, 20–61.

69 On the all-important economic significance of east Elbian agriculture in the middle of the nineteenth century, see R. H. Dumke, 'Anglo-deutscher Handel und Frühindustrialisierung in Deutschland 1822–1865', *Geschichte und Gesellschaft* 5 (1979), esp 182–4, 187, 191 and 194. See also the older but still important works by G. Hermes, 'Statistische Studien zur wirtschaftlichen und gesellschaftlichen Struktur des zollvereinten Deutschlands', in *Archiv für Sozialwissenschaft* 63 (1930), esp. 131–6; Jordan, esp. 17–82; and B. Brockhage, *Zur Entwicklung des preussisch-deutschen Kapitalexports 1817–1840* (Leipzig, 1910). From his studies of the last quarter of the nineteenth century, Puhle had extrapolated his thesis about the structural crisis of east Elbian large-scale agriculture on to the entire century. See *Von der Agrarkrise zum Präfaschismus* (Wiesbaden, 1972), 17, and idem, *Agrarbewegungen*, 47. In contrast to this, I would place myself with authors like G. Hermes who emphasize the radical change in the production capacity and total economic significance of east Elbian agriculture, and who contest at least for the period 1830 to 1860, the idea of a structural crisis or continual crisis susceptibility for east Elbian agriculture in general.

70 'Neuere deutsche Geschichtsschreibung', in idem, *Primat*, 258. See also Hermes, 135, and Rosenberg, 'Pseudodemokratisierung', 9.

71 On the economic and price trends in the 1870s, see M. Rolfes, 'Landwirtschaft 1850–1914', in *Handbuch der Deutschen Wirtschafts- und Sozialgeschichte*, Vol. 2 (Stuttgart, 1970), 495–526, esp 501–3.

72 See note 67.

73 A. Gerschenkron, *Bread and Democracy in Germany*, 2d ed. (New York, 1966), 37, 42ff.

74 Puhle, *Agrarbewegungen*, 36–9.

75 On this, Max Weber's works are still relevant. See his 'Arbeiten zur Lage der ostelbischen Landarbeiterschaft' and 'Entwicklungstendenzen in der Lage der ostelbischen Landarbeiter', in *Gesammelte Aufsätze zur Sozial- und Wirtschaftsgeschichte* (Tübingen, 1924), 470–507.

76 On noble liberalism in east Prussia, see Heffter, 223f.; W. R. Fann 'The Consolidation of Bureaucratic Absolutism in Prussia, 1817–1827' (diss., University of California, Berkeley, 1965), 146; Kehr, 'Das soziale System der Reaktion in Preussen unter dem Ministerium Puttkamer', in idem, *Primat*, 83–6.

77 Puhle, *Agrarbewegungen*, 50; see also Rosenberg, 'Funktion'.

78 Gerschenkron, 27; Puhle, *Agrarkrise*, 17; H.-U. Wehler, *Das deutsche Kaiserreich 1871–1918* (Göttingen, 1980), 234.

79 *Agrarbewegungen*, 41. On the political consequences see R. M. Berdahl, 'Conservative politics and aristocratic landholders in Bismarckian Germany', *Journal of Modern History* 44 (1972): 1–20.

80 H.-J. Puhle, *Agrarische Interessenpolitik und preussischer Konservatismus im Wilhelminischen Reich 1893–1914* (Bonn, 1975); idem, *Agrarbewegungen*, 63–8, 73; and Puhle's contribution in this volume which summarizes major arguments presented fully in these works.

81 Puhle, *Agrarbewegungen*, 50f. On Nazi agrarian policy, see also the contribution by J. E. Farquharson in this volume.

82 Rosenberg, 'Pseudodemokratisierung', 40.

83 *Kaiserreich*, 15 and 238f. See also Gerschenkron, 67.

84 *Agrarbewegungen*, 76; and word for word, the same in *Agrarkrise*, 52.

85 The opinions of East German historians are excluded here because of their much more obvious and political use of the Junkers as scapegoats. On several prevalent patterns of explanation and argumentation in East German historiography, see Kocka 'Staat'. They also do not have a general social history of the Junkers.

86 'Pseudodemokratisierung', 9, 34f. See also Büsch, 170; Birtsch, 90; B. Moore, *Social Origins of Dictatorship and Democracy. Lord and Peasant in the Making of the Modern World* (Boston, Mass., 1966), 433–52; D. Spring, 'Landed elites compared', introduction to idem (ed.), *European Landed Elites in the Nineteenth Century* (Baltimore, Md., 1979), 15–17; and James J. Sheehan, 'Conflict and cohesion among German elites', in idem (ed.), *Imperial Germany* (New York, 1976), 65, 82.

87 ibid., 16.

88 K. Kluxen, 'Der englische Adel im 18. Jahrhundert', in Vierhaus (ed.), *Adel*, 22.

89   Moore, 38.
90   Of course, the stereotype is never found in such a simplistic caricature. None the less it has an implicit effect.
91   For England, Kluxen, 12, 14, 16; Spring, 11; H. J. Habbakuk, 'England', in Goodwin (ed.), 15.
92   Spring, 103.
93   ibid., 2–6; for Prussia, Schissler, *Agrargesellschaft*, 161f.
94   H. Hattenhauer (ed.), *Allgemeines Landrecht für die Preussischen Staaten von 1794* (Frankfurt, 1970), Vol. 2/9, paras. 35f.
95   Habbakuk, 11; Kluxen, 17.
96   S. Pollard, 'Soziale Ungleichheit und Klassenstrukturen in England: Mittel- und Oberklassenn', in Wehler (ed.), 35f.; Moore, 29f.
97   Habbakuk, 11.
98   See Kocka, 'Staat'.
99   Otto Hintze tried to take the different development paths in English and Germany history and derive a unique constitutional model of 'monarchical constitutionalism' for them both. See 'Das monarchische Prinzip und die konstitutionelle Verfassung' and 'Das Verfassungsleben der heutigen Kulturstaaten', in idem, *Staat und Verfassung, Ges. Abh* I (Göttingen, 1962), 359–89, 390–423. On the present state of the discussion, see D. Langewiesche, 'Das deutsche Kaiserreich – Bemerkungen zur Diskussion über Parlamentarisierung und Demokratisierung Deutschlands', *Archiv für Sozialgeschichte* 19 (1979): 628–42.
100 On the importance of the upper house (Herrenhaus) as an instrument for securing the power and influence of the large landowners, see H. Heffter, 'Der nachmärzliche Liberalismus: Die Reaktion der 1850er Jahre', in H.-U. Wehler (ed.), *Moderne deutsche Sozialgeschichte* (Königstein, 1980), 188f.
101 Habbakuk, 16; F. M. L. Thompson, 'Britain', in Spring (ed.), 32; Koselleck, 515.
102 Pollard, 41; Moore, 37f.
103 Habbakuk, 2f.; Spring, 6f.
104 ibid., 6–10.
105 Due to the surfeit of relevant literature, I will not attempt to describe the essential differences, but only the central tendencies in this development.
106 Pollard, 35.
107 Kluxen, 12: Habbakuk, 1, 20; Pollard, 36; J. Blum, *The End of the Old Order in Rural Europe* (Princeton, N.J., 1978), 11.
108 Habakkuk, 18f.; Thompson, 33. However, it was *in principle* possible for representatives of the bourgeoisie to enter the peerage and gain a vote in the House of Lords. Pollard, 41.
109 Habbakuk, 12, 15f.; Kluxen, 19; Spring, 13; Pollard, 37.
110 The reasons for this are complex and of course cannot be reduced only to the Junkers' estate-based arrogance. It is not possible to analyse it any more precisely in this context. See my more detailed introduction to E. Kehr, *Preussische Finanzpolitik 1806–1810: Quellen zur Verwaltung der Ministerien Stein und Altenstein*, ed. H. Schissler and H.-U. Wehler (Göttingen, 1981).
111 Pollard, 37; Spring, 13; Kluxen, 19.
112 Pollard, 42–4. See also Pollard's thoughts on the principle of 'divide and conquer' which the English aristocracy employed with great success to integrate rising groups, pp. 43f.
113 E. Kehr, 'Zur Genesis des Königlich Preussischen Reserveoffiziers', in idem, *Primat*, 53–63.
114 Moore, 488–90.
115 See note 74.
116 Pollard, 38ff.; Moore, 31.
117 ibid., 20.
118 See, for example, H.-U. Wehler, *Bismarck und der Imperialismus* (Munich, 1976); and idem, *Kaiserreich*.
119 See Pollard, 40, 48; Moore, 31–6.
120 On the first, see Koselleck, 557–9; on the second, see Kehr, esp. 'Genesis', 'System'

and 'Die Diktatur der Bürokratie', in *Primat*, 244–53.

121   Pollard, 48f.

122   R. Bendix, *Kings or People. Power and the Mandate to Rule* (Berkeley, Calif., 1978), 598.

123   A modern social history of the Junkers, like the one Reif has now done for the West-phalian nobility, does not yet exist. Perhaps the forthcoming work of R. M. Berdahl will be of help. The well-researched study of F. Martiny on the Kurmark nobility is now over forty years old! A new undertaking of the social history of the Junkers would have to include the reflective and methodological demands of a social historical approach. It could continue the work of Rosenberg, Büsch and Koselleck while incor-porating revisions to the prevailing views put forward by H. Harnisch, H. H. Müller and others. It could include the older, yet still valuable work of Jordan, Stein, Zie-kursch and Czybulka. With the exception of Moore's work, there is in my view no other study which compares the history, role and function of the Junkers to other agrarian elites. At the present time, a comparative study of the Junkers and the southern planter class is being prepared by S. D. Bowman at the University of California. See also S. D. Bowman, 'Antebellum planters and *Vormärz* Junkers in comparative perspec-tive', *American Historical Review* 85 (1980): 779–808. The books edited by Vierhaus and Goodwin on the European nobility in the eighteenth and nineteenth centuries and the collection of essays edited by Spring are, with the exception of Spring's comparative introduction, the only individual studies. The same can be said for *Klassen in der euro päischen Sozialgeschichte* edited by Wehler which does not intend to give comparisons of countries, but rather gives an analysis of social inequality. Puhle's book, *Agrarbewe-gungen*, contains much important material for comparisons and its conceptual use of 'organized capitalism' also defines methodological dimensions for comparative work. However, it too does not intend to provide a social historical comparison of the agrar-ian leadership elites, but rather to find the specific characteristics of the political agrar-ian movements in those countries investigated by him in individual studies. Only sys-tematic comparison can make it possible to test existing assumptions about the role and function of the Junkers in Prusso-German history in a critical way.

2 Property and Wood Theft: Agrarian Capitalism and Social Conflict in Rural Society, 1800–50. A Westphalian Case Study

JOSEF MOOSER

I

The phases and forms of German agriculture's transition to capitalism from the eighteenth century onwards, the effect of this transition on the social position of different groups in rural society, and the relationship between agrarian capitalism and class formation have received very uneven treatment in the literature. The best-known case is the transformation of the Prussian feudal landed elite into capitalist landowners during the agrarian conjuncture and reforms of the late eighteenth and nineteenth centuries. In different phases and to varying degrees, agriculture was commercialized, that is, drawn into market relations, and noble holdings became the object of individual property transactions. The composition of the labour force on estates changed from peasants dependent on local power to free wage labourers. By 1848–9 at the latest, when the agrarian reforms were completed and the noble landed estates (*Rittergüter*) had lost most of their public sphere of influence through the nullification of patrimonial legal jurisdiction, capitalistic agricultural methods became quite prevalent on large estates. They had now become private enterprises which used wage labourers and individual profit calculations to produce for the market, even if they were still protected by remnants of political privilege for some time to come.[1]

This famous, or infamous, story of the Prussian 'Junkers' contrasts sharply with the much less well known and also less completely described history of the large and small peasantry and the landless agrarian lower classes. When and how did capitalist principles take hold of peasant agriculture? Did the great mass of peasants who held only small amounts of property usually tended by family members ever become capitalists? In what ways were the landless lower classes integrated into the market system? A primitive answer to these questions can be found in East German agrarian history, which is based on Lenin's sacrosanct theory of the 'Prussian path' towards the capitalist development of agriculture. According to this interpretation, peasants were emancipated from manorial control under the condition that the landed estate-owners would be compensated and could continue their politically privileged existence through the reform laws of 1807 and 1816. This toppled the agrarian population from the frying pan of feudalism into the fire of capitalism. Part of the peasantry was proletarianized and the rural population was subjected to both feudal and capitalist exploitation for at least half a century, thus inhibiting the growth of peasant capitalism.[2]

Empirical studies on the development of the agrarian reforms and systematic examination of social differentiation of the agrarian population, originating in the eighteenth century, suggest that this picture should now be revised. Large peasants, that is, those who owned horses and at least enough land to feed their families, were able to adjust fairly quickly to their emancipation and increase their yields despite unfavourable conditions. They were eventually aided by a definite accumulation of wealth stemming from small local and regional markets that had been established through the rapid growth of the land-poor and landless lower classes. These groups had to buy food products at more or less regular intervals and/or they had to lease land. In order to gather the resources for this, they made handicrafts, worked as seasonal wage labourers or took part in proto-industrial production for trans-regional markets. Under these conditions, which of course were subject to great regional variations, there were chances for the development of peasant capitalism before the reforms and in part independent of them. At least there were opportunities for an increasing commercial orientation in the upper levels of the peasantry, and their relative prosperity already in the late eighteenth century has frequently been documented.[3]

This study investigates only a small part of a long, gradual and often only partially enduring process through which peasants and landless labourers were drawn into capitalist agriculture. Taking the use of elementary agrarian resources – wood and the forest – as an index of changing class relations in the countryside, it investigates the success of individualistic property ownership and the effect this had on social relations among rural classes. Wood theft will be used as the indicator. It serves as a signal in two different ways. Administrative penalties shed light on the seigneurial regulations of a scarce resource and in particular on the ways in which the forest was changed into private property with the agrarian reforms. The Prussian law on wood theft of 1821, which replaced older individual provincial rulings, came into effect at the same time as the law governing the division of communal property (*Gemein-heitsteilungsordnung*) which provided the guidelines for ending common rights to forests and fields. This law, together with the dissolution of *Grundherrschaft*, was an important part of the liberal agrarian reforms that aimed to raise production through what Marc Bloch has called 'agrarian individualism'. The definition of a particular crime called 'wood theft' had this aim. When cut, prepared, or otherwise preserved wood was stolen, this was prosecuted as a 'common' theft and not as 'wood theft'. This latter category was reserved for the theft of uncut wood, waste wood, or wood which had fallen in storms. The extent to which the entire forest, or 'rational forestry', was to be protected was evident in a new version of the law in 1852 which increased the items for which one could be punished. The theft of grass, herbs, kindling and other things was now equated with wood theft.[4]

On another level, wood theft is a measure of protest or at least of tradi-tional resistance to the private control of wood and the forests. In fact, during the first half of the nineteenth century it probably was an increas-ingly common crime, much more frequent than ordinary theft. For example, in Prussia, excluding the Rhine Province, approximately 35,000 ordinary thefts were registered in 1850 as compared to 265,000 wood thefts.[5] Contemporaries increasingly understood wood theft as an ambiguous social phenomenon. On the one hand, even law-makers took into account the old adage that wood thieves were not really doing any-thing wrong. They differentiated between 'common' theft and wood theft because 'public opinion' made this distinction and 'in many cases' need and not greed was the 'main factor in the crime'.[6] On the other hand, however, especially as the demand for this increasingly scarce resource rose, wood theft became a 'vital question of the time' because it demoralized the impoverished lower classes and threatened to become a kind of school where they could learn to wage a 'war against those who were better off'.[7]

In this context of social protest, wood theft has entered the new social history of criminality together with other crimes like poaching, smug-gling, arson and especially *taxation populaire* during times of rising prices. All these themes have been investigated in the last few decades, particu-larly in English social history. In the Federal Republic, Dirk Blasius has followed this path in several important studies of 'criminality as social action' which pay particular attention to 'small' thefts of foodstuffs and wood. In such thefts, the tensions and conflicts in nineteenth-century rural society became apparent even though open revolt was remarkably rare, with the exception of the revolutionary years of 1848–9.[8] Blasius sees such offences as 'evidence of social change', or rather of the evolution of individualism in property ownership. A stiffening of the legal code to protect propertied society on the one hand confronted an 'offensive of the lower classes against efforts to write them off as a liability in modern society'. The kind of criminality which arose from the needs of everyday life and which (almost) became an everyday occurrence to handle those needs was therefore 'one of the basic processes towards the development of a proletarian self-consciousness'. In particular, the theft of wood in the agrarian realm 'set free . . . energy which the working class could draw on in their struggle for self determination during the industrialization process'.[9]

This essay cannot and should not examine Blasius's thesis in all its complexities. It can, however, critically question the thesis in an expanded case study. Was the class nature of wood theft so obvious? What were the principal lines of social conflict that characterized it? Who were the thieves and whom did they rob? Did it occur with the same frequency everywhere? How and by whom were the thefts repressed? These questions are easier to ask than to answer. The task is made even more difficult because of the imprecise nature of legal and criminal statistics that are given in aggregate form for regions with very different social structures. As in analyses of other forms of social protest, the best approach is to pursue a complex local or regional case study. The following is based on examples from the administrative area of Minden in Westphalia. It attempts to show the different types of wood theft which reveal a variety of conflicts in rural society during the period in which private property was established. Beginning with a few remarks on the use of wood and its changing value, it will conclude with examples of the surprisingly violent legal confrontations which ensued when the crime was prosecuted. Before these topics are examined, however, a few words must be said about the social position of the rural population in the regions under investigation.

The administrative region of Minden provides an excellent focus for a case study since it contained areas sufficiently different economically and socially to allow comparative conclusions.[10] It was composed of two regions, the old Prussian Minden-Ravensberg and the Paderborn bishopric which was secularized in 1803. Minden and especially Ravensberg were areas with a 'proto-industrial' agrarian textile industry which employed a property-poor or propertyless class. By 1800 the majority of the population consisted of small peasants and especially of so-called *Heuerlinge*. The latter had no property and rented houses and land from peasant owners. To obtain revenues, they often had to hire themselves out as day labourers together with their entire families for 'their' peasants in a fashion approximating the structure of peasant responsibilities to their lords before the agrarian reforms. They worked as flax-spinners, linen-weavers and agrarian labourers too. They also farmed small-holdings, raising poultry, rabbits, goats and, under the best of circumstances, a cow. Their very poor living conditions contrasted sharply with those of the often prosperous middle and large peasantry. The prosperity of the middle peasantry was based in part on rental and leasing income, on the low wages of the dependent *Heuerlinge* and on the sale of foodstuffs. In this case, a commercialization of peasant agriculture accompanied proto-industrialization.

In contrast to Paderborn, the noble estate economy in Minden–Ravensberg played an almost negligible role since the estates were often leased out in parcels. Here the peasants were the initiators of agricultural innovation and 'agrarian individualism' once community property was dissolved and collective forms of land use diminished. In Paderborn, on the other hand, the role of a relatively large number of noble estates, which of course were smaller in scale than those in East Prussia, was particularly important because they and the state owned a large part of the forest. In contrast to the rest of the population, composed mainly of small peasants, they formed the bridgehead of agrarian innovation. Remarkably, almost all the communal lands were divided in Minden–Ravensberg by 1800. In Paderborn, divisions did not even begin in earnest until the 1840s, causing bitter struggles in March of 1848. Small peasants clung that much more stubbornly to the collective economy and the rights to wood and forests which were associated with it because they comprised integral parts of the small farming system. In contrast to the situation in Minden–Ravensberg, the system in Paderborn could not be supplemented with income from industry. Spinning and weaving were not widespread and local handicraft production provided little supplementary income since the impoverished local population had limited purchasing power. Sometimes seasonal agricultural labour in Holland brought in extra income, but it only reproduced the local economic structure which was caught in a cycle of poverty.

Developments in the first half of the nineteenth century brought about a certain equalization of poverty with the majority of the population in both sub-regions, but for very different reasons. The agrarian crisis of the 1820s, poor harvests, rising taxes and legal suits with large landowners during the agrarian reforms threw the peasants of Paderborn into a life-threatening situation. A Prussian official at the time called Paderborn a 'German Ireland'. In Minden–Ravensberg, on the other hand, the situation of the sub-peasant class worsened when a crisis of the rural textile industry began in the 1820s and reached its high point in the 1840s. In the eighteenth century this region was often praised for its industriousness and called 'The Little Linen Country' (*Leinenländchen*); it was second only to Silesia as a centre of Prussian linen export. Now it became transformed into one of the poorest areas of the Prussian state. While the Silesian weavers' rebellion became a symbol of the Prussian pre-revolutionary crisis, there were no open rebellions in Westphalia until March 1848.

II

Pauperism, the inability of people to meet their basic needs no matter how hard they worked, shaped the lives of broad sectors of the population during the transition from a feudal agrarian society to a capitalist industrial economy. It was *one* reason for widespread crimes against property. Criminality was also encouraged by the special economic significance of the forest, especially of wood, and changes in the way in which forests were managed. Without considering these elements, we cannot fully understand the bitterness of the tensions and conflicts which emerged over the theft of wood. In the eighteenth century population increase and the expansion of industrial activities exacerbated the problems of forest management which had been evident since the late middle ages. A rising demand confronted a diminishing supply. Precisely for this reason, the supply had to be cultivated more 'rationally' in ways which would simultaneously destroy existing patterns of use.

Before the introduction of steam, coal, electricity and oil, wood was the most important and essential raw material and energy source in all areas of the economy. The forest was a many-faceted resource in animal husbandry; it served as pasture, and the foliage was used for feed, straw and fertilizer. Wood was the major source of heat particularly in the homes of the poor. In addition, it was an essential raw material for houses, furniture, tools and especially for handicrafts. Trade required wood for wagons and boats; foundries needed firewood; and finally the numerous linen-weavers had to cook their yarn in ashes to prepare it for weaving.

The drawback resulting from all this consumption was the fear of a scarcity of wood. Concerned voices were raised about this in government and economic discussions on population increase and 'the national wealth' in the late eighteenth century. An 'end to growth' appeared to be in sight.[11] The wood shortage and the alleged destruction of the forests through wood theft led an anonymous author writing in 1804 to predict a 'terrible future' for the heavily populated proto-industrial area of Ravensberg. The balance seemed to be destroyed between the natural resources and the expanding industrial population which had 'too many people'.[12] In this area, coal and peat to some extent had begun to replace wood as the main source of energy. In other places, such as the small peasant communities in Paderborn, the wood shortage already began to endanger certain trades. Many times during the eighteenth century communities located near glass works demanded that this industry which used so much wood should be closed down. They also complained that the glass workers took wood from the forest for their personal use and let their animals graze there. Eventually this resulted in violent confrontations between peasants and workers.[13]

The reaction of those in power to the actual or suspected wood shortage was 'to economize on the use of wood' (Sombart). This did not solve the conflicts but rather created more occasions for them. This reaction can be seen in the state's forest police laws (*Forstpolizeiordnungen*), enforced since the late middle ages, which aimed to protect the forest by limiting collective usage. The restrictions included periodic termination of animal-grazing and wood-gathering, as well as the rationing of commercial and firewood. They also included a redefinition of those who were entitled to take wood. This measure especially affected the lower classes since they had fewer rights in peasant communities and had to pay for their usage. Finally, parts of the forest designated for communal use were 'closed', and made into protected areas where new seedlings would not be endangered. All of these elements were part of 'rational' forestry.[14]

The 'economizing' process in the eighteenth century also aimed to increase output, since the sale of wood for commercial purposes brought in high profits due to the large demand. Because prices were rising, wood sales became a more important source of income for forest-owners than they had been before.[15] Tied to this was the gradual development of the modern notion of exclusive property control, which was challenged by peasant communities in many lawsuits. The climax and conclusion of this process was the introduction of liberal agrarian reforms which began at the end of the eighteenth century. They irrevocably converted property which had been divided between the peasant and the lord into indivisible 'private' property. The agrarian reforms were an enormous, slow process that aimed at restructuring usage rights. Their three parts – an expensive recompensation of noble landowners, the division of common property and the enclosure and redistribution of landholdings – eliminated the foundation of old forms of usufruct.

In the reform process, those needs for forest use which had formerly been satisfied by custom and by rights regulated through the lord and the community were now subject to market mechanisms. At the same time, this economic situation that encouraged and even provoked wood theft was further compounded by internal administrative reforms. The policing of forests was much more severely and effectively carried out in the nineteenth century than it had been in the seventeenth and eighteenth, when the absolutist state made claims to power but did not have the resources to translate those claims into action. The replacement of patrimonial courts, which were part of the *Grundherrschaft* legal jurisdiction, with a state justice system was part of the same process. The justice system and the police, which had changed from a provincial welfare administration into a primarily repressive security force, punished small offences much more frequently. This fact alone caused crime statistics to rise since the old patrimonial courts did not even record the crimes of some wood thieves, punishing them on the spot instead with a sound thrashing.[16]

This is, of course, an overstated and idealized description of developments during the first half of the nineteenth century. Their practical impact on day-to-day existence differed greatly from one place to the next and depended on the course of the agrarian reforms. It is, for example, not surprising that the first and clearest reports of market sales of wood at auctions came from Ravensberg and not from the Paderborn area. An 1801 newspaper article from this proto-industrial area describes how a peasant who was attuned to the market no longer brought wood into the city. Instead he auctioned off this scarce commodity on his farm for three times the market price. At that time, certain relationships within rural society were still taken into account. 'Those buyers from the area covered their needs for a bit less; but there were many new buyers there who had no connection to the peasant selling wood [*Holzbauer*] and for whom he did not feel obligated to lower the price; and with the small amount of wood it was not possible to help everyone.'[17] Thus, commercialization had not prevailed completely. Those buyers from the peasant's immediate vicinity and 'his' *Heuerlinge* obtained wood at a lower price in an almost patriarchal fashion. Thirty years later this had changed. In November 1835 the chronicle for Heepen in the Ravensberg district reported: 'Most well-to-do peasants now sell their wood at auctions. Many have taken place in the past few weeks which have brought high prices. Since no one seems to want to give the lesser people small quantities of wood afterwards, and since this lot cannot pay, the result will be a greater number of wood thefts.'[18]

Another limitation in the process of forest preservation and the commercialization of the wood trade came not from the slow pace of agrarian reforms but rather from their completion. When private property and free trade in land were established, it became possible for entire villages, not just individual peasants, to buy forest land. Thus the old patterns of usage could be continued on a smaller scale. In part, communal ownership of forests had already started before the reforms. The Paderborn community of Scherfede, for example, had already come to an understanding with its monastic landlord in 1794. Due to the cloister's constant problems with wood vandalism, the village gave up its right to the use of the entire cloister forest in return for a leasehold and full ownership of a section of it. This was a wooded area of over 2,000 Morgen (approximately 500 hectares), the use of which was reserved exclusively for the community. No inhabitant was allowed to sell or give away wood outside the community and any excess was to be sold by the village. In contrast to the Minden-Ravensberg area, where the size of both state and communal forests was relatively small, the rural communities in Paderborn controlled a significant amount of land, most of it forest. In the 1860s they held 20 per cent of 250,000 Morgen of forest land while the Prussian state in the region held 37 per cent. The remainder was in the hands of nobles. There was no significant forest property held by individual peasants, a characteristic which again distinguished it from Minden-Ravensberg.[19]

Thus, the typical situation where the state and former feudal lords shared most of the wooded property could in fact differ widely from place to place. This had an important impact on the class character of wood theft. It was not only the 'progressive alliance' of agrarian capitalist landowners, state officials and bourgeois land-lessees who stood in opposition to the mass of property-poor peasants and landless workers. Peasant communities and the different classes within the village were actors in this conflict as well. Communally owned forests were by no means spared from theft. In Paderborn, for example, there were approximately 1,000 thefts per year in the communal forests in the mid-1840s. Even in the community of Scherfede, wood pilferage did not stop, and in 1849 the village passed a law revoking residents' rights to cut down their wood allotments themselves. The old communal spirit collapsed because of inner rivalries. After 1849 wood could only be cut by village representatives who had consulted with a government forester. It was then sold to the highest bidder.[20]

III

On the basis of what has been presented thus far, it is clear that wood theft in fact incorporated many different kinds of crimes during the first half of the nineteenth century. These crimes reflected different social contexts and conflicts and were carried out by different perpetrators on varying fronts. Such socio-generic types of wood theft cannot be numerically compared using crime statistics. Instead they can only be characterized by individual cases. In what follows, wood theft will first be examined as part of the conflict between lords and peasants, and then as a form of resistance to agrarian modernization in the struggle between peasants and the landless lower classes. Through an interregional comparison, the relationship between pauperism and wood theft will also be closely examined.

A conflict between the Haxthausen estate and the community of Bredenborn reveals the close relationship of lawsuits over communal rights with wood theft and violence.[21] Both parties had contested the use of an 800 Morgen forest area since the sixteenth century. Rivalries among the local lord, von Haxthausen and the Paderborn chapter of the cathedral made it possible for the village to win a relatively good settlement at the regional court and the Supreme Court of Justice. However, these were of little value 'at home' due to conflicts among various noble families. At issue were the rights to wood and grazing in certain parts of the forest. The lord of the manor only conceded rights to fallen wood and other wood of little use, while the village demanded timber for construction as well, with the exception of oak trees. Through constant pilfering, the village had allegedly plundered the entire forest, including the oak trees, by the end of the eighteenth century. Perhaps behind this was an offensive attempt to guarantee their rights. It brought the estate-owners to the point of despair, and they demanded the 'unconditional dissolution' of the peasants' rights to wood.

If the peasant has a *right* to go into the forest and to exercise certain justified tasks there, then he never confines himself to these but rather expands them and takes everything he thinks he can take without danger. He ruins and destroys the forest in order to bring it within the sphere of his rights. It is quite impossible for the owner to provide strict surveillance, for to do this would almost require putting one forester beside every tree.[22]

The conflict heated up again in 1802 when von Haxthausen converted an eighth of the forest into a nursery. The community lodged a complaint at the episcopal court charging damages against common property, but it was denied. An appeal lodged in 1804 was successful to the extent that the first judgement was overturned pending renewed negotiations. However, this never took place due to the political upheavals caused by the secularization of the church government in 1803, the French occupation in 1807 and the Napoleonic Wars. When the legal complaints began, the state court took control of the disputed forest area. The community had to pay for forest access and for a forester. Both measures made the situation even worse. The local population treated the forester in a hostile way and even threatened to kill him. By 1819 the situation was so bad that he saw no option but to resign. The peasants were also unwilling to pay for wood usage 'because they claimed never to have been forced to buy wood', in the words of a district magistrate's report from 18 March 1820. This resulted in a number of fines. Although the amounts in this instance could not be documented, other evidence indicated that they

61

could be quite high. Von Haxthausen once admitted that he collected an average of 200 Taler a year in fines from the three communities in the period from 1778 to 1808.[23]

In 1820 the conflict between the estate-owner and the community was still so tense that the district magistrate recommended that a military command unit be stationed there to protect the forest and forester. This suggestion, however, was rejected by the government of Minden. In 1824 the community suffered a serious defeat. In a state decision, it was required to pay the large sum of 592 Taler in surtaxes for the disorderly appropriation of property which it had taken in 1807. In that year, von Haxthausen had ordered wood to be cut which promptly resulted in a *taxation paysanne*. Peasants would not allow the wood to be carried off or sold. Instead, they distributed it among the members of the community. The community even sought to legitimize its claims by presenting a formal list of everyone who had received wood in this action. None the less, this protest was unsuccessful. Despite these defeats, legal battles still continued on other fronts. In 1819 the community had received confirmation of its old rights to the forest. When 'shared' property ownership was finally dissolved in 1848, the village got a portion of the forest and a redemption payment from the landowner. Only then did the pillaging of wood and forest apparently come to an end.

In the south-eastern part of Paderborn where the village of Bredenborn was located, wood theft occurred more often than anywhere else in the region. It was an integral part of everyday life and an index of the unstable tug-of-war between the local landed elite and the impoverished small peasantry.[24] In her stories 'Die Judenbuche' and 'Bilder aus Westfalen' the poet Annette von Droste-Hülshoff, a member of the von Haxthausen family, gave an impressive description of the living conditions and behaviour of these peasants. In her view, the peasant saw the local lord as 'an archenemy and usurper of the property which really belonged to *him* [the peasant]. It was only out of cunning and self-interest that a true son of the land would flatter him [the landowner]; in every other way he would do him harm whenever possible.'[25]

The wood-pilfering described above was a consequence of the feudal ruling structure. The agrarian reforms, which brought with them the division of common lands, removed the justification for these acts. Of course, wood theft did not end, as the example from Scherfede shows. However, it now became a confrontation between two classes that had unequal chances to take part in economic modernization. In this class struggle, the 'wood thieves' were no longer simply defending the old rights of usufruct; they were defending their entire economic system – the family economy which was based on collective usage rights.

One example of this bitter struggle can be seen in a case of wood theft in Ravensberg around 1800 which was followed and avidly discussed in the regional press.[26] In proto-industrial Ravensberg, wood theft was not only promoted by wood shortages and the commercialization of the wood trade. Certain forms of it also reflected the changing relationship between peasants and *Heuerlinge* which accompanied the agrarian reforms and the division of communal land in the last decades of the eighteenth century. In this process, the paternalistic relationship between peasant and *Heuerling* eroded. At the same time, their class relationship, determined by the market, took on greater significance. When commonlands were divided, the pasture land once accessible to the *Heuerlinge* was at first only distributed among the peasants. The *Heuerlinge* sent complaints and delegations to Berlin with the result that certain parts of the pasture were to be set aside for their use. However, this was only achieved under certain circumstances and in particular areas since the peasants wanted the land for themselves.

From the peasants' perspective, the period of land division was a time of opportunity. However, the situation of the *Heuerlinge* only deteriorated. In a quick and effective manner, the peasants took advantage of the opportunities for free control over property. They transformed the former pasture land into fields and started to feed their livestock in stalls. By starting new plantings, they also began to lay the groundwork for private forests which would become a significant source of income. One official reported in 1809 that while the amount of land leased in part declined,

> the servitude of the poor *Heuerling* grew from year to year. Once the peasants started to increase their property, they then lost all goodwill towards their *Heuerlinge*, who lost the chance to use free pasture. The peasant gave them very little land, or none at all, to rent, in part because he wanted it for himself and in part because he did not want to give his *Heuerling* any time to cultivate since the peasant needed him [his labour power] for himself.[27]

The traditional economy of the *Heuerlinge* consisted of spinning or weaving, day labour and a family farm; its complex nature had guaranteed the family a certain amount of independence. Now, however, the system was threatened. Some *Heuerlinge* became strictly agricultural workers. Another part became renters and professional weavers or spinners who did not have sufficient property and could expect eviction when they opposed their peasant landlords. Apparently this happened fairly frequently because *Heuerlinge* finally started litigation against peasants to force them to guarantee their leaseholds for life. The demand to transform what had proven to be an unstable traditional and private rental agreement into government-protected tenure was at once conservative *and* revolutionary. In the final analysis, it was aimed against the market's control over the most fundamental necessities of life in rural society – land and property. None the less, it was rejected as 'unfair' and unjustifiable since the relationship between the peasant and the *Heuerling* was a 'private' one.

Apparently the conflict escalated into armed struggle, although the precise chronology cannot be reconstructed from press accounts. The newspapers reported that the spirit of the *Heuerlinge* 'resembled more and more an esprit de corps and wherever they could, they played the sansculottes while the peasants represented the aristocrats'. It was only the military in the nearby garrison in Bielefeld and the stationing of soldiers in the countryside which could prevent an open revolt, but it could not conceal the one taking place behind the scenes.

> At night gangs [of *Heuerlinge* and small peasants] go into the forest of a certain peasant whom they appear to have chosen specifically and use their thievish saws to cut down the most beautiful and best-grown trees. They even cut down the young oaks however they please, even two feet above the ground. They have caused such a panic among the owners, have threatened so loudly, and pursue their work so vociferously and openly that a peasant's life was never less safe than among the trees that he himself planted.

Indeed, when the thieves discovered one peasant they attacked him and tied him to a tree. He was found the next day partially frozen.[28]

In this case, the thefts were probably a case of impotent revenge in the face of legal defeats and attempts at military intimidation. They were none the less undertaken in a selective way against certain individual peasants and aimed to destroy the young plantings which were the tangible symbol of agrarian change. Thus they pointed clearly to the cause of the violence.

Bourgeois observers, lessees of landed estates and pastors, who were, like the peasants, victims of wood thefts, were also alarmed at the eruption of violence when communal property was divided. It touched on the principle of ownership in those areas where it had most recently been introduced. Thus it challenged the reformist understanding of private property as an element of progress because it would put an end to the 'nomadic economy' in village communities.[29] It was not only different interests which collided, but two different concepts of justice and the public good. Belief in the inviolable nature of property as a morally and economically progressive entity confronted notions of the right to subsistence, defined in terms of tradition. Both sides appealed to the state.

Defenders of private property demanded a more energetic prosecution of theft to the point of asking for 'martial laws' in the 'internal war',[30] while those appealing to traditional mores self-consciously invited the response of the socially responsible authorities, though never in the language of the radical democratic sansculottes from the French Revolution, which the authors cited above ascribed to the *Heuerlinge*.[31] It was both a convenient and a fearful response to see a connection between wood theft and the French Revolution or to think that the crime had spread because of developments in France.

At the same time, the only proposal to resolve the contradiction between the impoverished classes and those holding private property (or later between capital and labour) was 'strict justice' in order to protect property. The author of the following 'cry for help', written in Ravensberg in 1802, underscored the desire of property-owners for protection and thus invoked a theme which remained significant throughout the entire nineteenth century – the bourgeoisie's fear of revolution:

It is much better to prevent crimes of this kind than to find oneself forced to shoot with shrapnel afterwards. The number of those among us who do not think twice about a crime of this kind is very, very large, much too large for the state's true welfare to survive. This spirit has become the spirit of the people. Would the step to even greater crimes in fact be difficult? Our wood thieves see those who want to hinder them in their activities as their enemies and as enemies of poverty, against whom necessity empowers them. They have no wood, and the peasant has more than he needs, *ergo*. . . . Soon they will realize that the peasant has more rye than they do, and they will divide it with him; then they will discover people who have more money than they do and will take it from them; and still convinced of their justification, they will clear all those from their path who try to stop them. The little man sees no precise differences between one crime and another: anything the state lets pass his conscience permits him as well and he will not see it as evil. God protect us from the progression on which our people have now embarked, climbing higher and higher but still not reaching the top of the gallows! Only strict justice can save us now.[32]

Thus wrote a person educated in the Enlightenment, most likely a pastor in Ravensberg. And the peasants who were attacked? They implemented 'strict justice' in their own way through the drastic and brutal vigilante tactics of 'people's justice'. We will return to this topic below.

In contrast to the types of wood theft which have been described thus far, the criminal statistics reveal yet another type which was not directly part of the tensions and conflicts in rural society – theft stemming from undisguised, acute poverty. Quantitative measurements of criminality have many problems, including the likelihood that many offences, especially 'minor offences', were not recorded. In addition, the number of criminal charges reported may have increased due to the expansion of the security police force. None the less, close parallels do emerge between property theft, especially the theft of foodstuffs and wood, and the ups and downs of the economy. Particularly during the bad years when the grain price rose, the number of thefts also rose. A number of other factors also suggest this connection between pauperism and theft. The crimes had a seasonal character, and the majority of wood thefts took place in winter. Usually the thefts were very small and villages undertook pro-phylactic measures when times were bad. As a matter of course, commu-nities formed night patrols to protect their property in bad years or in times when the 'poorer classes' were unemployed since the police did not have the personnel to guarantee their safety.[33]

Poverty was in all likelihood the immediate cause for most of the offences. However, those wood thefts occasioned by need were also evi-dence of changes in rural social structure. They filled that vacuum created by the erosion of paternalistic support for the poor or by excessive charges to communal funds for the destitute in overpopulated villages. Thus wood theft varied with the capacity of other measures to confront poverty. When coal deliveries were made in the village of Heepen during the winter of 1840–1, the number of wood thefts declined drastically, reduced to less than 5 per cent of its previous level.[34] Given such a reversal, it might be argued that wood theft was a kind of self-help which replaced paternalism once that system had clearly collapsed.

Of course, one also should not overestimate pauperism as the cause of wood theft. The poor hardly demanded a 'right to theft'[35] as a matter of course without mitigating circumstances. It was rather a reaction which was tied to specific situations and social structures. As with hunger riots, poverty was an ever-present but not necessarily decisive factor. This con-clusion is suggested by the extreme variation in the frequency of wood theft and other forms of vandalism within the district of Minden. In 1837 in Paderborn, a region dominated by smallholding peasants, these crimes took place with a frequency twenty times greater than in the proto-industrial region of Minden-Ravensberg.[36]

Part of the explanation for this unequal distribution of theft lies in the larger forest area in Paderborn. In addition, the small peasants there had suffered through a difficult crisis which reached its peak in the 1830s. In Minden-Ravensberg, on the other hand, chronic poverty, especially among spinners, did not reach extreme levels until the 1840s. However, these figures do not necessarily represent real differences, because the variations in poverty were not that great. It is also unlikely that wood thefts were pursued more aggressively in Paderborn than in Minden-Ravensberg. In this instance, the interregional variations point to the notorious and infamous traditions of wood theft in the Paderborn region which had no parallel in Ravensberg despite the bitter conflicts there at the turn of the century. In contrast to the region which was dominated by small peasants, the proto-industrial area appeared to have found a structural solution to the conflict by 1800 by increasing peasant control over the lower classes. The solution hardly worked to the advantage of those without land. Commercial activity was offered as an alternative when all land use by the sub-peasant classes was suspended. The sale of yarn and linen brought money to the area and it circulated in local markets for agricultural products. Indeed, since the turn of the century the *Heuerling* class had divided in two – the old *Heuerlinge* who retained their usage rights and a semi-proletariat (*Einliegerproletarier*) that lived with small peasants and were *Heuerlinge* in name only. In fact they were yarn-spinners, linen-weavers and/or casual labourers.

In the Paderborn region, where there was no demand for a proto-industrial labour force, the same developments were not possible. In fact, it is not hard to imagine that wood theft supplied many small peasants and day labourers an equivalent for other sources of non-agrarian income. Many contemporaries were convinced of this fact. In the opinion of the Paderborn district magistrate, 'half of the wood sold at the twice weekly wood market in the city was stolen'.[37] The district forester Borchardt made a more precise differentiation between occasional wood thieves and three different types of 'professional' wood thieves. The latter were the landless local day labourers, the indebted smallholding peasants who tried to save their property by the sale of wood and an especially aggressive group of those who preferred 'the freest, the most carefree, unrestricted and loose life' to permanent residence and family.[38] The most characteristic thieves were the day labourers who found very little work. Their plight reflected the nature of the crisis of the small peasant village with particular clarity. For them, the 'wood theft system' was in fact a necessary condition for their survival. They learned the ins and outs of wood theft as children or as farmhands, employed by impoverished smallholding peasants. According to Borchardt, they married young and built their huts from stolen wood. They supported their families by stealing wood in organized gangs, by smuggling, with occasional day labour, and finally by keeping a few farm animals for which feed also had to be stolen since they had no arable land. Finally, they would burn down the house which had been insured against fire, take the money and begin the cycle again, building yet another house from stolen wood. As Borchardt explained, 'these people gain yet another advantage for themselves through such fires, since they have created the best opportunity for the favourable marketing and sale of the rest of the stolen wood'. The forester's unpleasant experiences during his often dangerous confrontations with wood thieves might have led him to exaggerate the situation. None the less, the very high number of insurance reimbursements for burnt buildings supports his account.[39]

There were no comparable developments in Minden-Ravensberg, although the course of wood theft did not disappear entirely in the *Vormärz* period. However, it no longer had the same socio-structural symptoms and significance as it did in Paderborn. In this proto-industrial area, criminality aimed solely at survival was particularly prominent. The punishment of children and young people, usually for field and garden thefts, increased continually up until 1850. Reports of 'common' thefts of foodstuffs indicated that they were probably more frequent in Minden-Ravensberg than in Paderborn.[40] Since the vast majority of the population was involved in textile manufacturing in some fashion, the price of yarn played the role of a crisis barometer played by the grain price elsewhere. An 1821 report from a small administrative area of only a few villages confirms this impression. The official described events during a month of particularly low yarn prices:

> Security police: bad situation. Everything is being stolen and burglarized. On the third and fourth of this month, the Pastor Weihe in Menninghüffen was robbed of old clothing, on the tenth and eleventh, the trader Hellman in Gohfeld had some coffee, bedding and linen stolen; on the 19th and 20th, the peasant Poggemüller in Holsen was robbed of two sides of bacon; on the 20th and 27th, the *Heuerling* Bochholz lost yarn and shirts and the peasant . . . in Oberbauerschaft had beds stolen.[41]

In contrast to wood theft, the traditional socio-structural lines of confrontation between thieves and their victims had disintegrated in these crimes. Not even the *Heuerling* was spared, although the property-owners of course were the most obvious victims.

Finding a class base for criminality becomes even more difficult when one includes yet another factor. A relatively small number of wood thefts was very characteristic for the social structure in Minden-Ravenberg, but so was a high number of civil court cases, almost twice as high as in Paderborn. These trials were an indication of the degree to which a money-based economy, with money transfers and money shortages, had become prevalent in everyday life. They usually originated with complaints over relatively small debts.[42] To be sure, the creditors who were trying to get their money back were often landowners, city merchants and of course wood dealers. In many cases, however, they were of almost the same social background as the debtors.[43] Small credit became an almost constant method of survival for the lower classes in an economy based on borrowing. Foodstuffs were increasingly only available for money, and money income was never sufficient. This allowed the development of debt fraud, yet another form of everyday criminality. Along with theft and commodity fraud, this became the most typical form of day-to-day confrontation between proto-industrial producers and merchants.[44]

The conflicts over debts reveal that money had an ambivalent meaning for the proto-industrial lower classes who were in the process of leaving behind the autarkic and barter economy. There was never enough money available, but a money economy opened up new modes of consumption, which were frequently labelled as frivolous and luxurious. This was probably the case because money, although it had now become a universal medium of exchange, still retained its former significance as a costly 'ringing coin' which was used to buy luxurious, prestige items in traditional society.[45] At any rate, a form of moral discipline within the money economy had yet to be established. This was carried out systematically 'from above' with a consistency and logic similar to that of the 'forest police' in their pursuit of wood thieves. The role which the forester played for thieves was played for petty debtors by the bailiff. In 1823 the majority of courts in Minden-Ravensberg decided that it was necessary to enforce a strict repayment of debts, even when it involved the complete expropriation of all property including the spinning wheel and bedding. The *Heuerling* would only remain credit-worthy when he feared losing these basic tools and supplies. It was only during a time of dire poverty in 1843 that the exception already demanded in 1823 finally came into effect, allowing at least bedding to be excluded from the court's orders.[46]

IV

Regional differences in prevailing forms of petty crime are also apparent in the penalties for wood theft. These often show a severity which is surprising for what was usually a harmless offence. The tactics of state prosecution, the resistance to them and extra-legal sanctions all point to a confrontation between the state and the impoverished lower classes. On the one hand, the state dissolved the practice of corporal justice under patrimonial jurisdiction, while on the other hand it provoked a direct collision of all parties in the form of vigilante justice outside the realm of the law.

During the nineteenth century, the legal sanctions against wood theft in Prussia were strengthened, and wood theft became similar to 'common theft'. Surely the tendency to criminalize wood theft shows that the state chose a 'path of repression'[47] to handle the social and political problem. In fact, this repression, which was indeed more effective, was carried out more by the administration than by the court. As with every law, the wood theft law limited the state justice system because it had to establish the facts of the matter and prove that a crime had actually occurred. It was often difficult to extract a wood theft, in the narrowly defined form, from an unclear and contested situation. It was difficult to make a distinction between that which was *still* a 'right' or custom, and that which was *already* a theft. The government, however, in its function as administrator and manager of the state forest, adopted strict police measures to regulate and even repeal customary rights.

The ineffectiveness of the justice system's punishments was the most important criticism of the 1821 wood theft law. On the one hand, complaints in Westphalia were directed against the judge's apparently strong commitment to providing evidence, which seems to have led to frequent acquittals.[48] On the other hand, when punishments were handed down, they often did not match the prevailing social realities. Since most of the fines levied could not be paid, the accused criminal was either taken into custody or sent for penal labour in the forests, or after 1834, to public works projects like road construction. However, penal labour was often more of a punishment for officials who had to control a large group of recalcitrant prisoners than it was for the prisoners themselves. When the work was in forests, it was often like sending wolves to guard the sheep since they found additional opportunities to steal.

Finally, the punishments had no value as a deterrent since they were often postponed when there were no suitable work opportunities. Those found guilty also allegedly claimed that they willingly accepted arrest 'because they had a chance to enjoy things living in jail which they didn't have at home'. Under these circumstances, those court days when forest crimes were handled perhaps did turn into scornful, satirical demonstrations against the justice system as the county and city court in Höxter described in 1836. The accused came in 'singing and whistling' and showed 'complete indifference towards every punishment' which was given, 'happy that the state still had to take care of them'.[49]

At least after the late 1830s, the Prussian state no longer allowed itself to be led around by the nose in this fashion, if indeed this was ever the case. From then on the flanks of the Prussian *Rechsstaat*, which already included patrimonial and police jurisdictions, were further extended to encompass military repression of forest vandals. Laws and statutes introduced between 1837 and 1839 facilitated the use of soldiers to protect the forest. They also sanctioned use of firearms against wood thieves and tightened controls on the sale of wood.[50] Ultimately, however, it was not the justice system and the police force with their reputation for ineptitude and corruption but rather the quasi-military management of forests which stemmed wood theft. The laws and regulations of 1837–9 confirmed the fundamental principle expressed by the Minden government – 'fear preserves the forest'. Already in 1840 the government determined that wood theft was on the decline.[51] More dramatic evidence of the change brought on by increased repression was the number of victims counted in bloody confrontations between wood thieves and foresters in the Minden district, especially in Paderborn. Between 1823 and 1837, before the laws were tightened, two thieves were wounded and three were killed in such confrontations, while nine forestry officials were wounded and two were killed. In the years from 1838 to 1848, this balance was reversed. During the shorter time period, eight thieves were wounded and five killed, but only four foresters received wounds, none of which were deadly. Indeed, the number of victims was probably larger, especially among the thieves, since in summary newspaper accounts it was sometimes only reported that numerous participants and victims were involved in confrontations.[52] This change in the state's repressive measures, coming on the heels of the agrarian reforms in the 1840s, also contributed to the forms of the March revolution in Paderborn forests. These revolts seem to show that the Minden government's plan to fill wood storage houses with cheap firewood while instituting the stricter forest laws was not very successful.[53] The balance of victims on both sides surely only represented the tip of the iceberg in the area of violence. It does in fact provide evidence of a 'spirit of resistance'.[54]

Of course, the forest administration responded decisively to the show of force 'from below'. Forceful confrontrations with the authorities were 'typically' initiated by organized gangs, but communal wood theft often resulted in violent confrontations as well. In 1798, after he had been employed for a year and a half on the Haxthausen estate, a new forester reported that he had discovered a wood theft by residents of the Bredenborn community. During this period, he had three experiences which must have made him fear for his life. 'Enraged' people chased him and his assistants through the forest, threatening them with axes, and at one point he saw 'death before his eyes'. It was only because of a warning shot, which wounded a Bredenborn resident, that he was able to keep his pursuers from him. It is not surprising that he soon requested either better protection or to be relieved of his duties because he would rather choose the beggar's staff 'than to abandon wife and children to the scorn of the mob after being murdered'.[55]

The same forester on the Haxthausen estate also received threatening letters which show the willingness of the rural lower classes to engage in violence. Judging by these documents, this was not just a trait specific to a marginalized group of rural vagabonds. They prophesied his death and, in particularly telling fashion, called him a Judas and the 'betrayer of his neighbours' who '[kept] the wood for Herr von Haxthausen'.[56] These accusations unrelentingly defined the forester as an advocate for the landlord. Thus they exposed the structural origin of the violence as a conflict between the landowner and the impoverished small peasants.

It becomes even clearer that this was the source of the violence when one looks at similar forms of insubordination by the rural lower classes that had limited resources and were heavily burdened with fees and taxes. The Paderborn region was infamous not only for wood theft, but also for its 'excesses' against local officials. 'Now someone's cow will be killed in the pasture, now another's forest planting will be ruined, now a third will have his grain cut while it's green.'[57] This destruction of property belonging to district secretaries, officials, police, court employees and meadow and forest guards was sometimes accompanied with attacks on houses and 'murderish treatment' of the victims. The violence was mainly directed against the state administration, that is, against the ever-increasing burdens of police forces and taxes which had been much weaker in the old ecclesiastic state.

Taking violence as an indication of the intensity of social conflict, the comparison of Paderborn with Minden–Ravensberg reveals that the almost 'modern' class conflict between peasants and *Heuerlinge* was no less severe than that between peasants and lords. In Minden–Ravensberg, thefts of wood and foodstuffs were often punished extra-legally by the 'people's justice' of the peasants themselves. In the interest of fairness, it is also worth noting that these extreme cases took place alongside normal state sanctions. There were also peaceful extra-legal measures, administered by peasant community leaders, where the thefts were punished by a recompensation of the victim.[58] In contrast, certain varieties of vigilante justice appear that much more brutal. They bear witness to an older form of vengeful justice in rural society which survived the legal reforms of the Enlightenment.

The author cited above who demanded 'martial law' also raised this issue in order to curb 'people's justice'. He wrote that the thrashing of thieves 'has been in style for many years', since the peasants were convinced that only corporal punishment, not money fines, would deter the thieves.[59]

Between 1800 and 1848 fourteen different cases of vigilante justice can be documented in Minden–Ravensberg. This violence took different forms, ranging from *charivari* to the destruction of property. However, the most frequently reported form of people's justice (eight cases) was murder. One example was described in horrible detail in the *Westfälischer Anzeiger* in 1806.

In the recent past once again [!] eight thieves appeared at the peasant Peterman's in the village of Versmold in the middle of the day. One thief was forced to accuse all the others, who were then taken from their houses and executed by the mob. According to an eyewitness from the area, the door-step ran with blood and the people lay around like butchered pigs.

Fifty peasants in the Minden area in 1847 treated five suspects with just as much brutality after a bed was stolen. Two people died and two were seriously wounded when they tried to force confessions with beatings.[60]

The willingness of peasants to use their social power to develop sustained tactics of intimidation is shown in yet another measure. What vigilante justice tried to accomplish through terror, the 'Association of Respectability and Morality' attempted to achieve through social control over the *Heuerlinge*. The peasants of Heepen in the district of Ravensberg tried to start this organization in 1840. In spite of the creation of a coal storage area, wood thefts still occurred and, in the opinion of the outraged peasants, 'the better-off inhabitants [believed] that they had done even more than the poorer class could demand, since in many other districts this had not taken place'. They felt 'that the unification of all upright men was needed to protect property and to teach the poor class to give up its laziness and its mode of illegal acquisition'. All landowners, from large peasants to smaller owners, should unite and agree only to rent housing and land to 'respectable' *Heuerlinge*. Indirectly, they also sought to control marriage by offering land and housing only to those who contributed ten Taler to the fund for widows and orphans before marrying and who postponed weddings until they were 25.[61]

This association was not legally recognized, however. Despite well-meaning support by the president of the province of Westphalia and one local official, the Minden government refused to approve the statute which 'in many ways contradicted the legal code'. Nevertheless, the peasants apparently did demand to see marriage licences. Though only limited in its impact, the intention behind this 'Association' shows the personal power of the peasants. Just like the nobility, they felt themselves to be the 'lords' over the propertyless class and in extreme cases, just like the nobility, even lords over life and death. If they happened to enter into competition with the state's monopoly on violence and justice in the process, they compensated for what they felt were weak spots in the state's justice system. The state, on the other hand, gave them power over the rabble in their role as landlords, which also included the right of 'discipline' by corporal punishment.

These measures of peasant control over the lower classes bring into sharp relief the forms of rebellion in 1848 and the courage of *Heuerlinge*

73

and small peasants who shared an almost chiliastic hope for a 'new age'. However, they also give an indication of the severity of the reaction against these rebellions. In Minden-Ravensberg, the riotous *Heuerlinge* who went from farm to farm requesting, not demanding, food often met peasants who gave out lashes instead of eggs and ham.[62] On the other hand, in the Paderborn region where the March revolts were much fiercer, 'anarchy' in the forests was repressed by the military and the peasants themselves. The conflict between village communities and landed estate-owners and forest-owners once again intensified. The villages demanded the restoration of the eighteenth-century rights. They destroyed tree farms, chased away foresters, burned down forest huts, reclaimed fines that had been paid and in general used the 'political confusion to fill people with fear and to force forest-owners to make exaggerated concessions which aimed at nothing but the destruction of the forest'.[63]

In those communities where wood and pasture rights had already been distributed, peasants and day labourers confronted one another as they did in Minden-Ravensberg. For example, after the division of a forest among three communities that used it, a Höxter official reported the following incident. 'From the 24th to the 25th [of November] a few inhabitants [of Amelunxen] who made their living by stealing wood from the sections that have now gone to the communities of Wehrden and Drenke, are assembling in the forest. They want to use force to expel the people from Wehrden, who have also assembled in the forest.' Only his appearance prevented a 'bloody conflict'. The 'negotiations' which followed surprised the district magistrate quite a bit, since they destroyed his image of rural dwellers as people 'unfamiliar with the state of daily affairs'. When he proposed that the forest be managed co-operatively by all three communities so that the needs of the day labourers could be taken into account, 'those involved from Drenke and Wehrden protested very vehemently and insisted on the justice of the laws. Using specific references to events in Vienna (*in the revolution of 1848, [Ed.]*), they asserted that Vienna was conquered even though it was 100 times larger and therefore they would not have any difficulties taking the restless proletariat in Ameluxen in hand.'[64]

This is how the peasants who had now become property-owners expressed themselves, although they had probably been experienced wood thieves themselves in the past. Given such attitudes on the part of the peasants, it is easy to imagine the reaction that a relatively small accomplishment of the revolution could arouse. On 26 June 1848 the king declared an amnesty for wood theft and forest vandalism[65] following the recommendation of the Berlin parliament, elected the previous May. The State Ministry gave only half-hearted support, expressing concern for the state forests. The apparent result was an 'exorbitant increase in wood thefts', according to the complaints of the Finance Minister Hansemann. The provisions were soon tightened and although the punishment for wood theft remained suspended, payments for damages were reinstatuted. In the spring of 1849 the 'most powerful execution' of the penal codes was again enjoined, namely rapid sentencing and carrying out the punishment. This included provisions to convert penal labour to a prison sentence if no suitable work opportunities were available. Judging from the rapidly rising number of prosecuted crimes, despite lower grain prices, one can assume that this pressure from above had an impact. And no doubt this satisfied those peasants who in December 1848 complained about the weakness of the police and courts as 'good and faithful subjects [*Untertan*] or, as one now says, as respected citizens [*Staatsbürger*]' demanding the 'protection of private property'.[66] Thus the amnesty probably had a paradoxical effect. It increased social tensions in the countryside and as a result it intensified peasant loyalties to the conservative forces against the revolution.

V

As police forces grew, urbanization came about and incomes rose, wood theft gradually declined in the second half of the nineteenth century.[67] Along with other forms of social protest, it none the less had a significance which was typical in the period before 1848. Therefore we will end the presentation here and briefly summarize the argument. Petty 'criminality as a social action' (Blasius) was definitely dependent on local and regional social structures in both its frequency and its form. Wood theft was a typical manifestation of social protest for the landless lower classes, especially in those places like Paderborn where changes in agrarian society had left the overburdened small peasant family economy in a dead end. The old conflict between the village and the lord over forest usage continued during and after the agrarian reforms, but now as a confrontation between different rural social classes. As population expanded, the lower class of small owners and day labourers increased. For them stealing wood and foodstuffs was an element of the 'economy of makeshift'.[68] As the lower level of wood theft in Minden-Ravensberg suggests, this was no longer typical for an agrarian society which had been penetrated by proto-industry in the first half of the nineteenth century, at least not after a transitional period of violent conflict when communal forms were disbanded. With the growth of the commercial economy, the lower classes here saw the possibility or felt the pressure to leave behind the agrarian realm. The proto-industrial lower class in the countryside was bound more strongly to a money economy. For them debt fraud was a frequent and common crime comparable to wood theft for the agrarian lower class. However, neither this crime nor petty theft of foodstuffs showed any signs of disappearing.

The regional character of petty criminality indicates the different opportunities for at least a partial development of peasant capitalism. Through wood theft, the small peasant in the Paderborn region before the agrarian reforms was also defending the family economy which was rooted in the community and depended on collective resources. The acclaimed good conscience of later wood thieves still was rooted in this tradition which was also in part continued through communal forest ownership. In Minden-Ravensberg, on the other hand, the middle and large peasants accommodated themselves to agrarian individualism very quickly. They developed their own modes of production within the limitations of the traditional family labour contract, now augmented by wage labour. This allowed them to increase their production largely for the local and regional agrarian markets. In this context, they learned to value personal control over land as private property, which is also shown in their treatment of wood thieves and other thieves. The extra-legal measures they took was proof that the state could depend on the support of these peasants-turned-landowners in its increasingly repressive measures of forest management.

The considerable violence of some of these thieves and the violence with which they were pursued bear witness to extreme social tensions in agrarian society during the first half of the nineteenth century which are not always apparent. A basic social and political problem was expressed through this seemingly harmless crime, namely, the polarization of social classes and the emancipation of rural lower classes from the peasant villages. This took place under the rubric of economic liberalism in a transitional era filled with massive poverty and economic crises. To this extent, widespread wood theft was a symptom of the individual self-determination of the lower classes.

Did this struggle also result in a 'proletarian class consciousness' as Blasius assumes? In the light of what has been presented here, this thesis must be viewed with careful scepticism. Wood theft was directed against a specific kind of private property, but its class nature was not so clear. Fellow village residents were also robbed, and it did not lead to any particular process of political education. Just as the wood thief looked to the past for his justification, he also remained fixated on a patriarchal authority which was obliged to care for the poor. Finally, in the light of the intimidating and probably successful repression, one could perhaps risk the opposite conclusion. The condition and experiences of the lower stratum in rural class society did not lead to the development of militant class consciousness. Instead, it was more likely that it led to that relative diffidence of the industrial working class emphasized by Barrington Moore.[69] Of course, this can only be called diffidence when measured against a revolutionary political programme. Seen somewhat differently, the workers' 'modest' demand for 'decent human treatment' showed a stubborn refusal to co-operate with liberal capitalism. In the same sense, we should not underestimate the resistance of wood thieves. They opposed the private, commercial control of a crucial commodity essential for warm feet and a heated meal.

Notes: Chapter 2

1 See the discussion and complete references in the article in this volume by Hanna Schissler; see also Hans Rosenberg, 'Die Pseudodemokratisierung der Rittergutsbesitzerklasse', in idem *Machteliten und Wirtschaftskonjunkturen. Studien zur neueren Wirtschafts- und Sozialgeschichte* (Göttingen, 1978), 83–102; on the concept of capitalism employed here, see Max Weber, *Wirtschaftsgeschichte* (Munich, 1933), 238ff.

2 See, for example, H. Bleiber, *Zwischen Reform und Revolution. Lage und Kämpfe der schlesischen Bauern und Landarbeiter im Vormärz 1840–1847* (Berlin/G.D.R., 1966). In this context, I can only allude to the discussion of the variations of the 'Prussian path' and the valuable studies on the agrarian reforms published by historians in the G.D.R. See the critical examination of this topic in Christian Dipper, *Die Bauernbefreiung in Deutschland 1790–1850* (Stuttgart, 1980), esp. 24ff. This also provides a good overview of the problems of agrarian reform.

3 The literature on this issue is very large and has grown considerably in the last decades. For an introduction and a general overview, see D. Saalfeld, 'Die ständische Gliederung der Gesellschaft Deutschlands im Zeitalter des Absolutismus. Ein Quantifizierungsversuch', *Vierteljahrschrift für Sozial- und Wirtschaftsgeschichte* 67 (1980): 457–83; P. Kriedte, H. Medick and J. Schlumbohm, *Industrialisierung vor der Industrialisierung. Gewerbliche Warenproduktion auf dem Land in der Formationsperiode des Kapitalismus* (Göttingen, 1977), (English translation, Cambridge, 1981).

4 For an overview of the legal regulations, see Ziegner-Gnüchtel, 'Der Forstdiebstahl', *Zeitschrift für die gesamte Strafrechtswissenschaft* 8 (1888): 222–315. For Prussia in particular, K. W. Hahn, *Das Holzdiebstahlgesetz vom 2. Juni 1852 mit Motiven, Kammer-Verhandlungen, Kommentar und Beilagen* (Breslau, 1852).

5 According to D. Blasius, *Kriminalität und Alltag. Zur Konfliktgeschichte des Alltagslebens im 19. Jahrhundert* (Göttingen, 1978), 81.

6 Hahn, 2.

7 S. M. Borchhardt, *Der Holzdiebstahl in seinen Ursachen, Folgen und Umfang. Nebst Mitteln zur Abhülfe, aus rein praktischer Erfahrung dargestellt* (Berlin, 1842), 2, 95.

8 See for example Blasius, *Kriminalität*; idem, *Bürgerliche Gesellschaft und Kriminalität. Zur Sozialgeschichte Preussens im Vormärz* (Göttingen, 1976).

9 The quotations are from Blasius, *Kriminalität*, 68, 18, 57.

10 In the following summary and for the social historical background of this presentation, I am drawing on my *Ländliche Klassengesellschaft 1770–1848. Bauern und Unterschichten, Landwirtschaft und Gewerbe im östlichen Westfalen* (Göttingen, 1984). Complete references can be found there, and I have limited myself to the most essential references in this essay. It is a revised and shortened version of ' "Furcht bewahrt das Holz." Holzdiebstahl und sozialer Konflikt in der ländlichen Gesellschaft 1800–1850 an westfälischen Beispielen', in *Räuber, Volk und Obrigkeit. Studien zur Geschichte der Kriminalität in Deutschland vom 18. bis zum 20. Jahrhundert*, ed. H. Reif (Frankfurt, 1984), 43–99. The translation was provided by Lynn Mally.

11 See W. Sombart, *Der moderne Kapitalismus*, 3 vols., 4th ed. (Munich, 1921), esp. 71, 'Das drohende Ende des Kapitalismus', in Vol. 2/2, pp. 1137–59; and J. Radkau, 'Holzverknappung und Krisenbewusstsein im 18. Jahrhundert', *Geschichte und Gesellschaft* 9 (1983): 513–43.

12 Grafschaft Ravensberg. Ueber Uebervölkerung', *Westfälischer Anzeiger oder Vaterländisches Archiv zur Beförderung des Guten und Nützlichen*, ed. A. Mallinckrodt et al. (henceforth cited as *WA*), 1804, cols. 342–6, 353–8, quotations from cols. 353 and 357.

13 U. Wichert-Pollmann, *Das Glasmacherhandwerk im östlichen Westfalen. Eine volkskundliche Untersuchung* (Münster, 1963), 124ff.

14 Sombart, 1149; K. Hasel, *Zur Geschichte der Forstgesetzgebung in Preussen* (Frankfurt, 1974).

15 See Sombart, 1064. On the significant value of wood export in comparison to the well-known export of grain from east Elbia, see R. H. Dumke, 'Anglo-deutscher Handel und Frühindustrialisierung in Deutschland 1822–1865', *Geschichte und Gesellschaft* 5 (1979), esp. 199. In general, see H. Rubner, *Forstgeschichte im Zeitalter der industriellen Revolution* (Berlin, 1967).

16 See, for example, Blasius, *Gesellschaft*, 24ff.; idem, *Kriminalität*, 19ff.; A. Lüdtke, '*Gemeinwohl', Polizei und 'Festungspraxis'. Staatliche Gewaltsamkeit und innere Verwaltung in Preussen 1815–1850* (Göttingen, 1982), esp. 209ff.; Borchardt, 35ff. Borchardt was a forest official in Paderborn.

17 *WA* 1801, cols. 113–26. The quotation is from col. 115.

18 Chronik der Gemeinde Heepen, in Stadtarchiv Bielefeld, Bl. 42.

19 W. Schwarze, 'Vom Waldbesitz der Gemeinde Scherfede', *Westfälischer Heimatkalendar*, 1959, pp. 157–9. The figures on property ownership are from A. Meitzen, *Der Boden und die landwirtschaftlichen Verhältnisse des preussischen Staats*, 8 vols. (Berlin, 1868–1908), 4: 82, 84, 428f. For property distribution in general, see Rubner, 111ff.

20 Statements for communal forests, estimated according to incomplete individual entries in Staatsarchiv Detmold (henceforth STAD) M1 IE 2914, 2915; for Scherfede, see Schwarze, 158.

21 The following is based on reports in STAD M1 IE 2917 and on the local historical background to Annette von Droste-Hülshoff's novel, *Die Judenbuche*. See K. Ph. Moritz, *Annette v. Droste Hülshoff. Die Judenbuche* (Paderborn, 1980), 19ff., 159ff.

22 A. Freiherr von Haxthausen, *Ueber die Agrarverfassung in den Fürstenthümern Paderborn und Corvey und deren Conflikte in der gegenwärtigen Zeit* (Berlin, 1829), 262f.

23 A letter of Werner von Haxthausen to the Minden government, 23 December 1819, STAD M1 Pr. 837.

24 Wernicke also sees wood theft as the 'most common' form of 'class struggle by the lower classes'. K. Wernicke, 'Untersuchungen zu den niederen Formen des bäuerlichen Klassenkampfes im Gebiet der Gutsherrschaft 1648–1789' (Diss., Berlin/G.D.R., 1962), 165ff.

25 A. von Droste-Hülshoff, *Bilder aus Westfalen* (1845), and *Die Judenbuche* are cited according to the edition of Droste-Hülshoff's *Werke in einem Band*, selected by R. Walbiner (Berlin/G.D.R., 1970), 344f.

26 Of course wood theft was not unknown in Minden-Ravensberg before this. In 1769 the war and estate court (*Kriegs- und Domänenkammer*) in Minden called it 'quite enormous' and promised to pursue 'indescribable trouble and work to end present disorders'. Quoted from H. Riepenhausen, *Die bäuerliche Siedlung des Ravensberger Landes* (Münster, 1938), 124.

27 Report of the steward Fischer from Schildesche near Bielefeld, 16 October 1809. Staatsarchiv Münster (henceforth STAM), Regierungskommission Bielefeld 25, Bl. 12.

28 J. N. 'Hülfe! Einbruch der vollständigsten Unsicherheit in der Grafschaft Ravensberg', *WA*, 1802, cols. 193–201, quotation from col. 196.

29 This was the expression of one of the great agrarian writers of the nineteenth century, J. N. Schwerz, *Beschreibung der Landwirtschaft in Westfalen und Rheinpreussen*, 2 pts (Stuttgart, 1836), here pt I, p. 320.

30 See the article 'Criminaljustiz. Mit Rücksicht auf die Grafschaft Ravensberg', in *WA*, 1805, cols. 439–43. Quotation from col. 440.

31 See Mooser, '"Furcht"', 61f.

32 See note 28, quotation from col. 199.
33 For these aspects, see Blasius, *Gesellschaft*, 140ff.; 'Jahresverwaltungsbericht der Regierung Minden, Abteilung Forstwesen für das Jahr 1838', STAD M1 Pr. 27; Ziegner-Gnüchtel, 243; Borchardt, 91, 93. There were frequent notices about patrols in monthly reports from the government of Minden in STAM Oberpräsidium (henceforth OP) 351, Vols. 1–7. On the police, see A. Lüdtke, 'Praxis und Funktion staatlicher Repression: Preussen 1815–50', *Geschichte und Gesellschaft* 3 (1977): 190–211; idem, *'Gemeinwohl'*, 143ff.
34 Poverty commission (*Armenvorstand*) of the community of Heepen in Ravensberg, 15 February 1841, in STAD M1 IE 2529. On the nature, functions and extent of community poverty programmes, see J. Mooser, 'Gleichheit und Ungleichheit in der ländlichen Gemeinde. Sozialstruktur und Kommunalverfassung im östlichen Westfalen vom späten 18. bis in die Mitte des 19. Jahrhunderts', *Archiv für Sozialgeschichte* 19 (1979): 231–62, esp. 255ff.
35 See Blasius, *Kriminalität*, 53ff.
36 According to locally differentiated figures which are not available for other years in Starke, *Justiz-Verwaltungsstatistik des Preussischen Staates* (Berlin, 1839), 365ff. See the aggregate figures for all of Westphalia in Blasius, *Gesellschaft*, 140ff.
37 District magistrate of the Paderborn district to the Minden government, 23 February 1836, STAD M1 IP 960, B1. 24. According to the leading Prussian statistician at the time, the firewood trade was a 'poor business' for 'small landowners'. J. G. Hoffmann, *Die Befugnis zum Gewerbebetriebe* (Berlin, 1841), 341f.
38 Borchardt, 18–34. The term 'profession' in this context did not imply professional criminality in the way we understand it today, but rather more-or-less regular theft as a part of income.
39 In the neighbouring Westphalian government district of Münster which had approximately 400,000 residents, only 30,266 Taler of insurance were paid out for fires in 1838, while in the four Paderborn districts, with 145,000 inhabitants, 78,093 Taler were paid. Consistent with this comparison, there were only 134 wood theft investigations in Münster in 1838, an area which had less forest land. Borchardt, 18ff., 26 (quotation), 28.
40 See the lists of punished children and adolescents in STAD M1 IP 289, 290; locally differentiated figures on 'common theft' are in STAD M1 IP 288.
41 Reports of the bailiff in the Ravensberg administrative district, Quernheim/Mennighüffen, 29 January 1821, Amtsarchiv Löhne, no. 17.
42 In 1837 there were 213 trials in Minden-Ravensberg per 1,000 inhabitants while in Paderborn there were 113. Starke, *Justiz-Verwaltungsstatistik*, 365ff.
43 Stressed by county and city court in Halle to the government of Minden, 2 February 1823, STAD M1 IIIE 180.
44 Commodity fraud meant pretending that a product was of very high quality. A description of this practice, also well known elsewhere, stresses that it had become 'habitual' but that it did not undermine 'the morality of the poorer inhabitants'. C. H. Bitter, 'Bericht über den Notstand in der Senne zwischen Bielefeld und Paderborn' (1853) in *64. Jahresbericht des Historischen Vereins der Grafschaft Ravensberg 1964/65*, 1–108, esp. 29ff.
45 See H. Medick's thoughts in Kriedte et al., *Industrialisierung*, 151ff.
46 See the reports and ordinances in STAD M1 III E 180.
47 Blasius, *Gesellschaft*, 109. On the details of the criminal law, see ibid., 103ff.; and Mooser, ' "Furcht" ', 70ff.
48 This was the criticism of the Westphalian parliament in 1832 and 1835, and especially that of the forester Borchardt. He made accusations against the apparently naïve judge and bitterly complained about the arrogance of lawyers towards subordinate forest officials.
49 There are many reports on the ineffectiveness of the justice system in STAD M1 IP 960, from which the quotation comes; also STAD M1 IE 2914; Borchardt, 65ff.
50 For details, see Mooser, ' "Furcht" ', 73.
51 Yearly administrative report of the Minden government, 1840, Abt. Forstwesen, STAD M1 Pr. 29.
52 The cases are only counted as having one victim. The figures given here came from

monthly reports from the Minden government, STAM OP 351, Vols. 1–7. More specific evidence on these events is no longer available at the regional level. Since one can imagine that the reports were selective and did not report all the victims, one can assume that the number of dead and wounded was higher.

53 Circular instruction from the Minden government, 14 September 1842, *Ministerial-Blatt für die gesamte innere Verwaltung in den Königlich-Preussischen Staaten* (henceforth *Ministerialblatt*), no. 3, 1842, 358ff. Notice of the Minden government, 7 January 1844, in ibid., no. 5, 1844, 9. Afterwards there were wood storage houses in five towns in the Paderborn region. On the revolution, see below, p. 73.

54 Blasius, *Kriminalität*, 56.

55 Borchardt, 33f.; quotations from the report of the forester Kirchhoff, printed in Moritz, 163ff.

56 Cited in Moritz, 168.

57 Minden government to Operpräsidium, 3 July 1823, STAM OP 689; additional reports in ibid., in STAD M1 IP 960, and M1 IP 1701, and also in the periodic reports of the Minden government.

58 See G. Engel (ed.), 'Tagebuch des Gemeindevorstehers Johann Cristoph Meyer zu Sieker, 1833–1835', *67. Jahresbericht des Historischen Vereins der Grafschaft Ravensberg*, 1970, 89–115, esp. 101, 108ff.

59 'Criminaljustiz. Mit Rücksicht auf die Grafschaft Ravensberg', *WA*, 1805, cols. 442f.; 'Volksjustiz. Grafschaft Ravensberg', ibid., cols. 1019–24; see also above, p. 65.

60 These periodic reports are to be found in the local press, the reports of the Minden government and in archival sources. See the complete references in Mooser, '"Furcht"', 77f.

61 This and the following references to this organization come from its statutes and the correspondence concerning it in STAD M1 IP 968.

62 Of course, this was not the only aspect of the revolution in the countryside. More important elements were legal, loyal behaviour, conservative electoral practices and appeals to the state to allieviate disorder. See W. Schulte, *Volk und Staat. Westfalen im Vormärz und in der Revolution 1848/49* (Münster, 1954); and Mooser, *Ländliche Klassengesellschaft*, 355ff.

63 The administrative commission of Prince Ratibor to the Minden government, 29 March 1848, STAD M1 IP 533, B1. 89f. On the revolt in the forests, see the reports in STAM OP 693 and STAD M1 III B 102 in particular.

64 Excerpt from the report of district magistrate from the district of Höxter to the Minden government, 28 November 1848, STAM OP 492, B1. 89ff. On similar tensions in the Warburg district, see the district magistrate's report to the Minden government, 2 May 1848, STAD M1 IP 533, B1. 181ff.

65 Order of the King's Cabinet, 26 June 1848, which was not included in the published laws. Instead the governments found out about it in a circular report. *Ministerial-Blatt*, no. 9, 1848, 216.

66 See *Ministerial-Blatt*, no. 9, 1848, 242, 352; ibid., no. 10, 1849, 145f.; Blasius, *Kriminalität*, 81; petition of community officials from Valdorf and Exter (Herford district) to the Minden government, 9 December 1848, STAD M1 IP 170 which carries sixty-four signatures from 'local residents'.

67 While wood theft still had a tendency to rise during the 1850s and 60s, by the 1870s it was on the decline, apparently due to the 'energetically conducted programme of forest protection'. W. Starke, *Verbrechen und Verbrecher in Preussen 1854–1878. Eine kulturgeschichtliche Studie* (Berlin, 1884), 29ff., 99.

68 O. H. Hufton, *The Poor of Eighteenth-Century France 1750–1789* (Oxford, 1974), esp. 11f.

69 See the interpretation of the German workers' movement in Barrington Moore, *Injustice. The Social Bases of Obedience and Revolt* (New York, 1978), 119ff.

3   Lords and Peasants in the Kaiserreich

HANS JÜRGEN PUHLE

I

The agrarian question was one of the most decisive economic, social and political issues confronting the Prusso-German state before the First World War. The distribution of landed property, the production methods and the profitability of agriculture were intimately connected with the patterns of social and political control in the countryside. In turn, these were related to the distribution of power within the Prussian state and to the historical role and social function of the dominant, largely grain-producing east Elbian Junkers and the bourgeois landowners who imitated them. All these factors had an impact on Prussian politics, while the state, because of its rapid economic growth, its overwhelming military strength and its able diplomacy, emerged as the uncontested hegemonic power in Central Europe after Bismarck became Prussian Minister President in 1862. They continued to play an important role in the politics of the North German Confederation and of the German Empire after its unification in 1871.[1]

The dominant position of Prussia in German politics expanded the general influence of the Prussian ruling elite, composed of large landowners, the military and the bureaucracy. Within this elite, the east Elbian landowners maintained an undisputed central role, despite the increasing integration of the 'younger' west German provinces. Their traditional predominance was the result of centuries-old, although sometimes modified, patterns of agrarian ownership and power. By the second half of the nineteenth century they had become an integral part of Prussian political and cultural institutions. Therefore the east Elbian landowners could retain their social and political privileges, albeit in a somewhat altered form, even though industrial and banking sectors were gaining power, and agriculture in general, particularly east Elbian grain production, was steadily losing its economic significance.[2]

The 'agrarian question', at least in the narrow sense of the term, must be discussed on two different levels – first with regard to the actual economic and social development of the agrarian sector itself, and second

81

with respect to the social and political implications of its history. Prussia–Germany had its own unique 'agrarian question' shaped by the peculiarities of agricultural development according to what Lenin called 'the Prussian path', combined with the traditional social leadership role of the east Elbian landowners, and forced industrialization starting in the middle of the nineteenth century. Through real estate and product markets, landed estates, particularly large estates, were integrated into a market system governed by capitalist principles. In the process, their susceptibility to crises increased.[3] This was immediately apparent in the period of the worldwide deflation between 1873 and 1896 which hit German agriculture very hard at the end of the 1870s and the beginning of the 1890s when price falls for the major products produced by the east Elbian growers were greatest. This meant that the east Elbian agricultural sector in particular was one of the 'losers' in the *structural* transformation brought about by economic development by the end of the century. *Economically* it was also weakened by these acute crises.

In other respects, the peculiar characteristics of the Prusso–German state allowed the deployment of specific *social* and *political* antidotes to help organized agriculture. In particular, the Junkers, together with the bureaucracy and military, enjoyed an unchallenged position in a ruling cartel in the Prussian state and in a society that had not yet been transformed by revolution. The Prussian tradition of interventionist politics and the peculiarities of the Bismarckian mode of state formation and domination offered agrarian interest groups unequalled opportunities to channel their organizational efforts.

As a result, by the turn of the century the major tendencies that would govern agrarian politics in the first half of the twentieth century were already apparent. The east Elbian landowners' well-organized pressure group dominated the corporative state organizations and the smaller independent agrarian groups. They controlled corporatist (*berufsständisch*) organizational structures, which communicated an anti-parliamentary *Mittelstand* ideology. In addition, large landowners tended to band together with large industrialists against the interests of the producers of consumer goods, the middle and small peasantry, and consumers, particularly the working class. Agriculture enjoyed the protection of the state through tariffs, trade, tax and pricing policies, all of which constituted one-sided subsidies of a particular economic sector. At the same time, the state undertook virtually no effective political measures to alleviate the prevailing structural crisis.[4]

The further development of this complex of problems well into the twentieth century, its long-term political effects and its significance in the spectrum of German proto-fascism cannot be investigated in detail here. This essay will essentially examine the contribution of the German agrarian complex to an unusual political situation: before 1914, the increasingly organized capitalist system had not called forth any considerable peasant movement with revolutionary or even progressive political goals and programmes. For the most part, German agrarian politics were located on the right, most often the extreme right, side of the political spectrum.

II

During the last quarter of the nineteenth century the significance of German agriculture measured in terms of its contribution to national wealth steadily diminished. The agricultural sector's production levels, trade volumes and share of employment, and the rural population in general were all declining. In short, the German economy was changing from an agrarian to an industrial system, with all the ensuing consequences. One special characteristic of the German transformation was that it started much later than in England, for example, and therefore its agrarian sector was more highly developed. It also took place in a peculiarly Prusso–German political environment where efforts were being made outside the agricultural sector to increase political participation and to create, somewhat belatedly, the institutions of a nation state. Precisely because of its late development, German industrialization took place very suddenly, accompanied by strong pressures and tensions, and above all at a substantially faster tempo than it did, for example, in France.[5]

The percentage of the working population employed in agriculture sank from 43·2 per cent in 1882 to 36·1 per cent in 1895 and 34·7 per cent in 1907. The share of those employed in agricultural wage labour decreased from 52·1 per cent in 1882 to 34 per cent in 1907. (By 1925 it was 26·5 per cent.) The number of independent agrarian producers fell from 46·7 per cent in 1882 to 25 per cent in 1907. Agriculture's contribution to the gross domestic product (using 1913 constant prices) fell from its 44·9 per cent average in the years 1860–4 to 29 per cent at the turn of the century, to a 23·4 per cent average in the years 1910–13. The agricultural share of all German exports fell consistently from the beginning of the 1880s, when it was 18·3 per cent, to the mid-1930s, when it was only 1 per cent. By the last quarter of the nineteenth century the grain-producing sector was already particularly affected by these developments.[6]

Because of a worldwide agricultural depression, farm prices sank drastically after 1873 and only began to recover after 1896. From that point until the First World War prices remained relatively stable, with a faint tendency to rise.[7] Although the number of farms increased continuously, this growth was mainly concentrated on very small holdings (under 2 hectares), and the land mass under cultivation actually decreased. Almost 60 per cent of all farms were in this category, while 35 per cent had from 2 to 20 hectares. For the most part, the number of large farms with over 20 hectares stagnated and even began to decline after 1895. Those large estates with over 200 hectares (0·2 per cent of all farms) controlled approximately 20 per cent of the arable land. (See Table 3.1.)

Table 3.1 *Agricultural Land-Holdings and Agriculturally Used Land in Germany, 1882–1907*

Size of holding in hectares	1882[1]		1895[1]		1907[1]	
	No. of holdings	Land mass (1,000 ha)	No. of holdings	Land mass (1,000 ha)	No. of holdings	Land mass (1,000 ha)
Under 2	3,061,831	1,825·9	3,236,367	1,808·9	3,378,509	1,731·3
2–5	981,407	3,190·2	1,016,318	3,286·0	1,006,277	3,304·9
5–20	926,605	9,158·4	998,804	9,721·9	1,065,539	10,421·6
20–50	239,887	7,176·1	239,643	7,113·2	225,697	6,821·3
50–100	41,623	2,732·0	42,124	2,756·6	36,494	2,500·8
100–200	11,033	1,521·1	11,250	1,545·2	10,679	1,499·2
Over 200	13,958	6,265·0	13,811	6,286·6	12,887	5,555·8
Total	5,276,344	31,869·0	5,558,317	32,517·9	5,736,082	31,834·9

[1] The compared categories are identical. Land mass = agriculturally used land; under 2 hectares = all holdings under 2 hectares.
    Sources: Statistik für das Deutsche Reich, Vol. 212, 2b: 'Berufs- und Betriebszählung v. 12.6.1907' (Berlin, 1912), 12ff.; Vol. 409, 'Volks-, Berufs- und Betriebszählung v. 16.6.1925' (Berlin, 1928), 60–3; *Statistisches Jahrbuch für das Deutsche Reich*, 1907, 1: 114–17; 1912, 34; 1924–5, 53–5.

On the other hand, the large east Elbian estates had traditionally been tied to *social* and *political* privilege. By the second half of the nineteenth century an increasingly homogeneous class of Junker and bourgeois estate-owners claimed membership in the ruling classes of the Prussian state, and thus could ensure agrarian interests politically, despite the declining economic significance of large landholdings. The landowners' 'objective class situation' was obscured by many things, including political tradition and what Hans Rosenberg has called a 'backward-looking consciousness as an estate' (*Standesbewusstsein*), that paralleled the 'neo-feudalized' political style of the Prussian ruling elite. At the same time, signs of the large landowners' 'embourgeoisement' were apparent in their market dependence and capitalist orientation.

By the end of the nineteenth century the importance of government-owned estates (*Domänen*) in Prussia had declined significantly compared to the beginning of the century. A large number of these estates, located primarily east of the Elbe, were transformed into *Rittergüter*. Most of their former tenant farmers (*Pächter*) now became independent owners, sometimes even receiving a noble title. The most secure properties were the entailed estates (*Fideikommisse*), regulated by a neo-feudal measure which ensured the inalienability of family property. The majority of these were established after 1850. By 1917 there were 1,369 entailed estates in Prussia, encompassing 7·3 per cent of all property, and 90 per cent of these were in noble hands.[8] In addition, the dominant form of landownership was the *Rittergut* which comprised the overwhelming majority of large landholdings in east Elbian Prussia. In 1866, 12,150 of the 18,197 large estates with over 133 hectares of land were *Rittergüter*. In 1885, 32 per cent of all land in the seven eastern Prussian provinces was divided into 6,454 large estates with holdings over 1,000 hectares; 68 per cent of these (4,393) were in noble hands.

Estate ownership brought with it definite privileges. Although the patrimonial courts and feudal hunting rights had been rescinded in 1848, the latter were replaced with neo-feudal ones. The decrees of 1850 controlling redemption payments ended the personal dependence of peasants on their lords, but the conversion of their remaining responsibilities into labour and money dues now made peasants economically dependent. Although the regulations for administrative districts (*Kreisordnung*) of 1872 and the rural community regulations (*Landgemeindeordnung*) of 1891 did suspend the lords' police powers to some degree, these laws and rulings hardly challenged the dominant role of the landowner in his own district, and the three-class voting system in the Prussian elections enabled estate-owners to weaken the most offensive measures. Until 1927 the *Rittergut* remained an independent communal and regional police district. Its owner was the judge in his own affairs, the head of the local election committee, the 'Herr im Haus', and often the local district administrator (*Landrat*). The antediluvian regulations governing the rights and duties of servants (*Gesindeordnung*) remained untouched and cemented the agrarian worker's dependence on his or her 'lord'. Even the democratization of the tax burden, initiated in 1861 with the abolition of tax exemptions for landownership, was reversed almost completely in Miquel's finance reforms after 1891.

Even though the east Elbian landed estates had a very privileged position, they were none the less in great difficulty by the end of the nineteenth century. In particular, they faced a long-term structural crisis in agriculture. The results of the 'peasant emancipation', with its regulations and redemption payments, the end of peasant protection laws, and frequent property transfers had all served to decimate the Prussian peasantry, and in the course of the nineteenth century expanded the size of a large 'sub-peasant' class. Agrarian real estate became a marketable product and large estates were increasingly integrated into the capitalist economy. The Prussian ruling class, particularly in east Elbia, had developed ruinous habits of conspicuous consumption, so well described by the writer Fontane.[9] There were also many other factors causing an increase in indebtedness and arrears, including massive speculation and short-sighted attempts to make profits, especially among the growing number of bourgeois owners, and a general disinterest in the nature of agricultural production. Many refused to make necessary reinvestments in their estates or to mechanize in a progressive fashion, a tendency encouraged through the indirect subsidies for a cheap and plentiful supply of foreign seasonal workers. The grain-producing east Elbian Junker and his bourgeois imitator had long since become accustomed to living from hand to mouth. They either ignored the structural problems, or they hoped for solutions through state aid, which they inevitably received. From the mid-1870s onwards explicit protectionism in favour of the east Elbian grain-producers was initiated. Protective tariffs increased five times from 1879 to 1887. There were also subsidies for rail and ship freight traffic, tax advantages, premiums, export subsidies for brandy, incentives for the import of foreign workers and later, even efforts to strengthen large holdings through colonization policies.

Given these circumstances, agriculture in east Elbia was much more economically susceptible to the *effects of industrialization* than in other German regions. With the exception of Berlin, Saxony and Upper Silesia, eastern Germany had missed the transition to industrialization. As early as 1890, industry's overall economic dominance began to make itself felt in economic competition, especially on the capital and labour markets.

In addition, east Elbian estates were directly dependent on short-term agricultural prices that only strengthened their tendency to overproduce. Because of their extensive monoculture, they were first of all dependent on the prices and transport possibilities for grain, and in the second instance, on the prices for potatoes, sugar beets and their derivatives, sugar and alcohol. Therefore they were especially sensitive to conjunctural changes in these product markets.

Towards the end of the century the situation was exacerbated by serious conjunctural crises, starting with an economic decline in 1875. This downswing began to touch the agrarian sector with real force when grain prices stagnated after 1878, and eventually east Elbian agriculturalists were more directly and seriously affected than industry. Therefore, the agrarians and their ideological spokesmen chronically tended to exaggerate the causal role of prices for the conjunctural change. This also led them to overestimate the impact of the state's trade and tariff policies for the expansion and direction of the economy.

Agricultural prices either declined or stagnated from 1878 until the peak of the agrarian crisis in 1894. At the same time, new trade agreements under Caprivi, instituted in 1891, led to a reduction in tariffs, even though the reductions were insignificant in the context of the whole economy. In early 1893 these developments delivered the ultimate incentive for the creation of the Agrarian League (*Bund der Landwirte*), a powerful organization which did not confine itself to economic matters alone.[10] After this point, conjunctural changes understandably ceased to have the same motivating character for the agrarians. By 1902 they passed a much stronger tariff law even though the economy had begun an upswing in 1898 which continued until the beginning of the First World War.

The effects of the crisis only served to increase the already prevalent political and social domination of the east Elbian estate-holders over the farmers and peasants in western and southern Germany. To some extent, these smaller landowners suffered less from the economic crisis than they did from the large agrarians' protectionism, which raised the price of livestock feeds. Those who were the least affected were the holders of relatively large, enclosed peasant farms in the north-western and south-eastern parts of the Reich. Of course, they had the same problems as other market-oriented producers – generally stagnating yields, slowly rising production costs, falling prices beginning in the 1870s and a growing dependence on prevailing economic trends. However, these well-established, labour-intensive, substantial family farms were usually spared the disastrous effects of land division by inheritance that prevailed in middle-sized and smaller holdings in south-western Germany, in the kingdom of Saxony and Thuringia, and that drastically reduced the farms' resistance to mortgage indebtedness and the regional profiteering of commercial middlemen. Moreover, the larger farms in western Germany gained additional stability in the crisis because they had a diversified crop system and livestock as well. Labour conditions in these regions were also traditionally more flexible than elsewhere and farms needed fewer workers, which insulated them from the so-called *Landflucht*, the migration of agrarian labourers to the cities. The same also applied to the large holdings in the marshes of Schleswig-Holstein.

There were great regional differences in German agricultural and labour conditions, including inheritance laws, production methods, land quality, cultivation methods and yields. All these different aspects cannot be fully investigated here. However, it is important to note that in Germany, in contrast to France, for example, specialized associations concerned with a single commodity did not gain an independent political voice, and thus were not able to influence the direction of the organized agrarian movement. The most important of these branch associations, especially in sugar and liquor production, were at best only old-style pressure groups. Working together with the large umbrella associations, they tried to advance their own particularistic economic goals within the government, the parliament and Agricultural Chambers (*Landwirtschafts-kammern*). But to some extent they needed the protection of large organizations which did not necessarily represent particular agrarian sectors. In France, on the other hand, it was just the opposite. The umbrella organizations could often only put down revolts from below with the help of the well-organized special interest groups (*associations spécialisées*).

Another important line of continuity in German agrarian politics was the constant increase of *state intervention* into the agrarian sector. There were many deep roots for this – the tradition of the Prussian state, east Elbian colonization policies and the protective laws for peasants and property, something which most German states had in common. The state also managed large agricultural holdings. Since the beginning of the nineteenth century, it encouraged the formation of scientific agricultural societies and agricultural associations (*landwirtschaftliche Vereine*). From mid-century onwards, these associations began to combine into central organizations at the regional level, which worked together closely with state authorities. With the state's aid, by the end of the century these bodies transformed themselves into legal, public, corporatist professional organizations called Agricultural Chambers (*Landwirtschaftskammern*). While some German states began this transformation somewhat earlier, in Prussia it took place in 1894, and in other states, between 1900 and 1906. By interlocking public and private organizational types, these interest groups and Agricultural Chambers had become privileged partners of the government by the turn of the century. They defined their interests in advance *within* the context of government policies, and not *in opposition* to them. Still, disregarding for the moment the vast infiltration of these organizations by regionally stronger, independent agrarian interest groups, a process which began in the 1870s and intensified in the 1890s, the Chambers could scarcely determine policy according to their interests. The same held for the umbrella organization of the Prussian *Landes-ökonomiekollegium*, founded in 1842, seventeen years before the establishment of the Ministry of Agriculture. It was also true for the German Agrarian Council, founded at the Reich level in 1872 from the Congress of Northern German Agriculturalists.

The protectionist agitation of the 1870s and the comprehensive demands of the Agrarian League for state intervention in the 1890s only strengthened these tendencies. Thus by the end of the nineteenth century agriculture's cries for state aid were no longer related to conjunctural trends; the call for tariffs was a reactionary, regressive and restorational demand. Unlike industry's demands in the 1870s, agriculture did not ask for temporary protection from new developments until it could find its own independent solutions. Rather, it demanded a system that would protect an entire production sector from market mechanisms in order to maintain the social status quo of agrarian producers. At a time when agriculture's loss of significance and prosperity was a decisive indication of structural change, not an accident, agrarians justified their claims by harking back to agriculture's once better position.

The tendency towards high levels of protectionism constituted a decisive problem for German agriculture in the twentieth century. Agriculture did not choose to transform production techniques or farm structure gradually or to find a profitable estate size. It did not diversify or specialize in certain crops to meet market demands, nor did it lower production costs through mechanization or the collective use of farm machinery. Instead, German agriculture relied on state intervention into the market. Until the 1950s (in the Federal Republic) agriculture depended on subsidies and price regulations and other measures to secure short-term profits. These were methods that mitigated the impact of all kinds of economic crises, but they could not remedy structural deficiencies for ever. The solution to the vital problems of German agriculture was permanently postponed. And this German tradition, together with a similar one in France, has decidedly influenced the unproductive policies of interventionism within the European Common Market which are so often criticized today.

III

The inability of estate-owners east of the Elbe to adjust to long-term economic changes contrasts sharply with their capacity to defend their status though political channels. Central to this process was the Agrarian League (*Bund der Landwirte*). After its formation in 1893, it quickly gained dominance over 'older' representatives of agrarian interests.

(1) It transformed the public-corporatist estate organizations, the old provincial and central associations and also the Agricultural Chambers, at least in non-Catholic areas. In addition, it inherited control over the Union of Tax and Economic Reformers (*Vereinigung der Steuer- und Wirtschaftsreformer*), a relatively exclusive east Elbian nobles' association founded in 1876. This group, together with the Central Association of German Industrialists (*Centralverband Deutscher Industrieller* or CDI), had waged the protectionist campaigns of the 1870s and 1880s. They had also organized a large parliamentary group in the Reichstag called the 'Free Economic Association' (*Freie Wirtschaftliche Vereinigung*).[11]

(2) The Agrarian League had a far more important and influential role in Berlin politics than the Catholic Christian Peasants' Associations

(*Christliche Bauernvereine*), although the latter were strong in the largely
Catholic areas of western and southern Germany where the League could
seldom penetrate. At the turn of the century these regional peasants' associations encompassed some 210,000 members expanding to 300,000 in
1906. They united to form the Federation of Christian Peasants' Associations (*Vereinigung der Christlichen Bauernvereine*) with seventeen and later
twenty-seven branches. However, within the general political spectrum
of the Kaiserreich, they played a relatively limited role. Their most
important political function was apparently to buttress the conservative
agrarian wing of the Centre Party. The largest associations, the Rhenish
branch, under the leadership of Freiherr von Loë, and the influential
Westphalian, Silesian and Bavarian Peasants' Associations, gained prominence within the Centre by the 1890s.[12] Of all these groups, only the
Westphalian Peasants' Association had a significant Protestant minority,
gained when it merged with the Minden-Ravensberg Association in
1887.[13]

Neither the predominantly Catholic associations nor the Catholic
Centre Party itself had a clear economic programme. With the exception
of the Rhenish Peasants' Association, they were all fellow travellers in the
agitation for protective tariffs. The explanation for this seems largely to
lie in the fact that the oldest and ideologically most influential association,
the Westphalian Peasants' Association, founded by Freiherr von
Schorlemer-Alst in 1862 and reorganized in 1871, served a region which
was less susceptible to structural and conjunctural crises. In Westphalia,
both the large peasant farms (from 20 to 100 hectares) and the big estates
(over 100 hectares) were of a profitable size. They were neither too small,
like many farms in southern Germany, nor too large, like many east
Elbian estates. Their mortgage debts were also comparatively low, and
diversified arable farming as well as animal husbandry decreased production risks. Traditional inheritance patterns, like the practice of
handing over property during the owner's lifetime in order to avoid
inheritance taxes, also limited excessive land divisions. Therefore,
peasant associations could concentrate on practical matters, like organizing credit and production co-operatives, insurance and arbitration
systems and similar self-help efforts. In Westphalia, not even the large
landholders wanted state aid. Their own association, with 13,000
members in 1878 and 23,000 in 1895, had experienced great difficulties
during the *Kulturkampf*. Afterwards, it took an overtly 'unpolitical' position and presented its aims as conservation, preservation and restoration.[14] Later attempts by the Agrarian League to form coalitions with
these influential peasant organizations in the Rhineland and Westphalia
were rejected many times.

In the other German states, especially in Baden and in Bavaria, where seven regional peasant associations had their origins in the 1860s, but did not form a united governing board until 1898. In these areas, the Christian Peasants' Associations were more like the older, unpolitical agrarian organizations than the new pressure groups emerging in the 1870s. However, they did try some modern tactics, like using their membership to launch a campaign to advance the 'preservation of property'. By 1900 they claimed almost 100,000 members. These associations, as well as the one in Trier, differed from groups in Westphalia, Silesia and the Rhineland because their leadership was largely made up of people who owned very little land or, in the case of clerics, no land at all. Therefore, the large land-holding interests were even less pronounced here. What united these groups and distinguished them from older agrarian associations was their distinctly Catholic, corporatist and anti-democratic ideology. They advocated a 'return to a healthy corporatist life' and opposed political parties as 'abstract unions of ideas'. In contrast, their organizations were 'real unions of interests', based not only on materialist concerns, but also on 'a foundation of positive Christianity' (Schorlemer).

The influence of these Christian Peasants' Associations was and remained limited because they retained their regional nature and were primarily limited to Catholics. In addition, they were not tightly organized and remained basically apolitical. The more powerful of them had to fight continuously to maintain any influence in the Centre Party, and by the turn of the century they were losing this battle. Unlike the German Conservative Party, for example, the Centre Party did not represent purely agricultural interests. It constantly had to strike a balance among the different groups that comprised it – peasants' associations, the clergy, the Christian Unions, Kolping Associations and the groups of the People's Association (*Volksverein*). Most importantly, these Christian Peasants' Associations could not muster the same kind of strength within the political structure of the Prusso–German state as could the Prussian Junkers.[15]

(3) The Bavarian Peasants' League (*Bayerischer Bauernbund*) was founded by the Frankish Peasants' League in 1895 to oppose both protectionism and the hegemony of the Catholic peasant groups. However, this regionally limited association was torn apart by internal rivalries and weakened with compromises. To be sure, at the local level a few of its groups sometimes articulated protests 'from below' by small peasants and the *Mittelstand*. The same tendencies, which several authors have called 'populist', were displayed by many regional groups of the Christian Peasants' Associations. These developments contributed decisively to the fact that the Centre Party in Bavaria, followed by the Bavarian People's Party and today's Christian Social Union (CSU), all became broadly based people's parties.[16]

(4) None of these peasants' associations could match the national significance of the Agrarian League, the dominant agrarian interest group between 1895 and the First World War. Founded as a radical opponent to Caprivi's policies favouring industrial development and trade, the League quickly became a mass organization. In 1894 it had 200,000, in 1901, 250,000 and by 1913, 330,000 members. The large landowners of east Elbia comprised less than 1 per cent of the membership, while 75 per cent was made up of small peasants. None the less, large owners controlled the organizational committees and the strictly run, financially independent bureaucratic structure that was tightly organized from the top down. From its inception, the League's decision-making bodies were controlled by professional politicians and aimed at agitational and political campaigns. At first the League was short on money and its leaders lacked influence on the government's decisions about economic policy. But it made up for this with its internal unity, free from leadership struggles and factional fights. Its manipulative popular ideological methods aimed at winning a mass base in the countryside and were masked by techniques which were tailored to meet individual needs. Its highly developed agitational strategies were publicized through the press and at political gatherings. Finally, it had a powerful campaign organization for elections and work in parliamentary lobbying.

The League paid for its own electoral campaigns, but only rarely did it run its own candidates, a practice which became even more infrequent after the defeat at the polls in 1903. Instead, it supported candidates of existing political parties, often providing massive assistance if they committed themselves to the League's platform. Once candidates accepted the League's mandate, their performance was monitored. Out of a total of 397 Reichstag representatives in 1898, 118 from five different political parties were committed to the League, and 76 of these were actual League members. In 1903 the figure was 89, in 1907, 138, and in 1912, 78. In the Prussian lower house, consistently more than one-third of the representatives were League members, and in 1908 they even constituted an absolute majority. The figure was somewhat lower for the lower house of the parliament in the state of Saxony before 1909.[17]

In its intransigent hostility to the Social Democrats and the left liberals, the League occasionally entered into unsuccessful tactical electoral agreements with the Centre Party, especially in the Rhineland and in Posen. Before the final break with the National Liberals in 1909, it sometimes formed alliances with regional branches of this party, especially in Hanover in 1897 and thereafter in Bavaria and western Germany. In general, however, the League relied on the unorganized majority of Free Conservatives and on the German Conservative Party in particular. Through complex personal and organizational ties, the League completely controlled this party's local organizations, candidate selection process, electoral campaigns and political direction. The League decisively transformed the Conservative Party's political style and platform in the twenty years from 1894 to 1914, especially during its oppositional phase before 1902. This brought many conservatives into conflicts of loyalty between the League, on one side, and traditional principles of conservative politics on the other.

From its inception, the League exerted an extraordinarily strong influence over the direction of economic legislation in general. In this endeavour, the political power position and privilege of the interests it represented in Prussia worked directly in the organization's favour. In addition, the League doubtless contributed more than any other association to the political polarization of the non-socialist forces, especially on social and constitutional issues. Largely because of the strong integrative power of its militant, neo-conservative, agrarian, *völkisch*-nationalistic ideology, it was able to pull groups without direct agrarian interests, like the 'old' *Mittelstand*, into the agrarian camp. While professing economic harmony, the League's ideology contained strong social Darwinist, *Mittelstand* and anti-Semitic characteristics. This conglomeration stemmed from many different sources. It combined the constant endeavour to justify the social and political status quo with a vehement revolutionary potential that had been set free not only on the left by the transition from an agrarian to an industrial society. The Agrarian League became a strikingly effective model of a new kind of political organization for property-owners. A mix between a political party and a pressure group, it pursued reactionary goals with direct democratic techniques and a proto-fascist ideology.[18]

(5) The ideological and propaganda efforts of the organized agrarians had considerable influence on the German Conservative Party. Occasional efforts to transform the party along more liberal or at least 'modern' lines were all unsuccessful. The Agrarian League played a decisive role in shaping the ideology of German conservatism. There were numerous other rightist organizations that modelled themselves on the League, for example, the German National Shopkeepers' Assistants' Association (*Deutschnationaler Handlungsgehilfenverband*), the Eastern Marshes Association (*Ostmarkenverein*, HKT), the Pan-German Association (*Alldeutscher Verband*) and the Navy League (*Flottenverein*). There were also many imperialistic agitational associations and organizations of the 'old' *Mittelstand*, like small shopkeepers and commodity-producers. In the post-Bismarck period, the opportunities for these organizations to play an active political role increased. Together with them, the League helped to take the general protectionist and social imperialist consensus prevalent in the 1880s and shape it into a fully articulated ideology of the property-owning classes. Moreover, the League helped to establish and

popularize this alliance with the political elite within the conservative milieu. Old conservative concepts like *individuality* (within an estate), *property*, *freedom*, *life* and *authority* were replaced by new ones. In their stead came *people (Volk)*, *people's community (Volksgemeinschaft)*, *Mittelstand*, *national labour in city and countryside*, *the struggle for existence*, *maintaining the race (Art)* and *politics of healthy people's sensibility (Politik des gesunden Volksempfindens)*. Biology, social Darwinism and myths of *Blut und Boden* had replaced history as the leading discipline to be converted into ideology. Conservatism was incorporated into a new, broad, *völkisch*-nationalist, social imperialist, militant and militaristic integrative ideology which contained organic, harmonious, *Mittelstand* and anti-Semitic elements. It used modern methods of direct democracy against parties and parliament. Because of its radically dichotomous view of society, directed primarily against liberals and socialists, it contributed substantially to the political polarization of German society and to the radicalization of political conflicts in the Kaiserreich.[19]

In particular, the carefully propagated *Mittelstand* ideology served to mask conflicts of interest with its unclear formulations. Its *berufsständisch* corporatist vocabulary was reminiscent of the old estates, while at the same time it suggested the Bonapartist solution of eliminating intermediate public bodies. This suited conservatism's increasing need to integrate and recapture anti-aristocratic, 'leftist' deviants. Because of expanding industrialization and universal male suffrage, at least in the Reich, the conservatives realized that they had to address the middle and lower classes.

Like almost all other elements of this new conservative (or rather neo-German) ideology, these individual characteristics had already been present before 1895, but it was through the disciplined co-ordination of the Agrarian League that they actually began to have a mass impact. This was especially true of anti-Semitism, which now became an integral part of the German right's *völkisch*-nationalistic ideology. A number of older, protest-oriented and rhetorically 'leftist' parties and splinter groups advocating a noisy kind of anti-Semitism had collapsed before the turn of the century, leaving some authors to assume mistakenly that anti-Semitism in Germany was on the wane. Instead, however, both the Agrarian League and the other *Mittelstand* agitation leagues channelled anti-Semitic feelings within the context of interest politics. This included both the older conservative type of anti-Semitism based on religion and economics as well as a newer brand of rowdy anti-Semitism based on biologistic myths. 'Jew-baiting' was now no longer the single or main purpose of the organization as it had been before; it was no longer a loud insistence, but rather a quiet, constant addendum to the association's more general agitation in pursuit of economic and political interests. Pre-

94

cisely for this reason, anti-Semitism became domesticated, acceptable for moderate conservatives and liberals, and thus much more dangerous. At a time when reason in general was denounced as a 'destructive' influence, this form of anti-Semitism, combined with the defence of agrarian interests, became a fundamental part of *Mittelstand* ideology and an element of anti-capitalist, anti-socialist and anti-liberal rhetoric.[20]

(6) Between 1893 and 1902 the Agrarian League was often radically opposed to the government and the so-called 'Caprivi system'. Within a very short period of time, the League organized almost half of the Reichstag's representatives against the trade agreements of 1893 and 1894. It pushed through the suspension of sliding tariff laws and export subsidies that together with the system of import quotas were aimed at increasing production. However, at first the League was not able to block the short-term continuation of Caprivi's foreign trade policies, which were intended to invigorate the German export industry and improve the situation of the urban labour market. Following the saying that Eugen Richter coined for them, 'learn to complain without suffering', the agrarians demanded much more than they could have realistically hoped to achieve.

The best example of this was the <u>Kanitz Bill</u> that was referred to by Kanitz himself as an 'outpost skirmish' and was designed to nationalize the export of grain. This proposal guaranteed fixed prices 'at a middle level' and aimed to socialize the production risks of a small group. Two other 'large demands' (*grosse Mittel*) included advocacy of bi-metallism and a proposal for commodity and stock market reform. The latter was largely incorporated in an 1896 law, although in reality the prohibition of the futures trade in grain was circumvented for some time to come. For the most part, the agrarians were relatively happy with their achievements.

The same was true for the anti-consumerist policies of the so-called 'small demands' (*kleine Mittel*) that favoured producers and were pushed through thanks to intensive propaganda and good connections to all of Prussia's Ministers of Agriculture and their staffs. These measures included animal health laws that aimed at banning imports temporarily, meat inspection laws, the regulation of railroad tariffs, the margarine law of 1897, a revision of the communal tax law in 1893, the maintenance of brandy subsidies (*Branntweinliebesgaben*), and new sugar laws. In addition, internal colonization laws in eastern Prussia were interpreted in a one-sided fashion that favoured large land-holders. The *Mittellandkanal* construction bill, supported by industry in particular, was at first delayed for years and finally substantially changed. By far the most important economic success for the Agrarian League was the trade-off of Junker support for the naval building programme in return for the promise of tariffs, a compromise achieved in 1902. This involved the agreement of agriculture, industry and the government to raise grain tariffs. For a very short time, the agrarians lamented the fact that they had not received more. On the whole, however, the League ended its opposition to the government's economic policies when the Kardorff proposal was accepted. Once their tariff demands were satisfied, the agrarians usually joined together with the ruling majority. They did, however, maintain their preference for alliances with the Centre Party, which meant an alliance of the conservatives of both religious confessions.

The Agrarian League's one-sided orientation in favour of large landholders was evident in its economic programmes and goals. The agrarian 'crisis' was to be mitigated through supports for agricultural products in the form of tariffs and tax advantages. The state was to guarantee that grain prices were kept high and that competition with industry on the labour market remained restricted. The agrarians had no serious intention of undertaking structural reform or rationalization on their estates. Instead, they saw agriculture as the first and most important estate in an organic and corporatist economic structure, entitled to direct public welfare payments to benefit the agrarian sector in the short term. They advocated, for example, financial relief for large estates, the reorganization of mortgage credit, radical debt write-offs, the restriction of communal and school taxes, and the reduction of worker protection laws, in addition to tariff credits and cash subsidies. Most important was their demand for high grain tariffs, which kept land values artificially high and certainly increased mortgage debts. In effect, the tariffs were a 'call to class struggle'.[21]

In order to ensure high prices, the east Elbian large landowners proposed an autarkic agrarian policy. To maintain their traditionally powerful position in Prussia, they fought against the cities and against liberalism which were seen as the breeding ground for free trade, capitalism, democracy and possible emancipatory movements. These were the agrarians' symbols of 'decay', even more than the working-class movement with which they had much less contact in practice than did the industrialists. For the agrarians, the 'social question' was often reduced to the problems of cheap importation of Polish seasonal workers. Their opponents were the 'red and golden internationals'. The latter included *international* industry, finance and commercial capital, and banks. They did not oppose the necessity of *national* industry, which for them meant mainly heavy industry.

(7) The Agrarian League developed its own variety of social imperialism, sharing in a basic consensus that prevailed in all associations of Wilhelmine Germany that represented property-owners. Social Darwinist, racist concepts, anti-Semitism, xenophobia and numerous elements

of radical, *völkisch*-biologistic nationalism had replaced traditional conservative beliefs. The agrarians did not have a high opinion of the Empire's colonial policies or of military expeditions in foreign countries because these ventures cost tax money and brought them no profits. None the less, they cultivated and propagated a special form of imperialistic missionary calling analogous to 'manifest destiny' or 'mission civilisatrice' in other nations. They wanted a 'national colonial policy' which would cost them nothing and bring them benefits, and in particular, they advocated the economic and military expansion of Prussia–Germany into East-Central Europe and Eastern Europe. For the Prussian agrarian 'Herrenmenschen' (F. Naumann) and their ideologues, the 'drive to the East' was the only profitable form of German imperialism and the only way to strengthen Germany's position in the world. This form of imperialist aggression was enthusiastically propagandized by the Agrarian League and other organizations. The League demanded the subjugation and colonization of large areas east of Prussia's borders, and dreamed of organizing disciplinary actions against 'Polish conditions', 'Tarnopoler Moral' and 'Galician judification'. The agrarians' demands were different from those of the Pan-Germans or the imperialist groups supported by industrialists. Together with the functionaries of the Eastern Marshes Society, which they supported, the agrarians aimed primarily at increasing land and property, enlarging their own estates, or acquiring new ones with new sources of cheap labour. They wanted to expand their personal sphere of influence into areas similar to those they already controlled in the hope of increasing their production levels and thus finding a solution to their economic woes and accumulated debts.

Therefore the fundamental *völkisch*-nationalistic consensus came to incorporate the inherited structural weaknesses of east Elbian estates. It included the agrarians' hopes for an improvement of their financial status and the widespread preconception that the acquisition of more land would not only enhance their prestige, but would also better their economic situation. The Agrarian League and the Eastern Marshes Association were the leading proponents of this position, and they were also in the forefront of those pursuing eastward-oriented colonial policies. They saw to it that one of the Kaiserreich's most volatile topics, summarized with the catchword 'Polish policy', remained at the centre of attention. Thus, the politics and ideology of the League and its concrete agrarian interests helped to shape a specific Prusso–German variant of imperialism before 1945 of which the 'drive to the East' was a much more important element than other colonial projects. In this respect, Germany's policies differed from the Western European model of colonialism or the 'informal empire' of the North Americans. These differences were largely due to the fact that the east Elbian agrarians, a pre-modern and pre-bourgeois elite, had a particularly weighty influence on the institutions and decision-making processes in German politics.[22]

IV

The dominant position of the Agrarian League reflected its ability to limit the possibilities for independent action by organizations outside its immediate sphere of influence. The way in which German agrarian interests formed political organizations had much to do with the long-term ineffectiveness, indeed the virtual absence, of peasant protest from below. From the very beginning, the Agrarian League sought to form a powerful, modern and well-organized machine that could integrate different regional and social interests. Although led by the east Elbian landed elite, the League could count on the mass support of small and middle peasants, even in southern and western Germany. Independent peasant protest could only surface for short periods of time in specific regions and had no major impact on the organization as a whole. Such revolts were only possible before the organizational structure was completely consolidated, as in the anti-Semitic agitation in Hesse and Franconia in the 1880s and 1890s, in which peasants were joined by artisanal workers and retailers. They could also break out when the organization suffered a leadership struggle or was weakened in a crisis, as was the case in the Schleswig-Holstein *Landvolkbewegung* at the end of the 1920s.[23] In both of these instances, however, quickly expanding large organizational machines were able to absorb and redirect the released energies. In the first case the Agrarian League took control, and in the second it was the agricultural division of the Nazi Party, together with those traditional agrarian groups which had come under its sway by the 1930s.

In Bavaria, there were many radical small peasant groups. They included the 'left' wing of the Bavarian Peasants' League, opponents of the large agrarians' protectionism and the often anti-Semitic, sometimes radically democratic representatives of small owners, called 'rural socialists' (*Landsozis*), whom the SPD hoped to integrate in the 1890s. But these small groups were unable to establish a united organization in Bavaria. Despite their occasional popularity, for example after 1918, their programmes had little influence and were for the most part atypical. Left liberals displayed only a sporadic and unsystematic interest in agrarian questions and rural agitation. Their partial involvement in the German Peasants' League (*Deutscher Bauernbund*), established in 1909 as an association of settlers from Posen and West Prussia, was only a passing phase.[24]

The Social Democratic Party also took no steps to mobilize peasant and smallholding supporters, thereby forfeiting a chance to split the united agrarian front under east Elbian leadership. Until well into the 1920s Kautsky's agrarian programme was the dominant party doctrine. According to this programme, the demise of small peasant farming was necessary, and the nationalization of land and property was put forward as a universal cure-all. There were some reform tendencies among SPD representatives in the southern German parliaments, and the theoretical discussions surrounding the agrarian issue found great resonance at the 1894 Frankfurt Party Congress. None the less, the party's basic position was only strengthened in response to Kautsky's 1899 writings and David's publications of 1903. On the whole, the party hardly took peasant interests into account. After 1909 it channelled some agitational efforts into the German Agrarian Labourers' Union (*Deutscher Landarbeiterverband*). Because of the party's misunderstanding of the role that property ownership played in peasant consciousness, it was surprised when its targeted appeals to east Elbian agricultural labourers as 'the key regiments of the Prussian army' met with little positive response.[25]

The SPD finally adopted a pro-peasant programme at the Kiel Convention in 1927, a revised version of a proposal rejected in 1895. But this was a hopeless effort, coming much too late to help the SPD compete with many parties and associations vying for peasant support. The German countryside, if we can use this general term, stayed on the right. This was not simply because leftist parties had forgotten it for so long; the explanation must also be found in agrarian conditions themselves and in a specific set of economic and political circumstances. For many reasons, the underprivileged small landowners of Prussia were more inclined to form coalitions with the ruling class, state power and large owners. The landed elite had a dominant position in the Prussian state and in the Prussian three-class voting system. The state itself had large agricultural interests and showed its obvious willingness to intervene on agriculture's behalf by its stance on colonization and resettlement issues, technical assistance and land redistribution. After Bismarck's decision to impose tariffs in the 1870s, the state also offered protection and price supports. Peasants could choose between an alliance with the state, from which they could reap potential benefits, and an alliance with a party suspected of revolutionary tendencies. The SPD also apparently wanted to overturn all rural traditions and values, and it had no foreseeable chance to take power. The same was true with some variations in the non-Prussian states. In addition, German peasants were usually not that badly off, even in the parts of southern Germany where land was divided equally among the children. They were not so poor, their holdings were not so small, divided, or unproductive, and their agricultural methods not so primitive as to push them over that threshold of misery which could lead to radicalization.

The comparatively good position of the peasantry and the leftist parties' limited interest in agrarian issues can both be traced mainly to Germany's fast pace of industrialization. The transition from an agrarian to an industrial society with the objective decline of agriculture's significance for the population as a whole took place very quickly. The rapidly rising demand for labour in cities and in industry drew agricultural workers away from the countryside more forcefully than, for example, in France and Russia. These economic developments spared the countryside the most extreme forms of poverty among small peasants, and at the same time convinced leftists that they did not have to worry about the peasant problem. By the end of the nineteenth century Germany was no longer an agrarian country, and therefore it would not be all that catastrophic for the leftist parties if they did not concern themselves with the countryside. Thus the political energies in rural areas continually flowed into organizational channels that were to the right of centre.

In every struggle for influence and power, the dominant large producers were able to assert themselves against the small peasants. At least on one level, the explanation of this is relatively straightforward, given the financial and organizational influence of large holders within the coalition of estate-owners and peasants. However, it is much more difficult to explain how the large organizations, controlled by the landed elite, could integrate small producers into their ranks despite the fact that estate-owning leaders and peasant constituents often had opposing interests. The large landowners wanted high product prices, for example, while the small landowners needed low livestock feed prices. The most common explanation given for the resolution of this apparent contradiction is the 'general agrarian' concern for high land prices, which were thought to be directly related to levels of agricultural protection that maintained German prices above world market levels.[26] Prussian land prices climbed an average of 17 per cent between 1895–7 and 1901–3 for all property sizes. From 1907–9 the prices climbed 33 per cent, almost twice as high as in the preceding period. This time, however, large land-holdings took the lion's share. Land prices for estates with 100 to 500 hectares rose 49 per cent in Prussia, and prices for estates over 500 hectares rose 53 per cent. Even middle and large peasant holdings experienced an above-average increase of 37 per cent.

This rapid rise of land values was not only the result of Bülow's tariffs passed by the Reichstag in 1902, which fixed the principal grain tariffs at 50–55 Marks per ton, that is, at levels that had prevailed before Caprivi's time; the increasingly favourable combination of economic circumstances on the world market and internal production increases played a role as well. None the less, it cannot be denied that tariff protectionism contributed greatly to the rising value of agricultural property in

Germany. The fact that prices already began to increase in 1902 after the Reichstag had decided to vote for the tariffs bill is ample testimony to this. Land values rose before the tariff came into effect in 1906 and long before agricultural prices were affected in 1907. In this instance, the 'objective' interests in tariffs of both large and small land-holders co-incided, although they could not profit to the same degree.

This can in part explain the attraction which the Agrarian League held for its mass following of small owners, at least in northern and central Germany. However, it does not explain its success in the southern and south-western areas that had partible inheritance patterns. In those regions, peasants were interested in relatively low land prices, yet even here the mechanisms of ideological integration and centralized organization brought them into the fold. A good example of this is the Württemberg state branch of the Agrarian League. Since the mid-1890s it had dominated the state Conservative Party and organized peasants who had once been liberal-minded politically. Because of the League's assistance, the Conservatives became a powerful party, second only to the Centre by 1912. This state branch that had given itself the name of a Peasants' and Winegrowers' League tried as hard as it could to meet the needs of the Württemberg electorate and distance itself from the Prussian landowners. None the less, on all important basic political issues, especially national issues, it followed the direction set by the central office of the Agrarian League.

On the whole, it is very difficult to determine to what degree small landowners were aware of the fact that land prices gave all agrarian pro-ducers a shared concern and a potential for unity. Although such percep-tions often existed, it would not alter the fact that agrarian protectionism, as established in the Kaiserreich, was a one-sided measure. Not even taking into account the cost of protection to consumers and tax-payers, in the long term tariffs completely stifled what little willingness there was for structural agrarian reforms. The large price discrepancies between western and eastern Germany remained, and large landowners profited from protectionism much more than others. Tariffs did little to stimulate agricultural export. Feed prices stayed at an unnaturally high level, and feed imports remained a central problem for western and south German producers before the First World War.

Most of all, however, the substantial increase in land prices after the turn of the century only encouraged more land speculation, sustaining the worst traditions of the nineteenth century. Inflated land prices worked against any attempts at a structural stabilization that might have helped large landowners to survive later crises. The significance and role of land prices in this context cannot be overestimated. Rising prices are not always the sign of healthy economic development. In the free trade countries of Denmark, Belgium and the Netherlands, land prices even fell after the turn of the century without causing any harm to agriculture. On the contrary, their fall brought about a willingness to intensify and diversify production methods, thereby laying the foundations for a structural modernization of the agrarian sector.

In Germany, in contrast, tariff protection was the one factor that united all agrarian organizations politically and ideologically, and stabilized the Agrarian League's dominant position among them. This in part also explained the participation of the Catholic Peasants' Associations as fellow travellers. Although the German Peasants' League, founded in 1909 as a liberal alternative to the Agrarian League, differed with the League on tax reforms, colonization policies and reform of the Prussian suffrage, it none the less argued that tariff protection laws should remain. The shared concern for state protection and support measures also explains the League's influence on non-agrarian organizations, like those of the declining 'old' *Mittelstand* formed after the turn of the century, which for the most part were inspired and supported by agrarian ideologues. Paradoxically, before the First World War the Agrarian League became the strongest and most active political organization for the 'old' *Mittelstand* in Germany before the First World War. The German National Shopkeepers' Assistants' Association was still rather weak and other *Mittelstand* groups were hopelessly divided. Additional factors also secured the Agrarian League's hegemony, including a general fear of revolution, anxiety over economic crises, a weakening of government leadership after 1890 and the political polarization of Wilhelmine society, promoted by the agrarians, the industrialists and even the majority of the working-class movement under Bebel and Kautsky.[27]

V

Agriculture had a much better starting position to gain political prominence and influence in the Prusso–German power elite than did industrialists. Even though on the whole irreversible economic trends ran against them, the agrarians' influence within the military and the government was traditionally much greater than that of other groups. They usually controlled local government east of the Elbe and the lower house of the Prussian parliament, which was often more important to them than the Reichstag. Out of all interest groups, they most clearly represented an unreconstructed feudal element in Germany, and the German state differed from its Western European counterparts precisely because such feudal relics could influence its social and political system. In addition, the agrarians could be sure that the state in principle was ready to give them the aid they demanded from it. Intervention, developmental aid and at times even elements of 'state socialism' were all part of the Prussian tradition, as was the practice of gaining 'the consent of all propertied classes' on issues that concerned them.[28] The only new factor in the last quarter of the nineteenth century was the intensification of state intervention and the state's willingness to play the role of economic stabilizer in an open fashion. This was explained largely by Germany's progression towards an advanced level of industrialization. Therefore, industrialists no longer needed the state's developmental aid, while, on the other hand, agriculture was placed even more on the defensive.

Agriculture's favourable starting position was further enhanced by the Agrarian League's uncompromising political, ideological and agitational radicalism. It advanced reactionary goals with the most modern techniques. The organized agrarians were not simply conservatives or reactionaries; they were radicalized conservatives. Their extremism and what they referred to as their 'hellishly sharp language' could channel aggressive feelings that already existed against cities, workers and 'mobile capital'. Their radical stance was nurtured not only by day-to-day political events but also by their realization that the threatening socio-economic changes taking place could not be stopped. They filled a need within Wilhelmine society for secondary integrative mechanisms, and at the same time contributed to a further polarization of political forces in the Empire. On the other hand, the agrarians' extremism and their oppositional stance meant that they had a chronically poor relationship with the central ministerial bureaucracy. Not even the more recent literature on the *Sammlungspolitik* points out that until 1902 the Agrarian League was in radical *opposition* to the government. This opposition was at times rekindled, especially during the First World War.

Any attempt to determine whether the agrarians or the large industrialists had greater influence confronts a number of unsolved problems. Even leaving aside the fact that we do not know enough about the contemporary influence of the military or the banks, for example, the question with which we began would have to be redefined from many different angles. The total economic potential of the relevant organizations would have to be carefully investigated, as would the methods they used to protect their interests and their traditional standing in the economic and social system as a whole. It would be necessary to determine their actual influence in government decisions and parliamentary affairs. One would also have to weigh the effects of their political interactions, their participation in the new wave of organizations and the ways in which they helped to shape the prevailing political style.

On the basis of the evidence presented here, it is possible to suggest answers to these questions along the following lines. The agrarians' political potential was much greater than their economic power. This allowed them to maintain the social and political status quo, including the restricted three-class suffrage in Prussia and the repression of the working-class movement. Because of their uncompromising stance and their demagogic techniques, their relationship to government and top bureaucrats was often worse than that of industrialists. But on the other hand, they had a much greater impact on public opinion and could define and direct the increasingly bellicose and irreconcilable style of political confrontation before the First War. They were largely responsible for formally enhancing the status of parliamentary politics in Germany and especially the Reichstag relative to the government and the bureaucracy.

At the same time, however, the League's anti-representational ideology and their direct techniques of mass manipulation effectively torpedoed all efforts to create a strong parliamentary state through Prusso–German constitutionalism. From the 1890s on, when the League went into open opposition against the government, the Reichstag and the Prussian lower house were the only means it had left to pursue its interest, and these arenas remained of paramount importance. In the state and Reich parliaments, the agrarians had a relatively strong and homogeneous basis of support, and heavy industry also occasionally had to rely on this basis. The agrarians used the mechanisms of parliament because they had no better alternatives, but they were not interested in refining or defending these tools. At any point in time, an authoritarian political system would have aroused greater sympathies if it had guaranteed agrarian interests. In comparison to industrialist interest groups, the Agrarian League benefited from a greater degree of organization and a more varied range of activities. During the Wilhelmine period these factors made it the most influential promoter of expansive *völkisch*-nationalism. They also made the League into a strong bastion against the process of democratization and the reform of the Prusso-German state system with all its instruments of power.

The large landowners were not particularly interested in the so-called *Sammlungspolitik*, that is, the co-ordinated efforts of the government, large industry and their parties to unite against the Social Democrats. Since their own basic political interests lay in areas other than those of the government and industry, the agrarians often had to be forced or even blackmailed into making compromises. They were not one of the protectors of the *Sammlungspolitik*, which remained for them a shaky coalition.[29] At most they were fellow travellers, often against their true feelings, as can be seen in the case of the naval building programme. The central government, the industrialists and the agrarians did not have the same notions of what *Sammlung* meant. They had different ideas about the political direction the *Sammlung* should take and about who should

104

assume the leading role within it. The government's leadership was certainly not generally acknowledged or respected, nor was there a 'bourgeois united front'.

As far as *economic* policies were concerned, the Agrarian League and the Central Association of German Industrialists were seldom in complete agreement. They shared an old alliance based on protectionism and had many other mutual concerns, like an interest in promoting synthetic fertilizers. But their preferences and priorities regarding tariffs, taxes and financial policies were rather different. In the area of *social* policy, the agrarians were in agreement with industrialists, middle-class artisans and small shopkeepers. They all wanted to remain 'Herr im Haus', maintaining patriarchal labour relationships. These priorities along with a common reaction against working-class demands served briefly to solidify the so-called Cartel of Productive Estates (*Kartell der schaffenden Stände*), a short-lived organization founded in 1913. This alliance of the Agrarian League, the Central Association of German Industrialists and the German Imperial *Mittelstand* Organization is testimony to the social and political consensus shared by these groups. Each had contributed to the *Sammlung* in its own way, but now they came together without the initiative or intervention of the state. Even though the cartel collapsed very quickly because of organizational differences among the industrialists, the basic consensus remained intact. It allowed a new, expanded version of the cartel to be formed during the First World War, namely, the proto-fascistic German *Vaterlandspartei*. It resurfaced again in Weimar with the formation of many new parties and associations, including the German National People's Party, the *Mittelstandspartei* and the National Socialist Party (NSDAP).[30]

Both genuine Prussian traditions and the specific economic effects of Germany's delayed industrialization helped to shape the reorganization of agrarian interests at the start of the 1890s. Together they allowed the Agrarian League to play a political role out of proportion to its economic weight. The effects of the agrarian crisis and the progressive decline of the old German Conservative Party in the early 1890s were important preconditions for its success. Even more important, however, was the fact that Bismarck's manipulative techniques had already created a 'political mass market', expanding the sphere of public politics and increasing popular political influence over parliaments and government. By the 1890s the Reich and Prussian governments could no longer carry out manipulative policies with the same decisiveness, and a power vacuum was created. A modern, well-organized, determined and radical interest group could easily fill this vacuum and exploit the situation to establish itself.

There were many 'neo-corporatist' (in an authoritarian sense) tendencies in agrarian politics. The agrarians toyed with the idea of economic councils and organizations defined by professions (*berufsständisch*), a policy they advocated more often than the industrialists,[31] and they opposed all democratization and parliamentarization. These tendencies provide clear indications of what could be called German proto-fascism. They reveal a society that did not possess a basic liberal-democratic consensus, something which can apparently only be achieved through preceding revolutions. In contrast, a consensus among the property-owning classes was revitalized in the peculiar configuration of the 1890s. Together with the consequences of Germany's late industrialization and retarded nation-building, these shared assumptions inhibited parliamentary democratization and social emancipation in the twentieth century. The movement to protect the economic and social status quo was closely tied to general political demands and desires. For this reason, the large agrarian interest organizations, under the leadership of the Agrarian League, became an important and fundamental element of proto-fascistic tendencies in Germany. Both industrialization and the transition to more organized forms of capitalism took place within 'the shell of a conservative, authoritarian state with a neo-feudal social structure', ruled by unbroken traditions and a prefigured political culture.[32]

Notes: Chapter 3

1 This essay is primarily based on two summaries of the problem which originally appeared in German: H.-J. Puhle, 'Die Entwicklung der Agrarfrage und die Bauernbewegung in Deutschland 1861–1914', in K. O. Frhr. von Aretin and W. Conze (eds.), *Deutschland und Russland im Zeitalter des Kapitalismus 1861–1914* (Wiesbaden, 1977), 37–59; idem, *Politische Agrarbewegungen in kapitalistischen Industriegesellschaften. Deutschland, USA and Frankreich im 20. Jht.* (Göttingen, 1975), esp. 58–77. The following does not contain detailed references. For a more thorough investigation of the problem, see other works by this author: H.-J. Puhle, *Agrarische Interessenpolitik und preussischer Konservatismus im Wilhelminischen Reich (1893–1914)*, 2d ed. (Bonn, 1975); idem, 'Der Bund der Landwirte im Wilhelminischen Reich', in W. Rüegg und O. Neuloh (eds.), *Zur soziologischen Theorie und Analyse des 19. Jhts.* (Göttingen, 1971), 145–62; idem, 'Parlament, Parteien und Interessenverbände 1890–1914', in M. Stürmer (ed.), *Das kaiserliche Deutschland*, 2d ed. (Düsseldorf, 1977), 340–77; idem, *Von der Agrarkrise zum Präfaschismus* (Wiesbaden, 1972); idem, 'Aspekte der Agrarpolitik im "Organisierten Kapitalismus"', in H.-U. Wehler (ed.), *Sozialgeschichte Heute. Festschrift für Hans Rosenberg* (Göttingen, 1974), 543–64; idem, *Politische Agrarbewegungen*. On the problems of continuity see also the recent works of J. Flemming, *Landwirtschftliche Interessen und Demokratie* (Bonn, 1978) and M. Schumacher, *Land und Politik* (Düsseldorf, 1978).
2 See M. Weber, 'Kapitalismus und Agrarverfassung', *Zeitschrift für die gesamte Staatswissenschaft* 108 (1952): 431–52; idem, 'Parlament und Regierung im neugeordneten Deutschland' (1918), in *Gesammelte Politische Schriften* (Munich, 1921), 3d ed. (Tübingen, 1971), 306–443; E. Kehr, *Schlachtflottenbau und Parteipolitik 1894–1901* (Berlin, 1930, repr. 1965); idem, *Der Primat der Innenpolitik* (Berlin, 1965); A. Gerschenkron, *Economic Backwardness in Historical Perspective* (Cambridge, Mass., 1962); H. Rosenberg, *Grosse Depression und Bismarckzeit* (Berlin, 1967); idem, *Probleme der*

deutschen Sozialgeschichte (Frankfurt, 1969); idem, *Machteliten und Wirtschaftskonjukturen* (Göttingen, 1978)'; W. F. Fischer, *Wirtschaft und Gesellschaft im Zeitalter der Industrialisierung* (Göttingen, 1972); H.-U. Wehler, *Bismarck und der Imperialismus* (Cologne, 1969); idem, *Krisenherde des Kaiserreichs 1871–1918* (Göttingen, 1970); idem, *Das deutsche Kaiserreich 1871–1918* (Göttingen, 1970); and a critique of this book, T. Nipperdey, 'Wehler's "Kaiserreich". Eine kritische Ausseinandersetzung', *Geschichte und Gesellschaft* 1 (1975): 538–60.

3   See C. Rodbertus-Jagetzow, *Zur Erklärung und Abhülfe der heutigen Creditnoth des Grund-besitzes*, 2 vols. (Jena, 1868).

4   Such proposals existed, for example Knapp's suggestion to 'westernize the East'. See G. F. Knapp, *Die Bauernbefreiung und der Ursprung der Landarbeiter in den älteren Teilen Preussens* (Leipzig, 1887); C. J. Fuchs, *Deutsche Agrarpolitik vor und nach dem Kriege*, 3d ed. (Stuttgart, 1927), esp. 71ff., 95f.

5   In particular, T. Veblen, *Imperial Germany and the Industrial Revolution* (first published 1915, repr. Ann Arbor, Mich., 1966), 174ff., 185f., 248f.; D. Landes, *The Unbound Prometheus* (Cambridge, 1969), 231ff.; Wehler, *Bismarck*, 112ff. See a more recent and differentiated treatment in H. Kaelble, 'Der Mythos von der rapiden Industrialisierung Deutschlands', *Geschichte und Gesellschaft* 9 (1983): 106–18.

6   See the *Statistisches Jahrbuch für das deutsche Reich*, 1907, 1: 36f., 48f.; W. G. Hoffmann et al., *Das Wachstum der deutschen Wirtschaft seit der Mitte des 19. Jhts.* (Berlin, 1965), 33, 153, 160.

7   Hoffmann, 552–5, 561f.

8   See G. Gothein, *Agrarpolitisches Handbuch* (Berlin, 1910–11), 236–47. For a comparison with earlier figures, see A. Meitzen and F. Grossmann, *Der Boden und die landwirtschaftlichen Verhältnisse des preussischen Staates*, Vol. 6/1 (Berlin, 1901), 550f. On entailments in general see also M. Weber, 'Agrarstatistische und socialpolitische Betrachtungen zur Fideikommissfrage in Preussen' (1904), in idem, *Gesammelte Aufsätze zur Soziologie und Sozialpolitik* (Tübingen, 1924), 323–93, esp. 328, 367.

9   See T. Fontane, *Der Stechlin*, first published in 1897. See also H. Rosenberg, 'Die Pseudodemokratisierung der Rittergutsbesitzerklasse' (1958), in his *Machteliten*, 83–101; J. Conrad, 'Agrarstatistische Untersuchungen', *Jahrbücher für Nationalökonomie und Statistik*, n.s. 16 (1888): 121–70, esp. 140, 146, 151; A. Meitzen, *Der Boden und die landwirtschaftlichen Verhältnisse des preussischen Staates*, Vol. 4 (Berlin, 1869), 498f.; Meitzen and Grossmann, 6/1: 554f., 557; 6/2: 138f.

10 On the founding of the Agrarian League, see O. von Kiesenwetter, *Fünfundzwanzig Jahre wirtschaftspolitischen Kampfes* (Berlin, 1918), and Puhle, *Agrarische Interessenpolitik*, 32ff.

11 See K. W. Hardach, *Die Bedeutung wirtschaftlicher Faktoren bei der Einführung der Eisen-und Getreidezölle in Deutschland 1879* (Berlin, 1967), Puhle, *Politische Agrarbewegungen*, 56–61.

12 See A. Crone-Münzebrock, *Die Organisation des deutschen Bauernstandes* (Berlin, 1920), 25ff.; K. Müller, 'Zentrumspartei und agrarische Bewegung im Rheinland 1882–1903', in *Festschrift für M. Braubach* (Münster, 1964), 828–57; H. O. Wesemann, 'Der Westfälische Bauernverein' (diss., Halle, 1927).

13 See the contributions by Robert Moeller and Jonathan Osmond in this volume.

14 See especially F. Jacobs, *Festschrift zur Enthüllungsfeier des Denkmals Frhr. v. Schorlemer-Alst* (Hiltrup, 1953), 30ff.; idem, *Von Schorlemer zur Grünen Front* (Düsseldorf, 1957).

15 See Schorlemer, *Promemoria und Motive*, quoted in Wesemann, 20f.; *Der Westfälische Bauer. Festnummer. 50 Jahre Westfälischer Bauernverein 1862–1912* 21 (1912): 357–462; E. Ritter, *Die katholisch-soziale Bewegung Deutschlands im 19. Jht. und der Volksverein* (Cologne, 1954).

16 On this topic see *Der Bayerische Bauernbund* (Munich, 1911); W. Mattes, *Die bayerischen Bauernräte. Eine soziologische und historische Untersuchung über bäuerliche Politik* (Stuttgart, 1921). See also several recent contributions, including I. Farr, 'Populism in the countryside: the Peasant Leagues in Bavaria in the 1890s', and D. Blackbourn, 'The problem of democratization. German Catholics and the role of the Centre Party', both in R. J. Evans (ed.), *Society and Politics in Wilhelmine Germany* (New York, 1978), 136–59 and 160–85; Farr's contribution in this volume; and D. Blackbourn, 'Roman

Catholics, the Centre Party and anti-Semitism in Imperial Germany', in P. Kennedy and A. Nicholls (eds.), *Nationalist and Racialist Movements in Britain and Germany before 1914* (London, 1981), 106–29.

17 On this, see in particular Puhle, *Agrarische Interessenpolitik* 37ff., 55ff., 63ff., 165ff., 201ff.

18 ibid., 184ff., 201ff. On the League's programme and ideology, see 72ff.; on the *Mittelstand*, 98ff.; on anti-Semitism, 111f.

19 See, for example, the contributions in *Handbuch der Deutsch-Konservativen Partei* (Berlin, 1911), compared to the *Konservatives Handbuch*, 2d ed. (Berlin, 1894), and also Puhle, *Agrarische Interessenpolitik*, 213–25; idem, 'Conservatism in modern German History', *Journal of Contemporary History* 13 (1978): 689–720.

20 Puhle, 'Conservatism'. See also R. Gellately, *The Politics of Economic Despair* (London, 1974), and S. Volkov, *The Rise of Popular Antimodernism in Germany* (Princeton, N.J., 1978). For a more traditional approach, see R. S. Levy, *The Downfall of the Anti-Semitic Political Parties in Imperial Germany* (New Haven, Conn., 1975).

21 Rosenberg, *Depression*, 187. For more complete references on this and the following topics, see Puhle, *Politische Agrarbewegungen*, 65ff.

22 See Kehr, *Schlachtflottenbau*, 310ff., 384ff., 430ff.; Wehler, *Bismarck*, 112ff., 142ff.; idem, *Krisenherde*, 107ff., 179ff.; Puhle, *Agrarische Interessenpolitik*, 85ff., 240ff., 255ff.; A. Galos et al., *Die Hakatisten. Der deutsche Ostmarkenverein 1894–1934* (Berlin, 1966).

23 See the discussion of agrarian splinter parties in the late 1920s in the contribution by Larry Jones in this volume.

24 See Mattes, and Ian Farr's contribution in this volume.

25 On this topic, see H. G. Lehmann, *Die Agrarfrage in der Theorie und Praxis der deutschen und internationalen Sozialdemokratie* (Tübingen, 1970), and the classics, K. Kautsky, *Die Agrarfrage* (Stuttgart, 1899), and E. David, *Sozialismus und Landwirtschaft* (Berlin, 1903).

26 This argument can already be found in R. Hilferding, 'Handelspolitik und Agrarkrise', *Die Gesellschaft*, 1924, pp. 113–29, esp. 114f. In addition, see W. Rothkegel, 'Die Bewegung der Kaufpreise für ländliche Besitzungen und die Entwicklung der Getreidepreise im Königreich Preussen von 1895 bis 1909', *Schmollers Jahrbuch* 34 (1910): 1685–1747; J. B. Esslen, 'Der Bodenpreis und seine Bestimmungsgründe', in *Grundriss der Sozialökonomik*, Part VII (Tübingen, 1922), 125–30.

27 See F. Aereboe, *Zur Frage der Agrarzölle* (Berlin, 1925), 5ff., 14ff.; M. Schumacher, *Mittelstandsfront und Republik* (Düsseldorf, 1972), 48ff.

28 Miquel in the Prussian Cabinet, 22 November 1897, cited in J. C. G. Röhl, *Germany without Bismarck* (London, 1968), 225. See P. C. Witt, *Die Finanzpolitik des Deutschen Reichs von 1903 bis 1913* (Lübeck, 1970), 63ff.

29 In general, I think the assumed unity within *Sammlungspolitik* has been somewhat exaggerated in the literature since Eckart Kehr. It was much more problematic than many historians have presented it recently. See Puhle, *Agrarische Interessenpolitik*, 155ff., esp. 158. Compare this to Kehr, *Schlachtflottenbau*, 172, 166f., and to what I consider to be a one-sided presentation in D. Stegmann, *Die Erben Bismarcks* (Cologne, 1970), passim; Witt, 58ff.; V. Berghahn, *Der Tirpitz-Plan* (Düsseldorf, 1971), 99ff., 150ff.

30 See the founding programme of the 'Cartel' in *Neue Reichskorrespondenz*, 25 August 1913, and Stegmann, *Erben*, 352ff.; idem, 'Zwischen Repression und Manipulation: Konservative Machteliten und Arbeiter- und Angestelltenbewegung 1910–1918', *Archiv für Sozialgeschichte* 12 (1972): 351–432, esp. 385ff.; H. Kaelble, *Industrielle Interessenpolitik in der Wilhelminischen Gesellschaft* (Berlin, 1967), 226ff. See also the discussion of agrarian splinter parties in Weimar's later years in this volume by Larry Jones.

31 See R. H. Bowen, *German Theories of the Corporatist State, 1870–1919* (New York, 1947); Puhle, *Agrarische Interessenpolitik*, 78ff., 98ff.; H. A. Winkler, *Mittelstand, Demokratie und Nationalsozialismus* (Cologne, 1972), 49ff.; S. Mielke, *Der Hansa-Bund für Gewerbe, Handel und Industrie 1909–1914* (Göttingen, 1975).

32 cf. Wehler, *Bismarck*, 122. The tendencies towards modernization and change in the Kaiserreich are, in my opinion, overestimated and the anti-democratic continuities underestimated in G. Eley, 'The Wilhelmine right: how it changed', in Evans (ed.), 112–35; idem, 'Some thoughts on the nationalist pressure groups in Imperial

Germany', in P. Kennedy and T. Nicholls (eds.) 40–67. To a great extent, Eley misinterprets 'völkisch' ideologies as 'populist' energies (which is not only a problem of translation); Eley's book, *Reshaping the German Right* (London, 1980), seems to me to disprove the author's own theses. On the state of the *Sonderweg* discussion, see D. Blackbourn and G. Eley, *Mythen deutscher Geschichtsschreibung* (Berlin, 1980); J. Kocka, 'Der "deutsche Sonderweg" in der Diskussion', *German Studies Review* 5 (1982): 365–79; R. G. Moeller, 'Die Besonderheiten der Deutschen?' *Internationale Schulbuchforschung* 4 (1982): 71–80; and idem, 'The Kaiserreich recast? Continuity and change in modern German Historiography', *Journal of Social History* 17 (1984): 655–83.

4 Peasant Protest in the Empire – The Bavarian Example

IAN FARR

Germany at the turn of the century was a society in transition. No longer a primarily agricultural nation, it was not yet a fully matured industrial state.[1] Rapid industrial growth and technological advances were helping to transform the German Empire into the most dynamic economy in Europe. Cities were multiplying in size and number as the demand for labour in industry and commerce expanded apace. Yet there were many parts of Germany which remained essentially rural and where the farm and the village shaped the rhythm and tenor of daily life. In 1900 more than twice as many Germans still lived in settlements of under 1,000 inhabitants as in the large cities of over 100,000 people.[2] Although the primary sector had ceased by the 1890s to be the predominant source of employment, it still sustained more than one-third of the German population. This meant, above all, a continued place in German society for the land-holding peasantry and the family farm. The proprietors of small and medium-sized holdings constituted the most important factor in Germany's agricultural production as well as a determining element in the social structure of the countryside.[3]

For these propertied peasants, as for their counterparts elsewhere in Europe, the socio-economic changes of the later nineteenth and early twentieth centuries presented new opportunities and unprecedented challenges. On the one hand, industrialization and the extension of the market economy offered the peasantry new possibilities of communication, collective action and political articulation. On the other hand, economic change dramatically reduced the contribution of agriculture and rural manufacture to the nation's output and accelerated the process of social polarization in the village.[4] These trends were hastened by the onset in the late 1870s of a long-term crisis in European agriculture occasioned largely by the emergence of new and relatively more efficient producers on the world market. Quite suddenly the buoyant prices and increasing demand which had so favoured landowners in the preceding decades were replaced by a more competitive market which highlighted some underlying weakness in the structure of German agriculture. The mood of optimism generated by the mid-century boom gave way to a climate of anxiety and resentment which drew the peasantry increasingly into the political arena.[5] The peasantry's capacity for durable political organization and influence was now enhanced by the wider range of experiences offered by specialized participation in the market, geographical mobility and communal political structures, but the changing economic and administrative priorities of the state, allied to the proliferation of powerful manufacturing and urban interests, threatened to shift the political balance irrevocably against the small farmer.[6] Throughout Europe peasants were confronted with the need for economic and political readjustment. But perhaps in no other country was the coincidence of rapid industrialization and sustained agricultural crisis so acute, nor its implications for the character of peasant politics so significant, as in late nineteenth-century Germany.

It is regrettable, therefore, that we know so little about the German peasantry in this period. Minimal efforts have been made towards a genuinely social-historical understanding of the structure, scope and direction of peasant politics in the Kaiserreich.[7] This is, in part, a reflection of a more generalized neglect which the modern European peasantry has traditionally suffered at the hands of historians. That omission is now being rectified, not least because the agrarian context of modern political revolutions has compelled historians to see peasants as more than the mere objects of history, immune to historical changes and contributing nothing to them.[8] But much of our knowledge of peasant politics in the age of industrialization is confined to Eastern Europe, largely because the experience of the peasantry there 'serves as something of a heuristic bridge between the well-worked soil of the third world and the all-but-uncharted terrain of the West'.[9] There are, however, further reasons, specific to German historiography, for the paucity of research into the peasantry of the imperial era.[10]

One is the limited degree to which local and regional history, which is probably well suited to the study of a peasant society as diverse as Germany's, is incorporated into the history of the Kaiserreich. It is no accident that recent works which interpret political developments in Imperial Germany from a non-Prussian perspective contain some of the best available discussion of pre-1914 rural politics.[11] A second and closely related factor is that German social history has been slow to embrace those disciplines, such as family history, demography, or social anthropology, which have sometimes enhanced historical consideration of the peasantry in other countries. The rehabilitation of such approaches from their unprincipled exploitation by Nazi racialism has only just begun.[12] This contrasts significantly with the central place accorded since the 1960s to models and concepts drawn from sociology and political science, particularly in analyses of Wilhelmine history. This is due to the recognition that, in the wake of the 'Fischer controversy', a systematic reinterpretation of the socio-political structures of Imperial Germany was urgently required. The product has been the consolidation in the Federal Republic of a social-scientific political history concerned to set the developments of the imperial period firmly in the context of the long-term failure of democracy in Germany. From it has come a formidable array of scholarly monographs on pressure groups, political institutions, power structures and decision-making processes, but virtually none of the problematics of rural and peasant society.[13]

The lack of conceptual or empirical work on the politics of the countryside has not, however, prevented certain assumptions about the nature of peasant political activity being built into recent historiography. Subsumed in many accounts of the Kaiserreich is a view of the peasantry as a socio-economic anachronism whose existence and politics were factors inhibiting Germany's transition to a modern pluralist democracy. The political behaviour of the peasantry was conditioned by traditionalism and an adherence to pre-industrial values. Peasant organizations remained exclusively contingent or subordinate to more powerful and durable interests.[14] As part of the so-called pre-industrial fabric of industrializing Germany the peasantry inevitably regarded rapid socio-economic change only as a threat which had to be repelled. These traditionalist instincts and resentments, it is argued, were exploited to service objectives inimical to the real interests of the small farmer. By succumbing to the blandishments of the Junker-dominated Agrarian League (*Bund der Landwirte*), the most powerful right-wing lobby in Wilhelmine Germany, peasants were drawn into a popularly based agrarian conservatism which set itself against more rational agricultural entrepreneurship and progressive political change. This pre-fascist agrarianism thus prevented not only the modernization of Germany's agriculture but also the political emancipation of German society from the inordinate influence of the landed aristocracy.[15] Symptomatic of the peasantry's supposed role as an agent, whether consciously or involuntarily, of elite designs was the support it gave to the cause of tarriff protection. The return to protectionism in 1879 and its reaffirmation in the 'agrarian-industrial' compact of 1902 is seen as the decisive factor in the preservation of the Junkers' economic and political power. The objective interests of peasant producers, which are customarily identified with animal husbandry, dairying and market gardening, were thereby sacrificed to the sectional interests of the east Elbian landowner. The level of protection against imported foodstuffs has therefore been interpreted as a yardstick against which to measure Germany's progress, or lack of it, towards democracy.[16]

There is certainly much to support this entrenched view of the peasantry as a section of society whose growing sense of resentment and alienation was successfully mobilized by forces implacably opposed to political change. As the economic crisis of peasant farming deepened in the 1880s and early 1890s so too did hostility towards any outsider who might be held responsible for rising production costs and diminishing returns. Rural animosity embraced an unresponsive central government and the over-zealous local official, the commodity speculators on the world's markets and the village cattle-dealer, as complex issues were rendered down into easily digestible slogans and targets for attack.[17] This susceptibility to demagogy was seized on by organizations such as the Agrarian League which ensured that otherwise inchoate protest serviced particular objectives. Numerous attempts to establish a coherent peasant interest independent of governmental direction or notable control foundered on misguided leadership, poor organization and lack of commitment.

Much of this also appears to substantiate the argument that peasant protest has always suffered from a fundamental inability to translate a recognition of wrongs into co-ordinated political action designed to rectify those grievances. The obstacles presented by the geographical dispersal and structural heterogeneity of the peasantry prevented any organization growing into a genuinely participatory movement. The more extensive it became, the more prone it was to fragmentation, and the less likely it was to remain in peasant hands. The nature of the peasant economy and the vertical segmentation of the peasantry into different communities, groups and interests, when compounded by the peasant's accurate appreciation of his own social and cultural inferiority, produced a state of 'low classness' which neutralized much of the peasantry's potential political leverage.[18]

Nevertheless, considerable doubts can be levelled against the view of the German peasantry briefly schematized here, and the assumptions guiding it. In the first place it comes uncomfortably close to the 'moral image' of the dependable and traditional peasant so assiduously promoted by nineteenth-century conservatives as a counter to the corrupt and immoral lifestyle of the urban proletariat and the attendant threat of revolutionary socialism.[19] The prototype of an instinctively dutiful and conservative peasantry dominated contemporary handbooks, infiltrated popular reading and sustained a legion of studies of peasant folklore which, in turn, cultivated spurious notions of continuity and persistence in peasant norms and behaviour.[20] Such preconceptions invade the treatment of rural politics in much agricultural history, where peasants are portrayed as the passive beneficiaries of the activities of prominent agrarian reformers.[21] They also prefigure many accounts of agrarian politics which devote uncritical and often misplaced attention to the careers of individual peasant leaders (*Bauernführer*).[22]

It is surprising that a new generation of 'critical' historians has not been more sceptical of these pervasive notions about the German peasantry. Some have tended to take the anti-industrial and anti-modern rhetoric of peasant protest too much at face value, without adequately considering the possibility that it was less a nostalgic rejection of capitalism than a way of facilitating the peasants' struggle to break into the capitalist system.[23] The widespread acceptance of the concept of modernization further tempts historians to regard the peasantry as a socio-economic anachronism, a relic of social changes against which it was bound to protest. Instead of treating peasant farming as a rational economic enterprise and therefore as an integral component of an industrializing society, it tends to be dismissed as a pre-industrial survival, unable and unwilling to 'modernize' in the way Danish agriculture did.[24] The traditionalism and pre-industrialism of the peasantry are forwarded as self-evident truths receiving and requiring no genuinely historical explanation. In the overall stress on the continuity of pre-industrial elements as decisive contributors to the ultimate collapse of German democracy, further assumptions are made about the relationship between political 'backwardness', fascism and the peasantry which are known to be oversimplified. The result is a tendency to interpret peasant politics in Imperial Germany almost exclusively as part of a direct lineage of tradition-bound authoritarianism which culminated in the victory of National Socialism.

Recent interpretations suggest, however, that peasant politics in Imperial Germany possessed a dynamic which cannot be explained in terms of peasant traditionalism or susceptibility to a carefully manipulated authoritarianism. Precisely at the time when the conservative mythology of the sturdy and reliable peasant was gaining ground, peasants themselves mounted a serious challenge to the established pattern of political relations in the countryside. Propelled by mounting economic grievances and by a determination to have their material interests more vigorously represented, peasants began to undermine the 'notable politics' (*Honorationenpolitik*) practised by the major parties. The most decisive period was the 1890s when higher election turn-outs, the increasing frequency of genuine electoral contests and, above all, a proliferation of political and non-political associations signified an unprecedented mobilization of agrarian sentiment. The established parties were compelled to construct entirely new organizational and ideological relationships with their rural constituents. The inability of the National Liberal Party to accommodate the newly politicized peasantry until the belated formation of the German Peasants' League (*Deutscher Bauernbund*) in 1909 contrasted sharply with the successful initiatives taken by the Conservative and Centre parties, which themselves had profound consequences for the course of Wilhelmine politics.[25]

Closer study of the peasantry in Bavaria will clarify some of these issues. This is not to claim that conditions here were representative of those throughout Germany, given the existence of a large Catholic majority, the enduring undercurrent of particularism and the singular relations between the ministerial elite and the political parties in Bavaria.[26] But Bavaria was a state where varieties of peasant farming, from dairying in the Allgäu or extensive grain-growing in the Danube valley to specialized hop cultivation in Franconia and marginal subsistence in impoverished upland areas, can be observed.[27] More importantly, no other part of Germany is more readily identified with the historical survival of a conservative peasantry. Such views do have some substance, since statistical comparison confirms that the peasant family farm was more prevalent here than elsewhere in Germany. More peasant holdings were owned exclusively by their proprietors and more relied solely on the labour input of the family than in any other state.[28] In Bavaria, therefore, resided an important concentration of landed peasants, including numerous of those 'middle peasants' identified by many historians as the primary agents of rural protest.[29]

The following analysis gives substantial weight to the view that the 1890s marked a dramatic watershed in rural politics in Germany. To be sure, it also reveals considerable evidence of the peasantry's inability to organize independent and sustained political action or to break the dominant mode of notable politics in the two decades after unification. It also demonstrates, however, that fundamental political changes occurred in rural Bavaria before 1914, sparked off by an unmistakable radicalization of the peasantry in the 1890s. This had serious consequences for the structure, priorities and style of the dominant political parties and had significant repercussions on the attitudes and politics of the Bavarian government. To appreciate the extent to which political relationships were transformed in the generation before 1914 the character of rural politics before 1890 has to be established.

The first point worthy of note is the absence in the 1880s of any sizeable or influential representation of peasant interests. Some organizations which had catered hitherto for the peasants of Catholic Bavaria were already in a state of terminal decline. These were the Patriotic Peasants' Associations (*Patriotische Bauernvereine*) formed in the late 1860s as part of the largely spontaneous popular protest against the apparently hegemonic aspirations of Bismarckian Prussia. In an unprecedented mobilization of public opinion peasants had joined the Catholic clergy in grass-roots activism against the threats to Bavarian sovereignty and religious freedoms which seemed imminent after Prussia's victory of 1866. Throughout 1860 the banner of 'For God, King and the Fatherland' had rallied peasants in south-eastern Bavaria to the burgeoning Patriotic movement.[30] An aggressive Catholicism had blended with a fierce resentment of Prussia and a dogmatic anti-liberalism to produce a public mood virulently hostile to the 'external taxation squeeze of military despotism'.[31] By 1872, however, it was clear that the *Bauernvereine* had lost their earlier momentum. Although the onset of the *Kulturkampf* appeared to confirm Catholic fears and increased popular disenchantment in Bavaria with the incumbent liberal ministry, the Prussian unification of Germany was irrevocable. It robbed the peasant organizations of their raison d'être. The frequency of meetings declined dramatically and many had to be abandoned in favour of drinking sessions.[32] Membership of the Deggendorf association slumped from 8,604 in 1870 to a nadir in 1882 when the annual assembly attracted only six participants. After a vain attempt to revive support by dispensing with the word 'Patriotic' it drifted quietly out of existence.[33] The only other branch of the movement to survive was that based in Tuntenhausen. It claimed a membership of some 2,000 in 1885. It relied entirely on a local clientele in the southern districts of Upper Bavaria, for whom it offered only sporadic meetings, negligible practical benefits and no political influence.[34]

The 1880s also witnessed repeated attempts to establish a permanent peasant organization in Franconia and Bavarian Swabia. These were due almost exclusively to the initiatives of Karl von Thüngen-Rossbach, a member of a large aristocratic family with considerable estates in Lower Franconia. He first came to public prominence in 1878–9 in the protectionist Union of Tax and Economic Reformers, where he was active in helping to secure Bismarck's conversion to agricultural tariffs.[35] He continued his agitation in Bavaria by forming a Franconian Peasants' Association in 1882. Alongside the insistence on the need for protective tariffs, Thüngen suggested curtailing the credit monopoly of rural moneylenders, reducing state expenditure and peasant taxation and demanded a state take-over of schemes for insurance, credit and mortgage debt. In succeeding years his campaign assumed a familiar routine as he tried to establish a network of subordinate associations designed to promote farmers' interests and to secure the election of more peasants and artisans to the legislature.[36] Some localized groups were established in central Bavaria but in the long run the only durable product of Thüngen's agitation proved to be the Central Franconian Peasants' Association. Founded in Gunzenhausen in 1885 by a local farmer, Friedrich Beckh, its prime function was as an electoral pressure group for Beckh and Friedrich Lutz, a brewer and landowner who soon assumed the leadership of the organization. It was instrumental in securing their election as Conservatives to the Bavarian *Landtag* in 1887.[37]

It has been suggested that these developments constituted a significant radicalization of the Bavarian peasantry in the early 1880s.[38] However,

neither the anti-Semetic rhetoric of Friedrich Beckh nor the reform programmes of Thüngen and the Patriotic Peasants' Associations attracted
sufficient members to sustain effective political campaigns or associational activities. The low level of participation in organizations was
reflected in the comparative dearth and uneven geographical distribution
of local credit co-operatives.[39] The only body claiming to represent
farmers' interests which continued to grow throughout the 1870s and
1880s was the explicitly non-political Agricultural Association (*Landwirtschaftlicher Verein*). Founded under governmental encouragement in 1810
to advance the practical education of the peasantry in more scientific
methods, it was monopolized from the outset by large landowners, officials and other non-farmers. In 1860 only 9,556 of the 21,733 members
were farmers, whereas 6,549 were officials. Successive revisions of the
statutes and reductions in the subscription helped to swell the membership to 56,467 by 1888, but the Association remained essentially a bureau
cratic mechanism for effecting legislative decisions and technical
improvements at the local level.[40] These preoccupations aroused considerable antipathy among farmers towards such manifestations of
'official' agriculture as winter courses, exhibitions and incomprehensible
lectures.[41] The bureaucratic influence, however, remained paramount.
Half of the district committees in 1882 were chaired by district officials,
and many others were presided over by priests, vets, or forestry
officers.[42] They were all determined to prevent any politicization of the
Association. As a result it came under increasing criticism for its failure to
act as a genuine representation of peasant interests, and for being 'incompatible with what is expected from a professional, co-operative organization of the peasantry'.[43]

This lack of peasant involvement in all but the most politically innocu-
ous of organizations contrasted quite sharply with some other parts of
Germany. In Westphalia the Catholic nobility had successfully transformed itself into a regional elite which, through the agency of von
Schorlemer's *Bauernverein*, enjoyed the confidence of many rural voters.
In other largely Catholic regions the example of Westphalia, and the
impetus provided by the *Katholikentag* of 1882, encouraged the formation
of a series of peasant associations. Many of these, such as the
30,000-strong Rhineland association, helped to secure the objectives of
the larger landowners while simultaneously ensuring continued peasant
allegiance to the Catholic Centre Party.[44] Meanwhile the peasants of
Hessen, disillusioned with the aloof *Honorationenpolitik* of the National
Liberals, were turning in increasing numbers to Otto Böckels *Mittel-
deutscher Verein* (Central German Association). Though an explicitly anti-
Semitic group, it ventilated a variety of grievances. According to
Massing, 'those who voted for Böckel ... were not enraptured by

notions of race superiority', but 'were concerned with more sober matters, such as cheaper industrial goods, cheaper government, cheaper credit, feed and Schnaps'.[45] By 1892 this body had 15,000 members organized into 400 local chapters and sharing a range of benefits from legal aid to cheap insurance and favourable terms for participation in co-operatives.[46]

Even this brief comparison demonstrates the quiescence of peasant politics in Bavaria before the 1890s. That immobility was determined partly by the lack of any effective agrarian lobby or assertive professional representation. Even more crucial was the absence of viable political alternatives in rural constituencies to the Catholic Patriotic Party. Popular animosity towards the *Kulturkampf* helped the Patriots to graft the Catholic parts of Franconia on to their heartland in Upper and Lower Bavaria and the Upper Palatinate, where they amassed over 75 per cent of the vote in every Reichstag election between 1874 and 1890, and monop-olized elections to the Bavarian *Landtag*.[47] At this time their only political rivals were the fragmented and largely moribund liberal parties whose sphere of activity was confined increasingly to the larger cities, Protestant districts and the educated and commercial bourgeoisie. The only part of rural southern Bavaria where the National Liberals retained parity with the Catholic Party before 1914 was the Allgäu. This was due to political traditions, dating back to 1848, which were sustained by close relations between town and country, long experience of independent communal responsibilities and by close interconnections between liberal and dairy-ing organizations.[48] Elsewhere, however, the justified identification of liberalism with the *Kulturkampf*, the economic interests of the urban bourgeoisie and a Bavarian regime closely tied to the Bismarckian Reich denied it any possibility of mass Catholic support. The perpetual liberal minority in the *Landtag* did, however, retain a political leverage lost by its counterparts elsewhere after 1879, because it was indispensable to the 'liberal-conservative, late-absolutist' elite which governed Bavaria. Having secured Bavaria's integration into the Empire this tightly knit and predominantly liberal ministerial oligarchy was devoted to neutralizing any Patriotic pressure for constitutional change and greater parliamentary accountability. In the absence of a genuine conservatism, National Liberalism was thus drawn into a prolonged state-conservative defence against the Catholic majority.[49]

The task was facilitated by the Patriotic Party's growing reluctance to mobilize its strength for a frontal assault on liberal dominance.[50] The party leadership was anxious to avoid an irreparable breach with the government because of the continuing friction in the 1880s between the Catholic Church and the Bavarian regime. This committed the Catholic Party to 'Cabinet-style politics' in defence of confessional interests and privileges. A devotion to religious issues was understandable in a state whose liberal government was antipathetic to the claims of the Roman Catholic Church and granted the 70 per cent Catholic majority only minimal access to political power. It also represented a policy on which all sections of the party could unite. The more the party turned to secular issues, the more likely it was to be fragmented by conflicting claims and priorities. Apart from ensuring a degree of unity within the parliamentary party, concentration on clerical matters helped to quell the more radical elements in Catholic politics. The ministerial elite and leading figures in the Catholic establishment distrusted political demands to improve the social and economic conditions of the subordinate classes in Bavarian society, since they constituted both a threat to the existing political order and an implicit challenge to the authority of the church. Conservative elements in the Catholic hierarchy thus negotiated a *modus vivendi* on church-political issues with an increasingly conciliatory ministry, but only by neglecting the urgent economic problems being faced by the Catholic *Mittelstand* and peasantry.[51]

Until the early 1890s the Patriotic or Centre Party survived the widening gulf between its clerical preoccupations and the secular concerns of its most important constituency by recourse to the well-tried principles of *Honorationenpolitik*. The key part here was played by the clergy, which, as a surrogate party bureaucracy, exercised considerable influence on the operations of rural politics. Prominent clergy were involved in the selection of suitable candidates and in the political dealing which accompanied the indirect suffrage used in *Landtag* elections until 1906.[52] A by-election in Stadtamhof in 1882 was one of the rare occasions when 'the peasant delegates turned their backs on the candidate acclaimed by the bishop's press and selected an independent candidate from their own midst'.[53] Local priests were also active during elections, helping to gather votes together and urging dilatory voters to the polls. In 'safe' constituencies notification of candidates in the local press and the occasional public appearance, backed up by admonitions from the pulpit, were deemed sufficient to maintain the link between Catholic politicians and 'their' voters.[54] The exclusion of the peasantry from all but a passive and acclamatory role did, however, have some important adverse effects. These included a steady decline in the proportion of Catholics voting for the party, as well as falling turn-out, particularly to *Landtag* elections.[55] Meanwhile, continued reliance on clerical *Honorationenpolitik* obscured the need for a comprehensive network of rural organizations, even after the incorporation of the Patriots into the Centre Party in 1887.[56] There was certainly enough residual Catholic loyalty to deter any transfer of political allegiance, but confessional solidarity and clerical persuasion now guaranteed only a minimal sympathy for the style and content of Catholic politics.

Even confessionalism, however, could not contain the challenge to deferential politics generated by the conjuncture of the 1890s, which brought substantial changes in the political life of the Bavarian peasantry.

Crucial to this conjuncture was an intensification of the economic problems confronting many agricultural producers. The deepening sense of crisis was occasioned first by a sharp downturn in grain prices from 1892 to 1895, following a brief recovery in the preceding two years from the lower price levels which had obtained since the early 1880s.[57] Mounting anxiety about the fall in cereal prices was heightened by a severe drought in the summer of 1893. The resultant acute shortage of fodder forced small farmers with limited reserves of cash or foodstuffs to sell off their livestock at unprofitable prices on local markets. The Bavarian government dispensed interest-free loans and substantial stocks of fodder to small farmers, particularly in Franconia, to mitigate the worst effects of the drought.[58]

These developments only highlighted the longer-term difficulties faced by many peasants in Bavaria who found their income being squeezed between static returns on staple products and rising production costs.[59] Many larger peasant farms, for example, were excessively dependent on income from grain, the staple product of Bavarian agriculture throughout the nineteenth century. Growing overseas competition revealed significant deficiencies in methods of cultivation, as well as the limited extent of diversification into animal-rearing and fodder crops. Efficient production was also hampered by the continued fragmentation of holdings, a problem which had only effectively been surmounted, with highly profitable results, in the Allgäu. Suitable credit facilities, which might have facilitated technical improvements, diversification and collective enterprises, were still few in number. Some factors influencing farmers' costs were outside their control. These included the comparatively high levels of taxation on rural property, which had long inhibited agricultural innovation in Bavaria. Significant increases in local, provincial and state expenditure since unification, as well as the continued imposition of levies still extant from the process of peasant emancipation, made considerable demands on rural producers. Farmers were also faced with costs for non-family labour, which rose markedly during the economic upswings of the early 1870s and 1900s, primarily in response to trends in the industrial labour market. In the vicinity of the larger cities peasants had to pay substantially more for permanent and seasonal workers than their counterparts in more remote districts.[60] The most conspicuous product of these accumulating pressures on many peasant households was undoubtedly the mounting level of unproductive indebtedness. This burden, which had its roots in the inflation of property prices in the 1860s, was aggravated by the continued susceptibility of farmers to seasonal dislocations and an undue reliance on informal types of credit to meet such emergencies. It was particularly prevalent on the larger impartible holdings of southern Bavaria where debts incurred on inheritance compounded the shortage of available capital. The foregoing analysis of the crisis in peasant agriculture should not be seen as justifying the alarmist warnings of contemporary agitators and ideologues who predicted the imminent eclipse of the German peasant. The number of bankruptcies, for example, remained relatively small.[61] There is, however, sufficient evidence to show that the exaggerated fears of many small farmers were based on real economic problems to which there were no instant solutions.

These anxieties were fuelled by the reorientation of Reich trade policy after 1890 under the auspices of Chancellor Caprivi's 'New Course'. By negotiating a series of new commercial treaties with Germany's neighbours, Caprivi's government effectively lowered the levels of protection against imports of both livestock and arable produce. These tariff reductions were only partially responsible for the fall in domestic prices after 1891, but for small landowners they constitued a more tangible and potent focus for grievance than shifts in world commodity prices. The apparent anti-agrarian bias of government policy also aggravated the sense of cultural inferiority and impotence felt by many farmers towards those who wielded economic and political power. The resulting groundswell of resentment was to prove a major factor in the mobilization of agrarian sentiment. Its principal product was the Agrarian League, whose immediate and dramatic political impact was itself a further spur to the politicization of the peasantry in the 1890s.

In Bavaria the initial victim of this rising tide of rural discontent was the Centre Party. Its *Fraktion* (delegation) in the Reichstag aroused distrust for the support it gave to the 1891 commercial treaties and to increases in military expenditure. By early 1893 popular animosity in Bavaria towards the forthcoming army budget, and the additional taxation it appeared to portend, posed a clear electoral threat to any representative who voted for a further expansion of the army.[62] Meanwhile, the gulf between the Catholic hierarchy and its mass rural constituency was highlighted by the Bavarian Centre's backing in 1892 for improvements in the salaries and conditions of priests and many government officials, at a time of deepening economic crisis for many farmers.[63] This grave tactical error was symptomatic of the party's persistent failure to recognize that, as one Swabian official noted, 'the interests of the agricultural population in confessional struggles have been completely superseded by economic issues'.[64]

The first indication of the Centre Party's problems came in the Reichstag election of 1893 when its share of the popular vote dropped to 42 per cent. Major inroads into Centrist strongholds in various parts of the countryside were achieved by the newly formed Bavarian Peasants' League (*Bayerischer Bauernbund*).[65] The new party secured some 9 per cent of the total vote and one in five of the votes cast in the constituencies which it contested. Particularly striking was the League's success in Lower Bavaria where its share of the vote exceeded that of a Centre Party which only three years earlier had commanded 85 per cent of the vote in the same province.[66] This bridgehead was confirmed in the *Landtag* poll only three weeks later. Despite urgent efforts by the Centre Party and local clergymen to meet this new challenge, the Centre suffered a 20 per cent drop in support, much of it in rural areas. Although still the largest *Fraktion* in the *Landtag*, it had forfeited its absolute majority. The *Bauernbund*'s tactics and programme again found their readiest response in Lower Bavaria, where eight candidates were successful.[67] This confirmed that the League had attained virtual parity with the Centre in one of the latter's acknowledged electoral citadels in southern Germany. Despite persistent problems in establishing a coherent and unified party out of its various provincial organizations, the *Bauernbund* continued after 1893 to threaten Centrist pre-eminence in south-eastern Bavaria. Some indication of its support was evident in the Reichstag election of 1898 when it supplemented its strength in the south by capitalizing on anti-Centrist sentiments among Protestant voters in Franconia. The League's share of the popular vote reached over 18 per cent comparable to that attained by the Social Democrats. In the twenty-two constituencies where *Bauernbund* candidates were in serious and direct opposition to the Centre party, that share was over 38 per cent compared to the Centre's 52 per cent.[68]

Most studies of the Bavarian Peasants' League suggest that these achievements were largely inconsequential.[69] At first glance that view appears justified. The Centre Party continued to be the dominant representative of rural Catholic voters. There were many villages and districts where the League was unable to loosen the clerical grip on peasant voters. The activities of its few parliamentarians were generally unco-ordinated and ineffectual. The *Bauernbund*'s success in 1898 was not to be repeated in any subsequent election before the First World War. Already in the *Landtag* election of 1899 it suffered significant reverses, despite the occasional deployment of intimidatory techniques such as threats to boycott shops and businesses.[70] The downward trend continued in every Reichstag poll until the war, a process accompanied by the organizational decomposition of the League into increasingly distinct provincial units. Membership of the *Bauernbund*, which had never reached more than modest levels, declined gradually from some 15,000 in 1896 to about

122

7,000 in 1913.[71] This compared unfavourably with the growth in Bavaria (excluding the Palatinate) of the Agrarian League whose membership rose from 6,584 in 1902 to at least 16–17,000 on the eve of the war.[72]

It would, however, be quite misleading to dismiss the *Bauernbund* as a transitory and marginal organization wielding minimal influence over the conduct of rural politics in pre-1914 Bavaria. This overlooks the League's genuinely catalytic effect in the political mobilization of the Bavarian countryside. Its emergence in 1893 signified the onset in rural Bavaria of that 're-casting of the political nation' which Blackbourn has identified as the hallmark of the 1890s.[73] The decade from 1892 to 1902 saw Bavarian politics dominated by agrarian agricultural issues, thrust to the forefront of the political stage by a distinctive radicalization of peasant sentiment. Although many of these issues subsided after the turn of the century, rural politics was never again to return to the patterns of quiescence and deference which had characterized the first two decades of the Kaiserreich. The Peasants' League shook the Bavarian government out of its previous complacency towards the peasantry and circumscribed the Bavarian activities of the Agrarian League. Above all, it was instrumental in forcing the Centre Party to reconstruct its vital agrarian base through the formation of new Christian Peasants' Associations (*Christliche Bauernvereine*), which grew rapidly to become one of the most powerful political interests in pre-war Bavaria. The *Bauernbund* thus had an impact far beyond that suggested by the statistical record. To understand this further, a brief examination of the movement is necessary.

The Bavarian Peasants' League, in common with many other expressions of peasant and popular protest in Imperial Germany, fits very uncomfortably into the categories conventionally used by historians.[74] Analytical confusion can be explained partly by the fact that the *Bauernbund* was rarely a unitary movement. It was characterized by erratic leadership, contrasting ideological and tactical emphases, and, therefore, by inconsistent relationships with other political parties and organizations. Another reason for the analytical confusion surrounding the League is the difficulty which historians with preconceived ideas often experience in coming to terms with popular movements which could equably embrace apparently irreconcilable objectives. For example, the rhetoric of peasant protest was undoubtedly suffused with social-protectionist sentiments which seemed implacably opposed to the 'predatory' forces of industrial modernization and may consequently have inhibited progressive political change. On the other hand, the egalitarian impulse in that protest militated against its manipulative deployment by forces committed solely to the preservation of privilege and to the exclusion of subordinate classes from the political process. These supposed incompatibilities were, in fact, a quite faithful reflection of the numerous material and political grievances which fuelled the peasant radicalism of the 1890s.

This can be seen in the range of measures the Peasants' League advocated to alleviate the economic problems faced by many Bavarian peasants.[75] Particular stress was laid on the need for political remedies to provide relief from some of the allegedly inequitable costs burdening peasant agriculture. We have already seen the extent of rural antipathy towards excessive or 'luxury' military expenditure, reinforced by the continued hostility of Bavarian Catholics towards Prussia and much of what it stood for. The military budget, and subsequently 'marinism', could be successfully portrayed as irrelevant extravagances, satisfying the appetites of Prussian militarists and heavy industrialists for grandiose projects funded by higher taxes levied against the hard-pressed small farmer. The *Bauernbund* also profited from growing rural disenchantment with the financial implications of the imperial insurance schemes of the 1880s. In many parts of Bavaria peasant employers tried to evade the requirements of the new legislation. Local petitions deriding the so-called *Wapperlgesetz* (Label Law) attracted thousands of signatures from peasants who saw the 1889 provisions for old-age and sickness insurance as inappropriate to the conditions of agricultural labour and who resented the additional financial outlay involved.[76] Throughout the 1890s the new agrarian movement campaigned for a revocation of some parts of the legislation. This led to changes in 1899 ensuring that contributors to the insurance scheme were not disadvantaged by the disproportionately high number of elderly people living in those rural areas which experienced a significant out-migration of younger wage-earners.[77] There were also demands for a fully progressive taxation system, to end what was seen as excessive discrimination against farmers and small producers. This attack on the financial privileges of the aristocracy was accompanied by calls for the abolition of entail on noble estates, and for large landowners, including the state, to allow greater access to forests for hunting and woodgathering, which were crucial supplements to peasant income in the upland districts of Bavaria. Resentment at the costs of credit and financial protection provided by moneylenders and private institutions fuelled a campaign for the state to introduce comprehensive schemes for property and fire insurance and credit distribution. The government was also urged to accelerate the development of railway branch-lines and local roads to facilitate access to wider markets. Characteristic of the League's aptitude in exploiting sensitive issues was its insistent pressure for the abolition of *Bodenzinse*. These were fixed annuities at 4 per cent interest contracted by peasants in 1848 to assist in the compensation of landlords for the loss of their remaining seigneurial rights. Despite attempts in 1872 to rectify the flaws inherited from the emancipation legislation of 1848–9, crucial anomalies, and an annual bill exceeding 14 million Marks, sur-vived. The removal of these levies would only have yielded marginal benefits to many farmers, but the financial aggravation they caused were less antagonizing than the sheer injustice of having to pay for freedoms granted half a century earlier. The campaign against the *Bodenzinse* was therefore very much a movement of political emancipation and it proved powerful enough to extract important legislative concessions in 1898.[78]

Reinforcing this campaign for radical changes in the tax structure and for systematic state intervention on behalf of peasant producers was insistent pressure for higher levels of protection against imports of grain, hops, meat and livestock. Although this demand united the various agrarian organizations in Bavaria, the League frequently adopted a more extreme stance than the rival *Bauernvereine*, as instanced by its espousal of the Kanitz plan for a state monopoly in imported grain. This was due partly to Thüngen's desire for a closer integration of the *Bauernbund* and the Agrarian League in Franconia. It also reflected popular sentiment in Lower Bavaria, where high levels of indebtedness on farms which depended heavily on marketing substantial surpluses of grain generated considerable sympathy for a monopoly which would guarantee farmers price support.[79] However, by favouring a scheme so blatantly engineered by the Agrarian League to advance the interests of the east Elbian estates, the *Bauernbund* did sacrifice internal unity and gave superficial credence to the Centre Party's charge that the League was a mere puppet of Prussian Junkerdom.

The economic measures advocated by the *Bauernbund* thus correspon-ded closely to the programmes of agrarian reform which had failed to elicit any widespread response in the 1880s.[80] Though given new impetus by developments in the early 1890s, these demands could not in them-selves break the established mould of rural politics. That transformation was sparked by combining an agrarian economic platform with a vocifer-ous campaign for political institutions to respect the objectives and griev-ances of the peasantry. This was to be achieved by absolute freedom of the press, speech and assembly, the abolition of the non-elected upper chamber (*Reichsratskammer*), universal male suffrage and a direct franchise for *Landtag* elections, and by the election of peasants rather than notables to represent peasant interests in parliament. There was no clearer chal-lenge to the principles of *Honorationenpolitik* than the *Bauernbund*'s deter-mination, evident in its earliest meetings and its first electoral campaign, to terminate peasant reliance on nobles, bureaucrats and priests. Only by mobilizing themselves behind candidates from their own midst could peasants expect any meaningful recognition of their particular needs.[81] This assault on elitism was conducted in a rumbustious style which further discomfited its victims. These included local officials, some of

125

whom were at a loss how to explain the truculent mood of the peasantry. They tended to blame the rebelliousness of the customarily deferential peasant on the 'terrorist' activities of the League's agitators, an indication of their insensitivity to the reservoir of resentment fuelling the demagogic politics of the *Bauernbund*.[82] Sporadic attempts by the League to infiltrate and politicize local branches of the Agricultural Association only heightened their consternation. In districts like Lower Bavaria the Catholic clergy bore the brunt of peasant rancour. Opposition to the Centre Party was articulated here through a vigorous anti-clericalism which condemned the exploitation of religion for political purposes, clerical control of education and the idea that a priest could be a legitimate political representative of the peasantry.[83]

As a new rural organization the *Bauernbund* clearly had difficulty in living up to its own maxim that only peasants could truly represent peasant interests. Some farmers, notably Franz Wieland and Georg Eisenberger, did occupy leading positions in the League. But they were accompanied at the forefront of electoral and campaigning activities by the journalists Johann Sigl, Anton Memminger, Alois Schwab and Georg Senftl, an aristocrat such as Thüngen, a writer and ex-priest Georg Ratzinger and by men with a substantial academic training, such as Albert Gäch or Leonhard Kleitner. Some had flirted previously with liberalism or Social Democracy. Others hoped to utilize heightened rural discontent to radicalize the Bavarian Centre Party into a genuine Catholic *Volkspartei* (People's Party).[84] However, few of these men were identified with the notable elite which had so alienated many rural inhabitants. Indeed, many used their record of convictions for slander and defamation as proof of their anti-establishment credentials. It is also clear from more detailed investigation that, in common with other agrarian movements of the period, the Peasants' League facilitated the emergence of a new brand of political leadership. Among the parliamentary candidates and in the local branches of the *Bauernbund* was a substantial proportion of peasants and farmers, who represented a clear break with the *Honorationenstruktur* which had previously characterized political relations in the Bavarian countryside.[85]

The *Bauernbund* thus introduced into Bavaria a new and essentially populist dimension which posed a fundamental challenge to governmental authority and to the political foundations of Centrist pe-eminence in southern Germany. Its volatile compound of agrarianism, political egalitarianism and peasant activism embarrassed a ministerial bureaucracy primed only to anticipate such insubordination from the urban proletariat. The government, seeking some explanation for the political radicalization of the peasantry, subjected agrarian meetings to close scrutiny while simultaneously instituting a range of inquiries into the state of the kingdom's agriculture. The immediacy of its reaction was in stark contrast to the apparent equanimity with which it had previously regarded the accumulating problems of the Bavarian peasantry. It now adopted a much more interventionist strategy, belatedly establishing a state-funded agricultural bank, providing greater co-ordination to co-operative initiatives and dispensing credit to facilitate diversification, mechanization and rationalization.[86]

The rapidity of the government's response was a reflection of the pressure exerted not only by the Peasants' League, but also by a Centre Party whose indispensable monopoly of rural politics in Catholic Bavaria had been eroded by the populism of the *Bauernbund*. Nothing is more illustrative of the League's enduring impact on the course of Bavarian and imperial politics than its effect on the structure, tactics and ideological orientation of the Bavarian Centre Party. What had been an unorganized party of notables excessively preoccupied with clerical issues was galvanized by 'the sparks from the incendiary torch of the Peasants' League' into a party patently committed to the economic and political interests of the Catholic *Mittelstand*.[87] Already in 1893 and 1894 Bavarian delegates in the Reichstag were spearheading opposition within the Centre *Fraktion* to the trade treaties with Romania and Russia. This heralded a new tension within the Centre Party between its Bavarian wing and a national leadership intent on working closely with the government to secure greater economic and civic parity for the Catholic minority. For example, consistent hostility among the Bavarian representatives to excessive military or naval expenditure, backed up by recurrent threats of a Bavarian secession, epitomized how far the Centre Party in the *Reichstag* was being inconvenienced by the threat from the *Bauernbund*.[88] That influence also accounts for the dramatic reduction of the aristocratic presence in the Bavarian *Zentrum*. Sensitivity to the Peasants' League's anti-elitist and anti-clerical pressure also resulted in a significant declericalization of the *Landtag* party, with the proportion of priests being halved between 1893 and 1912. Many of those who remained were younger clergymen from village backgrounds who were more sympathetic to the needs of the rural electorate. This was symptomatic of the much greater prominence attained within the Bavarian Centre by delegates drawn from the milieu of the peasantry and *Mittelstand*, which led to the temporary eclipse of the more conservative and notable elements in the party.[89]

The clearest indication of the transformation within the Centre Party induced by the *Bauernbund*, as well as by the grievances sustaining peasant protest, was the formation between 1893 and 1897 of the Catholic *Bauern-vereine*. Surprisingly little is known of these organizations. Both their essentially political character and the influence they exerted on the character and conduct of the Bavarian Centre tend to be underestimated.[90] Unlike their more established counterparts in the Rhineland and West-phalia, which merely serviced the militant and conservative agrarianism of the Catholic aristocracy, they were identified from the outset with the demands and interests of the peasantry. Despite continued and vituper-ative attacks on the Associations by the Peasants' League, their member-ship grew steadily to just under 38,000 in August 1898. By the end of 1907 membership had grown to over 120,000, organized in more than 3,000 local sections.[91] The *Bauernvereine* thereby became the cornerstone of the Centre Party's efforts to reconstitute its relationship with the newly politicized peasantry.

The striking success of the Christian Peasants' Associations in meeting, accommodating and ultimately utilizing the more radical sentiments in the peasantry can be attributed to a number of factors. The first was the way in which the *Bauernvereine*, in their urgent efforts to rehabilitate the Centre Party, simply appropriated the reform programme of the *Bauern-bund*. Although embellished with the familiar corporatism of Catholic social thought, the campaign of the Peasants' Associations was targeted on precisely the issues from which the Peasants' League had profited. More than one local official experienced difficulty in distinguishing between the rival groupings on questions such as rural taxation, *Boden-zinse*, the *Wapperlgesetz*, state-run insurance schemes and the need to curb profligate military and naval expendiure. Confessional preocupations survived only in the defence of church schools against demands for their abolition by some parts of the Peasants' League.[92]

Occasionally there was more than an ideological resemblance between the two movements. Clandestine discussions were held in 1894 between the respective leaders about the feasibility of a union between the *Bauern-vereine* and the *Bauernbund* in Catholic Franconia, but to no avail.[93] Further testimony to the extent of common ground between the two organizations was the sympathy expressed by Centrist leaders in Lower Bavaria for the amalgamation of the *Bauernbund*, Centre and *Bauern-vereine* into an independent Catholic *Volkspartei*, which could help to block any moves in the Reichstag towards 'Caesarist centralism'. This secessionist threat was always held in check by the realization that Bavarian Catholics could wield much greater power within a unified *Zentrum* that in any agrarian or separatist groupings. But Centrists like Söldner and Echinger continued to warn their party of the potentially high price of excessive identification with the Reich government, namely, further support from the Bavarian peasantry for the Peasant League.[94]

That prospect also ensured that the *Bauernvereine* associated themselves from the outset with the call for higher tariffs and for rigorous veterinary controls on imported meat and livestock. In the run-up to the vital tariff debates of 1901–2 they maintained pressure on the Centre Party and argued for oats and barley to be afforded the same protection as rye and wheat. It was the *Bauernverein*'s simple but carefully formulated demand for a 6 Mark tariff on all grains which united all agrarian organizations in Bavaria for the first and only time at a major peasant rally in Regensburg in October 1901.[95] The Association's dominant figure, Georg Heim, accumulated evidence to substantiate the view that most peasants benefited from higher tariffs. That claim is usually discounted by historians who, relying on Brentano's arbitrary calculation that protection only favoured the 25 per cent of German farms over 5 hectares in size, tend to attribute the strength of protectionist feelings among the peasantry to a mixture of Junker manipulation and peasant irrationality.[96] The revised tariff levels of 1902 undoubtedly did disadvantage many peasants by inflating land prices and aggravating the problem of indebtedness.[97] But a closer examination of the mixed farming practised on so many peasant holdings, and of the costs and risks involved in diversification into reputedly more profitable branches of agriculture, may show peasant assessments of protectionism to have been a great deal more sensible than is often assumed. Crude indications of the importance of grain to the Bavarian peasantry included the 3,000 metric tons sold by Heim's co-operative, whose 1,200 members were almost entirely small farmers, or the fact that, in eight of the twenty-four villages surveyed by the Bavarian government in 1895, 50 per cent of farms sold surplus grain on the market while only 21 per cent regularly purchased it.[98]

If the assumption that only a small number of peasants profited from greater protectionism perhaps requires more critical scrutiny, so too does the widely held view that peasant reliance on decisive political acts of economic subvention, such as higher tariffs, precluded adoption of more mundane measures to enhance the efficiency and competitiveness of their enterprises. Certainly more radical voices in the *Bauernbund* enjoyed a sympathetic hearing in the 1890s when claiming that practical reforms were futile without fundamental political initiatives. In the longer term, however, that emphasis on political solutions became more of a liability to the Peasants' League.[99] Another reason for the growth of the *Christliche Bauernvereine* was precisely their ability to supplement political action with comprehensive forms of practical assistance for the peasantry. That combination of agrarian populism and large-scale material aid to the small farmer is rightly associated with the name Georg Heim. It was largely on his initiative that the *Bauernvereine* introduced a wide range of financial, legal and technical services for its rapidly expanding membership, and that local functionaries acquired professional training and expertise. His entrepreneurial skills were crucial to the success of the

Association's Central Co-operative for the sale and purchase of agricultural products. Its turnover expanded almost fiftyfold between 1898 and 1913–14, by which time it had a reserve capital of 1.6 million Marks and a full-time staff of 270 at its Regensburg headquarters.[100] These activities also provided a solid institutional basis for Heim's successful political assault on the clerical and conservative notables within the Bavarian Centre Party.

The practical benefits and organizational backbone of the *Bauernvereine* gave the Centre Party a decisive advantage in the competition for the rural Catholic vote. As the economic outlook for the peasantry improved after the turn of the century, the *Bauernbund*'s failure to establish a coherent administrative and financial apparatus gravely impaired its electoral effectiveness. The League's increasing inactivity between elections contrasted unfavourably with the level of agitation sustained by the Peasants' Associations.[101] The latter, of course, had added support from the entrenched subculture of Catholic life, as well as the co-operation of younger clergymen intent on making their church more responsive to the socio-economic priorities of its parishioners. Priests did not monopolize the operations of the *Bauernvereine* to the extent often supposed, as closer investigation reveals, but they clearly represented an administrative resource not available to the Peasants' League.[102]

The electoral reverses and organizational incapacity of the *Bauernbund* also gave renewed encouragement to the Agrarian League, which, apart from its stronghold in the Palatinate, made little headway in Bavaria before 1900. Despite what one observer called its 'constant haranguing, incessant agitation, easy misrepresentation and Biedermeier-style reasoning', its influence remained confined to those districts where agrarian conservatism was already established, and to Protestant enclaves in Upper Franconia, where it attracted some 3,000 members by 1895.[103] Repeated attempts to extend into Catholic Bavaria foundered on the Agrarian League's identification with Prussia, militarism and the selfish interests of unprincipled Junkerdom. A measure of the difficulties it encountered in southern Bavaria was its growing reliance on Ludwig Wenng, a prominent anti-Semite in Munich, who saw the Agrarian League as the most appropriate vehicle for his style of politics.[104] From 1900 onwards, however, the League unfolded a more concerted campaign of meetings, propaganda and limited material assistance to substantiate its claim to be the standard-bearer of the entire *Mittelstand*. By diluting its political objectives in an economic programme which on issues like taxation and the *Bodenzinse* was specifically geared to peasant grievances in Bavaria, the Agrarian League was able to make some advances. Its radius of action, however, continued to be determined primarily by confessional factors.[105]

130

The steady expansion of the Agrarian League in Protestant Bavaria further weakened the *Bauernbund* cause in Franconia. Outflanked by the Catholic *Bauernvereine*, and then by the anti-liberal electoral pact between the radicalized Centre Party and the SPD, it was forced into a temporary and unprofitable accord with the Agrarian League. The resultant tensions within the *Bauernbund* were finally resolved by the formation of the liberal *Deutscher Bauernbund*, which occasioned an inevitable split in the Franconian sections of the Peasants' League. The Protestant and large landowning interests affiliated in 1911 to the Agrarian League, and the more democratically inclined majority joined the new liberal organization, whose membership in Bavaria reached 7,700 by 1912.[106] This allowed the Bavarian *Bauernbund*, which now operated only in the four southern provinces to resume its more radical anti-Centrist stance. It was thus in a position to capitalize on renewed popular discontent with a Centre Party in which conservative elements, intent on close co-operation with the government, had regained the upper hand since 1907. In by-elections in 1913 the Centre's vote was again being eroded, not least because, as one local newspaper commented, 'the time has passed when our voters are content with an annual appearance by their representative and say only "Ja" and "Amen"'.[107]

It has been one of the principal aims of this study to demonstrate why the politics of 'Ja' and 'Amen' no longer operated in many parts of the Bavarian countryside. They could not survive the significant and irreversible politicization of the peasantry which was such a characteristic feature of Wilhelmine Germany. Before 1890 peasants had largely been the passive objects of politics, restrained by deference and confessional loyalty from openly challenging the structure and priorities of liberal and Catholic *Honorationenpolitik*. That was to change irrevocably in the 1890s as mounting economic grievances and frustration with the clerical and bureaucratic elite kindled new forms of peasant protest, whose repercussions for political developments in both Bavaria and the Reich were more marked than is often supposed. The principal expression of rural dissent was the *Bauernbund*, a movement whose anti-elitist populism reflected a distinctive radicalization of peasant sentiment. In common with comparable organizations elsewhere in Germany the Peasants' League seriously embarrassed the established parties. Its agrarian emphasis, socio-political egalitarianism and demagogic rhetoric endangered in particular the Centre Party's previous monopoly of the Catholic vote in rural Bavaria. In due course factional disputes, ideological differences and an inability to establish an effective and co-ordinated administration tended to vitiate the threat posed by the *Bauernbund*. But that was not before the more radical elements in the Bavarian Centre Party, given new scope and leverage by rising peasant discontent, had begun the vital task of reconstructing the basis of their party's appeal to the rural voter. The ultimate success of that enterprise, which was crucial to the maintenance of the Centre's pivotal role in Wilhelmine politics, was due primarily to the alacrity with which the Catholic *Bauernvereine* incorporated the essential demands of the *Bauernbund*. Meanwhile the Peasants' League continued to serve as a reminder to the Centre Party not to default on its newly constituted commitment to peasant interests.

In the generation before 1914 Bavarian peasants became politically mobilized to a level inconceivable in the Bismarckian era. They joined organizations which were more durable and influential than any previous forms of rural association. These interest groups ensured that their members were acquainted with the most urgent political issues of the day.[108] Many rural constituencies were genuinely contested for the first time. Peasants voted in ever-increasing numbers in parliamentary elections for candidates whose selection was now rarely the sole preserve of unrepresentative notables. One should not, of course, overlook the extent to which deferential confessionalism or parochial perspectives continued to colour the outlook and behaviour of many small farmers. But even in this predominantly Catholic and less economically advanced part of Germany there are abundant indications that the peasantry had become very much a part of the nation's politics.

The evidence from Bavaria further suggests that one cannot reduce the politicization of the peasantry merely to a reflex protest against modernization which could only inhibit progressive political change. Certainly the appeal of all peasant organizations was imbued with an unrealistic agrarian romanticism directed against 'unfair' competition, the flow of migrants into the cities and the pernicious influence of the Jews. However, neither the anti-modern or anti-Semitic leitmotifs of the prevailing demagogy, nor the insistence on substantial subvention by the state, pre-empted the adoption of practical measures to improve the performance of the peasant farm. Membership of the Agricultural Association, and of other specialized institutions providing technical advice and assistance, expanded rapidly in the prewar decades. For example, the number of local credit associations grew from 448 to 2,745 between 1894 and 1913.[109] Furthermore, reactionary authoritarianism was not the sole or necessary beneficiary of a more politicized peasantry, as one is often led to expect. It was the democratic and egalitarian potential in peasant movements such as the *Bauernbund* which encouraged moderate socialists like Vollmar in their abortive campaign to make the SPD more responsive to the grievances of small farmers.[110] On the other hand, it is clear that the Centre Party's increasing need to articulate the socio-economic demands of its disproportionately influential petty bourgeois constituency was a major factor preventing its alignment in the Reich with progressive liberalism and Social Democracy.[111] In Bavaria, however, it was just such an electoral compact between the Social Democrats and a radicalized Centre Party which helped to extract electoral reform from an intransigent liberal ministry and paved the way for a greater degree of parliamentary accountability.[112] Such contrasting products of the rural protest of the 1890s serve as a warning not to treat peasant politics as a monolithic refuge of traditionalism. They suggest that the history of the German peasantry in the era of industrialization should be approached with the same sensitivity to subtle differentiations which is accorded automatically to the study of urban classes. Only then will we attain those deeper insights into the peasantry's political behaviour and consciousness which we so urgently need to advance our understanding of the course of recent German history.

Notes: Chapter 4

ABBREVIATIONS

AStAM	Allgemeines Staatsarchiv München (Bayerisches Hauptstaatsarchiv, Abteilung I, Allgemeines Staatsarchiv)
BdL	*Bund der Landwirte*
CEH	*Central European History*
CSSH	*Comparative Studies in Society and History*
GStAM	Geheimes Staatsarchiv München (Bayerisches Hauptstaatsarchiv, Abteillung II, Geheimes Staatsarchiv)
JCH	*Journal of Contemporary History*
JMH	*Journal of Modern History*
K.d.I.	Kammer des innern
M.Arb.	Arbeitsministerium
M.Inn.	Ministerium des Innern
M.L.	Landwirtschaftsministerium
Präs. Reg.	Präsidial-Registratur
R.A.	Regierungsakten
Reg.	Regierung
StAAg	Staatsarchiv Amberg
StABg	Staatsarchiv Bamberg
StAL	Staatsarchiv Landshut
StAM	Staatsarchiv München
StANg	Staatsarchiv Neuburg an der Donau
StAWg	Staatsarchiv Würzburg

1 H.-U. Wehler, *Das deutsche Kaiserreich 1871–1918* (Göttingen, 1973), 41–52. For contemporary awareness of this critical phase in Germany's development see K. D. Barkin, *The Controversy over German Industrialization 1890–1902* (Chicago, 1970).
2 *Vierteljahrsheft zur Statistik des deutschen Reiches*, Vol. 11, no. 3 (1902): 81–6.
3 In 1895 there were 2,254,765 farms between 2 and 50 hectares in size, occupying some 62 per cent of agriculture land. *Statistik des deutschen Reiches*, 112: 111. This category of farms embraced most of those who can reasonably be described as peasants, namely those for whom land husbandry was the sole or principal livelihood and for whom the

family farm constituted the basic unit of social and economic organization. For further discussion see E. R. Wolf, *Peasants* (Englewood Cliffs, N.J., 1966); T. Shanin (ed.), *Peasants and Peasant Societies* (Harmondsworth, 1971), 11–19.

4   T. Shanin, 'Peasantry as a political factor', in Shanin, *Peasants*, 256.

5   H. Rosenberg, *Grosse Depression und Bismarckzeit* (Berlin, 1967), 55–78.

6   D. F. Ferguson, 'Rural/urban relations and peasant radicalism: a preliminary statement', *CSSH* 18 (1976): 111–16; E. R. Wolf, *Peasant Wars of the Twentieth Century* (London, 1969), 279–94.

7   J. Flemming, *Landwirtschaftliche Interessen und Demokratie: Ländliche Gesellschaft, Agrarverbände und Staat 1890–1925* (Bonn, 1978), 1–4. Basic surveys include H.-J. Puhle, *Politische Agrarbewegungen in kapitalistischen Industriegesellschaften* (Göttingen, 1975), 28–112, and S. R. Tirrell, *German Agrarian Politics after Bismarck's Fall* (New York, 1951).

8   B. Moore, *Social Origins of Dictatorship and Democracy* (Harmondsworth, 1969), 453.

9   T. Judt, 'The rules of the game', *Historical Journal* 23 (1980): 182. Representative examples include Wolf, *Peasant Wars*; T. Skocpol, *States and Social Revolutions* (Cambridge, 1979); T. Shanin, *The Awkward Class* (Oxford, 1972); G. J. Gill, *Peasants and Government in the Russian Revolution* (New York, 1979); P. G. Eidelberg, *The Great Rumanian Peasant Revolt of 1907* (Leiden, 1974).

10   There is little to compare with E. Weber, *Peasants into Frenchmen: The Modernization of Rural France 1870–1914* (London, 1977); T. Judt, *Socialism in Provence* (Cambridge, 1979); T. Kaplan, *Anarchists of Andalusia 1868–1903* (Princeton, N. J., 1977); or, for Austria, E. Bruckmüller, *Landwirtschaftliche Organisation und gesellschaftliche Modernisierung* (Salzburg, 1977).

11   D. Blackbourn, *Class, Religion and Local Politics in Wilhelmine Germany: The Centre Party in Württemberg before 1914* (New Haven, Conn., 1980); D. S. White, *The Splintered Party: National Liberalism in Hessen and the Reich 1867–1918* (Cambridge, Mass., 1976); J. C. Hunt, *The People's Party in Württemberg and Southern Germany 1890–1914* (Stuttgart, 1975).

12   W. R. Lee, 'The German family: a critical survey of the current state of historical research', in R. J. Evans and W. R. Lee (eds.), *The German Family* (London, 1981), 19–50.

13   These works, as well as recent trends in the historiography of the Kaiserreich, are variously discussed in G. G. Iggers, *New Directions in European Historiography* (Middletown, Conn., 1975), 80–122; W. J. Mommsen, 'Gegenwärtige Tendenzen in der Geschichtsschreibung der Bundersrepublik', *Geschichte und Gesellschaft* 7 (1981): 149–88; J. Kocka, 'Theoretical approaches to social and economic history of modern Germany', *JMH* 47 (1975): 101–19; R. J. Evans (ed.), *Society and Politics in Wilhelmine Germany* (London, 1978), 11–39.

14   Puhle, *Agrarbewegungen*, 69ff.; H.-J. Puhle, 'Warum gibt es in Westeuropa keine Bauernparteien', in H. Gollwitzer (ed.), *Europäische Bauernparteien im 20. Jahrhundert* (Stuttgart, 1977), 603.

15   Puhle, *Agrarbewegungen*, 63–77; D. Gessner, 'Agrarian protectionism in the Weimar republic', *JCH* 12 (1977): 762–4. Indispensable for the Agrarian League is H.-J. Puhle, *Agrarische Interessenpolitik und preussischer Konservatismus im Wilhelminischen Reich 1893–1914* (Hanover, 1966).

16   This view is at its most explicit in A. Gerschenkron, *Bread and Democracy in Germany* (New York, 1966), 18–74. It is replicated in Rosenberg, *Grosse Depression*, 178–89; Wehler, *Kaiserreich*, 45–6; Barkin, *Controversy*, chs. 5 and 7; M. Kitchen, *The Political Economy of Germany 1815–1914* (London, 1978), 200–21; P. C. Witt, *Die Finanzpolitik des deutschen Reiches von 1903 bis 1913* (Lübeck and Hamburg, 1970), 63; E. Kehr, *Schlachtflottenbau und Parteipolitik 1894–1901* (Berlin, 1930), 253–70; Puhle, *Agrarische Interessenpolitik*, 235–54. The most important critiques of this view of protectionism are J. C. Hunt, 'Peasants, grain tariffs and meat quotas: Imperial German protectionism reexamined', *CEH* 7 (1974): 311–31, and R. G. Moeller, 'Peasants and tariffs in the Kaiserreich: how backward were the *Bauern*?', *Agricultural History* 55, no. 4 (1981): 370–84. See also T. Nipperdey, 'Organisierter Kapitalismus, Verbände und die Krise des Kaiserreiches', *Geschichte und Gesellschaft* 5 (1979): 422–5.

17 Blackbourn, *Class, Religion and Local Politics*, 236–8; Puhle, *Agrarische Interessenpolitik*, 83–140.
18 Shanin, 'Peasantry as a political factor', 253–5; E. J. Hobsbawm, 'Peasants and politics', *Journal of Peasant Studies* 1 (1973): 3–22; H. A. Landsberger, 'Peasant unrest: themes and variations', in H. A. Landsberger (ed.), *Rural Protest: Peasant Movements and Social Change* (London, 1974), 1–64.
19 The emergence of this stereotype is charted by J. G. Gagliardo, *From Pariah to Patriot: The Changing Image of the German Peasant* (Lexington, Ky., 1969). See also J. Ziche, 'Kritik der deutschen Bauerntumsideologie', *Sociologia Ruralis* 8 (1968): 105–41.
20 P. Zimmermann, *Der Bauernroman* (Stuttgart, 1975), 67–83; W. Emmerich, *Zur Kritik der Volkstumsideologie* (Frankfurt, 1971); W. Jacobeit, '"Traditionelle" Verhaltensweisen und konservative Ideologie', in H. Bausinger and W. Brückner (eds.), *Kontinuität? Geschichtlichkeit und Dauer als volkskundliches Problem* (Berlin, 1969), 67–75; W. Jacobeit, and H.-H. Müller, 'Agrargeschichte und Volkskunde', *Jahrbuch für Wirtschaftsgeschichte*, 1977, pp. 141–55.
21 This approach is exemplified by H. Haushofer, *Die deutsche Landwirtschaft im technischen Zeitalter* (Stuttgart, 1963). See the trenchant criticism of this tradition by H. Rosenberg, *Probleme der deutschen Sozialgeschichte* (Frankfurt, 1969), esp. 111–23.
22 Typical are G. Franz (ed.), *Bauernschaft und Bauernstand* (Limburg, 1970); F. Jacobs, *Deutsche Bauernführer* (Düsseldorf, 1958); F. Jacobs, *Von Schorlemer zur Grünen Front* (Düsseldorf, 1957).
23 G. Lewis, 'The peasantry, rural change and conservative agrarianism: Lower Austria at the turn of the century', *Past and Present* 81 (1978): 140. The need for caution in this area is admirably explained by D. Blackbourn, 'The *Mittlestand* in German society and politics 1871–1914', *Social History* 4 (1977): 409–33.
24 The Danish example is cited, among others, by Gerschenkron, *Bread and Democracy*, 38–9, and Gessner, 'Agrarian protectionism', 763. This tends to obscure the remarkable intensification of production which characterized Imperial German agricultural development. See particularly J. A. Perkins, 'The agricultural revolution in Germany 1850–1914', *Journal of European Economic History* 10 (1981): 75; G. Helling, 'Berechnung eines Index der Agrarproduktion in Deutschland im 19. Jahrhundert', *Jahrbuch für Wirtschaftsgeschichte*, 1965, pp. 125–51. See also D. Warriner, *The Economics of Peasant Farming* (London, 1964), 6–7, 140.
25 D. Blackbourn, *Class, Religion and Local Politics*, esp. 7–18; G. Eley, *Reshaping the German Right: Radical Nationalism and Political Change after Bismarck* (New Haven, Conn., 1980), esp. 9–40; G. Eley, 'The Wilhelmine right: how it changed', in Evans, *Society and Politics*, 116–21; I. Farr, 'Populism in the countryside: the Peasant Leagues in Bavaria in the 1890s', in ibid., 136–59. There has been a regrettable tendency for the ensuing debate to become oversimplified into one of 'manipulation' against 'self-activation' of the Wilhelmine peasantry – a misleading dichotomy, as this essay will attempt to demonstrate.
26 The best analysis is K. Möckl, *Die Prinzregentenzeit: Gesellschaft und Politik während der Ära des Prinzregenten Luitpold in Bayern* (Munich, 1972). See also D. Albrecht, 'Von der Reichsgründung bis zum Ende des ersten Weltkrieges (1871–1918)', in M. Spindler (ed.), *Handbuch der bayerischen Geschichte*, Vol. 4/I (Munich, 1975), 282–357.
27 G. Blondel, *Etudes sur le population rurale d'Allemagne* (Paris, 1897), 29.
28 65 per cent of Bavarian farms in 1895 were between 2 and 100 hectares in size, compared to 41·4 per cent in Germany as a whole. Full details on farm size, ownership and on the agricultural labour force are in *Beiträge zur Statistik des Königreichs Bayern* 81: 13–91.
29 Wolf, *Peasant Wars*, 291–2; Ferguson, 'Rural/urban relations', 114–15; T. Judt, 'The origins of rural socialism in Europe: economic change and the Provençal peasantry 1870–1914', *Social History* 1 (1976): 47–8, 55–65.
30 See the reports in AStAM, M.Inn., 66316, 73483; StAL, 168/5, 1072; StAM, R.A., 57826; StAAg, Reg., K.d.I. (1949), 13869. See also G. Windell, *The Catholics and German Unity* (Minneapolis, Minn., 1965), and T. Schieder, *Die kleindeutsche Partei in Bayern in den Kämpfen um die nationale Einheit 1863–1871* (Munich, 1936).
31 Windell, *Catholics*, 183; Schieder, *Die kleindeutsche Partei*, 203; AStAM, M.Inn., 66316.

32 StAAg, Reg., K.d.I. (1949), 13869.
33 AStAM, M.Inn., 38982, 38983, 66316.
34 AStAM, M.Inn., 38989, 66316, 73483; StAM, R.A., 57824, 57826.
35 H. Böhme, *Deutschlands Weg zur Grossmacht* (Cologne, 1966), 555–6; K. Hardach, *Die Bedeutung wirtschaftlicher Faktoren bei der Wiedereinführung der Eisen- und Getreidezölle in Deutschland 1879* (Berlin, 1967), 130–6.
36 Details of Thüngen's agitation are in AStAM, M. Inn., 38982–4, 38987, 38989, 66316; StAWg, Reg. 1943/5, 486; StANg, R.A., 9618; StABg, K 3, Präs. Reg., 850.
37 AStAM, M.Inn, 47329. On Lutz and Beckh see Möckl, *Prinzregentenzeit*, 449, and A. Schlögl, *Bayerische Agrargeschichte* (Munich, 1954), 857–9.
38 Möckl, *Prinzregentenzeit*, 200.
39 E. Hohenegg, *Die Landesorganisation des landwirtschaftlichen Genossenschaftswesens in Bayern* (Munich, 1927), 6–9.
40 StAM, Polizeidirektion, 4689; Schlögl, *Bayerische Agrargeschichte*, 559–60; A. Hundhammer, *Die landwirtschaftliche Berufsvertretung in Bayern* (Munich, 1926), 7–14; *Die Landwirtschaft in Bayern: Denkschrift nach amtlichen Quellen bearbeitet* (Munich, 1890), 782–7.
41 *Illustrierte bayerische Bauernzeitung*, 1 February 1880.
42 *Der landwirtschaftliche Verein in Bayern und die 'Bureaukratie'* (Munich, 1882), 1.
43 *Der fränkische Bauer*, 30 November 1894.
44 H. Reif, *Westfälischer Adel 1770–1860* (Göttingen, 1979), 429–31; Jacobs, *Von Schorlemer*, 7–26; K. Müller, 'Zentrumspartei und agrarische Bewegung im Rheinland 1882–1903', in K. Repgen and S. Skalweit (eds.), *Spiegel der Geschichte: Festgabe für Max Braubach zum 10. April 1964* (Münster, 1964), 829–31.
45 P. W. Massing, *Rehearsal for Destruction: A Study of Political Antisemitism in Imperial Germany* (New York, 1949), 101.
46 R. S. Levy, *The Downfall of the Anti-Semitic Political Parties in Imperial Germany* (New Haven, Conn., 1975), 59.
47 *Bayerns Entwicklung nach den Ergebnissen der amtlichen Statistik seit 1840* (Munich, 1915), 133. See also D. Thränhardt, *Wahlen und politische Strukturen in Bayern 1848–1953* (Düsseldorf, 1973).
48 Thränhardt, *Wahlen*, 71–8; K. Bachmann, *Die Volksbewegung 1848–9 im Allgäu und ihre Vorläufer* (Erlangen, 1954), 46–57.
49 Möckl, *Prinzregentenzeit* 30, 48–86; Albrecht, 'Von der Reichsgründung', 329; J. J. Sheehan, *German Liberalism in the Nineteenth Century* (Chicago, 1978), 126–7, 138, 209.
50 K. Bachem, *Vorgeschichte, Geschichte und Politik der deutschen Zentrumspartei*, vol. 4 (Cologne, 1928), 346.
51 Möckl, *Prinzregentenzeit*, 176, 200–1, 222, 339–47; H.-M. Körner, *Staat und Kirche in Bayern 1886–1918* (Mainz, 1977), 28–63.
52 U. Mittmann, *Fraktion und Partei: Ein Vergleich von Zentrum und Sozialdemokratie im Kaiserreich* (Düsseldorf, 1976), 157–8; T. Nipperdey, *Die Organisation der deutschen Parteien vor 1918* (Düsseldorf, 1961), 268–80.
53 AStAM, M.Inn., 38981.
54 Nipperdey, *Organisation*, 37. See reports of clerical activity in AStAM, M.Inn., 47329, and StAWg, Reg. 1943/5, 9141.
55 J. Schauff, *Die deutschen Katholiken und die Zentrumspartei* (Cologne, 1928), 84ff.; *Bayerns Entwicklung*, 132.
56 According to government figures, the number of Catholic political associations outside the major Bavarian cities remained static between 1883 and 1891. AStAM, M.Inn., 38984, 46133, 66320.
57 *Bayerns Entwicklung*, 72; *Die Massnahmen auf dem Gebiet der landwirtschaftlichen Verwaltung in Bayern 1890–1897* (Munich, 1897), 68.
58 AStAM, M.Inn, 66321; StAL, 168/5, 960; StABg, K 3, Präs. Reg., 748; StAWg, Reg. 1943/5, 419, 422, 427, 3093; Tirrell, *German Agrarian Politics*, 194–8.
59 The following is based on *Die Landwirtschaft in Bayern; Die Landwirtschaft im Regierungsbezirk Oberbayern* (Munich, 1885); *Untersuchung der wirtschaftlichen Verhältnisse in 24 Gemeinden des Königreichs Bayern* (Munich, 1895); *Bäuerliche Zustände in Deutschland, Schriften des Vereins für Sozialpolitik*, Vols. 22–4 (Leipzig, 1883), esp. 24: 113–206;

A. Kalchgruber, *Untersuchungen über wirtschaftliche speziell bäuerliche Verhältnisse in Alt-bayern* (Munich, 1885); AStAM, M.L., 4710; StAM, R.A., 61428; StAL, 168/5, 965; StAAg, Reg., K.d.I., 14506; StAWg, Reg. 1943/5, 2966; StABg, K 3, Präs. Reg., 613, 748, and K 3, F V a, 128.

60 *Bayerns Entwicklung* 68; *Zeitschrift des königlichen bayerischen statistischen Bureaus* 38 (1906): 326 and 45 (1913): 444–51. See also G. Ernst, *Die ländlichen Arbeitsverhältnisse im rechtsrheinischen Bayern* (Regensburg, 1907).

61 There were 31,772 compulsory sales of farms in Bavaria between 1880 and 1902.

62 GStAM, Gesandtschaft Berlin, 1063; StAL, 168/5, 1111; J. K. Zeender, *The German Center Party 1890–1906* (Philadelphia, Pa., 1976), 29–30.

63 Möckl, *Prinzregentenzeit*, 439–43; AStAM, M.Inn., 47332.

64 StANg, R.A., 9624. See also *Neue Freie Volkszeitung*, 13 January 1893.

65 Separate Leagues were formed in 1893 in Lower Bavaria, Upper Bavaria and Franconia and in 1894 in Swabia. Attempts at a formal union in 1895 proved fruitless. After a further effort to unite the various groupings in 1900 the differences between the League in Franconia and those in southern Bavaria became even more apparent. See the text for further details. The shifting alliances and leadership conflicts in the *Bauernbund* are overstressed in the partial account of A. Hundhammer, *Geschichte des bayerischen Bauernbundes* (Munich, 1924). The influence of Thüngen and large Franconian land-owners is exaggerated by Puhle, *Agrarbewegungen*, 62–3, and by H. Gottwald and W. Fritsch, 'Bayerischer Bauernbund 1895–1933', in D. Fricke (ed.), *Die bürgerlichen Parteien in Deutschland*, Vol. 1 (Leipzig, 1968), 66–78.

66 *Zeitschrift* 25 (1893): 76–90.

67 ibid., 99–123.

68 *Zeitschrift* 30 (1898): 118–23.

69 Puhle, *Agrarbewegungen*, 63; H. Haushofer, 'Der bayerische Bauernbund (1893–1933)', in Gollwitzer, *Europäische Bauernparteien*, 562–86. More perceptive is Möckl, *Prinzregentenzeit*, 446–77.

70 AStAM, M.Inn., 47335.

71 Gottwald and Fritsch, 'Bauernbund', 66.

72 Puhle, *Agrarische Interessenpolitik*, 67.

73 Blackbourn, *Class, Religion and Local Politics*, 18.

74 See also J. C. Hunt, 'The "egalitarianism" of the right: the Agrarian League in south-west Germany 1893–1914', *JCH* 10 (1975): 523.

75 For full details of programmes see StAM, R.A., 57824–5; StAL, 168/5, 1071; Hund-hammer, *Geschichte*, 219–31.

76 StAM, R.A., 60241; AStAM, M.Arb., 1239; A. Schmurbus, *Arbeit und Sozialordnung in Bayern vor dem ersten Weltkrieg* (Munich, 1969), 107; *Stenographische Berichte der Kammer der Abgeordneten*, 1893–4, 1; 145.

77 *Die Massnahmen auf dem Gebiet der landwirtschaftlichen Verwaltung in Bayern 1897–1903* (Munich, 1903), 304–5.

78 S. Hausmann, *Die Grundentlastung in Bayern* (Strasburg, 1892), 79–164; E. Jäger, *Kurze Geschichte des bayerischen Bauernstandes mit besonderer Rücksicht auf die Grundentlastung in Bayern* (Speyer, 1898), 46–58; K. Haff, *Die Bauernbefreiung und der Stand des Bodenzins-rechtes in Bayern* (Leipzig, 1910); A. Knapp, 'Das Zentrum in Bayern 1893–1912' (diss., Munich, 1973), 247–67; StAL, 168/5, 1113; *Bayerischer Bauernbund*, 9 January 1895.

79 StAL, 168/5, 1112.

80 Apart from Thüngen's programme see the proposals in G. Ratzinger, *Die Erhaltung des Bauernstandes* (Freiburg, 1883).

81 StAL, 168/5, 1071 and 1111; *Augsburger Allgemeine Zeitung*, 22 March 1893; *Neue Freie Volkszeitung*, 3 March 1893 and 14 July 1894.

82 StAL, 168/5, 971.

83 AStAM, M.Inn., 73455; StAAg, Reg., K.d.I. (1949), 5087; StANg, R.A., 9625–6; StAL, 168/5, 1111. For further discussion see I. Farr, 'From anti-Catholicism to anti-clericalism: Catholic politics and the peasantry in Bavaria 1860–1900', *European Studies Review* 13, no. 2 (1983): 249–68.

84 Bibliographical details are in AStAM, M.Inn., 73455 and StAL, 168/5, 1071. On

137

Memminger see also AStAM, M.Inn., 65689; StAWg, Reg. 1943/5, 538; on Sigl see
E. Schosser, *Presse und Landtag in Bayern von 1850 bis 1918* (Munich, 1968), passim;
StAM, R.A., 40813.

85 Haushofer, 'Bauernbund', 570. See, for example, the composition of local committees in Upper Bavaria detailed in StAM, R.A., 57791. For a penetrating analysis of
this and many other points in this essay I am deeply indebted to the paper by D. Blackbourn, 'Peasants and politics in Germany, 1871–1914', *European Studies Quarterly* 14
(1984): 47–75.

86 Full details are in *Die Massnahmen 1890–1897* and *Die Massnahmen 1897–1903*.

87 For a perceptive retrospective see *Allgemeine Zeitung*, 4 June 1910.

88 Tirrell, *Agrarian Politics*, 226–95; Bachem, *Zentrumspartei*, 5: 278–91, 351, 479–80;
Nipperdey, *Organisation*, 290–1; Blackbourn, *Class, Religion and Local Politics*, 45–51.

89 Knapp, *Zentrum*, 24–34, 55–7; Nipperdey, *Organisation*, 227, 228; Mittmann, *Fraktion
und Partei*, 168–70.

90 See the comments in Puhle, *Agrarbewegungen*, 58–60.

91 *Der fränkische Bauer*, 19 August 1898 and 2 November 1907. On the eve of the First
World War membership stood at 158,000. Provincial associations were formed in
1893 in Lower Bavaria and Lower Franconia, in 1894 in Swabia and Upper Franconia,
in 1895 in the Upper Palatinate, and in Central Franconia and Upper Bavaria in 1897.
They were formally united in October 1898 and their activities co-ordinated by a
central administrative office. See G. Heim (ed.), *Der bayerische Bauernverein in Ver-
gangenheit, Gegenwart und Zukunft* (Ansbach, 1906).

92 Full details in StAM, R.A., 57793; *Der fränkische Bauer*, 4 March 1898. For the views
of local officials see especially StAL, 168/5, 828.

93 *Bayerisches Bauernblatt*, 18 May 1909; *Neue Bayerische Landeszeitung*, 20 November
1894.

94 *Der niederbayerische Bauer*, 1 July 1897; *Neue Bayerische Landeszeitung*, 25 August 1894;
Der fränkische Bauer, 11 June 1897; *Der Bauer*, 2 April 1898.

95 AStAM, M.Inn., 73728.

96 L. Brentano, *Die deutschen Getreidezölle* (Stuttgart, 1910), 16–17. Brentano's assumptions are shared by Gerschenkron, *Bread and Democracy*, 26; Wehler, *Kaiserreich*, 55,
and many others.

97 L. Brentano, *Die Getreidezölle als Mittel gegen die Not der Landwirte* (Berlin, 1903), 26;
*Preisbewegung landwirtschaftlicher Güter in einigen Teilen Bayerns während der Jahre 1900
bis 1910, Schriften des Vereins für Sozialpolitik*, Vol. 148 (Berlin, 1914), passim.

98 *Der Bauer*, 6 April 1901; *Untersuchung der wirtschaftlichen Verhältnisse*, passim. The need
for more systematic explanations of the attitudes of small farmers towards tariff protection is rightly stressed by Hunt, 'Grain tariffs', 319–26; Flemming, *Landwirtschaftliche Interessen*, 28; H.-J. Puhle, 'Aspekte der Agrarpolitik im "Organisierten Kapitalismus": Fragen und Probleme vergleichender Forschung', in H.-U. Wehler (ed.),
Sozialgeschichte Heute (Göttingen, 1974), 554.

99 W. Mattes, *Die bayerischen Bauernräte* (Stuttgart, 1921), 30–9; F. X. Zahnbrecher,
'Landwirtschaftliche Vereine und Landwirtschaftskammern in Bayern' (diss.,
Munich, 1907), 29.

100 H. Renner, *Georg Heim: Der Bauerndoktor* (Munich, 1960), 57; *Der fränkische Bauer*, 1
April 1905; *Bayerisches Bauernblatt*, 9 February 1909.

101 *Niederbayerischer Anzeiger*, 5 February 1907.

102 Only 6 of 150 known local organizers of the *Bauernverein* in Lower Bavaria were
priests. *Der niederbayerische Bauer*, 1 December 1897 and 15 March 1898. For similar
trends elsewhere see StAM, R.A., 57791; *Der Bauer*, 19 February 1898; *Der oberfränkis-
che Bauer*, 15 March 1901.

103 StABg, K 3, 831xii.

104 StAM, R.A., 57825; Puhle, *Agrarische Interessenpolitik*, 134. See also StANg, R.A.,
9626–7; StAL, 168/5, 1114; StAAg, Reg., K.d.I., 13750, 14112.

105 K. Heller, 'Der Bund der Landwirte bzw. Landbund und seine Politik mit besonderer
Berücksichtigung der fränkischen Verhältnisse' (diss., Würzburg, 1936), 8–13, 36–42;
Bund der Landwirte (Königreich Bayern), 15 January 1905.

106 *Deutscher Bauernbund (Abteilung Bayern)*, 9 December 1911.

107 *Deggendorfer Donaubote*, 15 June 1913, commenting on a *Bauernbund* victory in Mallersdorf (Lower Bavaria).
108 The combined circulation of the *Bauernverein*'s two most important weeklies exceeded 100,000 by 1911. *Der fränkische Bauer*, 6 January 1912; *Bayerisches Bauernblatt*, 3 January 1911.
109 Hohenegg, *Landesorganisation*, 26–31.
110 G. von Vollmar, *Bauernfrage und Sozialdemokratie in Bayern 1893–1896* (Nuremberg, 1896). For fuller discussion see H. G. Lehmann, *Die Agrarfrage in der Theorie und Praxis der deutschen und internationalen Sozialdemokratie* (Tübingen, 1970); W. H. Maehl, 'German Social Democratic agrarian policy 1890–1895 reconsidered', *CEH* 13, no. 2 (1980): 121–57; A. Hussain and K. Tribe, *Marxism and the Agrarian Question*, Vol. 1 (London, 1981).
111 Blackbourn, *Class, Religion and Local Politics*, 233–5; D. Blackbourn, 'The problem of democratization: German Catholics and the role of the Centre Party', in Evans, *Society and Politics*, 160–85.
112 Möckl, *Prinzregentenzeit*, 465–534. Constitutional restraints on the *Landtag* limited the effect of the wider suffrage.

5 Economic Dimensions of Peasant Protest in the Transition from Kaiserreich to Weimar

ROBERT G. MOELLER

A social history of Germany in the post-First World War inflation must ultimately offer a balance-sheet which identifies winners and losers.[1] Historians who have ventured such calculations have typically counted peasant farmers among those who gained or at least suffered little relative to other social groups. Although during the war, agricultural producers like other Germans sustained serious losses and generally saw their standard of living decline, historians emphasize that peasant farmers none the less always controlled one vital resource – food. Unlike many urban dwellers, at least peasants always had enough to eat. In addition, the serious reductions in the food supply after 1914 caused by declines in domestic production and the Allied blockade of food imports created a constant upward pressure on prices which benefited producers. Attempts to control price increases through a system of maximum prices failed. In the alternative 'sub-economy', the flourishing black market, the sellers of agricultural products enjoyed a decided advantage over the buyers.

During the postwar inflation, historians stress, agricultural producers enjoyed high incomes which permitted them to recoup their wartime losses. The Mark depreciated more rapidly abroad than at home, keeping domestic prices below world market levels and serving as a barrier to food imports. The agricultural sector, still confronted by a demand which outstripped available supplies, found buyers for everything it could produce. Price controls were largely eliminated by the spring of 1921, and agricultural producers demanded and received the high prices that the market could bear under conditions of continued scarcity. After the suspension of essential controls, agricultural prices rose more rapidly than those for industrial goods, and this opening of the 'price scissors' in agriculture's favour only added to the profits of peasant producers.[2]

According to the standard interpretation, one particularly important inflationary gain for agricultural producers still must be added to this catalogue. Like all property-owning groups encumbered with mortgages before the war, agricultural producers could pay off long-term debts with inflated currency, a gain tantamount to the virtual elimination of agriculture's prewar debt burden. Interest payments on new loans were hardly significant, indeed might be negative, given the rate of inflation. In addition, as long as the value of the Mark continued to decline, taxes could also be paid in worthless paper money.[3] Thus, on balance and certainly relative to other social groups, peasant farmers fared better than most in the war and gained much from the inflation.

In 1923 Karl Wieskotten, a peasant farmer who lived on the outskirts of the Ruhr city, Gelsenkirchen, did not benefit from the hindsight of the economic historians who have studied the German inflation and who have assessed agriculture's fate so positively. As the hyperinflation gripped Germany, he certainly did not see himself in such rosy or relative terms. In fact, Wieskotten was so troubled by his personal circumstances that on a day in late January, he took the time to do something which undoubtedly would not otherwise have been part of his normal routine: he wrote a letter to his representative in the Prussian parliament, Franz von Papen, a conservative young Westphalian aristocrat, who was trying to establish his career as a defender of agrarian interests in the right-wing of the Catholic Centre Party.

Wieskotten rented a farm of about 30 hectares from a local mining company. Before the war, he had served the company for seven years as a coach-driver, advancing with his employer's loan of a horse to run his own carting business. His faithful service had also been rewarded with the opportunity to rent some property from the company. The low rent he paid, however, was not merely a reflection of the firm's altruism. Located in the immediate vicinity of the mine and thus constantly subject to a fall-out of industrial soot and smoke, the farm had been in sad shape when Wieskotten took it over.

Wieskotten had only just begun to undertake measures to improve the soil fertility on his farm when the war interrupted his efforts. The war also robbed him of key members of his labour force – three sons, one of whom had fallen in battle by the end of 1914. Sons were not the only losses occasioned by the war, and the military had requisitioned eight of the horses employed in Wieskotten's carting business. Still, throughout the war he had managed to maintain the farm, and by 1922, with the supplementary income from his revived hauling service in which he used seven new horses, he could support twelve people in his household, including his family and contractually bound workers.[4]

Despite his apparent success at recouping his wartime losses during the early postwar years, Wieskotten still felt that he had reason to complain. His recent notification that he owed the Prussian government 680,840

Marks had prompted his appeal to Papen. The money represented a fine imposed on Wieskotten by local authorities in Gelsenkirchen for his failure to deliver 8½ tons of bread grains from the 12·5 hectares he planted in cereals. The quota was part of a programme of grain requisitions instituted to replace the system of direct confiscations imposed under the state-controlled war economy and maintained into the early postwar period. On-going shortages of bread grains convinced national officials that a complete suspension of controls was impossible. Under the modified system, producers were expected to deliver only a set amount at fixed prices and were free to sell any surplus on the open market or to use it for their own needs. Wieskotten had not met his mandated quotas. He complained that given the poor quality of his soil, the assessment imposed on him was unrealistically high, over 300 pounds per morgen (approx. a quarter of a hectare), much more than the 200 pounds he had seen announced in the newspapers. As he assured Papen, it was certainly more than that expected of his neighbours, some of whom had been exempted completely.

Wieskotten had not turned to Papen before considering other options. The appeal to a national political figure was only the latest chapter in a long story of frustration and rejected petitions to local authorities. Moreover, it was not the first time that Wieskotten had protested his treatment under the controlled economy nor that he had appealed for redress of his grievances over perceived mistreatment by state authorities. A year earlier, he had written to the Prussian Minister of Agriculture to protest the confiscation of substantial reserves of bread grains and feeds, also due under the provisions of the grain levy system. His petition was rejected because of his failure to meet the appointed deadline for such appeals.[5] Tardiness had been held against him again in 1923, but obviously he hoped that Papen's intervention might succeed where his own appeals had failed. He was at great pains to convince Papen of the legitimacy of his claims, detailing his record of hard work and industry, and with a melodramatic flourish, he expressed his fears that 'Now possibly I will be brought to the poor house by these conditions'.[6]

Wieskotten's protest came at the height of the postwar German inflation. The record of his complaint is unusual in its completeness and few such detailed accounts of individual protest have survived in the archival record.[7] However, Wieskotten was hardly alone in counting himself among the losers in the inflation, and his discontent was shared by literally thousands of other agricultural producers who vehemently protested the grain levy system not with petitions but with outright refusals to meet mandatory quotas. How can we reconcile the positive picture of agriculture's fate in the inflation presented in the historical literature with the peasant protest which resounded in the German countryside in late 1922 and 1923? I will argue that by 1923, even relative winners could see themselves as losers. The source of perceived agrarian losses could be traced back to 1914, the suspension of a normally functioning market and the massive intervention of the state into the decisions of agricultural producers. By 1923 the source and object of peasant protest – the disruptive impact of the controlled economy, first initiated in 1914 – had still not been eliminated. It was this element of continuity which for peasant producers most clearly unified the period between the start of the First World War and the autumn of 1923 when the stabilization of the currency finally ended the hyperinflation.

This essay describes the impact of this decade on the economic behaviour of west German peasant producers and outlines the nature of their discontent, drawing heavily on evidence from the west German provinces of the Rhineland and Westphalia.[8] There are obviously limits to the generalizations which can be drawn from such a regional study. However, Jonathan Osmond's work on the Bavarian case as well as my own research in national archives which underlies my regional study strongly suggest that my findings for the Rhineland and Westphalian are far from unique. The forms of political protest among peasant producers in the early years of Weimar differed greatly from one region to the next, as Osmond's contribution clearly illustrates. The economic sources of peasant protest, however, were common to agricultural producers throughout Germany.[9]

For agricultural producers, the decade of war and inflation was characterized by a sustained atmosphere of political and economic instability, uncertainty and unpredictability. This contrasted sharply with the twenty years preceding the war in which the agricultural sector had not only enjoyed economic prosperity, based on steadily rising prices and expanding domestic markets, but had also been a privileged supporter of the conservative German government. The decade of war and inflation profoundly changed this situation. The bases of economic prosperity collapsed, and agriculture looked on as its interest were subordinated to those of workers and industrialists, believed to be more essential to the war effort and, once the war had ended, to the process of postwar reconstruction. Moreover, the end of ten years of war and inflation did not bring a return to the *status quo ante bellum*. The late 1920s were years of depression and crisis for the agricultural sector, and there was no return to the pre-1914 bases of prosperity. By 1933, for agricultural producers, it seemed that the prosperous pre-1914 years had been followed by almost twenty years of instability and crisis.

The search for a return to stability ended in peasant support for and acceptance of the economic solutions to their problems promised by a National Socialist regime. Rhenish and Westphalian peasants were not among those who earned dubious distinction as early supporters of the National Socialist movement, and for the most part, they continued to cast their votes for the representative of political Catholicism in Germany, the Centre Party, until the Nazis came to power. Still, they were never supporters of the Weimar Republic nor of those elements within the Centre Party which were sympathetic to the Republic and open to alliances with other parties who shared those sympathies. I will not address these political developments directly in this essay, and they are discussed in this volume in the contributions of Jonathan Osmond and Larry Jones. None the less, they remain clearly in the background of my analysis, and my purpose is to outline the economic dimensions within which peasant political discontent in the 1920s can more readily be understood.

The Bases of Prewar Prosperity

What was the nature of the pre-1914 economy which by the late 1920s seemed to peasants as distant as it was desirable? For peasant farmers in the Rhineland and Westphalia and in many other parts of Germany, the years from the late 1890s until the eve of the war represented a period of expansion and prosperity. Peasants in the imperial period are perhaps best known for their loud and incessant clamouring for the reintroduction of tariff protection, reduced in the 1890s under Bismarck's successor, Leo von Caprivi.[10] It was this action by Caprivi which had led to the greatly intensified agitation of agricultural interest groups in the Rhineland and Westphalia as they joined the east Elbian-dominated Agrarian League in chastising the government for abandoning the interests of agriculture.[11]

According to most interpretations, peasant support for tariffs was an irrational response to the 'Great Depression', the years of secular price decline which began in the early 1870s and continued for more than two decades. Protection was also a reaction against the threat of low-cost producers in the United States whose grain was reaching Germany cheaply by means of an improved international transportation system. Critics of tariffs charged that protection was a short-term response which impeded the adjustment of German agriculture to altered circumstances. They contended that protection increased the prices of imported feeds used by livestock farmers, and in addition, by raising bread prices, decreased the disposable income of consumers which could otherwise have been used to purchase the high-quality agricultural goods produced on peasant farms, particularly dairy and livestock products. Liberal and socialist opponents of tariffs in the Kaiserreich and liberal and socialist historians ever since have thus depicted peasants as refusing to adjust their production to the realities of the market, hiding instead behind tariff walls and shifting the costs for their intransigence to urban consumers.[12]

To be sure, tariffs instituted price subsidies for agricultural producers borne by consumers, but peasant acceptance of tariffs was not a measure of peasant resistance to economic change or the absence of clearly perceived self-interest.[13] Although west German peasants had never been as exclusively dependent on income from grains as estate-owners east of the Elbe, they marketed some grain, and could hardly object to price subsidies paid by consumers. Moreover, protection was endorsed as part of a policy mix which included minimal tariffs on imported livestock feeds. Of even greater importance to west German livestock farmers were the strict veterinary codes on imported livestock which followed the introduction of tariffs on grains, isolating west German markets from imports of Danish and Dutch pork and beef, more immediate threats to west German peasant farmers than the grain grown on the plains of the American midwest.[14]

Not only was the tariff system thus consistent with the economic concerns of west German peasants; in addition, it did not inhibit the ability of peasant farmers to adapt their production to the realities of expanding urban markets in other ways. Indeed, by 1914 west German peasants had proven themselves to be fully capable of responding to and benefiting from the growth of those cities which anti-urban agrarian rhetoric depicted in such threatening terms.[15] These changes in the organization of production reflected a clear adjustment to a capitalist market but did not require drastic departures from well-established patterns.

Production in these regions was typically organized around a form of mixed-farming, a variant of the three-field crop rotation, that hallmark of the agricultural revolution which was a familiar development throughout Western Europe by the end of the eighteenth century. This organizational scheme had originally permitted the expansion of cereal production Rather than leaving one-third of all land to lie fallow annually, essential under the three-field rotation to prevent soil exhaustion, peasant farmers planted that third either in legumes or root crops. This not only resulted in an increased winter feed supply for livestock, but in addition had beneficial effects on the soil because of the nitrogen-fixing qualities of many legumes and the care and increased fertilization given to root crops. Stall-feeding of livestock also permitted easy collection of manure, which could be used to fertilize arable land more efficiently. Fields planted in rotation in cereals thus yielded improved harvests. This system of production also reduced dependence on large inputs of seasonal wage labour, in scare supply in areas where the competition with industrial firms for workers was so great. Diversification of production permitted full employment of workers throughout the year and justified and allowed the full exploitation of the farm family and small numbers of contractually bound workers, often employed on a peasant farm and hired for an entire year.[16]

As long as grain prices continued to increase, as they did steadily into the 1870s, the primary function of cattle was as the provider of manure, literally a 'manure machine' (*Mistmaschine*) as contemporaries put it. As grain prices fell under pressure from international competition after the mid-1870s, one possible response was to lobby for tariffs. Another longer-term solution was to concentrate on other products within the mixed farming system for which prices either remained stable or moved upwards relative to grain prices, namely, dairy and livestock products. West German peasants aggressively pursued both alternatives.

Grains could still find their way to market, and protection only enhanced the attractiveness of a continued commitment to cereals, but for many peasant farmers, grains ceased to be a principal source of income. Grains which no longer reached the market were employed on the farm as livestock feed. Producers simply covered increased feed needs from their own production rather than turning to the market, and such self-sufficiency in basic feed production was prescribed as essential by agricultural economists. Grains could also be sold at protected prices to cover the costs of those purchased feeds not burdened with high tariffs – corn and barley, as well as protein supplements.

Increased concentration on livestock farming did not necessitate any major reorganization of production. It simply meant a shift in emphasis within those patterns already well established. Certainly after the middle of the 1890s, there was little incentive to abandon old patterns. The downward trend in prices for agricultural products was reversed, and with the exception of temporary setbacks at the turn of the century, prices for both grains and livestock products continued to increase steadily right up until 1914. The general improvement in the international economy coupled with the ever-increasing demand for agricultural products in expanding urban centres meant that in many parts of Germany and certainly in the vicinity of the Ruhr, peasants confronted a market that absorbed virtually everything they could produce.[17]

Rising product prices were not the only index of prewar prosperity. Data collected in an extensive survey conducted by the Prussian government in 1902 indicated that Rhenish and Westphalian farmers did not suffer from excessive indebtedness. The survey concluded that in the Rhineland, only 5 per cent of all agricultural producers were seriously in debt, and the class of largeholding estate-owners was overrepresented in this group. The same was true for Westphalia where the number of those considered to be in difficulty was only slightly higher, 6·7 per cent. Finally, although rising land prices reflected in part the speculative value of property in areas so near the Ruhr, they also provide additional evidence of the prosperity of the two prewar decades.[18]

This review of the years before the First World War suggests that by 1914 west German peasants had learned to live quite comfortably with the economic realities of an industrial society. A growing industrial sector competed with agriculture for labour, but those employed in industry had to eat, and the constantly expanding demand for all agricultural products made clear that industrialization was not without a salutary impact on agriculture. Certainly, rising land and product prices, expanding markets and tolerably low levels of indebtedness all justified the continued commitment to established patterns of production.

Admittedly, for agricultural producers, even if things are good, they can always be better, and peasant farmers are chronic and notorious complainers. In the almost two decades before the outbreak of the First World War, Rhenish and Westphalian peasants provided no exception to this rule. Most notably, their interest group representatives had joined in demands for the reintroduction of tariff protection in 1902. They were also vehement in their attacks on proposals for tax reforms which might threaten the privileged position of landed property, and could portray their allegedly deplorable circumstances in the darkest colours imaginable. Still, even by the turn of the century there was already substantial evidence that confirmed the judgement of the left-liberal Progressive Party politician Eugen Richter that German agricultural producers had 'learn[ed] to complain without suffering'.[19]

Agriculture in the Great War: Learning to Live with the Controlled Economy

In the years following August 1914 peasant discontent reflected not the desire to be faring even better, but rather the sense that the agricultural sector was rapidly losing ground. Peasant suffering was real, not imagined. Peasant farmers identified the source of their woes in the state-imposed controlled economy, a system of pricing and requisitioning policies intended to guarantee the supply and distribution of all goods during the war. A carefully co-ordinated system to ensure an equitable distribution of scarce necessities to consumers and fair prices to producers had not been part of the central government's prewar plans. Along with all other belligerent powers, the Germans had shared the illusion that the war would be over quickly. Rapidly rising prices, panic buying and fears of hoarding in the countryside presented immediate threats to the supply of food for the troops at the front and the domestic army of workers in war-related industries. State action was essential, and the government's initial response was to impose maximum prices in those instances where price increases threatened to exceed consumers' ability to pay.[20]

It soon became apparent, however, that maximum prices, if necessary, were not sufficient to guarantee adequate food supplies. Agricultural producers who chose not to comply with government regulations could simply withhold their products from the market altogether. Price controls were ineffective unless supplemented by a system of mandatory deliveries. The institutional form for such controls – imposed ultimately on virtually all products – first took shape in January 1915 when the government responded to fears of hoarding with the creation of the War Grain Office, charged with setting both prices and delivery quotas for producers. Using estimates of harvest yields and consumer needs for the coming year, this office generated a figure for the total grain supply required for the Reich. It also determined wholesale and retail prices and prescribed amounts which producers could keep for their own consumption and for livestock feeds. It then levied delivery quotas for each province, and provincial officials divided this amount among their administrative districts. Final responsibility for collection lay with the local official who set quotas for individual producers in his district.

Even as these measures were implemented, however, it was foreseeable that they would not suffice to secure the provisioning system nor to satisfy agricultural producers. In the absence of any comprehensive set of controls on *all* agricultural products, producers were left obvious opportunities to circumvent those controls which *did* exist. The forms this might take are not difficult to fathom, given the structure and organization of agricultural production on peasant farms before 1914. The system of mixed farming which had permitted flexibility in adjusting to shifting relative prices before the war became a means to circumvent a set of price and delivery controls introduced in a haphazard fashion after the war began.

The potential for such forms of resistance to controls had been apparent with the introduction of the earliest maximum prices for bread grains and restrictions on their use as feeds. At first, feed prices were left uncontrolled and quickly increased. Officials feared that price ceilings would block all imports. Neither appeals to national unity and patriotic obligation nor sanctions against using cereals and potatoes as feed for livestock numbed peasant responsiveness to these clear shifts in relative prices. Grains and potatoes quickly disappeared from the market to be used in lieu of expensive purchased feeds. The government countered not with a comprehensive system of relative prices but with the order in the spring of 1915 that thousands of pigs be butchered, eliminating them as competitors for basic food supplies.[21]

Such stop-gap measures were clearly not adequate to the task at hand.

In the absence of a unified control system, based on relative prices which reflected production costs, peasants exploited the flexibility of the mixed farming system, shifting acreage from cereals to feed grains, from arable to pasture, or from grains to other relatively higher priced products. It is difficult if not impossible to provide any aggregate estimate of the extent of such shifts of production, but their significance and the threat which they presented to the food supply registered clearly in the chronic complaints of local officials.[22]

From Bad to Worse: Shortages and the Black Market

By the time the Reich government instituted a set of comprehensive pricing policies, coupled in most cases with delivery quotas and backed when necessary by confiscation at the point of production – the farm – it was still too little and it came too late. The War Food Office, established in 1916 to co-ordinate policy at the national level, remained a 'dull sword', as Martin Schumacher has recently characterized it. It was never equipped with the thorough-going and comprehensive authorities let alone the personnel which might have allowed it greater effectiveness. Not surprisingly, it brought about no dramatic improvements in the provisioning system.[23]

Of course, by 1916 the problems confronting the War Food Office were not only those caused by the absence of an administrative network capable of enforcing what laws were already on the books. In addition, an already critical situation was complicated by two related developments: (1) acute declines in the output of all agricultural goods, attributable to diminishing supplies of *all* factors of production, particularly labour, fertilizer, draft animals and the absence of replacements for broken down machines; and (2) the emergence and rapid spread of a flourishing black market, an alternative to the malfunctioning system for collection and distribution established by the central government in Berlin.

Precise estimates of the declines in agricultural production do not exist, and officials candidly confessed that the 'passive resistance' of peasant producers to the war economy was directly reflected in underreporting of harvest yields and the acreage planted in specific crops.[24] Though published statistics may understate yields by as much as 10 per cent, the figures for the Rhineland and Westphalia, summarized in Table 5.1, provide at least some idea of the general trend in output and the reduction of acreage sown in grains. They are in line with national tendencies and indicate the tremendous losses in productivity and output, largely explained by the limited supply of many production goods and the com-

149

plete absence of others. The figures for livestock holdings, summarized in Table 5.2, reveal the dramatic decline in pig holdings, the major source of meat in the prewar period. The fact that cattle holdings declined relatively less indicated their importance as draft animals and producers of manure, essential given the shortages of synthetic substitutes. Moreover, absolute numbers say nothing of slaughter weights, and on this score, both the reports of local officials and published statistics were unanimous in recording dramatic declines.[25]

These real declines in domestic production meant that as the war

Table 5.1 *Major Grains: Yields and Output, 1913–24 (1913 = 100)*

		Wheat			Westphalia Rye			Oats	
Year	Ha	output	Tons/ ha	Ha	output (tons)	Tons/ ha	Ha	output (tons)	Tons/ ha
Base	(76,696)	(175,237)	(2·28)	(251,490)	(497,034)	(1·98)	(166,778)	(359,099)	(2·15)
1913	100	100	100	100	100	100	100	100	100
1914	94	82	87	100	92	92	108	104	96
1915	96	88	92	100	95	95	108	69	87
1916	70	54	77	81	61	75	77	64	84
1917	67	47	71	74	61	83	77	43	56
1918	68	51	76	76	63	83	72	46	64
1919	65	47	72	71	54	76	72	48	67
1920	75	53	71	76	53	69	81	53	65
1921	69	60	87	70	61	88	75	55	73
1922	64	37	58	69	47	68	82	43	53
1923	78	67	86	77	60	78	86	68	80
1924	81	49	61	79	53	68	96	55	58
					Rhineland				
Base	(79,625)	(206,220)	(2·59)	(151,562)	(343,045)	(2·26)	(146,639)	(383,854)	(2·58)
1913	100	100	100	100	100	100	100	100	100
1914	100	81	81	99	89	90	103	104	101
1915	103	106	103	97	99	101	104	72	69
1916	88	70	79	79	60	77	73	67	93
1917	80	57	71	70	58	82	71	49	69
1918	78	62	79	69	58	84	66	46	69
1919	73	48	66	59	39	65	62	41	66
1920	80	53	66	66	43	65	77	48	62
1921	82	78	64	62	48	77	71	41	58
1922	78	59	75	61	77	47	77	40	52
1923	91	74	82	66	82	54	82	71	87
1924	96	62	65	77	73	56	86	49	57

Source: *Vierteljahrshefte zur Statistik des Deutschen Reichs* (Berlin, 1913–25), 23/I:132, 134, 136; 24/II:220, 222, 224; 25/II:64, 66, 68; 27/I:45, 47, 49; 28/I:30, 32, 34, 48, 50, 52; 29/I:124, 126, 128; 30/I:18, 20, 22; 31/I:86, 88, 90; 32/I:6, 8; 33/I:28, 30; 34/I:36, 38.

Table 5.2   *Livestock Holdings, 1913–24*

Year	Households with livestock	Horses	Westphalia (1913 = 100) Cattle	Sheep	Pigs	Goats
Base	(375,110)	(175,306)	(751,114)	(132,210)	(1,546,087)	(220,533)
1913	100	100	100	100	100	100
1914	97	81	109	102	103	98
1915	92	76	100	91	62	94
1916	110	74	107	86	63	103
1917	119	76	98	93	39	108
1918	117	84	90	110	41	112
1919	119	95	89	131	49	114
1920	128	97	92	157	61	122
1921	132	101	93	129	67	126
1922	127	100	88	114	58	117
1923	114	*	92	138	78	120
1924	130	106	94	108	70	113
Base	(266,317)	(153,504)	Rhineland (647,586)	(53,484)	(745,292)	(186,776)
1913	100	100	100	100	100	100
1914	98	79	107	104	100	101
1915	92	71	95	81	63	98
1916	124	66	100	106	71	108
1917	146	68	94	99	42	117
1918	146	84	83	108	38	124
1919	143	88	74	121	47	123
1920	154	89	78	170	64	129
1921	163	91	77	152	72	132
1922	158	90	74	141	64	124
1923	115	*	80	183	82	132
1924	156	99	81	155	74	120

*Information on horses not available for 1923.

Source: *Vierteljahrshefte zur Statistik des Deutschen Reichs* (Berlin, 1913–25), 23/IV:56–9; 24/III:34, 35; 25/II:44–5; 26/IV:4–5, 8–9; 27/IV:10–11, 14–15, 40–1, 44–5; 29/II:90–1; 30/II:20–3; 31/III:88, 90; 32/III:64, 66; 33/II:16, 18; 34/III:20, 22.

continued, the amounts promised by local officials as rations for urban consumers might often reflect only good intentions. The alternative for consumers was illegal purchases directly from producers or from a supplier who made such purchases in bulk. The shorter rationed supplies were, the more attractive this option became. From the winter of 1915–16 there flourished a black market alternative to the regulated economy which involved virtually every part of German society. By the winter of 1916–17 the black market had taken on such substantial proportions that it threatened to undermine what slim chances for success remained for the controlled economy. For some products, the black market had become the only market, and it was generally acknowledged as an essential supplement to the legal provisioning system.[26]

The widespread violation of controls did little to improve a waning domestic morale.[27] It added to the general deterioration of respect for public authorities and the widely held belief that the government was incabable of containing a potentially disastrous situation. And it certainly widened the gap and heightened the antagonism between the producers and consumers of agricultural products. Whatever the extent of their grudging collaboration and direct confrontation on the black market, the system did nothing to improve relations between the two groups. Producers rejected consumer claims of inability to pay increased prices, given the ready supply of buyers on the black market, while consumers cited the black market as the clearest evidence of peasant subversion of the war economy.[28]

Despite the growing demands from many agricultural economists for higher fixed prices as the only means to undermine the black market and increase agricultural output, the government was unwilling to act on this advice. Certainly, such proposals were unacceptable to the national representatives of the socialist Free Trade Unions, the Social Democratic Party and other groups representing urban consumers, who argued that if prices were adjusted at all, it should be downward. In the face of the continued resistance of peasant producers, they insisted that the only acceptable policy was strict enforcement of existing controls and expansion of the regulatory network.[29]

Of course, by the winter of 1916–17 the government confronted an even more visible and immediate argument for tightening controls. Widespread industrial unrest and strike activity often focused on improvements in the food supply as a central demand.[30] Such organized collective action clearly demanded a decisive response from the state. Government officials candidly offered the Kaiser's 'Easter Message', the guarantee in April 1917 that meaningful political reform was on the immediate agenda, as an attempt to reward workers for their contributions to the war effort. As Wilhelm Groener, one of the more enlightened members of the General Staff, reflected, it was essential 'to feed the masses with ballots instead of meat and bread' as long as the provisioning system did not fulfill its purpose.[31]

Such verbal concessions were not the only steps taken to appease working-class discontent, however. The Berlin government promised to meet demands not only for ballots but also for bread. The introduction of additional controls on the grain harvest in the spring of 1917 was intended to achieve this goal. Within a year, these audits of reserves on peasant farms extended even into the farm family's living quarters, and control officials searched under beds and in closets for concealed reserves. To be sure, the discovery of any amounts however small served to confirm the suspicion of peasant perfidy, but even the most thorough farm-by-farm controls, conducted in the spring after the previous year's harvest had already been consumed, contributed more to the bitterness and resentment of peasant farmers than to the food supplies available for urban consumers.[32]

Ever-worsening shortages, consumer protest, urban unrest, tightened controls, producer resistance, the black market – these were all points on the vicious circle which characterized the provisioning system by the spring and summer of 1918. Undoubtedly no system of government controls could have broken out of this round. But by failing to achieve its goal of fair prices and equitable distribution, the state discredited itself in the eyes of both producers and consumers. Each side called on the government to control the other, and each believed that the government favoured the other's interests and consistently neglected its own.

The attempt to weigh the relative interests of consumers and producers preoccupied the government. Though tightened controls did not bring the desired results, they none the less suggested that the scales seemed to tip in the favour of urban industrial workers, particularly after the 'Turnip Winter' of 1916–17. In other respects as well, urban workers had commanded the attention of the government during the war. Trade union leaders and SPD representatives were included in important areas of governmental decision-making, including the realm of agricultural policy, the preserve of conservative agrarians before 1914.[33] Of course, such measures could not fill empty stomachs or guarantee an adequate supply of basic necessities for urban workers, but they did reflect a shift in the relative power of the interest groups of agriculture and industrial workers. For peasants, accustomed to a privileged and protected position before 1914, the war thus represented a relative decline in social and political status in addition to the obvious threat which it posed to their economic welfare.[34]

'The struggle for political and social advantage in the wartime economy', Gerald Feldman argues, 'was a struggle over the structure of society after the war.'[35] By 1918 it was a struggle in which agricultural producers were not among the winners. This shift in the relative power of the representatives of organized agricultural producers and industrial workers was, in the long term, a necessary development in an advanced industrial society. In Germany, it had been systematically postponed by a conservative government which granted agricultural producers a prestige out of all proportion to their numbers or their economic significance. But the shift in this balance of power under circumstances of extraordinarily heightened domestic social conflict during the war created enormous tensions and resentments on both sides of the producer–consumer divide.

Four years of controls on production had generated tremendous bitterness on the part of peasants towards industrial workers, their representatives and those civil servants who were condemned for collapsing before urban interests and forsaking the countryside. Caught between their loyalty to the old regime and fears of an uncertain future, conservative agrarian leaders attempted to shift the blame for the war economy away from the imperial government and on to industrial workers, who allegedly exploited their indispensable position to force an unwilling Kaiser's hand. In July 1917 one local administrator in eastern Westphalia summarized the feelings of the peasants in his district, stating that the 'central offices make their decisions in accord with the wishes of the industrial working class without paying any attention to producers. Evidence, they argue, is provided by . . . the much better treatment of industrial areas relative to areas where it is assumed that the population won't protest on account of its patriotic attitudes.'[36] By early 1918 such observations were by no means exceptional, and the monthly reports of government officials which stressed the faith of the rural population in the Kaiser and his army were increasingly at odds with the reality of a peasantry embittered and angered over the economic policies of that same Kaiser's government.

The Tumultuous Transition from War to Peace

In the winter of 1918–19 the November Revolution, the declaration of the Republic and the accelerated advance towards parliamentary democracy in Germany were radical breaks which profoundly shaped the forms of peasant collective action described in this volume in Jonathan Osmond's contribution. Peasant reaction to these political ruptures was also strongly influenced by important elements of continuity. Neither the end of the war nor the collapse of the Kaiserreich alleviated the crisis in the provisioning system. Controls remained essential. Indeed, supplies declined even more drastically in the months immediately following the end of hostilities, reflecting the belief widespread among many agricultural producers that with the war over, the controlled economy was no longer binding. Those producers still willing to deliver at fixed prices certainly had even less to offer than in the previous year. The government instituted after the November Revolution, the Council of People's Commissars, saw no option but to maintain controls on the agricultural sector, and it soon became clear that whatever the changes in government and its personnel, state intervention into the economic life of the peasantry was to remain official policy.[37]

Given what we know of peasant resistance to the controls imposed in the name of the Kaiser and justified with patriotic appeals, it is not surprising that peasant response to controls imposed by a socialist government was even more hostile. The expansion of the government to include the Catholic Centre and the liberal German People's Party after the election of a national constituent assembly in January 1919 made matters no better. The continued shortages of foodstuffs made it impossible for any government to consider suspension of controls, but nothing less could appease an angered peasantry. The division between consumers and producers remained an extremely important dimension of domestic social conflict in the transition from war to peace.

Throughout the spring and summer of 1919 the fears that labour militancy could easily be intensified by food shortages was a central consideration in the decision of the early Weimar governments to maintain controls on agricultural producers. Proposals for a relaxation of controls, consumer representatives argued, would result in price increases and an intolerable pressure on wages, disastrous not only for workers but for those who paid them. The consequence, according to Robert Schmidt, the Majority Socialist who held the posts of Minister of Economics and Prussian Commissar for the Food Supply in 1919, would be nothing less than 'chaos [and] Bolshevism with all its consequences, like we have seen it in Russia and Hungary'.[38] Schmidt's pessimistic assessment was hardly uncharacteristic in Majority Socialist circles and informed his decision to augment existing controls with additional checks and searches.[39] As one local official argued, Schmidt's scheme succeeded only in 'widening the gulf separating city and countryside,'[40] but politically acceptable alternative policies did not exist.

Resistance in the countryside to the maintenance of controls increasingly took on organized forms, and the controlled economy joined socialism and parliamentary democracy as favourite targets for the diatribes of conservative agricultural interest group leaders.[41] Indeed, in Weimar's early years all could conveniently be linked together, related symptoms of the disease infecting German society. Interest group attacks on the controlled economy did nothing to increase their constituents' desire to meet quotas. But even before 1919, when agrarian leaders had still exhorted their followers to fulfill their patriotic obligations, peasants had proved their ability to discover innovative means to circumvent controls without encouragement or direction. Forms of peasant 'passive resistance' to controls had existed as long as the controls themselves.

It was ultimately this continued resistance which undermined attempts to force deliveries at fixed prices. By late 1919 and early 1920 disregard for mandated prices and delivery quotas had simply become the norm. The end to direct controls on meat in October 1920 and milk in April 1921 thus merely made de jure a situation which had long existed de facto. In June 1920 the highest-ranking government official in Westphalia conceded that 'the controlled economy, specifically for meat, milk and butter, had already fallen apart'.[42] He undoubtedly would have concurred with the judgement of an official in the Reich Ministry of Agriculture that long before it was dismantled completely, '*the controlled economy* existed *only on paper*. Its suspension only represents an acknowledgement of conditions which already exist.'[43]

Agriculture in the Inflation: Controls after Decontrol

Still, despite the singular failure of controls, the government persisted in maintaining direct regulation of the grain supply and introducing price guidelines even for those products for which mandated prices were lifted. These steps were justified, officials argued, by the simple fact that the supply of almost all agricultural products still did not meet the demand for them. Domestic production remained below prewar levels, and in addition, the government consistently refused to meet domestic food needs with foreign imports, even after the suspension of the Allied blockade had made this a policy option.

The reluctance to turn to the world market for food, particularly for cereals, can only be understood if we consider the nature of the postwar inflation. Like the controls on the agricultural sector, the policy of deficit spending by means of the printing press was an innovation of the imperial government during the war, not the early governments of Weimar. Neither before nor after 1918 did the decision to print money to cover extraordinary costs not met by tax revenues directly reflect concern with the agricultural sector. Before 1918 it was a way to finance the war effort, a substitute for the politically unacceptable policy of increasing taxes and a supplement to the totally insufficient amounts which could be mobilized through the sale of war bonds. A deliberate policy of inflation was intended to postpone the day of reckoning, and of course it was hoped that when the war ended, a victorious Germany would make someone else pay its bills. The German defeat had shattered this illusion, and in the absence of other means to cover its budget, the new government of the German Republic continued to resort to a policy of inflation. The printing press remained a convenient source of ready cash to finance the sizeable costs of demobilization. Germany confronted other expenses as well.

Although a final figure for war reparations was left undetermined at the Paris peace talks in 1919, it was quite clear that Germany would have to pay substantial amounts.[44]

The alternatives to ending the inflation – either high rates of taxation and/or currency stabilization which might trigger economic recession and high unemployment – remained politically unacceptable precisely because they threatened to alienate organized labour and industry. A policy of inflation seemed to promise the smoothest possible path to economic recovery. In addition, the early governments of Weimar maintained that until the process of economic reconstruction in Germany and the revival of international commerce made possible real transfers to cover the costs of reparation, Germany had no option but to print money to pay the Allies. Finally, the depreciation of the currency permitted the government to deal with yet another liability, its debt to its own citizens, since war bonds could more easily be paid off in increasingly worthless currency.

The general agreement on a policy of inflation among government leaders along with representatives of labour and the business community created an 'inflation consensus' which blocked any moves towards stabilization until the summer of 1922. Labour was guaranteed the high rates of employment which accompanied the economic recovery from the war. Business benefited from labour peace and profited from the recovery boom. And the government won stability by placating labour and industry, in addition to the opportunity to rid itself of its war debt.[45] The disregard for agrarian interests in these calculations and agriculture's clear exclusion from this influential triumvirate provided yet another indication of the changing relative power positions of interest group representatives which had begun in 1914 and continued after the end of the war.[46]

Although none of the arguments favouring the continuation of the inflation had much to do with the immediate interests of agricultural producers, peasant farmers were clearly influenced by the inflation's consequences. The credits on agriculture's balance-sheet in the inflation were outlined in the introduction to this essay. There were significant debits as well. Peasant farmers had been loyal subscribers to war bond issues right up until 1918, and watched as the paper they held became worthless. To be sure, mortgages on landed property were also worth little, but this benefit of the inflation should not be exaggerated. During the war, in the absence of supplies of synthetic fertilizer, machinery and replacements to livestock holdings, peasants had used their incomes to make a considerable dent in their mortgage liabilities.[47] The postwar inflation thus accelerated a process already well underway before 1918. Moreover, complete elimination of mortgage indebtedness was not necessarily a highly desirable priority under all circumstances. Carrying some debt burden was considered sound business practice, and prewar experience indicated that some indebtedness was completely consistent with economic well-being and prosperity.

Thus, even some of agriculture's gains in the inflation were mixed blessings. In other respects, the inflation was unambiguously detrimental to the agricultural sector. It created an atmosphere of unpredictability over shifting relative prices and a general climate of uncertainty which created bases for production decisions fundamentally different from the steadily climbing prices of the pre-1914 period. Investments in livestock and machinery and other attempts to recoup wartime losses might consequently represent primarily the 'flight from the Mark' into real property rather than rational and carefully considered investment decisions.[48]

In addition, for agricultural producers the inflation meant the maintenance of controls on production in direct and indirect forms. The reality of the fitful, continuing depreciation of the currency made it exceedingly difficult to fathom the extent to which domestic price increases reflected the expansion of the money supply, the normal relationship of supply and demand under circumstances of continued scarcity, or as many consumers suspected, the peasantry's exploitation of an uncertain situation to charge usurious prices.[49] Price guidelines based in theory not only on production costs but also on 'social and ethical considerations' were instituted to resolve this dilemma and to respond to consumer discontent. Such measures proved entirely inadequate.[50] The inflation greatly complicated the work of the offices charged with this economic and moral calculus, and producers typically disregarded their recommendations anyway. Still, although officials failed in their attempts to establish informal guidelines for determining 'fair' prices, they fully succeeded in angering both consumers and producers. Such indirect controls generated more peasant resentment than they did deliveries at low prices, and served as a constant reminder that the controlled economy, though transformed, did not belong entirely to the past.[51]

An even more forceful and for peasants even less pleasant reminder of wartime controls was the continued regulation of the grain supply, and here too the justification of controls was directly related to the nature of the postwar inflation. The inflation was complicated by the fact that the Mark depreciated more rapidly abroad than it did within Germany. German domestic prices remained below world market levels. This situation had different consequences for different sectors of the German economy. Thus, heavy industrialists enjoyed an export advantage, and in the hope of improving Germany's balance of payments situation, the government did not discourage them from recapturing world markets lost during the war. For agricultural producers, the inflation imposed a barrier to imports even more impenetrable than prewar tariff protection and reversed prewar price relations in which German prices were consistently above world market levels (see Table 5.3). This discrepancy between domestic and world market prices also left the government unwilling to spend foreign currency for grain imports and convinced that controls on the German grain supply must be maintained. An end to controls, particularly on that critical nutritional staple, bread grains, could only follow an increase in imports, and an increase in imports could only follow an improvement in the state of Germany's currency.[52]

Table 5.3   *World Grain Prices (Dollar per Quintal [= 100 kg])*

	1921	*1922*	*1923*
	Wheat		
Germany	2·70	4·34	4·76
England	6·34	4·87	4·45
France	6·61	6·36	5·76
	Rye		
Germany	2·34	3·48	4·00
France	5·18	4·35	4·05
Belgium	5·38	4·36	3·52
	Barley		
Germany	2·44	3·78	4·07
England	5·56	4·90	4·21
France	6·03	5·24	4·11
	Oats		
Germany	2·25	3·69	3·64
England	4·67	4·55	4·32
United States	2·55	2·64	2·97
France	4·25	4·89	3·86

Source: International Institute of Agriculture, *Agricultural Problems in their International Aspect* (League of Nations, International Economic Conference, Geneva, May 1927, Documentation) (Rome, n.d.), 48–50, 64, 65, 69–71, 78–83, 94–7, 104–7.

The extensive resistance to direct controls did however lead by late 1920 to the decision to replace existing measures with the grain levy system. This alternative permitted producers to sell supplies in excess of mandated delivery quotas at open market prices or to use surplus supplies for feed. In short, the levy system created a dual market structure, forcing producers to deliver part of their harvest at fixed prices, while permitting them to sell the remainder on the open market at prices at least two to three times higher.[53] Officials conceded that such a two-tiered system would only underline the discrepancy between fixed domestic and world market prices for the producer, but from another perspective, the levy system was seen as a way to combat the black market by in effect institutionalizing it.[54]

In theory, the grain levy system, first implemented in the summer of 1921, was proposed as a useful transitional step towards an end to all controls and a way for the state to maintain its authority by making its demands more reasonable. In practice, delivery quotas once set evoked that chorus of protest from agricultural producers to which Wieskotten added his voice. Not only did regional variations in assessments cause particular distress. Even more infuriating was the failure of fixed prices to keep up with the rate of inflation.

None the less, the continuing depreciation of the currency which had accelerated in the air of crisis surrounding the assassination of Walther Rathenau in June 1922 only confirmed official opinion that it was 'absolutely the most unsuitable time to introduce the free economy'.[55] Over vociferous agrarian protest against the measure, the Reichstag approved, with minor modifications, the maintenance of the levy system for yet another year.

Certainly by now we have done much to illuminate the dimensions of Wieskotten's discontent as well as the discontent of thousands of other west German peasants in the winter of 1922–3. The hyperinflation, the rapid, uncontrollable deterioration in the value of the German currency which began in the summer of 1922 and took on astronomical proportions with the French invasion of the Ruhr in January 1923 did nothing to improve matters. An overheated printing press financed the costs of 'passive resistance' to French occupation, resulting in the final plunge of the currency. Wieskotten's fine had seemed high when first assessed in January. The impact of the inflation by late summer was clear in a reassessment, which reflected a reduction of the initial amount by half, but still left Wieskotten with a bill for 4,735,674 Marks, an amount which, according to local officials, Wieskotten was 'certainly in a position' to pay.[56]

By the summer German prices were approaching world market levels, and along with the value of the currency, the rationale for the controlled economy had disintegrated. By then many agricultural producers cared little that they were now free to demand world market prices for their entire harvest, and the destruction of the currency had fostered a barter trade in which Marks were not preferred as a medium of exchange. The final stage of the inflation had also brought with it hoarding and acute shortages, giving rise once again to the waves of urban scroungers, the black market and the exacerbation of conflicts between city and country-side.[57] Indeed, at the national level the danger of the complete collapse of the food supply was among the most compelling arguments in favour of an introduction of currency stabilization sooner rather than later, and by the time this action was taken in the autumn, conditions had deteriorated to a level comparable to the worst years of the war.[58]

The stabilization of the currency in November 1923 marked the end to almost ten years of sustained economic instability, characterized for peasant farmers by state intervention into agricultural production and the absence of a market capable of providing reliable price signals. Until 1920–1 for many products those signals were either dictated by the state or the caprice of the black market. Even for those products no longer directly controlled, the unpredictable dips in the value of the Mark disrupted normal market relations and made rational cost-accounting next to impossible. To be sure, the inflation allowed peasants to recoup some of the losses suffered during the war, but profits were achieved under conditions of unpredictability and uncertainty, circumstances favourable neither to future planning nor to optimal investment decisions. The nature of the inflation had also justified the maintenance of both direct and indirect controls on the agricultural sector, leaving peasant farmers in a rut of antagonism towards urban consumers and the state, seen to represent urban consumer interests, which dated back to 1914.

A Look beyond Stabilization towards 1933

Stabilization of the currency ended the inflation and the need for controls on agricultural producers, but it no more created conditions for prosperity than had the end of the war five years earlier. In fact, stabilization initiated a crisis in the agricultural sector, and although historians may disagree about the impact of the inflation on German agricultural producers, they do not question the severity of the agrarian crisis which began once the inflation ended.[59]

There is also little argument about the most important outlines of this crisis. It was triggered when income from the 1922–3 harvest proved insufficient to cover the costs of production for the coming year. In addition, agricultural producers who, like everyone else, had been spared the consequences of tax reform as long as the currency continued to depreciate, could no longer escape those consequences. Horses and machines purchased during the inflation could pay neither taxes nor the costs of production goods. This liquidity crisis forced many peasants quickly to assume new debts. Loans were, however, no longer available at the 4·5 per cent interest rates offered by agricultural credit co-operatives before the war. The inflation had eliminated the reserves of these credit co-operatives and dried up the steady stream of credits they had provided to their members before 1914. The situation was not reversed after 1924. By the late 1920s the total debt burden of agricultural producers still had not achieved prewar levels, but the greatest part of overwhelmingly short-term obligations at very high interest rates had been accumulated within the first two years after stabilization.[60]

Stabilization also ended the artificial protection for the agricultural sector created by the inflation, and domestic prices, after reaching world market levels in the hyperinflation, were well above those on the world market after 1924. Agricultural interest groups called for large doses of a familiar medicine – tariffs – bolstering their prewar arguments about the necessity to guarantee the viability of German agricultural producers by pointing to wartime shortages as evidence of the need for protection to achieve self-sufficiency in food production. The problem was, however, not only one of international competition from low-cost producers; it was, in addition, one of unpredictably fluctuating prices, a clear reflection of the international agricultural crisis of the mid-1920s, insoluble with protection, and far beyond the control or complete comprehension of the governments of Weimar, let alone the individual producer. The causes of economic instability were not the same as they had been in the period 1914–23. None the less, the realities of economic unpredictability were constant. A bad situation became worse in 1927–8 as prices fluctuated less and instead simply plummeted. And of course an already vulnerable agricultural sector was not spared the disastrous impact of the Great Depression in 1929.[61]

The severity of the agrarian crisis of the late 1920s is generally cited as a major factor in the peasantry's decision to turn away from Weimar and to National Socialism.[62] This essay has emphasized that by 1933 German agricultural producers had suffered not through five or six but rather through almost twenty years of uncertainty before they willingly entered the Third Reich. The political dimensions of this development have not concerned us here, but the account of the peasantry's economic fate in these two decades suggests why promises of stable prices and guaranteed markets, central parts of the National Socialist programme to revive the agricultural sector, should have appealed to peasant producers. Indeed, such goals had been writ large in the programmes of almost all agricultural interest groups in the late 1920s, and suggested the desire to return to the solid prewar bases of prosperity. Unlike other interest groups or political parties, the Nazis seemed capable of achieving these goals.

Obviously, these outlines of economic development can provide only part of an explanation of peasant antagonism towards Weimar and acceptance of National Socialism. However, any analysis of the political dimensions of this phenomenon is meaningful only against the background outlined here. We began with Karl Wieskotten and Franz von Papen. The latter's reception of and responsibility for the triumph of National Socialism are of course too familiar to bear detailing here. We cannot know if Wieskotten shared his erstwhile sponsor's enthusiasm for a government headed by Nazis, but the argument of this article strongly suggests that whatever Wieskotten's views of *Blut und Boden* and the ideology of the Thousand-Year Reich, he might well have welcomed the promise of an end to an extended period of economic instability dating back to August 1914.

Notes: Chapter 5

ABBREVIATIONS

BAK	Bundesarchiv Koblenz
HStAD	Hauptstaatsarchiv Düsseldorf
LAK	Landesarchiv Koblenz
OP	Oberpräsidium
Opräs.R	Oberpräsident für die Rheinprovinz
Opräs.W	Oberpräsident für die Provinz Westfalen
RB	Regierungsbezirk
Reg.	Regierung
RP	Regierungspräsident
StAM	Staatsarchiv Münster
VdRT	*Verhandlungen des Reichstags*

1 Research for this essay was funded by the German Academic Exchange Service (DAAD), the Social Science Research Council and the Stiftung Volkswagen. Earlier versions of the essay were presented to the Columbia University Economic History Seminar and to a conference on 'Rheinland-Westfalen im Industrie Zeit alter' held in Essen in June 1982. I profited greatly from the useful comments of the discussants on both occasions. In addition, particular thanks go to Jane Caplan, Gerald D. Feldman, Lynn Mally and Hans-Jurgen Puhle, all of whom offered excellent critical comments on earlier drafts. I have attempted to keep references to a minimum.

2 See, e.g., Franz Eulemberg, 'Die sozialen Wirkungen der Währungsverhältnisse', *Jahrbücher für Nationalökonomie und Statistik* 122 (1924): 763–6; Otto Auhagen, 'Ursachen und Wirkungen der Geldentwertung', *Schmollers Jahrbuch* 44 (1920): 93; Costatino Bresciani-Turroni, *The Economics of Inflation: A Study of Currency Depreciation in Post-War Germany, 1914–1923* (London, 1937), 229; Claus-Dieter Krohn, *Stabilisierung und ökonomische Interessen: Die Finanzpolitik des Deutschen Reiches 1923–1927* (Düsseldorf, 1974), 21.

3 An excellent summary and critical assessment of these arguments is provided by Jonathan Osmond, 'German peasant farmers in war and inflation, 1914–1924: stability or stagnation?', in *Die deutsche Inflation: Eine Zwischenbilanz*, ed. Gerald D. Feldman, Carl-Ludwig Holtfrerich, Gerhard A. Ritter and Peter-Christian Witt (Berlin, 1982), 289–307.

4 Letter dated 21 June 1923, StAM, Reg. Arnsberg I 15, no. 23.

5 Letter dated 22 January 1922, StAM, Reg. Arnsberg I 15, no. 21.

6 loc. cit.

7 On the general nature of agricultural protest over the so-called *Getreideumlagesystem*,

see Robert G. Moeller, 'Winners as losers in the German inflation: peasant protest over the controlled economy, 1920–1923', in *Die deutsche Inflation*, 255–88.

8 This study excludes the two southernmost districts of the Rhine province, RB Coblenz and RB Trier. These areas were characterized by generally smaller holdings, attributable to the practice of partible inheritance, and less market orientation, due to the absence of large, urban centres. By the late nineteenth century agricultural producers in the other three districts of the Rhine Province, RB Düsseldorf, RB Cologne and RB Aachen, had much in common with the peasants in the three districts of the province of Westphalia – production for nearby industrial markets and similarities in social structure – and together, these areas can be seen as an economic unity. In terms of the distribution of landholdings, and also proximity to and production for urban markets, these areas were quite similar to other areas predominated by peasant holdings, particularly the Prussian provinces of Saxony, Hanover, and Schleswig-Holstein. For comparisons, see Sigrid Dillwitz, 'Die Struktur der Bauernschaft von 1871 bis 1914: Dargestellt auf der Grundlage der deutschen Reichsstatistik', *Jahrbuch für Geschichte* 9 (1973): 56–61.

9 See Osmond, 'German peasant farmers'.

10 On the struggle over tariffs see in particular Kenneth D. Barkin, *The Controversy over German Industrialization 1890–1902* (Chicago and London, 1970), esp. 21–128; Steven B. Webb, 'Tariff protection for the iron industry, cotton textiles and agriculture in Germany, 1879–1914', *Jahrbücher für Nationalökonomie und Statistik* 192 (1977): 336–57; and Dirk Stegmann, *Die Erben Bismarcks: Parteien und Verbände in der Spätphase des Wilhelminischen Deutschlands: Sammlungspolitik 1897* (Cologne and Berlin, 1970), 80–91.

11 See the contributions by Farr and Puhle in this volume as well as Hans-Jürgen Puhle, *Agrarische Interessenpolitik und preussischer Konservatismus im Wilhelminischen Reich (1893–1914)* (Bonn-Bad Godesberg, 1975); Ian Farr, 'Populism in the countryside: the Peasant Leagues in Bavaria in the 1890s', in *Society and Politics in Wilhelmine Germany*, ed. Richard J. Evans (London, 1978), 136–59; David Warren Hendon, 'The Center Party and the agrarian interest in Germany, 1890–1914' (Ph.D. diss., Emory University, 1976); and idem, 'German Catholics and the Agrarian League, 1893–1914', *German Studies Review* 4 (1981): 427–45.

12 This interpretation comes up most frequently in discussions of peasant support for grain tariffs. See Alexander Gerschenkron, *Bread and Democracy in Germany* (Berkeley, Calif., and Los Angeles, 1943), 26–7, 57–8, 67, 75–6. Gerschenkron's analysis remains very influential. See, e.g., Barrington Moore, Jr., *Social Origins of Dictatorship and Democracy: Lord and Peasant in the Making of the Modern World* (Boston, Mass., 1966), 448–50; and Hans-Ulrich Wehler, *Das deutsche Kaiserreich 1871–1918* (Göttingen, 1973), 47, 55–6.

13 In general, for a reassessment of the impact of tariff protection, see J. A. Perkin, 'The agricultural revolution in Germany 1850–1914', *Journal of European Economic History* 10 (1981): 71–118; Steven B. Webb, 'Agricultural protection in Wilhelminian Germany: forging an empire with pork and rye', *Journal of Economic History* 42 (1982): 309–26; idem, 'Tariff protection'.

14 See Robert G. Moeller, 'Peasants and tariffs in the Kaiserreich: how backward were the *Bauern*?', *Agricultural History* 55 (1981): 370–84; and James C. Hunt, 'Peasants, grain tariffs and meat quotas: imperial German protectionism reexamined', *Central European History* 7 (1974): 311–31.

15 For examples of such conservative rhetoric and romantic descriptions of rural life, see Barkin, and Klaus Bergmann, *Agrarromantik und Grossstadtfeindschaft* (Meisenheim, 1970).

16 This and the following two paragraphs are based on the analysis in Moeller, 'Peasants and tariffs'.

17 Werner Heinrichs, 'Die Entwicklung der landwirtschaftlichen Betriebsverhältnisse in dem westlichen Teil des Hellweggebietes unter dem Einfluss der Industrie' (diss., Bonn, 1938), 116.

18 On indebtedness, see the results of a 1902 survey in *Preussische Statistik*, Vol. 191, Part III (Berlin, 1906), 41–3, 47–8, 50. On land prices, see Walther Rothkegel, 'Die Bewe-

gung der Kaufpreise für ländliche Besitzungen und die Entwicklung der Getreidepreise 1895–1909', *Schmollers Jahrbuch* 34 (1910): 1689–1747.

19 Puhle, *Agrarische Interessenpolitik*, 242.

20 See in particular Jens Flemming, *Landwirtschaftliche Interessen und Demokratie: Ländliche Gesellschaft, Agrarverbände und Staatt 1890–1925* (Bonn, 1978), esp. 80–105; Martin Schumacher, *Land und Politik: Eine Untersuchung über politische Parteien und agrarische Interessen 1914–1923* (Düsseldorf, 1978), 33ff.; Friedrich Aereboe, *Der Einfluss des Krieges auf die landwirtschaftliche Produktion in Deutschland* (Stuttgart, Berlin, Leipzig and New Haven, Conn., 1927); August Skalweit, *Die deutsche Kriegsernährungswirtschaft* (Stuttgart, Berlin, Leipzig and New Haven, Conn., 1927); Fritz Beckmann, 'Die Organisation der agraren Produktion im Kriege', *Zeitschrift für die gesamte Staatswissenschaft*, n.s. 7 (1916): 477–516, 611–26, 698–716, 771–98; and Robert G. Moeller, 'Dimensions of social conflict in the Great War: the view from the German countryside', *Central European History* 14 (1981): 147–51.

21 The so-called *Schweinemord* unleashed an extended debate in the press over food policy. See Beckmann, 'Die Organisation', 700, 703.

22 See the discussion in Moeller, 'Dimensions'.

23 Schumacher, *Land und Politik* 39–62; and for background on the creation of the *Kriegsernährungsamt*, Gerald D. Feldman, *Army, Industry and Labor in Germany, 1914–1918* (Princeton, N.J., 1966), 108–16. See also comments of Adolf von Batocki, head of the War Food Office, at a meeting in Berlin on the food supply attended by all Oberpräsidenten, 8 September 1916, LAK, 403/12317, Bl. 23.

24 The phrase 'passive resistance' was used by contemporaries. See, e.g., *Rheinische Zeitung*, 13 December 1916, clipping in LAK, 403/12701; and Skalweit, *Kriegsernährungswirtschaft*, 3. Underreporting was a constant theme in the reports of government officials at the local level which provide the richest single source for the evaluation of the impact of the controlled economy on the economic welfare of the peasantry. The problem of underreporting was also openly conceded in the government's official publications. See *Preussische Statistik*, Vol. 257 (Berlin, 1921), 76*–79*; and the discussion in Rudolf Berthold, 'Zur Entwicklung der deutschen Agrarproduktion und der Ernährungswirtschaft zwischen 1907 und 1925', *Jahrbuch für Wirtschaftsgeschichte*, Part IV (1974): 83–111.

25 The actual slaughter weights might be only slightly more than half of those used in official calculations. See, e.g., report of RP Arnsberg, 23 September 1917, RP Münster, 30 September 1917, RP Minden, 28 April 1918, all in StAM, Reg. Münster 4833; also, RP Aachen, 24 June, 1918, LAK, 403/12327/Bl. 697.

26 See the discussion with complete references in Moeller, 'Dimensions', 153–5.

27 Otto Baumgarten, 'Der sittliche Zustand des deutschen Volkes unter dem Einfluss des Krieges', in *Geistige und sittliche Wirkungen des Krieges in Deutschland* (Stuttgart, Berlin, Leipzig and New Haven, Conn., 1927), 26 and passim.

28 Moeller, 'Dimensions', 155.

29 Carl Legien for the General Commission of the Free Trade Unions to War Food Office (*Kriegsernährungsamt*) and Bethmann-Hollweg, February 1917, StAM, OP 3934; and in general, Feldman, *Army, Industry*, 97–116, 283–91.

30 Jürgen Tampke, *The Revolutionary Movement in the Rhenish-Westphalian Industrial Region 1912–1919* (Canberra, 1978), 33–66.

31 Feldman, *Army, Industry*, 369.

32 See in particular the description of controls on grains in Moeller, 'Dimensions', 155–9.

33 Jürgen Kocka, *Klassengesellschaft im Krieg 1914–1918* (Göttingen, 1973), 35.

34 Manfred Günther Plachetka, 'Die Getreide-Autarkiepolitik Bismarcks und seiner Nachfolger im Reichskanzleramt' (diss., Bonn, 1969), 455–6; Hans-Jürgen Puhle, *Politische Agrarbewegungen in kapitalistischen Industriegesellschaften: Deutschland, USA und Frankreich im 20. Jahrhundert* (Göttingen, 1975), 79–81; and Carl von Tyszka, *Der Konsument in der Kriegswirtschaft* (Tübingen, 1916), 19.

35 Feldman, *Army, Industry*, 4; also idem, 'Die Demobilmachung und die Sozialordnung der Zwischenkriegszeit in Europa', *Geschichte und Gesellschaft* 9 (1983): 156–77.

36 Landrat Halle, quoted in report of RP Minden, 22 July 1917, StAM, OP 3938. See a similar complaint from RP Münster, 27 May 1917, StAM, OP 3936.

37 See Schumacher, *Land und Politik*, 130–43, 317–53; and William Carl Mathews, 'The German Social Democrats and the inflation: food, foreign trade, and the politics of stabilization 1914–1920' (Ph.D. dissertation, University of California, Riverside, 1982), 533–78. These sources serve as well as the basis for the argument in the next paragraph.

38 To Otto Braun, at the time, Prussian Minister of Agriculture, BAK, R 43 I/ 1255, Bl. 117ff.; and Reichsministerium meeting of 16 June 1919, ibid., Bl. 153.

39 See the directive from 17 May 1919 in StAM, Kreis Siegen, Landratsamt 1674, and a similar directive to this effect from 6 June 1919 in StAM, OP 3970.

40 RP Minden, 17 October 1919, StAM, OP 3970. Still, these audits were to continue, at least for grain, until the spring of 1921. See the order of RP Aachen to Landräte und Oberbürgermeister, LAK, 403/13305, Bl. 485–87.

41 See Osmond's contribution in this volume.

42 Report of 19 June 1920 and the accompanying report from Kreisausschuss Lübbecke, 6 June 1920, StAM, OP 3947.

43 1 October 1920, BAK, R 43 I/ 1257, Bl. 259. Similar assessment from RP Düsseldorf, 21 May 1920, LAK, 403/13310, Bl. 331.

44 The brief discussion of the inflation in this and the next two paragraphs draws heavily on the excellent study of Carl-Ludwig Holtfrerich, *Die deutsche Inflation 1914–1923: Ursachen und Folgen in internationaler Perspektive* (Berlin and New York, 1980); and the older but still indispensable account of Bresciani-Turroni.

45 In general on the nature of the industrial recovery, see Gerald D. Feldman, *Iron and Steel in the German Inflation, 1916–1923* (Princeton, N.J., 1977); and idem and Heidrun Homburg, *Industrie und Inflation: Studien und Dokumente zur Politik der deutschen Unternehmer 1916–1923* (Hamburg, 1977); on the negotiations among these three groups on the policy to maintain the inflation, see also Gerald D. Feldman, 'The political economy of Germany's relative stabilization during the 1920/21 World Depression', in *Die deutsche Inflation*, 180–206.

46 The point is developed at greater length in Moeller, 'Winners as losers'.

47 RP Cologne, report of 31 October 1917 and 30 January 1917, StAM, Reg. Münster 4834. In general, see also Osmond, 'German peasant farmers'.

48 Osmond's comments in 'German peasant farmers' are highly instructive on this point.

49 See, e.g., Minister of the Interior to all OP, 14 September 1921, LAK, 403/13331.

50 On the demand for reinstitution of controls, see, e.g., report of a meeting of municipal government and trade union representatives in Düsseldorf, 16 November 1920, LAK, 403/13328; report of meeting of Arbeitskammer of Preisprüfungsstellen Westfalen, 7 October 1920, StAM, OP 3971; and another meeting of the same organization, 5 October 1920, HStAD, Reg. Düsseldorf 9075. And on the offices, established to determine price guidelines, see Goetz Briefs, 'Aufbau und Tätigkeit der Preisprüfungsstellen in der Praxis', in *Die Preisprüfungsstellen* (Berlin, 1917).

51 Landwirtschaftlicher Verein für Rheinpreussen to Prussian Minister of Agriculture, 23 May 1921, StAM, OP 4010. See also report of RP Cologne to Opräs.R, 25 August 1921 on the heated conflict over vegetable prices in Cologne, LAK, 403/13351, Bl. 489–91, and RP Cologne to Opräs.R, 19 August 1921, LAK, 403/13331.

52 This and the next four paragraphs summarize arguments developed at length in Moeller, 'Winners as losers'.

53 The system is described in Moeller, ibid.

54 Andreas Hermes, Reich Minister of Agriculture, speech to Reichstag, session of 16 June 1921, *VdRT, I. Wahlperiode 1920*, Vol. 349 (Berlin, 1921), 3906.

55 Anton Fehr, Hermes' successor, speech to Reichstag, session of 30 June 1922, *VdRT* 356:8189–90.

56 Letter from Oberbürgermeister Gelsenkirchen, 6 September 1923, StAM, Reg. Arnsberg, I 15, no. 23.

57 RP Düsseldorf to Opräs.R, 18 January 1923, LAK, 403/13308; RP Aachen to Prussian Minister of Agriculture, 5 February 1923, LAK, 403/13311; similar report of Opräs.W, 4 November 1922 and report from RP Minden, 23 December 1922, StAM, OP 3985. Also, *Münsterischer Anzeiger*, 3 December 1922 and report of Landrat Heinsberg, 26 February 1923, LAK, 403/13340, Bl. 1035.

58 See Hans Luther's comments at Kabinettsitzung, 15 August 1923, *Das Kabinett Strese-*

mann I u. II *(13. August bis 6. Oktober 1923)*, ed. Karl Dietrich Erdmann and Martin Vogt, Vol. 1 (Boppard, 1978), 4–7; also his letter to Reichskanzler, 22 August 1923, ibid., 60–3, and his comments at the Kabinettsitzungen, 30 August 1923 and 10 September 1923, ibid., 162–3 and 226–7.

59 See most recently, the account in Dieter Gessner, *Agrarverbände in der Weimarer Republik: Wirtschaftliche und soziale Voraussetzungen agrarkonservativer Politik vor 1933* (Düsseldorf, 1976); also the excellent study of Schleswig-Holstein by Rudolf Heberle, completed in the 1930s but published only in full thirty years later as *Landbevölkerung und Nationalsozialismus. Eine soziologische Untersuchung der politischen Willensbildung in Schleswig-Holstein 1918–1932* (Stuttgart, 1963). Also useful are Dieter Gessner, 'The dilemma of German agriculture during the Weimar Republic', in *Social Change and Political Development in Weimar Germany*, ed. Richard Bessel and E. J. Feuchtwanger (London, 1981), 134–54; and idem, 'Agrarian protectionism in the Weimar Republic', *Journal of Contemporary History* 12 (1977): 759–78. A useful overview is provided by Kim R. Holmes, 'The forsaken past: agrarian conservatism and National Socialism in Germany', *Journal of Contemporary History* 17 (1982): 671–88. The account in this and the next paragraphs draws on this literature.

60 Fritz Beckmann, 'Kreditpolitik und Kreditlage der deutschen Landwirtschaft seit der Währungsstabilisierung', *Berichte über Landwirtschaft*, n.s. 4 (1926): 79–140, 211–72.

61 See the discussion in the works cited above in note 59. On the interesting parallels with recent explanations of nineteenth-century agrarian discontent in America, see Robert A. McGuire, 'Economic causes of late-nineteenth century agrarian unrest: new evidence', *Journal of Economic History* 41 (1981): 835–52. And on the significance of these repeated crises, see the interesting discussion by Rudolf Vierhaus, 'Auswirkungen der Krise um 1930 in Deutschland: Beiträge zur einer historisch-psychologischen Analyse', in *Die Staats und Wirtschaftskrise des Deutschen Reiches 1929/1933*, ed. Werner Conze and Hans Raupach (Stuttgart, 1967), 158.

62 This is stressed in the work of Gessner. See also J. E. Farquharson, *The Plough and the Swastika: The NSDAP and Agriculture in Germany 1918–1945* (London and Beverly Hills, Calif., 1976), 25–42; and, e.g., Geoffrey Pridham, *Hitler's Rise to Power: The Nazi Movement in Bavaria, 1923–1933* (New York, Evanston, Ill., San Francisco and London, 1973), 224–36; and Horst Gies, 'NSDAP und landwirtschaftliche Organisationen in der Endphase der Weimarer Republik', *Vierteljahrshefte für Zeitgeschichte* 15 (1967): 341–76. On the agrarian splinter parties in Weimar's later year, see the contribution by Larry Jones in this volume.

6 A Second Agrarian Mobilization? Peasant Associations in South and West Germany, 1918–24

JONATHAN OSMOND

I

The mobilization of the agrarian interest in the 1890s has found a rightful place in analyses of German political development. The Protestant Junker estate-owners of the east, the Catholic landowning aristocracy of Silesia and western Germany, and large numbers of small peasant farmers organized and agitated on a scale hitherto unknown against falling agricultural prices and foreign competition. In the process they developed political purposes and methods which went beyond the strictly economic complaints of the farmer. The imperial administration, the regional state governments and bureaucracies, and the political parties were forced to take heed of agrarian demands articulated through large and forceful pressure groups. In 1893 the Agrarian League (*Bund der Landwirte*) was founded at the instigation of Junker grain-producers, but grew rapidly to incorporate substantial numbers of Protestant small farmers throughout Germany. Its demagogic tactics and its overt political role helped to influence agricultural policy and to draw the peasantry into an era of mass politics. A similar function was performed in a more diffuse manner by the Catholic peasant associations which emerged in the south and west of Germany and combined in 1900 to form the Federation of the Christian Peasants' Associations of Germany (*Vereinigung der christlichen Bauernvereine Deutschlands*).[1]

Less attention has been paid to the significant changes which followed the First World War and the revolution. In the same way that trade unions, political parties and other interest groups adapted and expanded in the immediate postwar period, so the peasants were drawn further into organizational and political life.[2] It is not enough to claim, as one scholar has, that 'toward the new state they adopted an attitude of reserve, favored the political parties on the right over those on the left, and in the main directed their attention to their long-neglected farms'.[3] In fact, the economic and political dislocation of the years 1918–24 involved a second crucial stage in the peasant mobilization begun in the 1890s and a dramatic crisis for the established bodies of agrarian representation. Precisely because they were concerned about their long-neglected farms, the peasants were stirred to exert pressure from below on their erstwhile leaders in the Agrarian League and the Catholic Federation. The war economy, its prolongation after the war and the revolution exploded the tenuous consensus which had been reached during the crises of the 1890s and in the immediate prewar period of relative prosperity, and revealed the organizational limits of the two main associations. The peasants rejected the apparent complicity of the League and the Federation in the wartime restrictions on production, prices and marketing, and either through the old organizations or through newly founded groups tried to combat the postwar controlled economy (*Zwangswirtschaft*).[4] Far from being passive, the peasants were even more vocal than they had been in the 1890s.

Dissatisfaction with the former leaders of the agrarian lobby was coupled with fears that revolutionary council government or even parliamentary rule under the Social Democrats would mean the socialization of farming property and the continuation of agricultural controls to the benefit of consumers rather than producers. Peasants may rarely have appeared as an overt counter-revolutionary force in these immediate postwar years, but their increased agitation had strong anti-socialist and anti-state impulses. State interference in production and marketing was particularly resented during the years of inflation, when it seemed that only price controls and compulsory food deliveries were preventing the farmers from exploiting their advantageous position as food-producers in a time of general privation and high demand. Here was a major difference both from the 1890s and from the depression which began in the later 1920s. From 1918 to 1924 farmers were angry, anxious and frustrated, but they were also conscious of some strength in their economic position. This may help to explain the characteristics of agrarian interest representation in these years: a huge mobilization of the peasantry, a professionalization and institutionalization of agricultural bodies and an affirmation of regional and local priorities.

Certain national features of the crisis of 1918–24 have emerged from recent literature. Martin Schumacher describes the heated postwar debates about agricultural policy and about the relationship between the political parties and the agrarian pressure groups. Jens Flemming discusses organizational developments, changing social relations in the countryside and the problems posed to farmers by the upsurge of organized agricultural labour. Hans-Jürgen Puhle draws a contrast between the tightly organized campaigns of the League before the First World War and its looser structure from 1921 as the more decentralized National Rural League (*Reichslandbund*).[5]

Essential for an understanding of these processes is a discussion of the regional experience. Both the Agrarian League and the Catholic Federation were built upon regional associations, and were in contention at local as well as at national level, since few areas were homogeneously Protestant or Catholic. Economic circumstances were regionally diverse, according to the types of farming practised, market structures and economic controls. Political structures too, despite the importance of national parties, were based on regional political communities, within which the farming associations played their part. Most important of all perhaps, the farmers' own experience of organized agitation was gained in regionally defined pressure groups. These have found treatment in the work of Jens Flemming on the central and eastern Prussian regions of Brandenburg, Saxony and Pomerania, in that of Robert Moeller on Westphalia and the northern Rhineland, and to a certain extent in the older pioneering study of Schleswig-Holstein by Rudolf Heberle.[6] It is the purpose of this article to adduce evidence of change in the regions of south and west Germany.

II

Germany west of the Rhine and south of the Main comprised the Prussian Rhine Province, Rhine Hesse, Birkenfeld, the Saar, the Palatinate, Baden, Württemberg, Hohenzollern and Bavaria.[7] These states and provinces were by no means uniform in structure, but they had sufficient in common to allow useful comparisons to be made between their experiences of agrarian politics in the prewar and postwar periods. They were also areas where both the Agrarian League and the Catholic associations had strongholds and were in competition with each other.

Confessionally there were great variations, and these were significant in view of the denominational allegiances of the agrarian associations. Only the tiny Prussian enclave of Hohenzollern could be described as homogeneous: almost entirely Catholic. The Rhine Province and the Saar were approximately two-thirds Catholic. Bavaria east of the Rhine was even more strongly so, but a distinction must be made between Catholic southern Bavaria and Lower Franconia and the Protestant regions of Central and Upper Franconia. Württemberg and Hesse were two-thirds Protestant, but in Baden and the Bavarian Palatinate the confessional mix was more even, with a Catholic preponderance in the former and a Protestant one in the latter. As important as these broad delineations, however, was the fact that within them were local confessional concentrations and also areas of mixed population. In localities of the latter type complexities of associational allegiance were particularly marked.[8]

The pattern of land tenure was likewise variable, and general regional differences were often offset by distinctive local characteristics. Inheritance laws differed considerably, providing for partible inheritance in much of the Rhineland and for entail in areas east of the Rhine. Other determinants were the nature of the cultivable terrain, the types of farming practised and general demographic movements. One aspect is quite clear, however: most of the agricultural land was owner-occupied. This was clearest in Württemberg and Bavaria, where the proportion was 92 and 95 per cent respectively, and least marked in the Rhine Province, where it was 80 per cent.[9]

About half of the agricultural land was in the form of holdings between 5 and 20 hectares in size, the lowest proportion being in the Rhine Province (44 per cent) and the highest in Bavaria (52 per cent). The whole of southern and western Germany was, therefore, characterized by the so-called medium peasant holding. The distribution of the rest of the land was more diverse. Dwarf-holdings of 2 hectares or less were significant in all areas except Bavaria and Hohenzollern, taking up between 10 (Württemberg) and 15 per cent (the Palatinate) of the land. Many of these tiny plots, especially near industrial centres, were cultivated by those whose main occupation was not agriculture, and they were rarely active in the peasant associations. Small peasant holdings of 2 to 5 hectares occupied between one-fifth (the Rhine Province) and one-third (Baden) of the land, except in Bavaria where the proportion was only 12 per cent. The large peasant farm of 20 to 100 hectares was important in Bavaria (30 per cent), the Rhine Province (21 per cent) and Württemberg-Hohenzollern (18–19 per cent), much less so in Baden, Hesse and the Palatinate (9–11 per cent). Estates of 100 hectares or more did exist in south and west Germany, and their owners were often prominent in agrarian politics, but their share of the land was very small.[10]

A distinction is often made between the grain-growing regions of eastern Germany and the dairy and livestock production of the west, but in fact grain was a major component even of the peasant economy.[11] Lower Bavaria, Hesse and the Palatinate were notable in this respect. The main arable crops were, however, almost without exception, potatoes, hay and oats, all pointing to a substantial livestock economy.[12] Dairy farming was a crucial facet of the small peasant farms, bringing in the farmers' regular income. It was prevalent in the Alpine regions and in areas supplying the large urban centres of the Rhineland.

Two speciality crops also deserve mention. Tobacco was produced on very small holdings in Baden and the Palatinate, and viticulture was a major feature of the landscape in many areas, particularly in the Palatinate and on the Moselle. The vineyards were generally very small, but could be very profitable.

171

The uneven urban and industrial development of the south and west affected the communications and market outlets of the peasants, the amount of farm labour available, the relative importance of the worker-smallholder sector and the attitude of the peasants to the urban consumer interest. It was in the Rhineland in particular that there were tensions between the cities and the rural hinterland. These promoted more radical farming movements in the Lower Rhine region, in the Saar and in the Palatinate.

For most of the period 1918–24 the whole of the territory west of the Rhine was under foreign, mainly French, military occupation. The Saar was actually separated from the rest of Germany, but even in other areas the French presence influenced the political and organizational life of the farming population and imposed greater economic strains on agriculture than elsewhere.

III

The terms 'agrarian politics', 'agrarian representation' and 'agrarian associations' cover a wide range of different and changing organizations, but in the context of the Weimar Republic they are used to refer principally to voluntary membership associations functioning as farming pressure groups or unions, and secondly to officially instituted agricultural bodies, elected or otherwise. The associations played their part within such bodies and exerted political influence on government and parties, but had an important immediate role for their members in providing information, economic and technical assistance, and social facilities. In such a form they were, however, still a relatively recent development.[13]

The nineteenth century had seen in most parts of Germany the development of official and semi-official agricultural bodies which were ostensibly non-political and concerned themselves with the economic and technical improvement of agriculture. The most notable of these were the Agricultural Associations (*Landwirtschaftliche Vereine*). They did solicit a popular farming membership, but they were dominated by civil servants and large landowners. The same was true of the state agricultural institutions which grew out of them in the 1890s, such as the Bavarian Agricultural Council (*Bayerischer Landwirtschaftsrat*) and the Agricultural Chamber for the Rhine Province (*Landwirtschaftskammer für die Rheinprovinz*) in Bonn.[14]

This reorganization of the official agricultural representation at the end of the century was largely a response to the economic problems of the 1890s and the growth of the so-called 'economic-political' organizations. These were the Peasants' Associations and the Agrarian League. The first

Peasants' Associations were founded as early as the 1860s, but it was in the 1880s and 1890s that they spread to most parts of the Catholic south and west and acquired a mass membership. It was in order to consolidate their position that they formed the Federation in 1900, but it remained a fairly loose grouping of disparate organizations. Meanwhile the Agrarian League made rapid progress in Protestant regions after 1893. Farmers were encouraged to join an association by the economic difficulties posed by Caprivi's policy of foreign trade accords, by the co-operative, technical, legal and insurance facilities offered by the local groups, and by the pressure which could be brought to bear at national level, particularly in the sphere of protection against foreign competition. The agrarian pressure groups also came to play an important role within political parties: the German Conservatives and the National Liberals in the case of the League, and the Centre Party in the case of the Federation. Thus in the space of a few years the organizational opportunities for the expression of the agrarian interest had changed significantly. New or revitalized 'economic-political' associations went out to seek the membership and support of the small farmers, and to increase the political clout of agriculture through overt intervention in official agrarian representation and in local and national politics.[15]

In the Rhineland the two most important organizations were the Rhenish Peasants' Association (*Rheinischer Bauernverein*, founded 1882) in the north and the Trier Peasants' Association (*Trierischer Bauernverein*, founded 1884) in the south. The former tended to be dominated by the Catholic nobility, in particular the Loë family. The latter was under greater clerical influence, the priests Dasbach and Schifferings taking the presidency at different times. The Agrarian League also made progress, but was limited by the predominantly Catholic nature of the region.[16]

One notable local phenomenon was the Hunsrück Peasants' Association (*Hunsrücker Bauernverein*, founded 1892), the creation of the clergyman Richard Oertel. Largely Protestant and not affiliated to the Federation, it made good headway in Prussian territory south of the Moselle and in the Oldenburg enclave of Birkenfeld, pursuing an uneasy path between the League and the Trier Association.[17]

The only organization to make any impact on the Bavarian Palatinate before 1914 was the Agrarian League, which helped to erode the previous political monopoly of the area by the National Liberals. The League brought matters of agrarian protection into the forefront of National Liberal debates, provoking intense internal wrangling and robbing the National Liberals of much of their rural support. By 1909 they had lost all six of their Reichstag seats for the Palatinate, two of them to the League. These political advances of the League were not matched, however, by spectacular membership gains. A figure of about 5,000 farmers was reached quickly, but then stagnated until the upheavals of 1918 and beyond. The Catholic farmers had no representation at all, despite an attempt to found a Peasants' Association in 1894.[18]

Agrarian politics in Hesse from the 1890s were characterized by the shifting relationship between the rural-based anti-Semitic party of Otto Böckel, the Agrarian League and the National Liberals, with the Catholic Hessian Peasants' Association (*Hessischer Bauernverein*, founded 1883) playing a minor role. The National Liberals, in the person of Waldemar von Oriola, dominated the League but, as in the Palatinate, there was dispute within the party about the extent to which the agrarian interest was coming to the fore. The League also had to take account of the hold which the anti-Semites had on the Protestant farming population, and in 1904 the anti-Semitic Hessian Peasants' League (*Hessischer Bauernbund*) merged with the League.[19]

In Baden, by contrast, it was the Catholic association which made the running. Although the Central Baden Peasants' Association (*Mittel-badischer Bauernverein*) of 1885 made little progress at first, it revived in the early 1890s and was refounded in 1892 as the Baden Peasants' Association (*Badischer Bauernverein*). It underwent a huge expansion from 1892 to 1897 and progressed steadily thereafter, reaching a membership of about 70,000 in 1913. Its success was built in part on the discontent of the small tobacco farmers and winegrowers. The Agrarian League also made some inroads, here too associated with the National Liberals.[20]

In Württemberg the agricultural constituency was fought over by the Württemberg Peasants' League (*Württembergischer Bauernbund*, founded 1893), which was the local organization of the Agrarian League, the People's Party (*Volkspartei*) and the Centre. The League made slow advances at first, overshadowed by the People's Party, but in later alliance with the Conservatives progressed to a membership of about 20,000 in 1914 and a strong presence in the *Landtag*. Meanwhile, the Centre Party concerned itself increasingly with the agrarian interest, although the Hohenzollern and Württemberg Peasants' Associations (*Hohenzollerischer* and *Württembergischer Bauernvereine*) were founded late: in 1898 and 1899 respectively. Progress was limited until reorganization in 1918.[21]

Each of the seven administrative districts of Bavaria east of the Rhine had from the 1890s its own Catholic Peasants' Association, these being united in 1898 under the title of the Bavarian Christian Peasants' Association (*Bayerischer Christlicher Bauernverein*). By the outbreak of war, it had achieved a massive membership of about 158,000 farmers. Dominated by the personality of the former teacher Georg Heim, the association provided a mass rural constituency for the Centre Party and received the support of the Catholic clergy. It could not be described as an establishment bastion, however, since its demands often brought it into conflict with the liberal ministries of Bavaria, and during the First World War Heim pursued a vehement campaign against Reich and state agricultural policy.[22]

In Protestant Franconia it was the Agrarian League which held sway, and for a short while it seemed that it might make incursions into Catholic Lower Bavaria. In the event the Bavarian Peasants' League (*Bayerischer Bauernbund*) established an independent existence in 1895 and developed into a major force in Bavarian agricultural politics, following a populist, anti-clerical and sometimes anti-Semitic line. One other organization also gained some ground: the liberal German Peasants' League (*Deutscher Bauernbund*, founded 1909), particularly in Lower Franconia.[23]

By 1914, therefore, the two main groupings of the League and the Federation had staked out for themselves most of the farming constituency of the south and west. Peasant pressure from below had in large measure been subsumed into voluntary associations and official bodies led by the Protestant and Catholic landowning aristocracy, bourgeois notables and the clergy. In the main the programme of agrarian protection met with at least the tacit approval of the small arable farmers, and concessions to the livestock producers over meat quotas placated them too. The protests of tobacco farmers and winegrowers could also be accommodated within the Catholic associations. Furthermore, the general rise in agricultural prices in the years preceding the First World War calmed some of the agitation of the 1890s.

The ground had not been uncontested, however, and it was by no means clear that the small farmers would subscribe without question to the view that their economic and political interests were consonant with those of the agrarian notables. Early challenges from the Bavarian Peasants' League and the Hessian anti-Semites, for instance, forced the League and the Federation to adopt more populist tactics. Local organizations continued a separate existence in Bavaria and the Hunsrück, and the foundation of the German Peasants' League in 1909 signified a dissatisfaction with the relationship between the Agrarian League and the small peasant farmers. Of greater significance was the fact that many, probably most, of the peasants of south and west Germany had not joined any association before 1914. The prominence of the League and the Federation by the eve of the war should not disguise the great disparity between their fortunes in different areas, nor the large numbers of peasants who were as yet unorganized.

IV

The changes which beset the prewar structure of agrarian representation in the early years of the Weimar Republic were the result of the problems

175

posed to German agriculture and the farmers' organizations by the First World War, the revolution and the inflation.[24] On the economic side, agriculture faced in the war and its aftermath great strains on its productive capacity and increasingly strict regulation of production, prices and marketing. Farmers resented the fact that they were no longer permitted free determination of their productive and consumptive priorities, and argued that the controls were endangering rather than promoting an adequate food supply. On the organizational side, the farmers' associations could not in the war operate as they had done hitherto. If they maintained opposition to governmental policy they were accused of disruptive and unpatriotic behaviour, but if they collaborated with the implementation of the war economy they faced the suspicion and anger of their membership.[25] This membership was itself weakened by the absence of so many men at the front. On the political side, the peasants' distrust of socialism was provoked by the apparent victory of the labour movement in the revolution. Farmers feared that agricultural production and marketing were to be subjected in perpetuity to state control, and that there was an immediate danger of the socialization or redistribution of farming property. These fears may have been ill founded, but they were no less real for that. To make matters worse, the bourgeois parties which might have been expected to stem the red tide appeared to be in disarray. It was these frustrations which prompted the peasantry to match the mobilization of the organized working class in town and country.[26]

In the Prussian Rhine Province the Rhenish and Trier Associations, the Agricultural Chamber and the Agrarian League came under pressure from above and below. From above, the new government of the Council of People's Commissars was stipulating changes in agricultural representation. The extent of its socialist agricultural programme was as yet unknown, but was viewed with trepidation. The French and Belgian occupying forces were also imposing restrictions on the freedom of action of the farming associations. The regionally prominent Centre Party meanwhile was rent between its conservative and democratic wings. From below came signs of new radical movements amongst the peasantry and of a fragmentation of the existing bodies. The latter were hard pressed to maintain control of the situation, and they did so with mixed success.

In November 1918 the provisional government announced that Peasants' and Farmworkers' Councils (*Bauern- und Landarbeiterräte*) should be established throughout Germany. They were intended to complement the revolutionary Workers' and Soldiers' Councils and to safeguard food supplies to the towns, but in practice they were generally constructed as counter-revolutionary instruments defensive of the farming interest.[27] In the Rhine Province it was the established agrarian repre-

176

sentation which took charge of the new bodies, forming in Cologne the Rhenish Peasants' Council (*Rheinischer Bauernrat*). This comprised the presidents of the Rhenish, Trier and Hunsrück Associations, the Agricultural Association and the Agrarian League. They were attempting to sustain their grasp on their own organizations and to consolidate a mass base for the Council by harnessing the peasant activism which was becoming evident in many areas. In the event, the French banned the council movement in the Rhineland, and the agrarian leaders had to seek other forms of organizational restructuring.[28]

The prewar associations were fragmenting at the local level, and hitherto unorganized farmers were joining new peasant groups. Even before the revolution, a committee of farmers was founded in Gladbach, near Düsseldorf, in September 1918. Shortly afterwards there was a local initiative in Schleiden, on what was to be the new Belgian border, a farmers' organization being founded in March 1919. The Hunsrück too witnessed a shake-up of its agrarian associations. Most significant were developments in the Moers area of the Lower Rhine, near the Dutch frontier.[29]

Moers, Cleve and Geldern were overwhelmingly Catholic districts, with a dense population of smallholders producing for the large local urban market. The area had been dominated by the Rhenish Peasants' Association. In January 1919 anger about the controlled economy, fear of socialism and dissatisfaction with the Rhenish Association prompted the calling of a farmers' meeting in Xanten, which attracted a large attendance and led to the formation of the 'Association to Protect the Economic Interests of Agriculture in the Moers Area'. The instigator of this was Josef Scholten, a local landowner. He was encouraged by this first foray and organized a propaganda campaign in surrounding areas and at a meeting of the Rhenish Association in Bonn. The result was the founding in March 1919 of the Free Peasantry (*Freie Bauernschaft*).[30]

The Free Peasantry was a new form of association, based on the notion that farmers should imitate the trade union organization of the industrial workers in order to assert producer against consumer interests. Its leaders disavowed party politics and swore to fight for the economic future of agriculture through activist means, including that of the produce delivery strike. Although they took their example from the Free Trade Unions and adopted a democratic union structure, the Free Peasants were vehemently anti-socialist and directed their efforts against state intervention in the agricultural economy and for the preservation of private property.[31]

The movement made rapid progress on the Lower Rhine. Within a couple of months twenty-six local groups were founded in the Moers district, and by 1921 the Free Peasantry had encompassed most of the farmers in the area and many in nearby Cleve and Geldern. It was very active in combating the controlled economy, establishing in June 1919 an economic commission to monitor farm prices and pressing the authorities, with some success, to raise prices, reduce delivery obligations, ensure adequate fertilizer supplies and provide compensation for requisitioned livestock. In 1919 negotiations with trade union consumer interests had an auspicious, but eventually disappointed, start, and the local farmers' needs were later helped by the foundation of a trading centre in Xanten.[32]

The potential of the new organization was soon recognized by the leaders of the Rhenish Association and the Agricultural Chamber. It was an opportunity to give fresh popular strength to the established bodies, but also a threat to their unity and more conservative stance. Clemens Freiherr von Loë-Bergerhausen, president of the Rhenish Association, was quick to make contact with the Free Peasantry; as early as February 1919 he staged a meeting of the Association in Xanten and voiced support for the incipient organization. He reported to the Chamber that the new movement posed no immediate threat, sharing as it did many of the aims of the established representation and showing no signs of party-political aberration. The Chamber for its part decided to welcome the new initiative and to promote it as long as it confined itself to legal tactics. The Free Peasantry would make possible the complete union of agricultural interests and provide an influx of new ideas from farming circles hitherto not reached by the official or the voluntary organizations. In the future it might indeed be the appropriate basis for elections to the Chamber.[33]

The following months saw the attempts of the Rhenish and Trier Associations to draw the Free Peasantry into their sphere of influence and to neutralize its more radical tendencies, and the attempts of the Free Peasants to take over the substructure of the Associations and to promote an activist stance on the controlled economy. The negotiations moved in fits and starts, with distrust and frustration on both sides. Loë's early contacts with Scholten were the basis of a provisional agreement on the recognition of the Free Peasantry as the substructure of the Rhenish Association, but this broke down in the summer of 1919 over questions of nomenclature, the division of responsibility between the 'trade union', the agricultural co-operatives and the Association, and the role of politics in the agrarian pressure groups. The Free Peasants insisted that their organization should abide by confessional and party-political neutrality, and this was seen by the Association as a threat to the hold of the Centre Party.[34]

An acrimonious debate developed in the press, and Loë appeared to distance himself from the Free Peasantry. Nevertheless, talks continued and in January 1920 in Cologne the Free Peasantry merged into the

Rhenish Association, while maintaining some measure of separate identity in its strongholds. The further intention of moving towards a full unification of agrarian representation in the Rhine Province was more difficult. The Trier Association was more wary of the Free Peasantry, and found itself losing ground to it. The Trier and Rhenish Associations also continued to exist separately, although in November 1920 they formed an umbrella organization called the United Rhenish Peasants' Associations (Rhenish and Trier Peasants' Association). Local accords were also reached with the Rural League, such as that between Scholten's group and the League in 1922, but there was no general amalgamation.[35]

The negotiations between the Rhenish Association and the Free Peasantry had been complicated from the beginning by a further associational novelty, the Christian Peasantry (*Christliche Bauernschaft*). This was spearheaded by Fritz Bollig of the Centre Party and was intended to assert peasant interests from within the party and to base them on 'true Christian principles'. This stress on Christian purpose was also to be found in the proclaimed objectives of the Free Peasantry, but the latter refused to be bound to Catholicism or Protestantism or to one political party. The Christian Peasantry also differed in that it took as its model the Catholic trade unions, rather than the Free Trade Unions. It did share the opposition of all the peasant groups to the controlled economy and to imagined attacks on private property, but by its more cautious stance and its insistence on operating within the Centre Party it alienated the Free Peasants, and was viewed with suspicion by Loë, who already had an uneasy relationship with the Centre. In May 1919 the Rhenish Centre Party welcomed the Christian Peasantry and, despite Loë's initial reservations, it was allowed in July to enter the Peasants' Association. This provoked a protest from the Free Peasantry, and liaison with Bollig's group was again revoked. At the local level there was tension between the Free and Christian Peasantries, as officials of the Agricultural Chamber tended to support the former and parish priests the latter.[36]

In the Hunsrück Oertel's Association likewise found itself under pressure from the Free Peasantry, here promoted by one Schössler, a renegade from the Hunsrück Association to the Agrarian League. Oertel was forced to amalgamate his organization with the Free Peasants and to see it affiliate in January 1921 to the National Rural League. A complete union of the local farmers' groups did not transpire, as the Trier Association maintained its distance.[37]

It was in the Bavarian Palatinate that the Free Peasantry scored its greatest successes and was to have its longest impact on agrarian politics. As in the rest of the Rhineland, the immediate postwar years saw a fragmentation and mobilization of the peasant interest. The Palatinate had lacked until now an organization for the Catholic farmers, but in

January 1918 a Palatine Peasants' Association (*Pfälzer Bauernverein*) was founded as a branch of the Federation and managed to capture the support of many smallholders, particularly winegrowers, in the eastern part of the province. Its progress was limited, however, by the appearance of the inter-confessional Free Peasantry, which absorbed Catholic farmers, many Protestant former members of the Agrarian League and also small peasant groups which had sprung up in 1918–19.[38]

The theory of the Free Peasantry was propounded in the Palatinate and the Saar by Heinrich Pflug, a landowner in that part of the western Palatinate now ceded to the Saar territory. He claimed that it was his observation of the strength of the Saar miners' unions which had provoked his intervention. In March 1919 he published for private circulation a pamphlet called 'Agriculture against Social Democracy: What Must Farmers Know about the Organization of the Industrial Workers in Order to Learn from It? Peasant Trade Unions'. This outlined the great successes of the Free Trade Unions in furthering the cause of urban workers and argued that the peasants must adopt similar tactics if they were to counteract this socialist power. Pflug interpreted these tactics as a relentless insistence on 'egoistic' demands, supported as necessary by delivery strikes. He criticized the existing agrarian organizations for their confessional and party-political ties and, as Scholten was saying on the Lower Rhine, insisted that a new farmers' union must be free of such inhibitions. Pflug's pamphlet was perhaps the most explicit written expression of the peasantry's conception of class struggle in this period, and gained appropriate notoriety.[39]

His ideas fell on fertile ground in the Palatinate, where there was mounting anger about the controlled economy, criticism of the inactivity of the Agrarian League and only rudimentary representation of the Catholic farmers. The confessional mix of the region also made the stress on inter-confessionality an attractive way of avoiding division. The Palatine Free Peasantry was founded early in 1920 and within a couple of months was locked in battle with the authorities over the controlled economy. A series of delivery strikes in the years 1920 to 1922 strengthened the position of the union amongst the small farmers, soured relations with the towns and with the Palatine and Bavarian governments, and threw the League and the Peasant Association into turmoil.[40]

The speed of Free Peasant progress in the Palatinate was extraordinary. Membership figures of the organizations show how agrarian politics in this small province were transformed. The Free Peasantry quickly gained a roll of some 15,000, which the League in competition came to match, The Peasants' Association stabilized at less than 3,000. These figures compare with a League membership before the war of some 5,000, and a total peasant population of about 50,000. Most of the small farmers were thus for the first time drawn into the pressure groups. The campaigning tactics of the Free Peasantry had forced the League and the Association to place much more importance on mass membership and to develop a much more forthright public stance. In the same way that further north the Rhenish Association took on board many of Scholten's ideas, so in the Palatinate the League and, to a lesser extent, the Association felt compelled to adopt the more aggressive vocabulary of the Free Peasantry.

Further comparisons with the Rhine Province are helpful. As the incursion of the Free and Christian Peasantries complicated the hold of the Centre Party, so the Palatine Free Peasantry compounded the existing confusion of the bourgeois parties. Before the war the National Liberals had had to adapt to the growth of the Agrarian League if they were not to lose even more ground in rural areas. After the war the agrarians and the National Liberals merged into one party, the German People's Party of the Palatinate (DVP *der Pfalz*), which stood closer to the DNVP than to Stresemann's DVP. Despite the Free Peasantry's avowed non-political stance, many of its leaders were active in the DVP, as were prominent figures from the Agrarian League. The rivalries between the farmers' associations were thus taken into the political party as well.[41]

In the Palatinate too there were attempts to forge unity between the agrarian factions, but here they failed. Negotiations led to the formation in January 1921 of the Palatine Peasants' League (*Pfälzer Bauernbund*), an amalgam of all three organizations, but disputes over the Free Peasantry's tactic of the delivery strike and the Association's wariness about absorption into the newly founded National Rural League fractured this unity within the month, and the new League became no more than the continuation of the Agrarian League under a new name, more appropriate to the decentralized Reich body. The Free Peasantry continued its advance, and poached a large local group from the Catholic Association.[42]

The Free Peasantry was to have more serious political repercussions in the Palatinate than elsewhere. The style of the organization and its debilitating effect on governmental authority attracted the French military command, which persuaded its leader, the demagogic Franz Josef Heinz, to throw in his lot with the growing Rhenish separatist movement. He proclaimed himself President of the Autonomous Republic of the Palatinate in November 1923 and enjoyed a brief reign until his assassination in January of the following year. His escapade split the Free Peasantry, but it survived into the late 1920s, albeit in a more muted form.[43]

Events in the Saar were not as melodramatic, but here too Pflug's ideas and the Free Peasantry made rapid headway. This Catholic region had before 1918 been dominated by the Trier Association, but its position was threatened by small activist groups, which were then taken over by the Free Peasantry. By 1921 elections to the Saar Agricultural Chamber gave the Free Peasantry seventeen seats, while the Trier Association could muster only seven. The chairman of the Saar Free Peasantry assumed presidency of the Chamber.

One of the reasons for the poor performance of the Trier Association was the limitation on its activity posed by the separation of the Saar from the Reich. The Bavarian and Reich authorities tried to cope with this problem in several ways, especially when they perceived a separatist danger in Free Peasant contacts with the Saar government and the French. One tactic was to sponsor the foundation of a new Christian Peasants' Association to counteract the Free Peasantry. When this made little progress, it was recommended that the Free Peasantry itself receive financial support in order to deter it from separatism! The Free Peasant leaders were adamant that their francophile appearance was a purely tactical aspect of their economic struggle, but the German authorities remained suspicious, particularly when Heinz accepted French patronage in the Palatinate.[44]

Developments in Hesse were similar to those already described, namely, the appearance of the Free Peasantry and moves towards agrarian unity. A distinction should be made between the Hessian provinces east of the Rhine and Rhine Hesse to the west, which had a higher Catholic population and was under French occupation. The Hessian Peasants' Association had most of its membership here, but the Free Peasantry made a formidable advance and soon outstripped the membership of the Association by about 15,000 to 4,000. Moves for unity produced in February 1921 the United Free Rhine Hessian Peasantry (*Vereinigte Freie Rheinhessische Bauernschaft*), which was an amalgam of the Free Peasantry, the Agricultural Association and parts of the Association and the League. As its title suggests, it was strongly influenced by Free Peasant ideas, and was a further example of the mobilizing and radicalizing role played by the new union. East of the Rhine the regional subsidiary of the National Rural League, the Hessian Rural League (*Hessischer Landbund*), proved more resilient, sustaining a membership of some 20,000. It had, as has been indicated above, already been subject to radical influence before the war.[45]

As in the Palatinate, there was in Hesse an accommodation of rural and urban Protestant bourgeois parties, in this case a union of the right wing of the DVP and the DNVP. In addition, in the *Landtag* elections of 1921 the Rural League put up a separate list, and helped to maximize the rural and urban conservative vote. In the 1919 election the DVP and DNVP had won twelve seats; in 1921 they took thirteen and the League eleven.[46]

In Baden the powerful hold taken before the war in Catholic areas by the Baden Peasants' Association was consolidated in the immediate postwar years, as more farmers were drawn in to swell the membership to about 91,000. The League on the other hand faced some initial difficulties as local activism reared its head. In 1919 two separate peasant leagues were established by former Agrarian League supporters, one in Freiburg in the south-west and one in Bretten further to the north. In 1921, as part of the formation of the National Rural League, these merged into the Baden Rural League (*Badischer Landbund*), with about 40,000 members. In the Baden elections of that year the League stood against the DNVP and achieved 8·3 per cent of the total vote. In 1925 the two parties combined in a right-wing bloc.[47]

In Württemberg there were signs of peasant discontent with the League, threats of delivery strikes and a realignment of agrarian representation. On the Catholic side the Peasant Association was reorganized in 1917, and in the following year the Central Agricultural Association for Württemberg and Hohenzollern (*Landwirtschaftlicher Hauptverband Württemberg und Hohenzollern*) was founded. These two merged in 1922 under the title of the latter. On the Protestant side the League had from its early years functioned as a political party and it continued to do so after the war. In 1919, however, it renamed itself the Württemberg Peasants' and Winegrowers' League (*Württembergischer Bauern- und Weingärtnerbund*) in an attempt to forestall any separate organization of the smallholders and winegrowers. It performed well in the *Landtag* elections of 1919, taking fourteen seats. During the early 1920s it was in opposition, but after 1924 it became a government party and its General Secretary, Theodor Körner, took office as *Landtag* president. He had steered the fortunes of the League since 1895, and played a further political role as a postwar member of the Reichstag for the DNVP.[48]

Developments in Bavaria included all the features found elsewhere: strong League and Association presence, challenged in the postwar years; Peasants' Councils; an agrarian political party; political realignment; and peasant radicalism. The Bavarian Christian Peasants' Association remained by far the strongest of the agrarian organizations, providing as it did an effective press, numerous facilities and popular spokesmen. Heim had relinquished the presidency in 1913, but he remained the leading personality. The Association benefited too from church support and generally from governmental and administrative approval. It was far from acquiescent, however, in the face of the controlled economy and the inflation, and its local meetings could be as stormy as those of the more radical groups.[49]

The role of the Association was crucial in the crisis of the Bavarian Centre Party, which went further than the difficulties in the Rhineland. Heim had for a long time chafed at the link with the national Centre Party, since he saw the agricultural interests of Bavaria being subordinated to the industrial base of the party in the Rhineland. He also resented the democratic trend associated with Matthias Erzberger, and it was the latter's 1917 peace resolution in the Reichstag which pushed the Bavarians closer to separation. In November 1918 at an Association meeting in Regensburg Heim and other Association leaders founded the Bavarian People's Party (*Bayerische Volkspartei*), a much more conservative and agrarian-dominated Catholic party than the Centre Party of the Weimar Coalition. At first the Bavarians maintained a working arrangement with the Centre in the National Assembly, but Heim continued to push for complete separation. He was particularly hostile to Erzberger's policies at the Finance Ministry. The break came in January 1920.[50]

The Bavarian Rural League (*Bayerischer Landbund*) appeared to weather well the storms of the postwar years, with a huge membership increase and expanded activity in many districts. This regeneration was, however, a response to peasant discontent with the controlled economy and to challenges from the Bavarian Peasants' League and the Free Peasantry. Before the end of the war, membership had stagnated at about 17,000, but from 1920 to 1922 it rose from some 22,000 to some 42,000. This spectacular growth signified not only a consolidation of the League's position in its Franconian strongholds, but also an incursion into more southerly areas. There was vociferous League propaganda in the north of Bavarian Swabia, northern Upper Bavaria and the Upper Palatinate. The intensity of activity in 1922 and the danger of illegal incitement to non-delivery of foodstuffs prompted both the Ministry of the Interior and the president of the Rural League to investigate the behaviour of the radical ringleaders. The Peasants' Association and the Bavarian Peasants' League were also disturbed by this outburst of agitation against the controlled economy of grain, the latter particularly when its Upper Palatine branch defected to the Rural League.[51]

Despite such setbacks, the Bavarian Peasants' League also made rapid headway amongst the rural population. In the revolution of 1918–19 it played a role unusual for an agrarian interest group. Its radical wing was led by Karl Gandorfer, a landowner and mayor from Lower Bavaria whose brother Ludwig was a member of the USPD and a close associate of Kurt Eisner, Prime Minister of Bavaria after the revolution. Ludwig died within days of the revolution in a road accident, but Karl continued to collaborate with the left. He and Eisner promoted the foundation of a Central Peasants' Council (*Zentralbauernrat*) in Munich, which was dominated by radical members of the Peasants' League. The Peasants' Councils in Bavaria were indeed the only ones in Germany to show revolutionary sympathy, although this did not meet with the approval of the bulk of the Peasants' League membership. The other farmers' groups were unremittingly hostile and attacked the League for years afterwards for its revolutionary complicity.[52]

The Peasants' League enjoyed a huge membership increase from about 7,000 in 1914 to about 50,000 in 1921. It performed well too in the 1919 elections. With 9 per cent of the vote it sent sixteen representatives to the Bavarian *Landtag*, and with slightly less it gained four seats in the National Assembly. These were substantial improvements on the 1912 results. Nevertheless, the voice which it had in Bavarian agricultural affairs was still disproportionate to its size. Gandorfer and his colleagues had taken on the role which might have been expected to fall to the much larger Peasants' Associations, first through their dominance of the Peasants' Councils, and then through the League's participation in government. After Eisner's death the League furnished the Bavarian Minister of Agriculture from 1919 to 1930, excepting two brief spans in 1919–20 and 1923–4. In 1922 Anton Fehr of the Bavarian Peasants' League for eight months occupied the post of Reich Minister of Agriculture.[53]

This ministerial responsibility did not, however, fall to the radical wing of the League. Steiner and Wutzlhofer, Ministers of Agriculture in 1919 and 1920–3 respectively, had been members of the Council Government in Munich in 1919, but they did not generally take the radical and populist Gandorfer line. Fehr, who served as Minister of Agriculture from 1924 to 1930, was on the moderate wing of the party. The maverick Gandorfer, once excluded from power, concentrated his considerable energies and demagogic skills on inciting pressure from below, particularly in his home territory of Lower Bavaria, where his constituency gave him a *Landtag* and a Reichstag mandate.

The initial target of his agitation was the controlled economy, which in Lower Bavaria, the 'bread basket' of Bavaria, aroused particular ire because of the long-lasting restrictions on bread grain production and marketing. Agitation reached its peak in the years 1921 to 1923, by which time the controls on most produce had been lifted and there remained only the new grain levy, under which farmers had to deliver a certain proportion of their crop at fixed prices. Gandorfer's fulminations against this legislation were taken up in even more vehement form by incursors from the Free Peasantry.[54]

The Bavarian Free Peasantry was different in many respects from its counterparts in the Rhineland. Its main agitators were not indigenous to the area, but speakers from the Palatinate or non-farmer renegades from other organizations. It also became associated with racist groups, including the National Socialists. These aspects, plus its agitation against the controlled economy and its 'trade union' image, caused the Bavarian authorities great concern. They feared that it would reduce even further rural respect for the law and the state and lead the farmers into undesirable political channels.[55]

The Free Peasantry may have been something of an intruder in Bavaria, but that did not prevent it stirring up trouble and winning support. It built upon the Bavarian Peasants' League's long tradition of rural agitation and pushed the Gandorfer wing further towards radicalism. Gandorfer himself frequently spoke out strongly against the Free Peasantry, but this was because he feared its encroachment into his support. He often tried to outbid its demands. Both organizations called for grain delivery strikes in Lower Bavaria, and although these met with less success than those in the Palatinate, there was disruption of the food supply through deliberate delay of delivery.[56]

Criticism of the grain levy did lead to attacks on the authorities in general. In peasant meetings in Lower Bavaria there were repeated condemnations of the tax offices, the local administration and the price control boards. Some Free Peasant speeches crossed the line of legality and there were prosecutions for incitement to criminal action. The imprisonment of the speakers increased the wrath of their supporters. It was noticeable too that Heim and the Peasants' Associations were often denounced for their association with the BVP and hence with the government.[57]

Lower Bavaria was the scene of most activity on the part of the Bavarian Peasants' League and the Free Peasantry, but other Bavarian regions were far from immume. The Free Peasants intervened in Swabia and in the poor smallholding area of the Rhön in Lower Franconia, and the Peasants' League and the Rural League fought it out in many districts.[58]

Competition for farming support was highlighted by the ill-fated attempts to unify the agrarian associations in Bavaria. In 1920 talks between the Peasants' League and the Christian Peasants' Association foundered, as did discussions in the following year between the Peasants' League and the German Peasants' League. All the associations felt sufficiently strong to spurn uncomfortable compromise.[59]

V

It has been necessary to describe these intricate local disputes, because the organizational maelstrom was a major symptom of discontent and of the difficulties facing the Agrarian League and the Catholic Federation in the immediate postwar years. They could not hope to contain tensions in a uniform manner from above; each region had its particular problems and characteristics, which could only be dealt with at local level. Nevertheless, it is clear that certain trends lay beneath the confusion. The task must now be to identify these trends, to attempt to explain them and to estimate their longer-term significance.

186

One of the most striking features of the period was the huge increase in the membership figures of the peasant associations. The established organizations were now faced with a more vociferous mass base and with rival activist groups. Table 6.1 gives an approximation of membership of the main organizations in the early 1920s, compared with the prewar figures (in parentheses).[60]

Table 6.1 *Membership of Major Agrarian Associations: South and West Germany*

	Agrarian/ Rural League	Peasants' Association	Free Peasantry	German Peasants' League	Bavarian Peasants' League
Rhine Province Saar	43,000 (?) —	131,000 (90,000) 5,000 (2,500)	30,000 (—) 15,000 (—)	? —	— —
Palatinate	15,000 (5,000)	7,500 (—)	15,000 (—)	—	—
Hesse	20,000 (?)	8,000 (?)	15,000 (—)	?	—
Baden	40,000 (?)	91,000 (70,000)	—	?	—
Württemberg	48,000 (20,000)	30,000 (?)	—	?	—
Bavaria	42,000 (17,000)	141,000 (158,000)	12,000 (—)	10,000 (7,700)	50,000 (7,000)

Membership statistics of the pressure groups are notoriously difficult to establish, and those cited here are tentative and incomplete. Nevertheless, taken in conjunction with contemporary official and unofficial writings on agrarian organization and some indications from the reports of the associations themselves, they testify to a surge of small farmers into organized activity. Only in the case of the Bavarian Christian Peasants' Association does one detect a stagnation or even a decline in membership, but this is not surprising in view of the extraordinary success of that organization before the war and its consequent vulnerability to inroads by competitors afterwards.[61] All the other associations grew substantially, and the Free Peasantry in particular represented a new force independent of the established groups. This expansion of membership was on the face of it a boost to the League and the Federation but, as the accounts above have shown, many of the new recruits were initially attracted by local initiatives competing with the older associations. Even where these new foundations merged into the league or one of the Peasants' Associations they signified an organization of the previously unorganized and an appeal for more campaigning tactics. This meant changes in the established associations, even if they continued to operate under their prewar titles.

One such change was the adoption by the associations of more democratic, efficient and professional organizational structures. Pressure from an expanded membership led the associations to try to establish closer links between that membership and the leadership and to develop the provision of tangible assistance. Before the war the Agrarian League had had an ostensibly democratic structure, but in practice tight central control and limited local activity discouraged wide participation in League affairs.[62] The constitutions of the postwar associations permitted a greater degree of membership involvement, and the evidence suggests that this did in fact occur. Certainly leadership groups did establish themselves, but they were drawn from a wider section of the local communities and were more clearly accountable to their members.

Similarly, the tasks performed and facilities offered by the associations developed from their prewar level. Some organizations, particularly the Catholic associations in Bavaria, were already quite advanced in this respect, but after the war more of them followed suit, by establishing permanent bureaucracies of so-called 'peasant secretaries' (*Bauernsekretäre*) and panels of expert advisers on technical, legal and financial matters. Advice sessions and general meetings were held more frequently, and the newspapers and other publications of the associations proliferated. The agricultural co-operative and savings bank network, so important to the small farmers, was developed further, partly under the aegis of the 'economic-political' organizations. Agricultural employers' federations were founded in several areas in response to the legalisation of farmworkers' unions and their insistence on properly negotiated wage tariffs, and there was considerable overlap between the leadership of such bodies and that of the peasant associations.[63]

These activities were aspects of the way in which agrarian politics were entering more fully the public domain. This process had been in train well before the First World War, but was now accelerated by state intervention in the food economy during and after the war, by the increased participation of farmers in open debate of agricultural matters and by the elements of democratization heralded by the change of regime in 1918. There were several institutional innovations which reflected these developments.

Before 1914 there had been no Reich ministry of agriculture, but from the middle of the war the vital role of food and agriculture was accorded greater recognition at ministerial level. The War Food Office of May 1916 was developed in peacetime first as the Reich Food Office of November 1918, then as the Reich Food Ministry of March 1919 and eventually as the Reich Ministry for Food and Agriculture of April 1920. In the federal states too official agricultural bodies were founded. Of the states under discussion here, only Prussia had a Ministry of Agriculture before 1918. In 1919, however, a Ministry of Agriculture was established in Bavaria, a Ministry of Food in Württemberg and a Food Office in Hesse. The Saar, which was now outside the administration of the Reich, also acquired a Minister of Agriculture. The agrarian associations in some cases furnished the ministerial personnel of the new bodies, and in all cases were involved in negotiations with them.[64]

At subordinate levels of administration too there was an expansion of public agricultural representation. First there had been the short-lived Peasants' Councils, but these were succeeded in 1920 by Peasants' Chambers (*Bauernkammern*) at district, province and state level. They enlarged the network of facilities available to farmers and provided a forum for the debate of agricultural affairs. Based on a peasant franchise and contested elections, they were an area in which the rivalry of the voluntary associations could come to the fore.[65]

Another feature of the period was the assertion by the peasant associations of local and regional autonomy. The decentralization of the *Reichslandbund* (National Rural League) in 1921 was symptomatic of this, but by no means the sole example. Explanations of this phenomenon can be given at various levels. In the first place, farmers were conscious of their economic difficulties in local terms. They might well attach blame to the agricultural policies of Reich governments or to the impositions placed on Germany by Versailles, but they more easily identified their immediate problems with local antagonists: the French occupying troops, regional government, the local tax office, cattle-traders and the trade unions and factories in nearby towns. They might also feel that they could achieve more through direct action or negotiation within their regional community than they could through giving support to east Elbian magnates. Furthermore, the economic problems in one area might be very different from those elsewhere. There was no clear common cause between, say, a middling cereal farmer in Lower Bavaria, a dairy farmer in Swabia, a tobacco-producer in Baden and a winegrower on the Moselle. The occupied Rhineland in particular had marketing problems posed by French restrictions on the flow of goods to unoccupied territory. Such variations also help to explain why the timing of agitation differed. Price controls and other economic difficulties varied over time. Hence the Palatine milk and potato delivery strikes came before Lower Bavarian protest against the grain levy, and disturbances by winegrowers in several areas later still.

Differences of timing and activity were matched by a fluidity of membership between the organizations. Farmers were sometimes members of more than one peasant association, and there are also numerous examples of defections by individuals or local groups from one association to another. This applied even to the leaders, who might switch allegiance or be compelled to do so. Heinz was for a time active in the Palatine Peasants' League, Gandorfer was briefly expelled from the Bavarian Peasants' League and Scholten became a local leader of the Rhenish Peasants' Association.

Local leadership was an important feature of the associations. Whenever newspaper or police reports draw attention to radical peasant activity, they associate it with an individual agitator. These men both drew on local peasant discontent and in turn promoted it through their attested demagogic skills. Many of them were significant figures in their own communities: Heinrich Pflug was a retired major and owner of two sizeable farms and a brickworks; Karl Gandorfer likewise owned a brickworks as well as his substantial farm and was mayor of Pfaffenberg. There were differences, however, between the social standing of many of the new activists and their prewar *Honoratioren* counterparts. More of them were actually farmers, and although they often came from the category of the large peasants, they were not great estate-owners. Generational differences also played a part; in many cases activism was promoted by younger farmers or agrarian ideologues from rural backgrounds, people who had not previously been active in the peasant associations. They had often only recently returned from military service, and it is not too much of an exaggeration to talk of a 'front generation' of peasant politicians. Similarly, rank-and-file agitation was usually associated with younger farmers.[66]

Distinctions of confession, generation and political or organizational allegiance led to calls by many participants for a unification of the peasant interest at least at regional level. Although in one sense the divisions represented strength, in that they showed that the associations could rely on sufficient support to maintain their separate identities, it was felt by the agrarian leaders that their cause was ill served by a fragmented constituency. Their endeavours to promote unity met with mixed success. The early development and strong presence of the Rhenish Peasants' Association in the northern Rhineland meant that it could absorb the Free Peasantry, even if it had to adapt itself in the process. In the Palatinate a vacuum in agrarian organization before the war allowed the Free Peasantry to make such headway that it could afford to maintain a competitive independence. In Rhine Hesse it could itself take over the other organizations. In Bavaria, Baden and Würtemberg confessional divides made union impossible. Beyond that, the participation of the Bavarian

Peasants' League in the revolution made it an unwelcome ally for the BVP and the Catholic associations. In the south and west generally, the public image of the National Rural League remained that of a Junker group, and the other organizations were discouraged from too close a cooperation.

A further feature of regional diversity and autonomy was the appearance of separatism in the Rhineland and Bavaria, in both cases associated with the agrarian interest. This found its clearest expression in the Palatinate, where there was considerable peasant hostility to the Reich and Bavarian authorities and discontent with the chaotic conditions of the hyperinflation. Heinz and some of his supporters were lured by French promises of monetary stability and sympathetic treatment of agriculture. Heinz, who saw his plan as a form of counter-revolution, was initially successful, but his sponsorship by the French alienated his conservative peasant support, and his demise was greeted with general relief.[67] In Bavaria, Heim was asserting not only a conventional Bavarian particularism, but also opposition to a Reich agricultural policy which, he claimed, endangered what was a predominantly rural and agricultural state. The separation of the BVP from the Centre was only the first sign of Bavarian autonomist tendencies.

These were only the most prominent examples of the political repercussions of the peasant associations. The agrarian interest played a large part in party political crises in all areas: within the Rhenish and Bavarian Centre parties, and within and between the Protestant bourgeois parties of the Palatinate, Hesse and Baden. Two peasant associations, the Bavarian and Württemberg Peasants' Leagues, operated as political parties themselves, and prevented a consolidation of the bourgeois vote.

The political motivation of most farmers was clear. Without necessarily seeking open counter-revolution or a restoration of the old order, they hoped to combat state intervention in agriculture and to deflect dangers of socialist planning. Only the Bavarian Peasants' League seems to diverge from this pattern, but members of the League did not collaborate with the revolution to the same extent as Gandorfer and a few others. Even he was fundamentally conservative, but used a populist and anti-establishment rhetoric and was prepared to work with Eisner in order to assert the interests of agriculture. He and his supporters did make some play of calling for the division of the large entailed estates in Bavaria, but he was careful not to suggest the redistribution of more agricultural property than that.[68]

The economic origins of the postwar peasant activity are also evident. Farmers were in a relatively advantageous position but felt constrained in various ways. Demand for food was high and supply short, farmers were protected by the inflation from serious foreign competition and their debts were being wiped out. However, they were prevented from exploiting the full potential of their situation by the economic controls of the war and the *Zwangswirtschaft*, by the high prices of essential production goods such as fertilizer, fuel, machinery and seed, and by pressure from the consumer interest for lower food prices.[69] This combination of strengths and weaknesses helps to explain the nature of the peasants' organizational response: they were strong enough to organize but had sufficient complaints on which to base concerted campaigns.

VI

The events of 1918–24 can contribute to an analysis of the role of agrarian discontent in German political change from the 1890s to the rise of National Socialism. The combination in the Wilhelmine Empire of an allegedly backward political and economic agrarian stance with 'modern' forms of mobilization has been used to establish links with the appeal and tactics of the NSDAP in the rural sector. The Agrarian League in particular has been seen as an expression of 'pre-fascist' ideology and political practice. This made it prey to Nazi influence and infiltration when economic conditions deteriorated for farmers from the mid-1920s onwards.[70] Essential to an understanding of this process is a recognition of the changes which took place in the intervening period.

From 1918 to 1924 the peasant associations of south and west Germany gained significantly in membership, developed forms of organization which were more efficient and professional, became open to a wider participation of different types of farmers, and launched quite successful campaigns against aspects of German agricultural policy. The cooperatives and savings banks were developed, as were various forms of public representation for agriculture. The agrarians also played an important part in reshaping the political parties of the centre and right.

The hyperinflation and stabilization began to change all this. After 1923 German agriculture faced renewed competition from foreign produce of a higher quality and lower price than domestic goods, high interest rates soon overshadowed the gains of the inflation and placed farmers once more in serious debt, and agricultural prices began to sink. Farm foreclosures increased and demonstrations against the agricultural crisis became more frequent and more violent.[71]

From 1924 and in some cases even earlier, the membership figures of the associations began to decline appreciably. By the late 1920s farmers were evidently unwilling or unable to pay subscription dues to the associations, and they saw less purpose in acting through them. This was partly because of differential effects of the depression on sectors of peasant production. Hence there was a proliferation of small fractions devoted to the interests of particular farmers (winegrowers, tobacco farmers, and so on), and of peasant political parties. This development fits into a familiar pattern of the central period of the Weimar Republic, namely, the fragmentation of the bourgeois parties and the growth of splinter pressure group parties.[72]

In 1929 the main agrarian associations seemed to have retrieved something from their predicament, when they formed the so-called Green Front (*Grüne Front*) at national level. Regional amalgamations took place at the same time.[73] However, this long-hoped-for union of the agricultural interest was a reflection of the weakness rather than the strength of the associations. They had lost many members and were faced with sectoral fragmentation of their constituency. They had also lost, or were in the process of losing, many of the advantages achieved during the inflationary period. Ministries of agriculture in the states had been abolished or amalgamated with other ministries. Elections to Peasants' Chambers were not held because of the desire to save money. Worst of all, perhaps, the co-operative network had been severely damaged. Local funds had been eroded or erased during the hyperinflation, and the co-operatives and other financial institutions wound up or bailed out from Reich funds. In place of co-operatives in the hands of the peasant associations and responsive to local needs was a centralized agricultural co-operative system.[74]

The 'second agrarian mobilization' of 1918–24, therefore, had a pivotal role in the transition from the agrarian populism of the pre-1914 period to the Nazi progress in rural areas of the late 1920s and early 1930s. The apparatus of agrarian representation which had made strides in the prewar period was further reshaped and invigorated in the early postwar years. The contrast between these advances and the decline thereafter became part of the vacuum in the 'middle' of German politics which could be filled by the extreme right.[75]

Notes: Chapter 6

1   See particularly: A. Gerschenkron, *Bread and Democracy in Germany* (Berkeley, Calif., and Los Angeles, 1943); S. R. Tirrell, *German Agrarian Politics after Bismarck's Fall: The Formation of the Farmers' League* (New York, 1951); H.-J. Puhle, *Agrarische Interessenpolitik und preussischer Konservatismus im wilhelminischen Reich 1893–1914* (Hanover, 1966); J. Flemming, *Landwirtschaftliche Interessen und Demokratie* (Bonn, 1978); F. Jacobs, *Von Schorlemer zur Grünen Front* (Düsseldorf, 1957), D. W. Hendon, 'The Center Party and the agrarian interest in Germany 1890–1914' (Ph.D. diss., Emory University, Georgia, 1976).

2   G. D. Feldman, *Iron and Steel in the German Inflation 1916–1923* (Princeton, N.J., 1977), 102, speaks of 'a veritable organizational mania in Germany' in 1918–19.

3   W. T. Angress, 'The political role of the peasantry in the Weimar Republic', *Review of Politics* 21, no. 4 (1959): 536.

4   See: R. G. Moeller, 'Winners as losers in the German inflation: peasant protest over the controlled economy 1920–23', in G. D. Feldman, C.-L. Holtfrerich, G. A. Ritter and P.-C. Witt (eds.), *Die Deutsche Inflation: Eine Zwischenbilanz* (Berlin and New York, 1982), 255–88, and his contribution to this volume.

5   M. Schumacher, *Land und Politik: Eine Untersuchung über politische Parteien und agrarische Interessen 1914–1923* (Düsseldorf, 1978); Flemming, *Landwirtschaftliche Interessen*; Puhle, *Agrarische Interessenpolitik*, 303–7.

6   Flemming, *Landwirtschaftliche Interessen*, 198–229; R. G. Moeller, 'Peasants, politics and pressure groups in war and inflation: a study of the Rhineland and Westphalia, 1914–1924' (Ph.D. diss., University of California, Berkeley, 1980); R. Heberle, *Landbevölkerung und Nationalsozialismus* (Stuttgart, 1963).

7   Alsace and Lorraine are not treated here in view of their postwar incorporation into France. The Saar territory is included, since organizational developments there form part of a general south-west German pattern.

8   *Statistisches Jahrbuch für das Deutsche Reich 1924/5* (Berlin, 1925), 11.

9   *Statistisches Jahrbuch für das Deutsche Reich 1927* (Berlin, 1927), 52.

10 *Statistisches Jahrbuch für das Deutsche Reich 1913* (Berlin, 1913), 36–7; *Statistisches Jahrbuch für das Königreich Bayern 1911* (Munich, 1911), 69.

11 cf. J. C. Hunt, 'Peasants, grain tariffs, and meat quotas: Imperial German protectionism reexamined', *Central European History* 7 (1974): 311–31.

12 *Statistisches Jahrbuch für das Deutsche Reich 1920* (Berlin, 1920), 41–2. This assesses the crops in terms of area cultivated and the size of the harvest.

13 For definitions and theoretical analysis of the relationship between official bodies, voluntary associations and the state see H. A. Winkler, *Pluralismus oder Protektionismus? Verfassungspolitische Probleme des Verbandswesens im Deutschen Kaiserreich* (Wiesbaden, 1972).

14 cf. A. Schlögl (ed.), *Bayerische Agrargeschichte: Die Entwicklung der Land- und Forstwirtschaft seit Beginn des 19. Jahrhunderts* (Munich, 1954), 556–60; Nordrhein-Westfälisches Hauptstaatsarchiv Düsseldorf (NWHStA), RW 152 87: Organisation des landwirtschaftlichen Berufsstandes. On the Agricultural Association in Bavaria see also I. Farr, 'Populism in the countryside: the Peasant Leagues in Bavaria in the 1890s', in R. J. Evans (ed.), *Society and Politics in Wilhelmine Germany* (London, 1978), 137; also Farr's essay in this volume.

15 See particularly Puhle, *Interessenpolitik*; Hendon, 'Center Party'; Farr, 'Populism in the countryside'; Farr's contribution to this volume; and D. Blackbourn, 'Peasants and politics in Germany', *European History Quarterly* 14 (1984): 47–75.

16 Jacobs, *Von Schorlemer zur Grünen Front*, 26–32; H. Muth, 'Zur Geschichte des Hunsrücker Bauernvereins', *Jahrbuch für Geschichte und Kunst des Mittelrheins und seiner Nachbargebiete* 20/21 (1968–9): 184.

17 Muth, 'Hunsrücker Bauernverein', 178–219.

18 Landesarchiv Speyer (LA S), T63 193: Bund der Landwirte 1893. For Palatine politics before 1914 see E. O. Bräunche, *Parteien und Reichstagswahlen in der Rheinpfalz von der Reichsgründung 1871 bis zum Ausbruch des Ersten Weltkrieges 1914* (Speyer, 1982). For the agrarian interest in the Palatinate before and after the First World War see my forthcoming doctoral thesis for Oxford University, 'The Free Peasantry and Agrarian Politics in the Bavarian Palatinate during the Weimar Republic'.

19 D. S. White, *The Splintered Party: National Liberalism in Hessen and the Reich, 1867–1918* (Cambridge, Mass., and London, 1976), especially 130–1, 134–47, 171–2.

20 Hendon, 'Center Party', 62–4, 138–41, 147, 327.

21 D. Blackbourn, *Class, Religion and Local Politics in Wilhelmine Germany: The Centre Party in Württemberg before 1914* (New Haven, Conn., and London, 1980), 89, 91, 198–200, 210–13; J. C. Hunt, *The People's Party in Württemberg and Southern Germany 1890–1914* (Stuttgart, 1975), especially 89–110; J. C. Hunt, 'The "egalitarianism" of the right: the Agrarian League in southwest Germany, 1893–1914', *Journal of Contemporary History* 10 (1975): 513–30; Hendon, 'Center Party', 83.

22 cf. A. Hundhammer, *Die landwirtschaftliche Berufsvertretung in Bayern* (Munich, 1926),

34–56; F. Münch, 'Die agitatorische Tätigkeit des Bauernführers Heim. Zur Volksernährungsfrage aus der Sicht des Pressereferates des bayerischen Kriegsministeriums während des Ersten Weltkrieges', in K. Bosl (ed.), *Bayern im Umbruch: Die Revolution von 1918, ihre Voraussetzungen, ihr Verlauf und ihre Folgen* (Munich and Vienna, 1969), 301–44.

23 Hundhammer, *Landwirtschaftliche Berufsvertretung*, 56–87; A. Hundhammer, *Geschichte des Bayerischen Bauernbundes* (Munich, 1924); Farr, 'Populism in the countryside'.

24 For discussion of agricultural production problems in this period see particularly A. Skalweit, *Die Deutsche Kriegsernährungswirtschaft* (Stuttgart, Berlin, Leipzig and New Haven, Conn., 1927); F. Aereboe, *Der Einfluss des Krieges auf die landwirtschaftliche Produktion in Deutschland* (Stuttgart, Berlin, Leipzig and New Haven, Conn., 1927); J. Lee, 'Administrators and agriculture: aspects of German agricultural policy in the First World War', in J. M. Winter (ed.), *War and Economic Development: Essays in Memory of David Josslin* (Cambridge, 1975), 229–38; Moeller, 'Peasants, politics and pressure groups', 'Winners as losers in the German inflation' and his contribution to this volume; J. Osmond, 'Peasant farming in south and west Germany during war and inflation 1914 to 1924: stability or stagnation?', in Feldman et al. (eds.), *Die Deutsche Inflation* 289–307.

25 cf. Puhle, *Interessenpolitik*, 303–5; Münch, 'Die agitatorische Tätigkeit des Bauernführers Heim'.

26 On agricultural labour see J. Flemming, 'Grossagrarische Interessen und Landarbeiterbewegung. Überlegungen zur Arbeiterpolitik des Bundes der Landwirte und des Reichslandbundes in der Anfangsphase der Weimarer Republik', in H. Mommsen, D. Petzina and B. Weisbrod (eds.), *Industrielles System und Politische Entwicklung in der Weimarer Republik* (Düsseldorf, 1974), 745–62.

27 cf. H. Muth, 'Die Entstehung der Bauern- und Landarbeiterräte im November 1918 und die Politik des Bundes der Landwirte', *Vierteljahreshefte für Zeitgeschichte* 21 (1973): 1–38.

28 NWHStA RW 152 87, pp. 25–30: 'Zur Bildung der landwirtschaftlichen Berufsvertretung' (1919); Muth, 'Entstehung', 24–5, 34–5.

29 Muth, 'Entstehung', 33; NWHStA RW 152 87, 31: Schmitz to *Landwirtschaftskammer*, 5 January 1919; Muth, 'Hunsrücker Bauernverein', 217–18.

30 B. Schlütter, 'Die Freie Bauernschaft am linken Niederrhein (in den Kreisen Mörs, Kleve und Geldern, unter besonderer Berücksichtigung des Kreises Mörs)' (diss., Hamburg, 1924); NWHStA RW 152 87, pp. 61–3: G. Reuter, 'Die Organisation der Bauern am Niederrhein' (March 1919).

31 For a fuller discussion of Free Peasant ideology see my forthcoming thesis, 'The Free Peasantry', ch. 3.

32 Schlütter, 'Die Freie Bauernschaft', 45–52.

33 NWHStA RW 152 87, p. 33: Lee to Reinhardt, 8 March 1919, pp. 23–30. reports by *Landwirtschaftskammer*, 1919.

34 NWHStA RW 152 87, for reports of negotiations; see also Schlütter, 'Die Freie Bauernschaft', 53–5, and Moeller, 'Peasants, politics and pressure groups', 300–3.

35 NWHStA RW 152 87, for correspondence and newspaper articles; see also Landeshauptarchiv Koblenz (LHA K), 441 25519: Der Rheinische Bauernverein, 1905–28; Schlütter, 'Die Freie Bauernschaft', 57–8; and Moeller, 'Peasants, politics and pressure groups', 300–3.

36 NWHStA RW 152 87, p.. 64; Schlütter, 'Die Freie Bauernschaft', 55–6; Schumacher, *Land und Politik*, 399–403; Moeller, 'Peasants, politics and pressure groups', 296–300.

37 Muth, 'Hunsrücker Bauernverein', 217–18.

38 A contemporary view of Palatine agrarian politics is to be found in F. J. Rohr, 'Die freien erwerbswirtschaftlichen und wirtschaftspolitischen Organisationen der pfälzischen und saarländischen Landwirtschaft in der Kriegs- und Nachkriegszeit' (diss., Heidelberg, 1922). See particularly in this connection pp. 78–9 amd 91–5.

39 H. Pflug, *Landwirtschaft gegen Sozialdemokratie* (Baltersbach, 1919).

40 LA S H3 10 415–16: Lieferstreik der pfälzischen Landwirte, 1920; F. Revol, *Le Syndicalisme paysan et les grèves paysannes de 1920, 1921 et 1922 dans le nord du Palatinat Rhénan* (Paris, 1923).

41 Bayerisches Hauptstaatsarchiv München (BHStA) ML 3639: Bäuerliche Organisationen in der Pfalz 1920–33, Heckmann to Ministry of Trade, 5 March 1924; A. Crone-Münzebrock, *Die Organisation des deutschen Bauernstandes* (Berlin, n.d.), 18; Bundesarchiv Koblenz (BA K) NL 227: Nachlass Albert Zapf, no. 9: Vereinigung des BdL, Abteilung Pfalz, mit dem Nationalen Liberalen Verein der Pfalz zur DVP der Pfalz. For political contacts between the parties and the agrarian groups see, for example, R. Hamm, *Freie Bauernschaft, Heinz-Orbis und Separatismus* (Deileisterhof, 1930); BA K NL 227: no. 3: Jung to Zapf, 4 February 1924; private papers of R. Hamm: Jung to Zapf, 30 October 1924.

42 *Freier Bauer*, 2, 9, 20, 27 February, 13 March, 15, 22 May, 19 June 1921.

43 cf. Hamm, *Freie Bauernschaft*; BHStA MA 107 668: Heinz-Orbis, 'Präsident der autonomen Republik Pfalz': seine Erschiessung und andres, 1924–32; G. E. R. Gedye, *The Revolver Republic: France's Bid for the Rhine* (London, 1930), 214–40.

44 BHStA MA 108 212–13: Christlicher Bauernverein Saar, 1921–2, Freie Bauernschaft Saar, 1921–33.

45 Revol, *Syndicalisme Paysan*, 170–1, 174, 179, 181–2.

46 K.-G. Faber, 'Die südlichen Rheinlande von 1816 bis 1956', in F. Petri and G. Droege (eds.), *Rheinische Geschichte* (Düsseldorf, 1976), 2:34; Flemming, *Landwirtschaftliche Interessen*, 325.

47 J. H. Grill, *The Nazi Movement in Baden, 1920–1945* (Chapel Hill, N.C., 1983), 25–8, 139–41, and elsewhere for discussion of the agrarian interest in Baden.

48 Schumacher, *Land und Politik*, 70, 310–11; A. Panzer, 'Parteipolitische Ansätze der deutschen Bauernbewegung bis 1933', in H. Gollwitzer (ed.), *Europäische Bauernparteien im 20. Jahrhundert* (Stuttgart and New York, 1977), 538–40; K. Heger, *Die Deutsche Demokratische Partei in Württemberg und ihre Organisation* (Leipzig, 1927; repr. 1970), 67–9; Jacobs, *Von Schorlemer zur Grünen Front*, 38.

49 Hundhammer, *Landwirtschaftliche Berufsvertretung*, 34–56; BHStA ML 3638: Bayerischer Christlicher Bauernverein.

50 K. Schönhoven, *Die Bayerische Volkspartei 1924–1932* (Düsseldorf, 1972), 17–21, 28–9, 33–7.

51 Hundhammer, *Landwirtschaftliche Berufsvertretung*, 63; Staatsarchiv Neuburg an der Donau (StA N/D): Bezirksamt Neuburg 6776: Bund der Landwirte und ähnliche Gesellschaften 1921–3; BHStA ML 1876: Organisation der Freien Bauernschaft im rechtsrheinischen Bayern 1922–6: Ministry of Interior to provincial governments, 13 December 1922; *München-Augsburger Abendzeitung*, 7 November 1922.

52 cf. A. Mitchell, *Revolution in Bavaria 1918–1919: The Eisner Regime and the Soviet Republic* (Princeton, N.J., 1965), 156–8; W. Mattes, *Die Bayerischen Bauernräte: Eine soziologische und historische Untersuchung über bäuerliche Politik* (Stuttgart and Berlin, 1921).

53 Hundhammer, *Landwirtschaftliche Berufsvertretung*, 68–81; M. Spindler (ed.), *Bayerische Geschichte im 19. und 20. Jahrhundert 1800 bis 1970* (Munich, 1978), 2:1292, 1298–9.

54 Spindler, *Bayerische Geschichte* 2:1294; BHStA MA 102 139–40: Wochen- und Halbmonatsberichte des Regierungspräsidenten von Niederbayern, 1919–25; BHStA ML 1875: Bayerischer Bauernbund, 1920–6.

55 BHStA ML 1976: Organisation der Freien Bauernschaft.

56 loc. cit.

57 Staatsarchiv Landshut (StA L), Rep. 167/2: Landgericht Landshut – Strafakten.

58 cf. StA N/D: Bezirksamt Neuburg 6776; Staatsarchiv Amberg: Akten des Amtsgerichts Cham; Staatsarchiv Würzburg: Landratsamt Hofheim 2760, Die Freie Bauernschaft.

59 BHStA ML 3638: report of general meeting of *Christlicher Bauernverein*, 3 February 1920; *Augsburger Postzeitung*, 8 February 1921.

60 These membership statistics are culled from numerous sources of varying reliability: Hundhammer, *Landwirtschaftliche Berufsvertretung*; Revol, *Syndicalisme Paysan*; Hamm, *Freie Bauernschaft*; D. Fricke (ed.), *Die Bürgerlichen Parteien in Deutschland* (Berlin, 1968); Hendon, 'Center Party'; *Reichslandbund Jahrbuch* 1926; Schlögl, *Bayerische Agrargeschichte*; Rohr, 'Organisationen'; Schlütter, 'Freie Bauernschaft'; Grill, *Nazi Movement in Baden*; Hunt, *People's Party in Württemberg*; Bräunche, *Parteien und Reichstagswahlen in der*

Rheinpfalz; and miscellaneous archival sources. The following points should also be noted: the figure of 48,000 for the Agrarian League in Württemberg is from 1928, but the figure for the early 1920s would probably have been of this order, perhaps even higher; the figure for the Palatine Peasants' Association soon dropped to 2,500; the figure of 30,000 for the Free Peasantry in the Rhine Province is very much an approximation, and probably overlaps with that for the Rhenish Peasants' Association; the figures for the Free Peasantry in the Saar and Bavaria are in each case the higher of two estimates.

61 The two figures are from different sources, and the apparent decline in membership may be misleading. What is clear is that there was no great increase in membership.

62 cf. Puhle, *Interessenpolitik*, 39–41.

63 See, for example, the archive of the *Verband der pfälzischen Industrie* in Neustadt a.d. Weinstrasse for the records of the *Kreisarbeitgeberverband für Land- und Forstwirtschaft, Wein- und Gartenbau*, 1921–34.

64 cf. M. Schumacher, 'Quellen zur Geschichte der Agrarverbände und Agrarpolitik (u.a. Landwirtschaftskammern) in der Weimarer Republik', in T. Trumpp and R. Köhne (eds.), *Archivbestände zur Wirtschafts- und Sozialgeschichte der Weimarer Republik* (Boppard R., 1979), especially 126–35.

65 cf. Schlögl, *Bayerische Agrargeschichte*, 574 5; NWHStA RW 152–87, passim; BHStA ML 120 and 3993: Wahlen zu den Bauernkammern, 1920–8 and 1929–33.

66 Interviews with R. Hamm (1978) and present owner of Baltersbacherhof, Pflug's former farm (1983); BHStA ML 2698: Gandorfer, Carl; StA L Rep. 167/2: Landgericht Landshut – Strafakten; BHStA MA 107 991: Palatine government to Bavarian Ministry of Agriculture, 25 November 1919.

67 For a fuller discussion of Palatine separatism and the agrarian interest, see my forthcoming thesis, 'The Free Peasantry', ch. 5.

68 cf. BHStA MA 102 139–40: Wochen- und Halbmonatsberichte des Regierungspräsidenten von Niederbayern, 1919–1925, passim; Mitchell, *Revolution in Bavaria*, 156–8.

69 cf. Moeller, 'Winners as losers in the German inflation' and Osmond, 'Peasant farming in south and west Germany'.

70 cf. H.-J. Puhle, *Von der Agrarkrise zum Präfaschismus* (Wiesbaden, 1972).

71 cf. Heberle, *Landbevölkerung und Nationalsozialismus*; D. Gessner, *Agrarverbände in der Weimarer Republik* (Düsseldorf, 1976); J. E. Farquharson, *The Plough and the Swastika: The NSDAP and Agriculture in Germany 1928–45* (London and Beverley Hills, Calif., 1976).

72 cf. L. E. Jones, 'The dissolution of the bourgeois party system in the Weimar Republic', in R. Bessel and E. J. Feuchtwanger (eds.), *Social Change and Political Development in Weimar Germany* (London, 1981), 268–88.

73 For example, the union of the Free Peasantry and the Palatine Peasants' League as the Palatine Peasantry (*Pfälzer Bauernschaft*) on 1 October 1929.

74 cf. BHStA MA 100 600: Landwirtschaftliches Genossenschaftswesen.

75 cf. L. E. Jones, '"The dying middle": Weimar Germany and the fragmentation of bourgeois politics', *Central European History* 5 (1972): 23–54; Jones, 'Dissolution of the bourgeois party system' and his contribution to this volume; J. C. Hunt, 'The bourgeois middle in German politics, 1871–1933: recent literature', *Central European History* 11 (1978): 83–106; T. Childers, 'Inflation, stabilization, and political realignment in Germany 1924 to 1928', in Feldman et al., *Die Deutsche Inflation*, 409–31.

7 Crisis and Realignment: Agrarian Splinter Parties in the Late Weimar Republic, 1928–33

LARRY EUGENE JONES

By the end of the 1920s the German party system had become so fragmented along social, economic and ideological lines that none of the established bourgeois parties were capable of offering effective resistance to the rise of National Socialism. The founding of the Business Party of the German Middle Class (*Wirtschaftspartei des deutschen Mittelstandes* or WP) in the first half of the decade and of the Reich Party for People's Justice and Revaluation (*Reichspartei für Volksrecht und Aufwertung*) in the summer of 1926 both represented attempts on the part of the urban middle classes to stem their declining social and economic fortunes through the creation of new political parties that placed primary emphasis upon the representation of middle-class economic interests. A barometer of the increasing disenchantment which the more traditional elements of the German middle class felt towards the existing party system, these efforts quickly spread to the German countryside with the founding of two national agrarian parties, the German Peasants' Party (*Deutsche Bauernpartei* or DBP) and the Christian-National Peasants and Farmers' Party (*Christlich-Nationale Bauern- und Landvolkpartei* or CNBLP) in the spring of 1928. Although regional agrarian parties had existed in various parts of the country ever since the end of the previous century, it was only as a consequence of the acute economic distress which the German agricultural community experienced during the second half of the 1920s that farm leaders throughout the country began to organize themselves into agrarian parties with a national rather than a regional profile. But as the fate of these parties between 1928 and 1933 so clearly revealed, neither was capable of providing effective relief from the increasingly desperate economic situation in which German agriculture found itself during the final years of the Weimar Republic. With the resultant radicalization of the German countryside, both the DBP and the CNBLP sustained increasingly heavy losses to the National Socialist German Workers'

198

Party (*Nationalsozialistische Deutsche Arbeiterpartei* or NSDAP) and entered a period of rapid decline that was to culminate in their virtual disappearance from the political scene by the middle of 1932.[1]

The efforts to create a national agrarian party during the last years of the Weimar Republic were confined almost exclusively to the Protestant sections of the country and with the exception of certain parts of Bavaria never enjoyed widespread support among the Catholic peasantry. Moreover, they received their strongest support in those areas where the local rural population consisted primarily of small and middle-sized peasant proprietors with a long tradition of economic independence. In the Prussian provinces to the east of the Elbe River, for example, the labourers who had traditionally worked on the large Junker estates were conspicuously lacking in the self-confidence necessary to organize themselves politically and remained more or less subservient to political manipulation by the local rural elites. Regional agrarian parties had flourished in Bavaria, Württemberg and other parts of the country ever since the severe agricultural crisis of the mid-1890s, although at the national level the German agricultural community continued to pursue its social and economic objectives by working within the framework of the established bourgeois parties. The National Rural League (*Reichs-Landbund* or RLB), which had been created on 1 January 1921 through the merger of the prewar Agrarian League (*Bund der Landwirte*) and the newly founded German Rural League (*Deutscher Landbund*), not only enjoyed particularly close ties to the leadership of the right-wing German National People's Party (*Deutschnationale Volkspartei* or DNVP), but had its allies within the German People's Party (*Deutsche Volkspartei* or DVP) as well. By the same token, the Federation of German Peasants' Associations (*Vereinigung der deutschen Bauernvereine*), which had been founded in 1900 as a counter-weight to the Junker-dominated Agrarian League, maintained a close alliance with the German Centre Party (*Deutsche Zentrumspartei*) both before and after the First World War. The weakest of the major interest groups within the German agricultural community, however, was the German Peasants' League (*Deutscher Bauernbund* or DBB), an organization founded under liberal auspices in 1909 in an attempt to mobilize peasant opposition to the protectionist tariff policies of large landed agriculture. Though originally affiliated with the prewar National Liberal Party (*Nationalliberale Partei*), Karl Böhme and the leaders of the DBB transferred their allegiance to the newly founded German Democratic Party (*Deutsche Demokratische Partei* or DDP) immediately after the end of the war in hopes that it offered the best bulwark against the twin dangers of social revolution and feudal reaction.[2]

The network of alliances or *Querverbindungen* that had developed between the different sectors of the German agricultural community and Germany's non-socialist parties after the end of the First World War constituted an essential feature of Germany's political structure through the middle of the 1920s. But with the virtual collapse of Germany's agricultural economy in the wake of the inflation and subsequent stabilization of the Mark in 1923–4, these alliances came under increasingly heavy strain before they eventually broke down towards the end of the decade.[3] The first alliance to crack under the strain of these developments was the alliance between the German Peasants' League and the Democratic Party. The DDP's reluctance to support organized agriculture in its efforts to dismantle government controls over the grain industry in 1921–2 did much to antagonize its supporters within the German Peasants' League and left both it and the DBB exposed to sharp attacks from the DNVP and its allies within the National Rural League.[4] Relations between the DBB and DDP suffered a further blow in October 1924 when Böhme and several of his associates seceded from the party in protest against its supposed lack of independence vis-à-vis the Social Democrats. Though ostensibly triggered by the DDP's refusal to join a coalition government in which the DNVP was also represented, Böhme's resignation was motivated to a far greater extent by his fear that the free trade interests which had become so deeply entrenched on the DDP's left wing would not support the DBB's demands for a selective agricultural tariff when Germany regained its tariff autonomy at the beginning of 1925.[5]

Following his resignation from the DDP, Böhme joined the German People's Party and campaigned actively on its behalf in the December 1924 Reichstag elections.[6] Whatever repercussions this may have had upon the DDP's performance at the polls, however, were minimized by the fact that many of the DBB's leading officials, including its president Friedrich Wachhorst de Wente, refused to follow Böhme's lead and quickly reaffirmed their loyalty to the DDP.[7] As it turned out, the principal casualty of Böhme's break with the Democratic Party was not the DDP but the German Peasants' League. For as Böhme intensified his attacks against the DDP during the course of 1925, a severe split developed between Böhme and those like Wachhorst de Wente who had remained loyal to the DDP.[8] The crisis within the DBB drew to a head in August 1926 when Böhme was forced to resign as its secretary-general amid allegations of embezzlement and financial impropriety. Not only did this leave the DBB on the verge of a complete financial collapse, but its predicament was compounded by the defection of a large part of its Berlin staff to the rival National Rural League in February 1927 and the loss of more than half of its 18,000 members by the middle of the year.[9] The DBB's demise was irreversible, and in October 1927 what still remained of its national organization merged with the Bavarian Peasants'

League (*Bayerischer Bauernbund* or BBB) and an association of twelve regional peasant unions known as the National Federation of Small and Middle-Sized Agricultural Enterprises (*Reichsverband landwirtschaftlicher Klein- und Mittelbetriebe*) to found a new agricultural interest organization entitled the German Peasantry (*Deutsche Bauernschaft* or DBS) under the chairmanship of the BBB's Anton Fehr.[10]

With an initial membership of approximately 200,000, the German Peasantry represented a loose coalition of fifteen independent peasant unions, the largest and most influential of which was the 30,000 member Bavarian Peasants' League.[11] Although the DBS was quick to proclaim a policy of bipartisan neutrality towards the existing political parties, the fact that the Bavarian Peasants' League had run its own slate of candidates in state and national elections ever since its founding in 1893 could only have presaged a further loosening of ties between the independent peasantry and the various political parties through which it had traditionally sought to achieve its social and economic objectives. In terms of its basic ideological orientation, the BBB not only accepted the republican form of government, but evinced a deep-seated hostility to the highly concentrated form of capitalism that had developed in Germany since the end of the previous century.[12] But while the war had done much to radicalize the BBB to the point where several of its leaders actively supported the Bavarian revolution of 1919, the runaway inflation of the early 1920s had forced the BBB to shift its attention away from questions of national policy to the social and economic issues that were pressing so heavily upon the Bavarian peasant. In an attempt to extend its influence into the towns and small cities that dotted the Bavarian countryside, the BBB officially changed its name to Bavarian Peasants and Middle-Class League (*Bayerischer Bauern- und Mittelstandsbund*) in November 1922 and entered into closer ties with middle-class organizations from other parts of the country.[13] At the same time, the leaders of the BBB strongly denounced the 'Draconian' measures which the national government had taken to stabilize the Mark in 1923–4, and in the ensuing election campaign they demanded the immediate repeal of those facets of the government's stablization programme that posed an unacceptable burden to Germany's rural and urban middle classes.[14] Not only did this strategem produce tangible benefits in the Bavarian and national elections that were held throughout 1924, but between 1924 and 1928 the BBB belonged to a special coalition in the Reichstag known as the Economic Association (*Wirtschaftliche Vereinigung*) in which the Business Party and the German-Hanoverian Party (*Deutsch-Hannoversche Partei* or DHP) were also represented.[15]

Fehr's ultimate objective as the BBB's most prominent national leader was to transform the Bavarian Peasants and Middle-Class League into a national peasants' party with the newly founded German Peasantry as its organizational nucleus. The prospects for the creation of such a party had been greatly enhanced by the disintegrative effect which the general course of Germany's economic development during the second half of the 1920s had had upon relations between the German agricultural community and the existing bourgeois parties. Following the stabilization of the Mark in 1923–4, the German farmer encountered economic difficulties that were to prove even more severe than those he had experienced during the inflation. For not only had many farmers sold their 1923 harvests for paper Marks that were soon rendered all but worthless by the introduction of the *Rentenmark* in November 1923, but the inflation had also destroyed the capital assets of those private credit co-operatives through which the German farmer had traditionally obtained the inexpensive, short-term loans he needed for the purchase of seed, fertilizer and machinery. As a result, those farmers who had not already disposed of their harvests had no alternative but to sell their crops at the earliest possible opportunity in order to secure the capital they needed to prepare for the next planting season. Combined with the virtual collapse of agricultural prices on the world market, this helped to depress domestic prices for German agricultural products from 1924 to 1929 to their lowest level since the outbreak of the First World War. Moreover, this coincided with a dramatic increase in the costs of fertilizer, fuel and farm machinery, thereby creating a severe price squeeze that left the German farmer with no alternative but to go into debt once again. By the end of the decade, agricultural indebtedness had climbed so rapidly that whatever gains the farmer might have experienced as a result of the inflation had been completely wiped out.[16]

In January 1925 Germany regained the authority to levy tariffs on agricultural and industrial imports. Over the course of the next three years the German government, buoyed by the support and participation of the right-wing DNVP, proceeded to implement a series of selective agricultural tariffs aimed at protecting the domestic market from excessive foreign competition. But whatever benefits the German farmer was supposed to receive from a return to protectionism were systematically undercut by the bilateral trade treaties which the German Foreign Office negotiated from 1925 to 1927 in an attempt to develop new markets for Germany's surplus industrial production.[17] Moreover, these policies did little to help the small farmer, who found himself confronted with mounting production costs and a domestic market saturated with imported meat and dairy products. The failure of the government's protectionist policies became fully apparent in the winter of 1927–8 when the bottom fell out of domestic pork prices, and peasants, particularly in the north and north-central parts of Germany, took to the streets in protest.

Peasant unrest reached a dramatic climax on 28 January 1928 when more than 140,000 farmers from the province of Schleswig-Holstein demonstrated against high taxes, high interest rates and foreign imports.[18] This was followed by similar, though less impressive demonstrations in Thuringia, Württemberg and other parts of the country as local rural elites tried to contain the growing wave of peasant discontent to which the deepening agricultural crisis had given rise.[19] These developments were particularly alarming to the leaders of the DNVP, which of all of the established bourgeois parties was most heavily dependent upon peasant support. Fearful that the radicalization of the peasantry might destroy their party's chances in the forthcoming national elections, the leaders of the DNVP rushed forwards with an emergency farm programme, the central features of which were provisions for tax relief, credit assistance and tighter controls over the import of pork and other meat products.[20]

It was against the background of these developments that Fehr and the leaders of the Bavarian Peasants' League took the first steps towards the creation of a national agrarian party. Speaking at a demonstration of the Silesian Peasants' League (*Schlesischer Bauernbund*) on 12 February 1928, Fehr announced that the BBB would present a full national slate of candidates under the name German Peasants' Party in the Reichstag elections that were scheduled to take place later that spring. Fehr's announcement came in response to an appeal which the leaders of the Silesian Peasants' League had issued in August of the preceding year for the creation of a national peasants' party and marked the end of the BBB's collaboration with the Business Party.[21] In making such an announcement, Fehr no doubt assumed that the newly-formed German Peasantry would serve as the new party's organizational nucleus. But these plans ran into strong opposition from peasant spokesmen with close ties to the DDP, who used their influence within the German Peasantry to undercut Fehr's position as the DBS's national chairman. As a result, the DBS proceeded to dissociate itself from the efforts to found a new agrarian party and reaffirmed its policy of bipartisan neutrality at an emergency meeting of its executive committee on 22 March. This was accompanied by Fehr's resignation as chairman of the German Peasantry's national organization in favour of Emil Marth, an undistinguished Pomeranian farmer with no national political ambitions whatsoever.[22] Undaunted by this turn of events, Fehr and the other five members of the BBB's delegation to the Reichstag formally reconstituted themselves as the German Peasants' Party and proceeded with their plans to run a national slate of candidates in the forthcoming Reichstag elections.[23]

The founding of the German Peasants' Party aroused widespread apprehension within the ranks of Germany's conservative agrarian elite. Not only did the Bavarian Peasants' League, the driving force behind the new party, represent a nascent agrarian populism for which Germany's more conservative farm leaders had little sympathy, but they feared that the creation of the DBP foreshadowed a further radicalization of the German countryside. But the decentralized structure of the National Rural League, the principal bastion of agrarian conservatism in the Weimar Republic ever since its founding in 1921, made it difficult for Germany's conservative farm leaders to formulate a concerted response to the radicalizing effect which the deepening agricultural crisis had had upon Germany's rural population. Moreover, several of the RLB's regional affiliates – most notably those in Thuringia and Württemberg – had run their own slate of candidates in virtually every state and national election since the founding of the Weimar Republic and exercised considerably more influence over their local constituencies than the RLB itself. In November 1927 the leaders of the Thuringian Rural League (*Thüringer Landbund* or TLB) petitioned the RLB's national leadership on behalf of a national agrarian ticket for the Reichstag elections that were scheduled to take place early the following year.[24] This proposal, however, encountered fierce opposition from the RLB leaders with close ties to the DNVP, and it was shelved at a meeting of the RLB executive committee on 14 December 1927 in favour of a resolution which left the question of electoral strategy to the discretion of the RLB's state and regional affiliates.[25] The subsequent demonstration by 36,000 Thuringian peasants in Rudolstadt on 7 February 1928 and Fehr's announcement five days later that the Bavarian Peasants' League would present a national slate of candidates in the forthcoming Reichstag elections convinced the leaders of the TLB that they could ill afford to wait for the official sanction of the RLB leadership in Berlin. On 17 February Franz Hänse and Karl Friedrich Döbrich from the Thuringian Rural League along with Wilhelm Dorsch from the Hessian Rural League (*Hessischer Landbund*) decided to take matters into their own hands by announcing their resignation from the DNVP Reichstag delegation and the founding of a new agrarian party subsequently entitled the Christian-National Peasants and Farmers' Party.[26]

The fact that the three principals involved in the founding of the Christian-National Peasants and Farmers' Party – Hänse, Döbrich and Dorsch – were all former members of the DNVP Reichstag delegation gave rise to immediate allegations that the new party was nothing but a Nationalist front organization created for the purpose of duping unwitting peasants into voting for candidates who, once they had been elected, would rejoin the Nationalist Party.[27] The new party's credibility, however, was greatly enhanced when the three former Nationalist deputies were joined several days later by Karl Hepp, a member of the DVP Reichstag delegation from Hesse–Nassau and a farm leader of truly national stature. Having served as one of the RLB's two national presidents ever since the organization's founding in 1921, Hepp had long sought to organize the small and middle-sized farmers from central and south-western Germany into a force sufficiently powerful to prevent the RLB from falling under the domination of the large landowning interests from east of the Elbe River.[28] But Hepp's relations with the DVP had become increasingly strained following the appointment of party chairman Gustav Stresemann to the chancellorship in the late summer of 1923. Not only was Hepp adamantly opposed to Stresemann's willingness to head a coalition government in which the Social Democrats were also represented, but like most of Germany's agricultural leaders he was openly critical of the way in which German trade policy between 1925 and 1928 had consistently favoured the interests of German export industry at the expense of the independent farmer.[29] Coming on the eve of the 1928 Reichstag elections, Hepp's defection threatened the DVP with the loss of what still remained of its badly decimated agrarian wing and severely damaged the party's electoral prospects in central and south-west Germany.[30]

Buoyed by Hepp's defection and outspoken criticism of German trade policy since the middle of the 1920s, the official founding of the Christian-National Peasants and Farmers' Party took place in the Thuringian capital of Weimar on 8 March 1928.[31] While the leaders of the right-wing DNVP were extremely apprehensive that this foreshadowed a further radicalization of the German peasantry and feared that the CNBLP might join forces with Fehr and the newly-founded German Peasants' Party,[32] the impulse that lay behind the founding of the CNBLP was profoundly conservative and had little in common with the agrarian populism of the Bavarian Peasants' League. As Ernst Höfer, chairman of the Thuringian Rural League, explained in an article written shortly after the CNBLP's founding, the party to which he and his associates had given birth was essentially an attempt to contain the wave of agrarian unrest that was spreading throughout the countryside by providing the German farmer with the effective political representation he needed in order to survive the deepening agricultural crisis. Given the way in which all of Germany's non-socialist parties had consistently sacrificed the welfare of the German farmer to that of other social groups, it was only through the consolidation of the entire agricultural community into a united agrarian party that the radicalization of the German countryside could be held in check.[33] Arguments to this effect, however, did little to dispell the deep-seated misgivings with which the leaders of the DNVP and their allies within the National Rural League had greeted the founding of the new party and only served to dramatize the sharp political cleavages which the deepening agricultural crisis had produced within the ranks of Germany's conservative agrarian elite.

In its initial response to the CNBLP's founding, the RLB executive committee had done little more than reaffirm its traditional policy of bipartisan neutrality with respect to all political parties and leave the decision to support or reject the new party in the hands of its regional affiliates throughout the country.[34] A feeble compromise which only reflected the RLB's decentralized organizational structure, this decision ran into strong criticism from the leaders of the DNVP, who began to press for a stronger and less equivocal stand against the efforts to create a separate agrarian party.[35] In view of Hepp's position as one of the RLB's two national presidents, however, this posed a severe danger to the RLB's internal solidarity and threatened to drive a permanent wedge between those of its organizational affiliates which supported the DNVP and CNBLP respectively. The situation within the RLB was further aggravated by the fact that the DNVP tried to halt the spread of the new party by entering into electoral alliances with the RLB's regional affiliates in those areas of the country where the CNBLP had not yet established itself.[36] When this tactic failed to deter the founders of the CNBLP from expanding their party's campaign into areas where local farm leaders had remained loyal to the DNVP, the fragile truce which the leaders of the National Rural League had tried to establish between the two parties collapsed into an open conflict that threatened to destroy the very foundations upon which the RLB had always rested.[37]

The May 1928 Reichstag elections bore dramatic testimony to the increasing disaffection of Germany's rural electorate from the various non-socialist parties through which it had traditionally sought to achieve its social and economic objectives. Between them, the CNBLP and the DBP received over a million votes and elected seventeen deputies to the Reichstag. Most of these gains came at the expense of the DNVP, which according to one Nationalist estimate lost approximately 420,000 votes to the CNBLP and German Peasants' Party.[38] But the CNBLP's success was confined almost exclusively to areas like Thuringia and Hesse where it received strong organizational support from the RLB's regional affiliates. In Thuringia, for example, the CNBLP received 127,000 votes, while in the two Hessian districts it polled nearly 180,000. In the three Saxon districts, on the other hand, the CNBLP received only 16,500 votes as the leaders of the Saxon Rural League (*Sächsischer Landbund*) closed ranks behind the DNVP in an effort to halt the spread of the new party. By the same token, the CNBLP was generally unsuccessful in East Prussia where the RLB's local affiliates were under the control of conservative landowners with close ties to the DNVP.[39] Yet in spite of the fact that the CNBLP received over half of its nearly 600,000 votes in

Hesse and Thuringia, its performance still eclipsed that of the German Peasants' Party by approximately 120,000. As in the case of the CNBLP, the DBP received the bulk of its support in areas where it enjoyed the support of local agrarian organizations. Not only did the four Bavarian districts provide the DBP with more than three-quarters of its 480,000 votes, but the only other region in which the DBP registered any notable success was Silesia, where it received strong support from the local peasant unions. Otherwise, Fehr's hopes of transforming the Bavarian Peasants' League from a regional into a national agrarian party failed to materialize.[40]

Immediately after the elections the leaders of the German Peasants' Party approached the CNBLP about the formation of a parliamentary coalition or *Fraktionsgemeinschaft* in the Reichstag. When these efforts were abandoned in the face of strong opposition from the leaders of the National Rural League,[41] Fehr and his associates proceeded to renew the parliamentary coalition which they had formed with the Business Party during the preceding legislative period.[42] At the same time, representatives from the DNVP's agrarian wing tried to reach an accommodation with the CNBLP in hopes of preventing a further fragmentation of the German right along class and vocational lines.[43] But these hopes quickly evaporated in the wake of Alfred Hugenberg's election as DNVP party chairman in the fall of 1928. Hugenberg was an uncompromising opponent of the republican system of government and sought to free the DNVP from the control of those special economic interests which had seduced it into entering the government first in 1925 and then again in 1927. Hugenberg's assault against the position which special economic interests had held within the DNVP ever since the middle of the 1920s, however, came just as the leaders of the German agricultural community were beginning to band together for more effective representation of their own economic interests and set him on a clear collision course with the National Rural League and the leaders of his own party's agrarian wing. In August 1928 the leaders of the RLB had undertaken a major overhaul of their organization's leadership structure, with the result that responsibility for the formulation and execution of RLB policy now lay in the hands of a three-man presidium consisting of Hepp, Martin Schiele and Albert Bethge. The key figure in the newly reconstituted RLB presidium was Schiele, a member of the DNVP Reichstag delegation who had served as Minister of Agriculture in 1927–8 and who was regarded as a political moderate more interested in practical results than unproductive polemics.[44] In March 1929 Schiele took an important step towards the more effective representation of agricultural interests by bringing the leadership of the RLB, the Christian peasant unions, the German Peasantry and the German Agricultural Council (*Deutscher Landwirt-*

schaftsrat) together into a loose coalition of agricultural interest organizations known as the 'Green Front'.[45] From the very outset, the impulse which lay behind the creation of the 'Green Front' ran counter to the whole thrust of Hugenberg's political agenda and threatened to drive a permanent wedge between the DNVP and the leaders of its agrarian wing.[46]

Fears that Hugenberg's extremism might cause permanent damage to the DNVP's ties to organized agriculture were hardly assuaged by the role which the party played in the campaign against the Young Plan in the summer and fall of 1929. In July 1929 Hugenberg met with the leaders of a number of other right-wing organizations to form the National Committee for the German Referendum (*Reichsausschuss für das deutsche Volksbegehren*) for the purpose of mobilizing public opinion against the new reparations plan which the German government was in the process of negotiating with the Entente. Both the National Rural League and the Christian-National Peasants and Farmers' Party joined the National Referendum Committee, and both actively supported efforts to block ratification of the Young Plan by popular referendum. But relations between the three organizations became severely strained in late August 1929 when the more radical elements within the National Referendum Committee succeeded in persuading Hugenberg to incorporate a special paragraph stipulating that all of those officials responsible for the Young Plan should be tried and punished for treason under the committee's pretentiously entitled 'Freedom Law against the Enslavement of the German People'. When Hugenberg subsequently refused to delete or modify the offending paragraph for fear of losing the support of Adolf Hitler and the more radical elements within the National Referendum Committee, Schiele and the leaders of the RLB issued a public statement indicating that while they would continue to co-operate with the National Referendum Committee in its struggle against the Young Plan, they could not support those provisions of the 'Freedom Law' which called for the trial and punishment of government officials deemed responsible for the signing of the Young Plan.[47]

As relations between the DNVP and organized agriculture continued to deteriorate through the autumn of 1929, the situation within the RLB became increasingly volatile as Hepp and those farm leaders with close ties to the CNBLP began to press for a complete break with Hitler and the more radical elements within the 'national opposition'.[48] At the same time, the CNBLP began to expand its organizational base into Nationalist strongholds such as Saxony, Pomerania and East Prussia. Here the principal figure was Günther Gereke, a former Nationalist Reichstag deputy who as founder and president of the German Chamber of Rural Municipalities (*Deutscher Landgemeindetag*) had built up a wide range of personal contacts in central and eastern Germany. Gereke's efforts received considerable financial support from conservative industrialists intent upon breaking Hugenberg's hold over the DNVP, and even General Kurt von Schleicher, the Reichswehr's political specialist, encouraged the growth of the CNBLP.[49] The CNBLP's crusade against Hugenberg reached a preliminary climax in the campaign for the county and municipal elections that were scheduled to take place throughout Prussia on 17 November 1929. In a particularly sharp attack on Hugenberg a week before the elections, Gereke asserted that the crucial question facing the German farmer was not so much the struggle against the 'Weimar System' as the damage which Hugenberg's jingoistic fantasies and divisive political tactics had done to the German agricultural community. What the CNBLP offered in the place of Hugenberg's irresponsible fanaticism, claimed Gereke, was a sober, objective *Realpolitik* which concerned itself first and foremost with the material welfare of the German farmer. Maintaining that the course of German economic development since the middle of the previous century had consistently favoured large urban areas at the expense of Germany's rural population, Gereke and his associates pledged themselves to a programme of greater austerity on the part of local government and to a tax reform aimed at redistributing the burden of government financing more equitably among the various sectors of the population.[50]

The CNBLP scored significant gains at the expense of the DNVP not only in the Prussian municipal elections on 17 November, but also in the Thuringian *Landtag* elections three weeks later. In the meantime, the CNBLP's political future had been greatly enhanced by the secession of twelve Nationalist deputies, including agricultural specialist Hans Schlange-Schöningen, from the DNVP in early December 1929.[51] Schlange immediately affiliated himself with the CNBLP and worked to re-establish the close ties between organized agriculture and the German conservative movement which Hugenberg's policies as DNVP party chairman had done so much to destroy.[52] But in the critical negotiations that took place between the secessionists and their followers in January 1930, those agrarian leaders like Gereke and Schlange-Schöningen who favoured closer ties with the other groups that had broken away from the DNVP found themselves completely thwarted by the obstinacy of those in control of the CNBLP.[53] Particularly outspoken in his opposition to the cultivation of closer political ties with the dissident Nationalists was Hepp, who insisted throughout these negotiations that the primary responsibility of the CNBLP lay not in reconstituting the German right, but in consolidating the German agricultural community into a united agrarian party capable of providing the 'Green Front' with the effective parliamentary backing it both deserved and needed.[54] Consequently, the

209

Christian-National Coalition (*Christlich-nationale Arbeitsgemeinschaft*) which the CNBLP and the twelve Nationalist secessionists formed in December 1929 as a means of achieving official delegation status was never seen as anything more than a temporary expedient which infringed in no way whatsoever upon the CNBLP's political and organizational integrity.[55]

The CNBLP continued to expand its organizational base through the spring of 1930 as more and more embittered Nationalists switched parties.[56] In fact, one of the most serious problems that confronted the leaders of the CNBLP in the first half of 1930 was the task of creating an organization sufficiently comprehensive to absorb all of the disillusioned farmers who were abandoning the DNVP.[57] In this respect, however, the leaders of the CNBLP soon found themselves confronted with a second and even more formidable rival for the loyalty of the German farmer in the form of the National Socialist German Workers' Party. The NSDAP had been quick to capitalize upon the radicalizing effect which the deepening agricultural crisis had had upon Germany's rural population, and in the second half of 1929 it scored a series of electoral triumphs in Baden, Thuringia and other parts of the country that testified to its increasing popularity among precisely those groups to which the CNBLP hoped to appeal.[58] All of this caused considerable alarm within both the RLB and CNBLP. For although they had both co-operated with the NSDAP under the auspices of the National Committee for the German Referendum, the conflict over the imprisonment paragraph of the so-called 'Freedom Law' had done much to alienate Schiele and the more moderate representatives of Germany's conservative rural elite. Following the referendum's rejection by the Reichstag in December 1929, the RLB officially resigned from the National Referendum Committee and called for its immediate dissolution.[59] At the same time, the leaders of the Thuringian Rural League used the campaign for the state *Landtag* elections on 17 December 1929 as the occasion for a general broadside against the NSDAP in which the Nazis were portrayed as social and political radicals whose constant flirtations with the German working class made them totally unreliable as a vehicle for the representation of agricultural economic interests.[60] Scarcely less spirited was the defence which the National Rural League took up in February 1930 against Nazi charges of 'agrarian Marxism' and failure in the struggle against the Young Plan.[61]

As battle-lines for the struggle over the loyalty of the German farmer were drawn with increasing sharpness in the spring of 1930, the more moderate elements within Germany's rural elite found themselves caught on the horns of an increasingly painful dilemma. The founding of the 'Green Front' in the spring of 1929 had been predicated upon the assumption that the struggle for the more effective representation of agricultural economic interests was not fundamentally incompatible with the struggle against the 'Weimar system'. Though questionable, this assumption was at least plausible as long as the Social Democrats remained in control of the national government. But with the formation of the Brüning government in the spring of 1930 it was no longer possible for Germany's conservative farm leaders to avoid a choice between the policies of the 'Green Front' and those of the 'national opposition'. For not only did Brüning select Schiele, the one man most closely identified with the formation of the 'Green Front', as his Minister of Agriculture, but he set the goal of agricultural recovery as one of his government's highest domestic priorities.[62] Regarding this as tangible vindication of the policies which the 'Green Front' had pursued since its creation a year earlier, the leaders of the CNBLP immediately endorsed the formation of the Brüning government and pledged to support it in its struggle for agricultural recovery.[63] Within the DNVP, on the other hand, the formation of the Brüning government was accompanied by a severe internal crisis that nearly resulted in the secession of the party's entire agrarian wing. By urging its parliamentary representatives, including those who sat in the DNVP Reichstag delegation, to support the new government in the vote of confidence that was scheduled to take place on 3 April,[64] the RLB executive committee openly challenged Hugenberg's leadership of the party and forced him to reverse the strong stand which he had initially taken against the Brüning Cabinet so that it might have an opportunity to enact its farm programme. But party unity, temporarily salvaged by Hugenberg's strategic retreat, quickly collapsed when Brüning proceeded to combine his government's farm bill with the introduction of new taxes aimed at providing the revenue necessary to fund it. In two successive votes – the first on 12 April and the second two days later – the leaders of the DNVP's agrarian wing defied Hugenberg's instructions as party leader and voted with the government parties to secure passage of the controversial farm bill.[65]

Only the mediation of Schiele and the former Nationalist party chairman Count Kuno von Westarp prevented a general exodus on the part of the DNVP's agrarian wing from taking place in the aftermath of the April crisis.[66] A final break, therefore, did not materialize until the summer of 1930 when Hugenberg's decision to support a Social Democratic motion of no confidence against the Brüning government forced the dissolution of the Reichstag and triggered a secession on the DNVP's left wing that was far more extensive than the one that had taken place the previous December. Among those who left the DNVP in the second secession of July 1930 was none other than Schiele himself, who proceeded to join the CNBLP along with Heinrich Lind, Walther von Keudell and a number of

other former Nationalist deputies.[67] The immediate effect of these developments was to enhance the CNBLP's credibility and attractiveness as a
national agrarian party and to clear the way for closer co-operation
between it and the National Rural League. On 22 July the RLB executive
committee signalled a radical departure from its standing policy of
bipartisan neutrality by calling upon its affiliates throughout the country
to throw their support behind separate agrarian tickets at the state, provincial and national levels.[68] Over the course of the next several weeks, the
RLB's regional affiliates in Saxony, Württemberg and Franconia – all
former Nationalist bastions in the countryside – transferred their allegiance from the DNVP to the CNBLP.[69] Only in Hanover and several of
Germany's larger eastern provinces such as Pomerania and East Prussia
were Hugenberg's confederates able to prevent the RLB's local
organization from going over to the CNBLP.[70]

In spite of the strong support which it received from the National Rural
League and its regional affiliates throughout the country, the CNBLP
still encountered two major problems in its campaign for the 1930 Reichstag elections. In the first place, the CNBLP's close identification with
Schiele's agricultural programme severely hampered the party in its
efforts to attract support from farm circles that stood outside the RLB's
immediate orbit. Not only did the Federation of German Peasants' Associations under the leadership of Centrist Andreas Hermes explicitly dissociate itself from the RLB's appeal for agrarian solidarity,[71] but the
deep-seated hostility which the German Peasantry and the independent
peasant unions from the northern and western parts of Germany felt
towards the tariff policies of large landed agriculture militated against the
conclusion of an electoral alliance between the CNBLP and the German
Peasants' Party.[72] The second problem which plagued the CNBLP
during the 1930 election campaign was a split within the party leadership
over the question of its relationship to the German conservative
movement. For while Schiele, Schlange-Schöningen and Gereke were
political conservatives who ultimately sought to reintegrate the CNBLP
into a greater German right,[73] the forces around Hepp, Döbrich and
party chairman Ernst Höfer defined their party's objectives almost
exclusively in vocational or corporatist terms and remained adamantly
opposed to the establishment of close political ties with the other groups
that had broken away from the DNVP.[74] Even though Gereke, armed
with promises of financial support from German heavy industry,[75] was
able to win approval at a meeting of the CNBLP executive committee on
29 July 1930 for an electoral alliance with the fledgeling Conservative
People's Party (*Konservative Volkspartei* or KVP) which Westarp and
other dissident Nationalists had founded four days earlier,[76] hopes that
this might pave the way for the CNBLP's participation in a bourgeois

unity ticket associated with the name of Reich President von Hindenburg foundered on the strong opposition of Hepp and his supporters.[77]

Though critical of the way in which the German party system had developed during the course of the 1920s, the leaders of the CNBLP were careful to distinguish their critique of the Weimar state from the anti-republican demagoguery of Germany's radical right. For Gereke and his supporters, the purpose of the campaign was not to secure a mandate for the destruction of the Weimar Republic, but rather to forge a conservative parliamentary majority that would make it possible for the Brüning government to complete the reform of Germany's social, political and economic life it had begun in April under the mantle of Reich President von Hindenberg. In spite of reservations about Brüning's tax and social policies, the leaders of the CNBLP hailed Schiele's farm programme as a vital step towards restoring the profitability of German agriculture and assailed Hugenberg, Hitler and the so-called 'national opposition' for resorting to obstructionist tactics that only delayed agriculture's economic recovery.[78] For the most part, however, the central theme in the CNBLP's campaign for the 1930 Reichstag elections was the struggle against Marxism. Not only did party propagandists hold Germany's working-class parties responsible for the desperate situation in which the German farmer currently found himself, but they cited the emancipation of the state from Marxist influence as an essential prerequisite for the success of the Brüning-Schiele programme.[79] The vehemence of the CNBLP's crusade against Marxism was matched by an equally deep-seated antipathy towards Hitler and the NSDAP. To the party's more conservative leaders, the NSDAP was little more than a socialistic workers' party whose programme and revolutionary rhetoric left it virtually indistinguishable from the Communists and Social Democrats. Particularly offensive was the NSDAP's constant evocation of the Peasants' War of 1525 as an example which the present generation of German farmers should follow. Categorically rejecting the 'Kata-strophenpolitik' pursued by Hitler and his associates, the leaders of the CNBLP portrayed their party as a pillar of patriotic and Christian conviction whose loyalty to home and hearth precluded participation in the sort of revolution which the Nazis were trying to incite.[80]

The anti-Marxism that was such a prominent feature of the CNBLP's campaign for the 1930 Reichstag elections was almost totally absent from the election appeals of the German Peasants' Party. There was, however, a curious discrepancy between the campaigns which the DBP conducted in Bavaria and the other parts of the country. In the north, where the DBP's support was confined to a thin strata of family farmers and small peasants stretching from Silesia through western Prussia to Lower Saxony, the party eschewed anti-socialism in favour of a sharp attack on the large landowning and monarchistic circles in control of the CNBLP. At the same time, the leaders of the DBP's northern wing espoused an unconditional commitment to the republican form of government as embodied in the Weimar Constitution.[81] This diverged in several significant respects from the campaign which the DBP's Bavarian affiliate, the Bavarian Peasants and Middle-Class League, conducted in the southern parts of the country. For while the BBB endorsed the republican form of government and dissociated itself from the 'Katastrophenpolitik' of Hugenberg and the 'national opposition', it also qualified its support of Germany's republican institutions by calling for a reform of the Weimar Constitution that would ensure the independence and financial integrity of the individual German states.[82] Combined with a pronounced emphasis upon the 'preservation of genuine Christian culture', this helped provide the BBB with a decidedly more conservative profile than that displayed by the DBP's northern wing. Adding to the confusion was the fact that in Franconia and the Palatinate – the two Bavarian districts in which the BBB was least well organized – the Bavarian Peasants' League merged its ticket with that of the CNBLP in an otherwise unparalleled example of agrarian solidarity.[83]

The Reichstag elections of 14 September 1930 constituted a crucial turning-point in the efforts to create a national agrarian party. In the final analysis, however, neither the German Peasants' Party nor the Christian-National Peasants and Farmers' Party succeeded in establishing itself as a viable alternative to the existing bourgeois parties. This was most immediately apparent in the case of the DBP, which lost nearly 30 per cent of the votes it had received in 1928 and saw its strength in the Reichstag slip from eight to six deputies. Moreover, the fact that no less than six out of every seven votes which the DBP received came from Bavaria underscored the failure of the Bavarian Peasants' League to expand its organization and influence into other parts of the country, while in its traditional strongholds in Upper and Lower Bavaria it suffered losses in the neighbourhood of 15 to 20 per cent. In contrast to the DBP's unequivocal defeat at the polls, the leaders of the CNBLP could point to the fact that their party had doubled both its 1928 popular vote and its number of Reichstag seats as proof of a major electoral triumph.[84] Such a claim, however, conveniently ignored the fact that the CNBLP's performance in the 1930 Reichstag elections fell far short of the expectations with which Schiele, Hepp and other party leaders had originally entered the campaign. Instead of the forty Reichstag mandates which the leaders of the CNBLP had hoped their party would win, the CNBLP emerged from the campaign with a mere nineteen, discounting the three which it had received in Württemberg by virtue of its alliance with the local Peasants and Vintners' League. Not only had the CNBLP failed to dislodge the DNVP from its traditional strongholds east of the Elbe River, but it also suffered disconcerting reverses of its own in those areas which in 1928 had been the first to rally to its banner.[85]

The big winner in the struggle for control of the German countryside in the 1930 Reichstag elections was not the CNBLP, but the National Socialist German Workers' Party. In many rural precincts, particularly in areas with predominantly Lutheran populations, the NSDAP received as much as 40 per cent of the total popular vote, while in several districts in Schleswig-Holstein and Lower Saxony it received an absolute majority of all votes cast. The reasons for the Nazi victory were essentially two fold. In the first place, the outbreak of the world economic crisis at the end of the 1920s had done much to aggravate the difficult situation in which German agriculture had found itself ever since the middle of the decade and had radicalized Germany's peasant population to the point where it was no longer content to follow the lead of the traditional rural elites. Moreover, the farm programme which Schiele had introduced with such fanfare in the spring of 1930 had produced little in the way of tangible benefits to the beleaguered German farmer. Had the elections taken place at the time of Schiele's appointment to the Brüning government, then it is conceivable that he and his conservative supporters in the National Rural League might have been able to contain the wave of rural discontent to which the deteriorating agricultural situation had given rise. But the relative ineffectiveness of Schiele's farm programme in the period between April and September 1930 severely undercut the position of those farm leaders who had allowed themselves to become too closely identified with the Brüning government and created a situation which the Nazis were able to exploit with consummate skill. The second factor which helped account for the NSDAP's success in the 1930 Reichstag elections was the elaborate organization which the party had built up throughout the country since the middle of 1928. Even before the creation of the Agrarian Political Apparatus (*Agrarpolitischer Apparat*) under R. Walter Darré in the summer of 1930, the Nazis possessed a party organization which none of their rivals in the countryside could match. By combining this with a highly sophisticated political propaganda, the Nazis were able to translate peasant dissatisfaction over the deteriorating agricultural situation into a storm of rural protest which virtually overwhelmed the less radical agrarian parties.[86]

The outcome of the 1930 Reichstag elections – and particularly the magnitude of the Nazi victory in the countryside – came as a rude shock to the leaders of the DBP and CNBLP and raised severe doubts within both parties as to their legitimacy and future course of action. In the case of the German Peasants' Party, this manifested itself in a mood of general resignation that spread throughout the party in the aftermath of the election.[87] As it became increasingly clear that their efforts to establish the DBP as a national agrarian party had failed, the leaders of the Bavarian Peasants' League tried to salvage what still remained of their political position by joining the CNBLP in a special parliamentary coalition entitled the German Rural Folk (*Deutsches Landvolk*).[88] The formation of this alliance met with strong criticism from the northern wing of the party, and in December 1930 August Hillebrand, the party's only deputy to have been elected outside Bavaria, sealed its virtual demise by affiliating himself with the left-liberal German State Party (*Deutsche Staatspartei*) under the leadership of Schiele's predecessor as Minister of Agriculture, Hermann Dietrich.[89] Coinciding with a decision by the leaders of the German Peasantry to sever their organizational ties to the BBB,[90] Hillebrand's action meant the end of the German Peasants' Party as a national political entity. Not only had the Bavarian Peasants' League failed to establish itself as the crystallization point around which a national peasants' party could form, but the differences between the northern and southern wings of the party to which it had given birth had proved too great to bridge.

The demise of the German Peasants' Party was paralleled by an equally destructive leadership crisis within the Christian-National Peasants and Farmers' Party. The leaders of the CNBLP were deeply disturbed by the fact that in many parts of the country their party had finished a distant third behind the DNVP and NSDAP in its bid for the support of the German farmer. The election results were particularly upsetting to Hepp, who held the party's close identification with Schiele's agricultural programme responsible for its disappointing performance at the polls. In a frame of mind which his rivals described as hysterical, Hepp allied himself with Heinrich von Sybel and Albrecht Wendhausen, two of the CNBLP's most outspoken government critics, in an effort to change the direction in which Schiele and Gereke were leading the party.[91] The immediate consequence of this was that Schiele, who in the recent elections had headed the CNBLP's ticket in five separate districts, declined to accept his Reichstag mandate so as not to compromise his party's freedom of movement.[92] At the same time, Schiele came under such heavy fire from Hugenberg's supporters in the National Rural League that he was obliged to resign his position as one of the RLB's three presidents. With Schiele essentially neutralized within both the CNBLP and RLB, the forces around Hepp, Sybel and Wendhausen were able to gain the upper hand within the CNBLP Reichstag delegation. On 1 October 1930 they secured the passage of a resolution that denounced the government for its lack of initiative in the reparations question and called for its reorganization as a government of national concentration in which all right-wing parties, including the National Socialists, would be invited to participate.[93] Claiming that the government's dependence upon the Social Democrats prevented it from implementing Schiele's farm programme, the CNBLP then proceeded to support right-wing motions of no confidence in the Brüning government and voted against its request for a parliamentary recess when its own refusal to support the Cabinet had resulted in government inaction on the Schiele programme.[94] By this time, Gereke and other party moderates such as Heinrich Lind and Baron Schenk von Stauffenberg had become so thoroughly disgusted with the obstructionist tactics employed by Hepp and his supporters that they launched into a bitter attack on the way in which the party was being led at a stormy caucus of the CNBLP Reichstag delegation on the night of 18–19 October. Only an announcement by Schiele that he intended to secure enactment of his programme by presidential decree prevented a major secession on the part of Gereke and other CNBLP moderates from materializing.[95]

The future of the Christian-National Peasants and Farmers' Party was ultimately decided by developments within the National Rural League. Schiele's resignation from the RLB presidium represented a major triumph for Hugenberg's supporters on the organization's extreme right wing, and they were determined to keep it from falling back under the influence of those associated with the CNBLP. Their primary concern was that Hepp might succeed Schiele as the RLB's managing president, thereby leaving the organization in the hands of those close to the CNBLP. But Hepp's recent behaviour had severely damaged his credibility with RLB moderates who feared that his election would lead to a further radicalization of the Rural League and its regional affiliates. Consequently, when the RLB executive committee met on 22 October 1930 to choose Schiele's successor, the organization's more moderate elements rallied behind the candidacy of Count Eberhard von Kalckreuth, a former German Nationalist who had left the DNVP earlier in the year, in hopes that he might be able to contain the forces of social and political radicalization that were at work within the RLB.[96] When Kalckreuth was subsequently chosen to succeed Schiele as the RLB's managing president, the severely shaken Hepp claimed that the RLB had fallen under the domination of the large landowning interests from east of the Elbe and announced his resignation from the RLB presidium in protest against the way in which the choice of Kalckreuth discriminated against the small and middle-sized farmers from western and central Germany.[97] In a related move Ernst Höfer, the first chairman of the Thuringian Rural League and the CNBLP's national chairman, proceeded to resign from the RLB executive committee after efforts to reach a reconciliation with Hepp had failed.[98]

The changes which took place in the RLB leadership in the autumn of

1930 constituted a devastating blow to the leaders of the CNBLP and deprived them of the strong organizational support which they had come to expect from the National Rural League. Not only had the departure of Schiele and Hepp from the RLB presidium removed two of the CNBLP's most ardent supporters from their positions of influence within the RLB, but Kalckreuth, Schiele's successor as the RLB's managing president and the most influential single person within the RLB organization, was far more sympathetic to the goals and methods of the 'national opposition' than his predecessor had been. By the same token, the CNBLP's Heinrich Lind, who in December 1930 was elected as Hepp's replacement on the RLB presidium, was a weak and uninspiring figure who lacked the internal support necessary to halt the RLB's drift to the right. As a result, Hugenberg's associates at the provincial and state levels of the RLB's national organization were able to initiate a purge of those RLB officials who had supported the Schiele strategy during the recent campaign. In Silesia, Brandenburg, Saxony and Hanover, Hugenberg loyalists succeeded in driving CNBLP supporters from their posts within the RLB's local affiliates and were thus able to re-establish their own position within the RLB's national organization. This, in turn, was accompanied by a marked radicalization of the tactics which the RLB used in its agitation against the policies and programmes of the Brüning-Schiele government.[99]

With the triumph of the radicals within the RLB, the situation within the CNBLP became increasingly strained. To be sure, the party continued to oppose the Brüning government and resolutely voted against the Emergency Decree which it presented to the Reichstag on 1 December 1930.[100] But as developments over the next several months were to reveal, the party's internal unity was far too fragile to withstand the pressures generated by the increasing radicalization of the German countryside. On 2 February 1931 the National Rural League used the demonstration celebrating the tenth anniversary of its founding as the occasion for a new round of attacks against Schiele and the Brüning government.[101] This came on the heels of a severe setback which Schiele had just suffered in the Cabinet on the question of agricultural tariffs, and it was only with the greatest difficulty that the RLB's more moderate leaders were able to prevent the adoption of a motion of no confidence in Schiele's performance as Minister of Agriculture.[102] The frustration which the leaders of the RLB felt with respect to Schiele's ineffectiveness as a member of the Brüning government carried over into the CNBLP, where on 10 February four members of the party's Reichstag delegation – Sybel, Wendhausen, Karl Heinrich Sieber and Martin Haag – joined the DNVP and NSDAP in walking out of the Reichstag as a means of demonstrating its lack of legitimacy in the eyes of the nationalist right.[103]

The leaders of the CNBLP were quick to dissociate themselves from this move, and at a meeting of the party executive committee on 12 February they insisted that the four dissident deputies return to the Reichstag or face expulsion from the party. Haag, a member of the Württemberg Peasants and Winegrowers' League (*Württembergischer Bauern- und Wein-gärtnerbund* or WBWB), agreed to accept this ultimatum, but the other three deputies refused to reconsider their action and resigned their Reichstag mandates.[104]

The schism that had been developing within the CNBLP ever since the September elections had finally erupted into public view. At the heart of this split lay the fact that while the CNBLP continued to associate itself with the so-called 'national opposition', it also refused to engage in demagogic activity such as the secession from the Reichstag that might compromise the effectiveness with which it could represent agricultural economic interests. In this respect, the leaders of the CNBLP openly criticized the decision to walk out of the Reichstag on the grounds that the absence of the DNVP and NSDAP made the passage of new laws aimed at agricultural recovery virtually impossible.[105] Yet in spite of the tactical differences that separated it from the more radical right-wing parties, the CNBLP readily endorsed the referendum for the dissolution of the Prussian *Landtag* which the Steel Helmet (*Stahlhelm*), a right-wing veterans' organization with an estimated 280,000 members, initiated in the spring of 1931.[106] By ending the Social Democratic domination of Prussia, the leaders of the CNBLP hoped that it would be possible to end Brüning's dependence upon the Social Democrats and force a reorganization of the national government. But the CNBLP's experience as a member of the alliance which the Steel Helmet had organized for the purpose of conducting the referendum was hardly reassuring. For, as in the case of the referendum against the Young Plan, the CNBLP found itself the target of constant abuse from groups more radical than itself that sought to discredit it as a member of the 'national opposition'.[107]

As the leaders of the CNBLP came to realize that their party was ill equipped to compete with the more radical elements on the German right, they proceeded to dissociate themselves as inconspicuously as possible from the 'national opposition' and discreetly moderated their criticism of the Brüning government. In the speech that accompanied his election as the CNBLP's national chairman in August 1931, Wolfgang Hauenschild-Tscheidt carefully avoided any reference to the 'national opposition' and confined his criticism of the Brüning government to a reiteration of the CNBLP's refusal to support any government that remained hostage to the Social Democrats in Prussia.[108] An even more remarkable indication of the CNBLP's move to the middle was the willingness of Hauenschild, Schlange-Schöningen and other CNBLP moderates to participate in the efforts of politicians from the other bourgeois parties to undertake some sort of concerted action on behalf of the Brüning government when the Reichstag reconvened in October 1931. At a meeting of representatives from the various bourgeois parties between the Centre and the DNVP on the evening of 15 September, Schlange stressed that only the close co-operation of all responsible Germans, regardless of their present party affiliation, could prevent a collapse of the German state, and outlined a seven-point programme which, among other things, provided for a joint declaration in the Reichstag on 13 October, a sharp line of demarcation with respect to both the left and the right and an unequivocal statement of support on behalf of the Brüning government.[109] But Schlange's enthusiasm for closer political ties with the other parties of the middle and moderate right did not extend to the CNBLP's more conservative leaders, who forced Hauenschild into withdrawing from the negotiations and the action that had been planned for the opening of the Reichstag.[110] To underscore their party's aloofness from the entire project, the leaders of the CNBLP Reichstag delegation then presented Brüning with a series of demands upon whose fulfilment their support would depend.[111]

Throughout the crisis that accompanied the reorganisation of the Brüning government in the autumn of 1931, the CNBLP steered a singular course between those parties that continued to support the Chancellor and those that sought to bring him down. For although the CNBLP continued to press for a reorganization of the national government and voted against the Cabinet which Brüning presented to the Reichstag on 13 October,[112] its leaders did not take part in the demonstration which Hitler, Hugenberg and the forces of the 'national opposition' had held in Harzburg two days earlier. Moreover, the CNBLP's relations with the National Rural League, under Kalckreuth a proud and resolute member of the 'national opposition',[113] had all but collapsed as a result of the growing influence which the more radical right-wing parties were able to exercise at the upper echelons of the RLB's national organization. Instead of attacking the RLB outright as they had done in the case of the CNBLP,[114] the leaders of the NSDAP had sought to subvert the National Rural League from within in hopes that pressure from the organization's rank-and-file membership would force it into affiliating itself more and more closely with the 'national opposition'. Not only Kalckreuth's appearance at Harzburg, but also the election of the NSDAP's Werner Willikens to the RLB presidium in December 1931 bore dramatic testimony to the success of this strategy and underscored the CNBLP's increasing isolation within the German agricultural community.[115]

At no time was the rift between the CNBLP and RLB more apparent than in the campaign for the presidential elections that took place in the spring of 1932. The CNBLP was one of the first parties to openly endorse Reich President von Hindenburg's re-election to the office which he had held for the past seven years, and Gereke played a major role in his campaign as an official of the 'Hindenburg Committee' which had been formed under the chairmanship of industrialist Carl Duisberg in late February 1932.[116] The National Rural League, on the other hand, took umbrage at the fact that the bulk of Hindenburg's support seemed to be coming from those parties that were most closely identified with the hated 'Weimar System' and publicly urged the leaders of the 'national opposition' to reject Hindenburg as a candidate for re-election.[117] When the 'national opposition' failed to agree upon a candidate to oppose Hindenburg, the RLB called upon its members to vote for either Hitler or Theodor Duesterberg, whom the Steel Helmet and the DNVP had nominated as a candidate of the Harzburg Front. In the run-off election on 10 April the RLB's national leadership threw its full support behind Hitler.[118] Not only did this endorsement dramatize the gulf that had developed between the CNBLP and RLB, but many of the RLB's more moderate regional affiliates were so offended by the decision to endorse Hitler that they refused to follow the organization's national leadership. In Prussian Saxony the leaders of the RLB's regional affiliate voted overwhelmingly to support Hindenburg's bid for re-election,[119] while the executive committee of the Thuringian Rural League rallied its supporters against Hitler's candidacy with the slogan 'No socialist Reich President'.[120] At the same time, Theodor Körner alt of the influential Württemberg Peasants and Winegrowers' League announced his support of Hindenburg's candidacy with a sharp attack against Hitler as a political neophyte whose party's success at the polls stemmed from the fact that it had not yet been saddled with responsibility for translating its promises into reality.[121]

Although the leaders of the CNBLP were no doubt relieved by Hindenburg's re-election, they could hardly draw solace from the fact that in most parts of the country Germany's rural population had given its overwhelming support to Hitler's bid for the presidency. Neither this nor the rift that had developed between it and the RLB's national leadership augured well for the CNBLP's prospects in the state elections that were scheduled to take place in Prussia, Bavaria and Württemberg on 24 April 1932. In Prussia the leaders of the CNBLP tried to avert an electoral disaster by joining the Business Party and an amorphous group calling itself the 'Young Right' (*Junge Rechte*) in the formation of a loose electoral alliance headed by Westarp and entitled the National Front of German Estates (*Nationale Front deutscher Stände*).[122] At the same time the CNBLP categorically rejected Hugenberg's offer to accept candidates from the various parties to the right of centre on the DNVP's state ticket (*Landesliste*) provided that the deputies who were elected through this arrangement agreed to affiliate themselves as guests (*Hospitanten*) with the DNVP *Landtag* delegation.[123] The outcome of the election, however, only confirmed the worst fears of the party's leaders as the CNBLP received less than 1 per cent of the total popular vote and failed, as did the other members of the National Front of German Estates, to elect so much as a single deputy to the *Landtag*.[124] In the meantime, the party's electoral prospects in Bavaria and Württemberg had already received a devastating blow when the RLB affiliates that had supported it in the 1930 Reichstag elections decided to renew their former ties to the DNVP, thereby condemning the CNBLP to certain defeat in both states.

By dramatizing the CNBLP's loss of popular support, the outcome of the April 1932 *Landtag* elections accelerated the party's organizational collapse and helped prepare the way for an even more disastrous defeat in the national elections that were to be held later that summer. Particularly damaging to the CNBLP's election prospects was the collapse of its organizational base in Hesse and Thuringia, the two areas from which it had traditionally received its strongest support. In June the Hessian Rural League announced that it would support the DNVP in the forthcoming Hessian state elections and explicitly dissociated itself from the bourgeois unity ticket which the CNBLP had formed with other middle-class splinter parties.[125] Shortly thereafter, the leaders of the Thuringian Rural League, claiming that the CNBLP had compromised itself by virtue of its support for Brüning and Schiele, voted unanimously to present their own slate of candidates in the Reichstag elections that had been scheduled for 31 July 1932.[126] As the CNBLP found itself increasingly isolated from those forces in the German agricultural community to whose initiative it owed its very existence, the party's leaders became deeply divided as to the course of action they should pursue. Schlange-Schöningen and the leaders of the CNBLP's more moderate wing were convinced that the party's only future lay in a merger with other bourgeois groups and actively supported the efforts to found a united middle party that took place following the dissolution of the Reichstag in early June 1932.[127] Hauenschild and his supporters, on the other hand, sought to align what still remained of the CNBLP with the forces of the 'national opposition' and entered into secret negotiations with both the DNVP and NSDAP for an electoral alliance in the July elections.[128] Although his neogitations with the Nazi party leadership eventually broke down as a result of the strong opposition which the proposed alliance encountered from Willikens and the NSDAP's agrarian spokesmen,[129] Hauenschild was able to negotiate an agreement with Hugenberg whereby the DNVP would be entitled to all votes (*Reststimmen*) which the CNBLP did not need for the election of its own candidates at the district level.[130] Consequently, the CNBLP's campaign in the July 1932 Reichstag elections displayed remarkable reserve in its treatment of the radical right. Not only did the CNBLP abstain from its customary attacks against Hugenberg and the DNVP, but it was only after the Nazis had tried to embarrass the CNBLP by leaking reports of their negotiations for an electoral alliance that the party publicly criticized the NSDAP for its unfair campaign methods.[131]

If the leaders of the CNBLP hoped to salvage their party's declining electoral fortunes by stressing their solidarity with the goals of the radical right, they were still unable to compensate for the glaring deficiencies that had developed in their party's national organization. For example, the CNBLP was able to present candidates in only twenty-five of Germany's thirty-five electoral districts, and in former strongholds such as Thuringia and Württemberg it deferred to the wishes of the local RLB affiliates and refrained from running its own slate of candidates. More-over, some of the party's most familiar names – including those of Hepp, Schlange-Schöningen and Gereke – were conspicuously absent from the list of candidates which the CNBLP presented at the national and district levels.[132] None of this augured at all well for the party's chances at the polls, and the CNBLP proceeded to go down to a defeat even more devastating than the one it had suffered in April. Outside Thuringia and Württemberg where local agrarian organizations ran unaffiliated tickets, the CNBLP received less than 40,000 votes – or less than a quarter of what it had received in Prussia alone just three months earlier – in the July 1932 Reichstag elections.[133] Nor did it fare any better in the next electoral round on 6 November 1932. For although the CNBLP conducted a vigorous campaign structured around the slogan 'With Hindenburg for a New Germany' and attacked the NSDAP far more aggressively than it had done in the previous campaign,[134] it failed to capitalize upon the growing disenchantment which many German farmers were beginning to feel with respect to National Socialism and managed to improve upon its performance in the July elections by a mere 9,000 votes.[135]

The CNBLP had ceased to be a factor in Germany's political life well before the Nazi seizure of power on 30 January 1933. The failure of the CNBLP to establish itself as a permanent force in the German country-side stemmed from a variety of factors. In the first place, the CNBLP owed its existence to essentially negative circumstances and would never have been founded had it not been for the deepening agricultural crisis and the inability of Germany's more established bourgeois parties to provide organized agrarian interests with the effective political repre-sentation to which they felt entitled. Secondly, the CNBLP was too heavily dependent upon the support of the RLB's regional affiliates and never succeeded in developing an effective national organization of its own. As a result, the CNBLP remained more or less frozen in the mould of a classical *Honoratorienpartei* and as such was ill equipped to meet the challenge of a truly modern political party like the NSDAP. Thirdly, the CNBLP's close identification with the agricultural policies of the Brüning-Schiele government severely compromised its political effectiveness during a period of increasing economic hardship. Not only did this leave the CNBLP's more moderate leaders exposed to the agitation of radical anti-government parties such as the DNVP and NSDAP, but it also led to a serious erosion of the party's relationship with the National Rural League. The fate of the CNBLP was effectively decided in the fall of 1930 when the party's disappointing performance at the polls made it possible for Hugenberg's associates from east of the Elbe River to torpedo first Schiele's position and then that of Hepp and Höfer within the RLB's national leadership. The subsequent split in the CNBLP Reichstag delegation in February 1931 signalled the end of the party's parliamentary effectiveness and exposed it to another round of attacks from the radical right. Caught between the economic demands of the 'Green Front' and the agitation of the 'national opposition', the leaders of the CNBLP steered an unsteady course that only accelerated the party's organizational collapse and set the stage for its electoral eclipse in the spring and summer of 1932.

Still, the history of the CNBLP offers a valuable corrective to the vast body of literature which has traditionally sought to establish a causal connection between the politics of Germany's rural elite and the establishment of the Nazi dictatorship in January 1933.[136] To be sure, no one would seriously dispute the central role which the east Elbian Junkers played in the destruction of the Weimar Republic or in Hitler's appointment as Chancellor. But to focus so one-sidedly upon the political machinations of the large landowners from east of the Elbe River is to overlook the fact that the German agricultural elite was badly divided on the eve of the Nazi seizure of power and that many of Germany's most conservative farm leaders were profoundly disturbed by the series of events which culminated in the installation of the Hitler-Papen government. For all of their professed hostility to the Weimar Republic, the leaders of the CNBLP never shared the dictatorial aspirations of Germany's radical right and struggled desperately, if ineffectively, to prevent the German countryside from falling under Nazi influence. What the leaders of the CNBLP sought was a conservative regeneration of the German state, a goal which in their minds held little in common with the cheap demagoguery and obstructionist tactics of the NSDAP. That the effectiveness of their opposition was undercut first by the intrigues of Hugenberg's associates within the National Rural League and secondly by the radicalizing effect which the world economic crisis had upon the German peasantry should not be allowed to obscure the fact that they not only represented a significant body of opinion within Germany's conservative rural elite, but harboured a visceral distrust of National Socialism right up until the last days of the Weimar Republic.[137]

In a broader sense, the emergence of agrarian splinter parties in the second half of the 1920s constituted an important chapter in the dissolution of the Weimar party system. For while both the German Peasants' Party and the CNBLP proved remarkably adept at enticing disgruntled farm voters away from the more established bourgeois parties, neither succeeded in establishing itself as an agrarian party with a truly national profile. From the very outset their appeal was regional rather than national, their success confined to those areas where they enjoyed the support of local agricultural organizations, and their effectiveness limited by both the confessional as well as the structural diversity of the German agricultural community. Not only were agrarian splinter parties notably unsuccessful in their efforts to mobilize the Catholic sector of Germany's rural population, but the conflict of interests between small family farmers who had responded to the vicissitudes of the world market by diversifying production and large landowners whose economic fortunes were still tied to the rise and fall of international grain prices militated against the creation of a national agrarian party which purported to represent the German agricultural community as a whole. Yet, having staked their existence upon the defence and promotion of agricultural economic interests, both the DBP and CNBLP were hampered by an unresolved contradiction between the need to work within the framework of the existing political system in order to promote the welfare of those they claimed to represent and the 'anti-system' bias that had become such an essential component of their basic ideological orientation. Unable to legitimize themselves by the success of their efforts on behalf of agricultural economic interests, they were destined to serve as little more than conduits for the transmission of disaffected rural voters from the more traditional bourgeois parties to that arch-enemy of the Weimar system itself, the NSDAP.

Notes: Chapter 7

ABBREVIATIONS

BA	Bundesarchiv Koblenz
BBB	Bayerischer Bauernbund/Bayerischer Bauern- und Mittelstandsbund
CNBLP	Christlich-Nationale Bauern- und Landvolkpartei
DBB	Deutscher Bauernbund
DBP	Deutsche Bauernpartei

DBS	Deutsche Bauernschaft
DDP	Deutsche Demokratische Partei
DHP	Deutsch-Hannoversche Partei
DNVP	Deutschnationale Volkspartei
DVP	Deutsche Volkspartei
KVP	Konservative Volkspartei
NL	Nachlass
NSDAP	Nationalsozialistische Deutsche Arbeiterpartei
PA	Politisches Archiv des Auswärtigen Amts, Bonn
RLB	Reichs-Landbund
TLB	Thüringer Landbund
WBWB	Württembergischer Bauern- und Weingärtnerbund
WP	Wirtschaftspartei des deutschen Mittelstandes
ZStA	Zentrales Staatsarchiv Potsdam

The completion of this essay would not have been possible without the financial support of the Alexander von Humboldt-Stiftung and the Deutscher Akademischer Austauschdienst, and I would like to take this opportunity to express my appreciation for their generosity. I am also deeply indebted to Friedrich Freiherr Hiller von Gaertringen, who not only made available the papers of his grandfather, Kuno Graf von Westarp, but also facilitated access to several valuable collections of pamphlets, newspaper articles and other materials in the possession of the heirs of Theodor Körner alt, Friedrich von Holtz and Franz Freiherr Schenck von Stauffenberg. For his support and generous assistance I remain profoundly grateful.

1 In the interests of economy, extensive references to secondary sources have been deleted. I am, however, deeply indebted to two seminal studies by Dieter Gessner, *Agrarverbände in der Weimarer Republik. Wirtschaftliche und soziale Voraussetzungen agrarkonservativer Politik vor 1933* (Düsseldorf, 1976), and *Agrardepression und Präsidialregierungen in Deutschland 1930–1933. Probleme des Agrarprotektionismus am Ende der Weimarer Republik* (Düsseldorf, 1977), which provide much of the background for this investigation. The only scholarly account of agrarian splinter parties is Arno Panzer, 'Parteipolitische Ansätze der deutschen Bauernbewegung bis 1933', in Heinz Gollwitzer (ed.), *Europäische Bauernparteien im 20. Jahrhundert* (Stuttgart and New York, 1977), 524–42, although Hans-Jürgen Puhle, *Politische Agrarbewegungen in kapitalistischen Industriegesellschaften. Deutschland, USA und Frankreich im 20. Jahrhundert* (Göttingen, 1975), 28–103, has also dealt with this topic as part of a comparative study of agrarian movements in the twentieth century.

2 For further details, see Martin Schumacher, *Land und Politik. Eine Untersuchung über politische Parteien und agrarische Interessen 1914–1924* (Düsseldorf, 1978), 387–494.

3 For an excellent example of this, see the contribution by Jonathan Osmond in this volume.

4 For example, see Joseph Kaufhold, *Die Sünden der Demokratischen Partei und des Deutschen Bauernbundes an der Landwirtschaft*, Deutschnationale Flugschrift, no. 134 (Berlin, 1922), 9–18. For further details on the background of this conflict, see Robert G. Moeller, 'Winners as losers in the German inflation: peasant protest over the controlled economy, 1920–1923', in Gerald Feldman, Carl-Ludwig Holtfrerich, Gerhard A. Ritter and Peter-Christian Witt (eds.), *Die deutsche Inflation. Eine Zwischenbilanz/The German Inflation Reconsidered. A Preliminary Balance* (Berlin and New York, 1982), 255–88.

5 Böhme to Koch-Weser, n.d., in *Deutscher Bauernbund* 16, no. 42 (16 October 1924): 349–50. See also Karl Böhme, *Der Bauernstand in Knechtschaft und Freiheit* (Berlin, 1924), 121–4.

6 Böhme, 'Der Deutsche Bauernbund im Kampf', in *Deutscher Bauernbund* 16, no. 48 (27 November 1924): 402–3. See also Karl Böhme, *Der nationale Liberalismus und die Bauern*, Flugschriften der Deutschen Volkspartei, no. 69 (Berlin, 1927).

7 Remarks by Wachhorst de Wente before the DDP executive committee, 21 October

1924, in the records of the German Democratic Party, Bundesarchiv, Koblenz, Bestand R 45 III (hereafter cited as BA R 45 III), 19/96–7.

8   Remarks by Wachhorst de Wente before the DDP executive committee, 10 October 1925, BA R 45 III, 19/120–22.

9   For a highly coloured account of these events, see Karl Böhme, *Zum Streit der landwirtschaftlichen Organisationen! Ein Wort zur Abwehr* (Leipzig, n.d. [1928]), 3–19.

10 Lübke and Müller to the Reich Chancellery, 1 October 1927, in the records of the Reich Chancellery, Bundesarchiv, Koblenz, Bestand R 43 I (hereafter cited as BA: R 43 I), 1301/2–3.

11 'Aufbau und Ziele der Deutschen Bauernschaft', n.d., Bundesarchiv, Koblenz, Nachlass Jakob Kaiser, 221.

12 The secondary literature on the BBB is quite extensive. In addition to the contribution by Ian Farr in this volume, one should also consult Heinz Haushofer, 'Der Bayerische Bauernbund (1893–1933)', in Gollwitzer (ed.), *Europäische Bauernparteien*, 562–86, and Ian Farr, 'Populism in the countryside: the peasant leagues in Bavaria in the 1890's', in Richard J. Evans (ed.), *Society and Politics in Wilhelmine Germany* (London and New York, 1978), 136–59, as well as the contemporary study by Alois Hundhammer, *Geschichte des Bayerischen Bauernbundes* (Munich, 1924).

13 For the general outlines of the BBB's postwar development, see Hundhammer, *Geschichte*, 168–89, and Puhle, *Agrarbewegungen*, 85–7.

14 See Fehr's speeches from the spring of 1924 as reported in *Der Bündler. Organ für fortschrittliche Bauern und Mittelstandspolitik* 6, no. 4 (27 January 1924): 2–3, and no. 11 (16 March 1924): 1–3.

15 In this respect, see Fehr to Bredt, 9 May 1924, as well as the protocol of an agreement between the BBB, DHP and WP, 5 November 1924, both in the unpublished Nachlass of Johann Victor Bredt in the private possession of his daughter, Frau Dr. Ada Rambeau of Marburg.

16 For further information, see Dieter Gessner, 'The dilemma of German agriculture during the Weimar Republic', in Richard Bessel and E. J. Feuchtwanger (eds.), *Social Change and Political Development in Weimar Germany* (London and New York, 1981), 134–54.

17 For further details, see Arno Panzer, 'Das Ringen um die deutsche Agrarpolitik von der Währungsstabilisierung bis zur Agrardebatte im Reichstag im Dezember 1928' (Ph.D. diss., Kiel, 1970), 24–51, and Dirk Stegmann, 'Deutsche Zoll- und Handelspolitik 1924/5–1929 unter besonderer Berücksichtigung agrarischer und industrieller Interessen', in Hans Mommsen, Dietmar Petzina and Bernd Weisbrod (eds.), *Industrielles System und politische Entwicklung in der Weimarer Republik. Verhandlungen des Internationalen Symposiums in Bochum vom 12.–17. Juni 1973* (Düsseldorf, 1974), 499–513.

18 Gerhard Stoltenberg, *Politische Strömungen im schleswig-holsteinischen Landvolk 1918–1933. Ein Beitrag zur politischen Meinungsbildung in der Weimarer Republik* (Düsseldorf, 1962), 107–12.

19 In this respect, see *Der Thüringer Landbund. Thüringer Bauernzeitung für die im Thüringer Landbund zusammengeschlossenen Bauernvereinigungen* 9, no. 12 (11 February 1928): 1, and Württembergischer Bauern- und Weingärtnerbund (ed.), *Der württembergische Bauernfreund. Ein Wegweiser und Jahrbuch für unseren bäuerlichen und gewerblichen Mittelstand für das Jahr 1929* (Stuttgart, n.d. [1929]), 90–1.

20 Kuno von Westarp, *Bauernnot – Volksnot. Das Arbeitsprogramm des Reichstages und das landwirtschaftliche Programm der Deutschnationalen Volkspartei*, Deutschnationale Flugschrift, no. 317 (Berlin, 1928).

21 Paul Hiltmann, 'Tatsachen und Probleme der Bauernbewegung', in *Die grüne Zukunft. Zeitschrift für deutsche Bauernpolitik* 1, nos. 1–2 (October–November 1928): 2–5, 18–24. For the text of Fehr's speech, see *Bayer. Bauern- und Mittlestandsbund. Beilage der "Neuen freien Volkszeitung" in München*, 22 February 1928, no. 5.

22 *Deutsche Bauernzeitung. Zentralorgan der Deutschen Bauernschaft* 2, no. 14 (1 April 1928): 157–8, and no. 16 (15 April 1928): 181–3. See also Wachhorst de Wente's remarks before the DDP executive committee, 6 March 1928, BA R 45 III, 20/128–9.

23 Hiltmann, 'Tatsachen und Probleme der Bauernbewegung', 24.

24 Resolution from the executive committee of the Thuringian Rural League, 24

November 1927, appended to a circular from the RLB presidium, 23 December 1927, in the published Nachlass of Luitpold von Weilnböck (hereafter cited as NL Weilnböck) in the private possession of Frau Konrad Frühwald of Neustadt an der Aisch.

25 Report on the meeting of the RLB executive committee, 14 December 1927, NL Weilnböck.

26 *Thüringer Landbund* 9, no. 15 (22 February 1928): 1.

27 Rudolf Lantzsch, 'Bauernparteien?', in *Der Demokrat. Mitteilungen aus der Deutschen Demokratischen Partei* 9, no. 6 (18 March 1928): 164–5.

28 Hepp to Stresemann, 4 September 1921, in the Politisches Archiv des Auswärtigen Amts, Bonn, Nachlass Gustav Stresemann (hereafter cited as PA NL Stresemann), 231/141458–60.

29 In this respect, see Hepp to Stresemann, 24 May 1925, PA NL Stresemann, 93/172762–3, and Hepp's speech in *Der 8. Reichs-Landbund-Tag. Die Reden der Präsidenten und des Ernährungsministers Schiele* (Berlin, n.d. [1928]), 8–9.

30 Kempkes to Stresemann, 24 February 1928, PA NL Stresemann, 99/173883–9.

31 *Thüringer Landbund* 9, no. 20 (10 March 1928): 1.

32 Stauffenberg to Westarp, 24 February 1928, NL Westarp.

33 Ernst Höfer, 'Zur Gründung der Christlich-Nationalen Bauernpartei', in *Thüringer Landbund* 9, no. 23 (21 March 1928): 1. See also Karl Dorsch, 'Zur Gründung der Christlich-Nationalen Bauern- und Landvolkpartei', ibid., no. 32 (21 April 1928): 1, and Erwin Baum, 'Was will die Christlich-Nationale Bauern- und Landvolkpartei?', in *Nassauische Bauern-Zeitung. Organ und Verlag der Bezirksbauernschaft für Nassau und den Kreis Wetzlar e. V.*, 5 May 1928, no. 105.

34 *Reichs-Landbund. Agrarpolitische Wochenschrift* 8, no. 8 (25 February 1928): 101.

35 Westarp to Wilmowsky, 23 February 1928, NL Westarp. See also Schmidt-Stettin to Hepp, 26 March 1928, and Richthofen to Hepp, 25 April 1928, both in NL Weilnböck, as well as Lothar Steuer, *Die deutsche Landwirtschaft und die politischen Parteien. Eine Wahlkampfbetrachtung* (Kassel, 1928), 12–15.

36 In this respect, see the protocol of an agreement between the Bavarian Rural League (*Bayerischer Landbund*) and the DNVP, 3 March 1928, NL Weilnböck, and Lüttichau to Westarp, 24 March 1928, NL Westarp.

37 For example, see Feldmann to Höfer, 27 March 1928, NL Westarp, and Hopp to the RLB presidium, 8 May 1928, NL Weilnböck.

38 Memorandum from the German National Workers' League (*Deutschnationaler Arbeiterbund*), 12 June 1928, NL Westarp. See also Lothar Steuer, *Die deutschnationale Wahlniederlage am 20. Mai 1928. Ihre Ursachen, Zusammenhänge, Folgerungen* (Anklam, 1928), 17–20.

39 For an analysis of the CNBLP's performance in the 1928 elections, see the lengthy memorandum from Kriegsheim to the members of the RLB executive committee, 6 June 1928, NL Weilnböck, as well as 'Nach der Wahl', *Reichs-Landbund* 8, no. 21 (26 May 1928), and 'Zur Reichstagswahl', *Thüringer Landbund* 9, no. 42 (26 May 1928): 231–2.

40 For a district breakdown of the DBP's performance in the 1928 elections, see *Die Grüne Zukunft* 1, no. 2 (November 1928): 30.

41 Memorandum dated 14 June 1928, NL Weilnböck.

42 *Die Grüne Zukunft* 1, no. 2 (November 1928): 28. See also Fehr's report at the BBB's state convention, 27–9 October 1928, in the *Bayer. Bauern- und Mittelstandsbund. Beilage zum 'Schwäbischen Volksblatts'*, 31 October 1928, no. 1.

43 In this respect, see Richthofen to Hepp, 6 July 1928, as well as Richthofen to Westarp, 6 and 16 July 1928, all in NL Westarp.

44 Wilmowsky to Krupp, 2 August 1928, in the Historisches Archiv der Friedrich Krupp GmbH, Essen (hereafter cited as Krupp-Archiv), FAH 23/502.

45 Wilmowsky to Krupp, 20 March 1929, Krupp-Archiv, FAH 23/502. For further information, see Gessner, *Agrarverbände*, 96–128, as well as Heide Barmeyer, *Andreas Hermes und die Organisation der deutschen Landwirtschaft. Christliche Bauernvereine, Reichslandbund, Grüne Front, Reichsnährstand 1928–1933* (Stuttgart, 1971), 80–120.

46 Lind to Hugenberg, 6 May 1929, NL Westarp.

47 Resolution adopted by the RLB executive committee, 25 September 1929, NL Weilnböck. See also Schiele to the headquarters of the National Referendum Committee, 13

September 1929, NL Westarp, and to the members of the RLB executive committee, 13 September 1929, NL Weilnböck, as well as Wilmowsky to Krupp, 14 September 1929, Krupp-Archiv, FAH 23/503. For further information, see the superbly researched dissertation by Elizabeth Friedenthal, 'Volksbegehren und Volksentscheid über den Young Plan und die deutschnationale Sezession' (Ph.D. diss., Tübingen, 1957), 64–75.

48   See Hepp's remarks at a meeting of the RLB executive committee, 1 November 1929, in the records of the Reichs-Landbund, Zentrales Staatsarchiv, Potsdam, Bestand 61 Re 1 (hereafter cited as ZStA Potsdam 61 Re 1), 120a/135–7. See also Wilmowsky to Hugenberg, 11 October 1929, ibid., 148–9 (also in Krupp Archiv, FAH 23/503). These and other documents on the crisis within the RLB in the fall of 1929 are to be found in Dieter Gessner '"Grüne Front" oder "Harzburger Front". Der Reichs-Landbund in der letzten Phase der Weimarer Republik zwischen wirtschaftlicher Interessenpolitik und nationalistischem Revisionsanspruch', *Vierteljahrshefte für Zeitgeschichte* 29 (1981): 110–23.

49   On Gereke's activities in the summer and autumn of 1929, see Günther Gereke, *Ich war königlich-preussischer Landrat* (East Berlin, 1970), pp. 148–55, as well as the published reports in *Der Landbürger. Kommunalpolitisches Organ der Christlich-nationalen Bauern- und Landvolkpartei* 4, no. 15 (2 August 1929): 225, no. 17 (2 September 1929): 258; no. 19 (2 October 1929): 290.

50   In this respect, see 'Einfachheit und Sparsamkeit. Die kommunalpolitischen Richtlinien der Christlich-nationalen Bauern- und Landvolkpartei', in *Der Landbürger* 4, no. 19 (16 October 1929): 306–10, as well as the reports of Gereke's speeches in Wiehe und Querfurth, 10 November 1929, ibid., 4, no. 22 (16 November 1929): 341–2.

51   For further details, see Friedenthal, 'Volksbegehren', 113–31.

52   *Nassauische Bauern-Zeitung*, 5 February 1930, no. 30. See also Hans Schlange-Schöningen, *Am Tage danach* (Hamburg, 1946), 40–2, as well as the entry in the diary of Karl Passarge, 30 January 1930, in the Bundesarchiv, Koblenz, Nachlass Passarge (hereafter cited as BA: NL Passarge), 2/25–6.

53   See the entries in Passarge's diary for 5, 12 and 30 January 1930, BA: NL Passarge, 2/10–26.

54   Speech by Hepp in Münster, 24 February 1930, in *Der Landbürger* 5, no. 6 (16 March 1930): 82–3.

55   For further details, see the speech by Gereke in Halle, 21 December 1929, in *Der Landbürger* 5, no. 1 (2 January 1930): 2, as well as G. R. Treviranus, *Auf neuen Wegen*, Volkskonservative Flugschriften, no. 2 (Berlin, 1930).

56   See the reports of Nationalist defections in *Der Landbürger* 5, no. 6 (16 March 1930): 83, and no. 7 (2 April 1930): 98.

57   Entry in Passarge's diary, 16 March 1930, BA: NL Passarge, 3/58–9.

58   Research on the Nazi courtship of the German farmer has been quite extensive. In addition to the contribution by J. E. Farquharson in this volume, see Horst Gies, 'NSDAP und landwirtschaftliche Organisationen in der Endphase der Weimarer Republik', *Vierteljahrshefte für Zeitgeschichte* 15 (1967): 341–76, and J. E. Farquharson, *The Plough and the Swastika. The NSDAP and Agriculture in Germany 1928–1945* (London and Beverly Hills, Calif., 1975), 1–42.

59   *Reichs-Landbund* 10, no. 3 (18 January 1930): 27–9. See also the report of the meeting of the RLB executive committee, 15 January 1930, ZStA Potsdam 61 Re 1, 120a.

60   Otto Weber (ed.), *Nationalsozialismus und Bauerntum. Ein Handbuch zur Klärung der nationalsozialistischen Frage* (Weimar, 1929).

61   Reichs-Landbund e.V., 'Reichs-Landbund und Nationalsozialismus', 8 February 1930, Bundesarchiv, Koblenz, Nachlass Leo Wegener, 35. See also 'Das nationalsozialistische Agrarprogramm', *Reichs-Landbund* 10, no. 11 (15 March 1930): 129–31.

62   In this respect, see Schiele's memorandum from 29 March 1930, Bundesarchiv, Koblenz, Nachlass Herman Pünder, 131/231–4, as well as the undated memorandum on the formation of the Brüning government by Westarp, April 1930, NL Westarp.

63   *Nassauische Bauern-Zeitung*, 4 April 1930, no. 79.

64   Hepp, Bethge and Kriegsheim to the RLB organization, 16 April 1930, NL Westarp.

65 For further details, see the undated memorandum by Westarp, 'Niederschrift über die Spaltung der DNVP vom Jahre 1930', NL Westarp.

66 Westarp, 'Betr. Trennungsabsichten', n.d. [May 1930], NL Westarp.

67 *Nassauische Bauern-Zeitung*, 6 August 1930, no. 180.

68 *Reichs-Landbund* 10, no. 30 (26 July 1930): 360.

69 For example, see Alwin Domsch, 'Reichstagsauflösung und Neuwahl', *Sächsische Bauern-Zeitung* 37, no. 31 (3 August 1930): 316–17.

70 In this respect, see the DNVP campaign brochure, *Der Landbund im Wahlkampf* (Berlin, n.d. [1930]).

71 Hermes to the German Peasants' Associations, 29 July 1930, in the Schorlemer-Archiv, Westfälisch-Lippischer Landwirtschaftsverband, Münster, vol. 1 Ov.

72 In this respect, see *Deutsche Bauernzeitung* 4, no. 32 (10 August 1930): 357–8, and Wirtschaftsverband für bäuerliche Veredelungsarbeit e.V., *Bauernpolitik oder Landbundpolitik?* (Bremen, n.d. [1930]), as well as the article by the DBP's August Hillebrand, 'Vom alten zum neuen Reichstag', *Die grüne Zukunft*, 3, nos. 7/8 (July–August 1930): 81–6. On the negotiations between the CNBLP and DBP, see the report in *Der Landbürger* 5, no. 16 (16 August 1930): 248–9.

73 Schiele to Seeckt, 20 August 1930, Bundesarchiv, Militärabteilung Freiburg, Nachlass Hans von Seeckt, 131. See also Schiele, 'Schliesset die Reihen', *Reichs-Landbund* 10, no. 33 (16 August 1930): 385, as well as the report of Gereke's speech in Halle, n.d., in *Der Landbürger* 5, no. 16 (16 August 1930): 241–2.

74 For further details, see the report of Höfer's speech in St. Goarshausen, 27 July 1930, in the *Nassauische Bauern-Zeitung*, 29 July 1930, no. 173, and of Hepp's speech in Usingen, 28 August 1930, ibid., 30 August 1930, no. 200, as well as Höfer, 'Wir marschieren', *Thüringer Landbund* 11, no. 62 (2 August 1930): 1.

75 Protocol of a meeting between Gereke, Sogemeier and Blank, 28 July 1930, in the Historisches Archiv der Gutehoffnungshütte, Oberhausen, Nachlass Paul Reusch, 4001012024/7.

76 Wilmowsky to Krupp, 1 August 1930, Krupp-Archiv, FAH 23/504.

77 See Gereke's remarks at a meeting with leaders of the other moderate bourgeois parties, 7 August 1930, in 'Bericht über die Verhandlungen mit der DVP wegen Zusammenwirkens für das Hindenburg-Programm', n.d. [August 1930], NL Westarp.

78 [Günther Gereke], *Die Sendung des Landvolks*, ed. Landbürger-Verlag (Berlin, n.d. [1930]), 3–12. See also Franz Döbrich, 'Christlich-nationale Bauern- und Landvolkpartei und Neuwahlen', *Thüringer Landbund* 11, nos. 69–70 (27 and 30 August 1930), and the campaign flyer from the Württembergischer Bauern- und Weingärtnerbund, 'Wahlaufruf zur Reichstagswahl am 14. September 1930,' n.d., in the Nachlass of Friedrich von Holtz (hereafter cited as NL Holtz) in the private possession of the Holtz family.

79 For example, see Willy Ohm, *Der Schicksalsruf: Bauern, an die Front* (Berlin, n.d. [1930]).

80 Theodor Körner alt, 'Bauernbund und Nationalsozialisten', ed. Württ. Bauern- und Weingärtnerbund (Flugblatt no. 16), NL Holtz. See also Theodor Körner, *Was hat das Landvolk von der Nationalsozialistischen Deutschen Arbeiterpartei zu erwarten? Fragen und Antworten zur nationalen Bewegung* (Stuttgart, n.d. [c. 1930–1]).

81 'Die Deutsche Bauernpartei ruft auf', n.d. [August–September 1930], Bayerisches Hauptstaatsarchiv, Munich, Abt. V, Flugblätter-Sammlung, F 129. See also 'Ein Wahlaufruf der Deutschen Bauernpartei', *Die grüne Zukunft*, 3, nos. 7/8 (July–August 1930): 96–8.

82 'Der Bayerische Bauern- und Mittelstandsbund (Die Deutsche Bauernpartei) ruft auf zur Wahl am 14. September!', n.d. [August–September 1930], Bayerisches Hauptstaatsarchiv, Munich, Abt. V, Flugblätter-Sammlung, F 64.

83 Hillebrand, 'Neue Fraktionsbildung im Reichstag', *Die grüne Zukunft*, 3, nos. 11/12 (November–December 1930): 133.

84 Höfer, 'Das Wahlergebnis', *Thüringer Landbund* 11, no. 76 (20 September 1930): 1–2.

85 The data upon which the foregoing analysis was based was taken from Bureau des Reichstags (ed.), *Reichstags-Handbuch. V. Wahlperiode 1930* (Berlin, 1930), 204–7. See also *Der Landbürger* 5, no. 20 (16 October 1930): 311–12.

86 The secondary literature on the Nazi breakthrough into the countryside is quite exten-

sive. In addition to the standard regional studies by Rudolf Heberle, *From Democracy to Nazism. A Regional Case Study of Political Parties in Germany* (Baton Rouge, La., 1945), 32–89, Jeremy Noakes, *The Nazi Party in Lower Saxony, 1921–1933* (Oxford, 1971), 147–55, and Geoffrey Pridham, *Hitler's Rise to Power. The Nazi Movement in Bavaria, 1923–33* (London, 1973), 78–145, see the recent monograph by Zdenek Zofka, *Die Ausbreitung des Nationalsozialismus auf dem Lande. Eine regionale Fallstudie zur politischen Einstellung der Landvolkbevölkerung in der Zeit des Aufstieges und der Machtergreifung der NSDAP 1928–1936*, (Munich, 1979).

87 'Was nun?', *Die grüne Zukunft* 3, nos. 9/10 (September–October 1930): 101–3.
88 *Bayer. Bauern- und Mittelstandsbund. Beilage zum 'Schwäbischen Volksblatt'*, 3 December 1930, no. 6.
89 Hillebrand, 'Fraktionsbildung', 133.
90 *Deutsche Bauernzeitung* 4, no. 49 (7 December 1930): 493–4.
91 On the situation within the CNBLP Reichstag delegation, see Westarp to Schulenburg, 28 September 1930, NL Westarp.
92 *Bayerischer Landbund* 32, no. 39 (28 September 1930): 2.
93 *Nassauische Bauern-Zeitung*, 3 October 1930, no. 229. See also Heinrich von Sybel, 'Zum Regierungsprogramm', *Reichs-Landbund*, 10, no. 41 (11 October 1930): 447–9, and H. Sieber, 'Rechtskurs', *Nassauische Bauern-Zeitung*, 14 October 1930, no. 238.
94 Hepp, 'Gebot der Stunde', *Nassauische Bauern-Zeitung*, 23 October 1930, no. 246.
95 Westarp, 'Meine Verhandlungen zwischen dem 18. Juli und 18. Oktober 1930', n.d. [October 1930], NL Westarp.
96 Wilmowsky to Krupp, 28 October 1930, Krupp-Archiv, FAH 23/504.
97 *Nassauische Bauern-Zeitung*, 25 October 1930, no. 248. See also the report in *Reichs-Landbund* 10, no. 43 (25 October 1930): 507.
98 *Thüringer Landbund* 11, no. 88 (1 November 1930): 1–2.
99 For further details, see Gessner, *Agrarverbände*, 239–42. On Lind's election, see *Der Landbürger* 5, no. 24 (16 December 1930): 377.
100 Speech by Höfer at the CNBLP's national party congress in Berlin, 2 December 1930, in the *Nassauische Bauern-Zeitung*, 4 December 1930, no. 280. See also the speech by Gereke, 4 December 1930, in *Verhandlungen des Reichstags* 444: 280–4.
101 *Reichs-Landbund* 11, no. 6 (7 February 1931): 75–82.
102 Wilmowsky to Krupp, 2 February 1931, Krupp-Archiv, FAH 23/504.
103 *Nassauische Bauern-Zeitung*, 11 February 1921, no. 34.
104 *Der Landbürger* 6, no. 4 (16 February 1931): 54–5.
105 Gereke, 'Landwirtschaft und Opposition', *Bayerischer Landbund* 33, no. 8 (22 February 1931): 2–3. See also the report of speeches by Hepp in Weilburg, 17 February 1931, in the *Nassauische Bauern-Zeitung*, 18 February 1931, no. 40, and Gereke in Kassel, 16 February 1931, in *Der Landbürger* 6, no. 5 (2 March 1931): 69–70.
106 *Nassauische Bauern-Zeitung*, 6 February 1931, no. 30.
107 Gereke to Dingeldey, 2 April 1931, in the records of the German People's Party, Bundesarchiv, Koblenz, Bestand R 45 II, 22/137.
108 *Nassauische Bauern-Zeitung*, 15 August 1931, no. 197. For the complete text of Hauenschild's speech, 13 August 1931, see BA R 43 I, 2687/10–24.
109 Entry in Passarge's diary, 15 September 1931, BA NL Passarge, 6/13–21. For further details, see Larry Eugene Jones, 'Sammlung oder Zersplitterung? Die Bestrebungen zur Bildung einer neuen Mittelpartei in der Endphase der Weimarer Republik 1930–1933', *Vierteljahrshefte für Zeitgeschichte* 25 (1977): 275–6.
110 Passarge to Schlange-Schöningen, 29 September 1931, BA NL Passarge, 6/39–45.
111 'Notforderungen des Deutschen Landvolks (Christlich-nationalen Bauern- und Landvolkpartei)', n.d. [29 September 1931], BA R 43 I, 1140/235–40.
112 Speech by Döbrich, 15 October 1931, in *Verhandlungen des Reichstags* 446: 2150–2. See also the *Nassauische Bauern-Zeitung*, 1 October 1931, no. 226, as well as the letter from Stauffenberg to the members of the WBWB, n.d. [c. October–November 1931], NL Holtz.
113 *Reichs-Landbund* 12, no. 5 (30 January 1932): 49–52.
114 For example, see Willi Seipel, *Landvolkpartei oder Hitler-Bewegung?* (Munich, 1932).
115 Gies, 'NSDAP und landwirtschaftliche Organisationen', 359–68.

116 In this respect, see *Der Landbürger* 7, no. 4 (16 February 1932): 54, and the *Thüringer Landbund* 13, no. 14 (20 February 1932): 1, and no. 16 (27 February 1932): 1.

117 *Reichs-Landbund* 12, no. 8 (20 February 1932): 121–2.

118 Gessner, *Agrardepression und Präsidialregierungen*, 182–3 n. 96. See also *Reichs-Landbund* 12, no. 12 (19 March 1932): 161–2.

119 Wilmowsky to Goerdeler, 1 April 1932, in the Historisches Archiv der Gutehoffnungshütte, Oberhausen, Nachlass Paul Reusch, 400101290/39.

120 *Thüringer Landbund* 13, no. 26 (2 April 1932): 1.

121 Theodor Körner alt, 'Hindenburg oder Hitler? Nüchterne Betrachtungen zur 2. Reichspräsidentenwahl am 10. April 1932', n.d., in the Nachlass of Theodor Körner alt (hereafter cited as NL Körner) in the private possession of the Körner family.

122 *Der Landbürger* 7, no. 8 (16 April 1932): 145. On the negotiations which led to the formation of this front, see Wilmowsky to Krupp, 24 March and 1 April 1932, Krupp-Archiv, FAH 23/506, as well as Jones, 'Sammlung oder Zersplitterung?', 279–81.

123 *Nassauische Bauern-Zeitung*, 1 April 1932, no. 75.

124 E. Keinast (ed.), *Handbuch für den Preussischen Landtag. Angabe für die 4. Wahlperiode (von 1932 ab)* (Berlin, 1932), 388–95.

125 'Hessisches Landvolk!', 13 June 1932, NL Körner. See also the *Nassauische Bauern-Zeitung*, 17 June 1932, no. 138.

126 *Thüringer Landbund* 13, no. 53 (6 July 1932): 1, and no. 54 (9 July 1932): 1–2.

127 On Schlange's involvement in these efforts, see his letters to Passarge, 3 June 1932, BA NL Passarge, 6/189–92, and Westarp, 5 July 1932, NL Westarp. For further details, see Jones, 'Sammlung oder Zersplitterung?', 283–92.

128 In this respect, see the draft of an agreement between the CNBLP and NSDAP, 21 June 1932, and Hauenschild to Frick, 27 June 1932, both in the NSDAP Hauptarchiv, Bundesarchiv, Koblenz, Bestand NS 26 (hereafter cited as BA NS 26), 551, as well as the entry in Passarge's diary, 24 June 1932, BA NL Passarge, 9/216–17.

129 Frick to Hauenschild, 11 July 1932, BA NS 26, 551. See also Willikens to Frick, 28 June and 9 July 1932, and Reibing to Frick, 6 July 1932, ibid.

130 *Deutsches Landvolk. Nachrichtenblatt der Christlich-Nationalen Bauern- und Landvolkpartei* 5, no. 27 (22 July 1932): 1–2.

131 ibid., no. 28 (27 July 1932): 2.

132 ibid., no. 27 (22 July 1932): 2.

113 Bureau des Reichstags (ed.), *Reichstags-Handbuch. VI. Wahlperiode 1932* (Berlin, 1932), 13–25.

134 *Deutsches Landvolk* 5, no. 32 (14 October 1932): 1–4; no. 33 (20 October 1932): 1–2. See also Christlich-nationale Bauern- und Landvolkpartei, *Weg und Ziel des Landvolks* (Berlin, n.d. [1932]), 1–2, 8–10.

135 Bureau des Reichstags (ed.), *Reichstags-Handbuch. VII. Wahlperiode 1932* (Berlin, 1933), 192–3.

136 For example, see Werner Braatz, 'Die agrarisch-industrielle Front in der Weimarer Republik 1930–1932', *Schmollers Jahrbuch für Wirtschafts- und Sozialwissenschaften* 91 (1971): 541–65, and David Abraham, *The Collapse of the Weimar Republic. Political Economy and Crisis* (Princeton, N.J., 1981), 85–115, 316–18.

137 For an example of such sentiment as late as early 1933, see the pamphlet by the WBWB's Gottlob Muschler, *Die neue politische Lage* (Stuttgart, n.d. [1933]), 3–6, 12–14.

8 The Agrarian Policy of National Socialist Germany

J. E. FARQUHARSON

L'aspect moderne de Nazisme ne doit point faire oublier que ses buts et ses nostalgies plongent souvent dans un passé plus ancien.[1]

The above quotation, although intended as a general analysis of National Socialist ideology, could well serve at least to some extent as a resumé of the general agrarian policies which the NSDAP followed. Here it will be maintained that this was especially true of the law on Hereditary Farm Entailment (EHG) and of the settlement programme pursued in the Third Reich which together with the Reich Food Estate (*Reichsnährstand* or RNS) formed the three pillars of National Socialist agricultural policy. Although internally coherent and to no small degree well within the mainstream of traditional right wing agrarian thought, the National Socialist programme came to a Germany already too far down the path of industrialization to be ultimately succesful. This may well have proved to be the case even had Germany won the war, although clearly this latter contention is disputable.

What complicates any assessment of the Hitler party's agricultural plans in any case is that they collided almost immediately with the demands of pragmatism, in that priority was given in the Third Reich to rearmament, at least from 1935 onwards. The conflict between ideology and short-term needs make evaluation of the original agrarian programme a difficult matter, but none the less it can be said that it represented an aspect of the Third Reich which looked backwards for its models, rather along the lines that some historians have described as 'neo-feudal'.[2] Indeed, it has been stigmatized as the expression of utopian anti-modernism.[3]

There is no doubt that many party members were to some genuine extent anti-urban. City life was seen as the source of most contemporary socio-political maladies such as Marxism or liberalism, stigmatized by Heinrich Himmler as 'asphalt intellectualism'.[4] In the 1920s he was himself a member of a 'Back to the land' movement called the Artamanen in Bavaria. At the other end of Germany, in the Göttingen area, Herbert Backe, a future Minister of Agriculture in the Third Reich, was describing

233

how two-thirds of all Germans lived in cities and only 34 per cent under what he called 'natural conditions', a value judgement which is surely revealing.[5] Already in the early days of the NSDAP therefore a strong anti-urban current can be distinguished in many party circles, with a tendency to glorify the peasantry as its logical concomitant. On the Right politically in Germany there had been a long tradition of 'peasant Romantik', and here the NSDAP has to be seen in the context of German conservatism since the nineteenth century. (The question will be raised at the end as to whether anti-urbanization and a peasant ideology necessarily entails anti-modernism as such.)

Hitler himself was not exempt from this influence. Schoenbaum has suggested that national 'Blood and Soil' ideology was very much part of the *Führer*'s mental world, rather than mere tactical necessity.[6] Certainly *Mein Kampf* is full of vague allusions to the link between the sword and the plough, where the task of the former is to win soil for peasants to cultivate in order to establish a sound relationship between the population of Germany and its living-space (*Lebensraum*). Such considerations would presuppose the maintenance of the peasantry; that the farming population tended to be conservative and thus represented a bulwark against liberalism and Marxism was no doubt another reason for its advancement. This is not, however, to suggest that Hitler had worked out any precise plans as to how this was to be achieved in practice, since he took little interest in the practical side of farming.

Until March 1930 the nearest thing the NSDAP had to an agrarian programme were two articles by Werner Willikens in its annual Yearbook in 1929 and 1930. A farmer himself, Willikens was the NSDAP spokesman on agriculture in the Reichstag after March 1928. He denied reports that the party aimed at land expropriation, and promised a settlement programme in eastern Germany and a reform of farm inheritance laws, together with an end to speculation in land. None of this was very exactly formulated, but the real significance lay in the general principles adopted. These foreshadowed the later programme, published in March 1930, above all in the emphasis on farming land in the interests of the nation as a whole, and not purely for private gain. This was precisely the point of departure for the NSDAP and marks its divergence from any liberal system, where agricultural interests were allowed to build lobbies of their own.

Thus even prior to 1933 the Hitler movement was really saying two things to farmers: first, we regard you as a necessary foundation in our state, to which end we shall maintain you; second, in return for this you must serve the whole nation. It then followed that the prerequisite for agrarian prosperity was a recovery of the entire national economy, in which agriculture had a vital part to play.

The proclamation of the actual party farming programme, a somewhat fuller version of Willikens's two articles, was followed almost at once by the acquisition of a new agrarian expert, Richard Walther Darré.[7] Although he had never been a farmer, Darré, like Himmler, was a qualified agronomist. He offered basically two propositions. The first was the decisive contribution, as he saw it, of the Nordic 'race' to European culture, a process in which the peasant base of Nordic society had played a leading part.[8] The second was the notion that the existing elites had failed, and a new one emanating from the peasantry was required to revitalize Germany. Whatever the provenance of these ideas, they fitted in very neatly with existing National Socialist principles. Some historians have gone further and suggested that with his 'Blood and Soil' ideology Darré made an enormous contribution to the party's thought overall.[9] It has even been averred that he widened the existing values-system of the movement to the point where it became a peasant-oriented party.[10] The further implication here is that he also was chiefly responsible for mobilizing the farm vote, but this is in both respects to claim too much for him. First, due to its anti-liberal bias and the concept of 'the common good before individual gain', the NSDAP had given clear indications via Werner Willikens and the programme of March 1930 what the general thrust of its agrarian thinking would entail, by linking duties to rights and privileges. Secondly, the Hitler movement had already begun to break through on the land prior to Darré's arrival, and it is to this that some reference now must be made.

By 1928 the general situation of German agriculture was deteriorating rapidly, as Brandes, president of the influential German Agricultural Council, pointed out in a gloomy speech in February of that year.[11] According to him only between 50 and 60 per cent of holdings were making a profit, and the yield per hectare was down to 8 Reichsmark (RM) as opposed to 53 in the financial year 1924–5. By 1932 the farm price index for cattle was only 63 per cent of the 1913 figure, and that of butter little more than half that in 1929. The unevenness of the price fall accentuated difficulties for peasants, who produced more meat and dairy produce than did the grain-cultivating estate-owners. The world economic crisis increasingly pushed the Weimar regime to state intervention of one sort or another, but in an unco-ordinated and unsystematic fashion. Eventually in response to energetic lobbying by agrarian associations, piecemeal grain regulations were unified and German cereal prices stabilized simply by being cut off from the world market.[12] This did not, however, apply to meat or dairy produce, which in 1930–1 accounted for 68 per cent of farm incomes. Farmers attributed government inaction in this area to what they perceived as the one-sided policy of furthering German industrial exports. What they understood by this was the apparent fear in ruling circles that duties on food imports would lead to retaliation against the export of German manufactured goods. Peasants saw themselves as being sacrificed to industrial needs. The outcome of the piecemeal approach adopted by successive Weimar governments combined with the general fall in prices for farm products was that the agrarian price index in 1931–2 was 85 for crops and plants and only 67 for animal produce (1928–9 = 100).[13]

It was against this background, where peasants suffered more than estate-owners, that unrest began to grow sharply. A huge demonstration in Schleswig-Holstein in January 1928 was what the then Minister of Agriculture called 'the writing on the wall'.[14] The NSDAP slowly began to react to farm radicalization, especially in north-west Germany. There are indications that until then, the peasantry had tended to view the party with suspicion, probably due to the word 'Socialist' in its title, which was taken to imply Marxism. In April 1928 the NSDAP tried to clear up any misunderstanding about Point 17 of its original 1920 programme, which called for land expropriation: Hitler explained to the peasants (a month before the Reichstag elections) that this applied only to property gained by speculation, and not to agricultural holdings as such. Possibly due to this the NSDAP gained a fairly substantial vote in some rural districts in north-west Germany.[15]

Clear indications now existed that a large number of farm votes could be captured which may well account for Willikens's two articles in 1929 and 1930, as well as for the party's agrarian programme in March 1930. It would, however, be an error to assume that the latter should be interpreted solely as an electoral device: doubtless this played some part in its formulation, but the views of Hitler, Himmler, Backe and Willikens suggest that the supposed inherent conservatism of the peasantry and the party's anti-urban ethos would have combined sooner or later to produce some kind of specific agrarian goals. However much the onset of the world economic crisis may have affected the timing, it did not fundamentally alter the *Weltanschauung* to which National Socialists already subscribed. Above all, the nationalism explicit in their own views meant that a propaganda appeal to the peasantry based on protectionism represented a genuine conviction as much as a desire to win votes.

Hitler commissioned Darré to build up an agrarian cadre within the NSDAP in July 1930.[16] Initially at least Darré did not necessarily see this as being confined to legal methods. In August 1930 he suggested to party headquarters that if all food-producers were organized under NSDAP control, it would be possible to blockade the cities and so destroy the Republic. Since, however, in the following month the party won 107 seats in the Reichstag, possible illegality had been overhauled by events. There was now a clear chance of winning power by mobilizing the discontented rural population. Beginning in October 1930, Darré erected a new apparatus of professional farm experts and propagandists at Munich. By the spring of 1932 Saxony alone had some 1,200 staff engaged at various levels in the regional agrarian cadre.[17] The party's verbal warfare against the Republic could now be centrally directed down through regions and districts to the villages, with the whole propaganda campaign co-ordinated in Munich. This is not to say that progress, despite peasant unrest, was everywhere swift and even; local circumstances seem to have determined NSDAP success in the final analysis.[18]

But in general, although elements of other sectors of German society voted for the NSDAP, it is difficult to think of any which did more to help the Hitler movement to power. Why were peasants so prone to National Socialist propaganda? By 1927 many had already become disillusioned with the Republic, which they blamed for their economic problems. Clearly, the price fall after 1928 merely intensified this feeling, especially due to the expense to them, as employers, of social insurance which had increased from RM8·70 per hectare in 1913 to RM26·39 in 1927.[19] Such financial burdens were especially irksome to smaller peasant holdings, whose owners were proportionately, at least in Schleswig-Holstein, more likely to vote for Hitler than were estate-owners or agricultural labourers.[20] Thus the apparent failure by successive Weimar governments to help the peasantry intensified, and led to a feeling of betrayal to industrial interests. Disillusion with Schiele as Minister of Agriculture between 1930 and 1932 was particularly acute, as he had been seen as an agrarian nominee. Lavish help given to eastern landowners under the Osthilfe scheme (to aid distressed agriculture) merely added to peasant grievances.

National Socialist propagandists were able to use resentment all the more effectively through their infiltration of existing farmers' associations. This was particularly true of the Landbund (the right-wing Rural League) which was the main vehicle of farm agitation against the Republic. By December 1931 at least two members of its executive committee (including Werner Willikens) were National Socialists. In April 1932 the Landbund actually supported Hitler as a candidate in the presidential elections.

Given that the electoral breakthrough on the land was so rapid, why did the party's efforts in the countryside start so relatively late? The NSDAP originally was a small party, and until the late 1920s simply lacked financial resources. Both factors inhibited activity on the land as well as elsewhere.[21] Secondly, the party seems to have been largely obsessed by the desire to win the industrial workers for the 'national idea', which meant defeating Marxism on its own ground, the urban areas. Not until late 1927 did any reorientation begin slowly to take place, and then until Darré's arrival in a patchy and uneven way. In 1929 the deputy Gauleiter of Bavaria was complaining to party headquarters in Munich about the shortage of propaganda material for peasant indoctrination.[22] In other words, only when the movement had failed in urban working-class areas did it turn to winning the farmers. Here the time-factor is clearly important, which is the third point, since the policy realignment towards the middle classes, especially on the land, coincided temporally with the onset of a real economic crisis. Without this, success in rural areas would no doubt have been more limited.

Eventually the peasantry played a genuine part in assisting the NSDAP to power. After January 1933 the promises made to the peasantry in return – to give it back profitability and restore its waning social prestige in an industrial country – had now to be made good. The party needed the support of the farming population *tactically*, as an instrument for consolidating National Socialist power. *Operatively* the agrarian sector could provide Germany with a high degree of self-sufficiency in food, which would enable Hitler to pursue an independent foreign policy. Finally, the NSDAP, especially the group in the agrarian cadre around Darré, could begin to realize its long-term *strategic* aim of 'Blood and Soil' to restore the peasantry to its rightful place in German society.[23]

When Darré took over as Minister of Agriculture in June, some agrarian recovery had already taken place.[24] For him the real departure was the beginning of a genuinely National Socialist policy which aimed at making German agriculture the foremost sector of German life, rather than one merely equal to the others. Basically, his programme rested upon two premisses: most importantly, the peasantry was the 'life-source' of the German nation as a whole.[25] This belief was based on the assumption that the rural birth-rate, higher than that in urban areas, had to replenish the entire population, since the city dwellers were simply not reproducing themselves quickly enough to sustain their own population levels. In the 1920s there had been a lively debate over this whole matter, in which a former head of the Reich Statistical Office had joined.[26] His voice naturally lent an air of scientific respectability to the discussion, so that the conviction that urban life was almost literally the death of Germany was not confined to the NSDAP. When Hitler told peasants at the Harvest Festival in 1933 that the demographic future of the German people depended on maintaining the peasantry, he was voicing an opinion which at the time was relatively widespread.

Peasants thus had to be protected against possible economic downfall. Here Darré diverged widely from previous policies in his commitment to the principle that higher prices alone were not the solution. In addition, the preservation of the peasantry demanded an end to speculation overall, since exposure to free market forces could ruin the very people on whose existence Germany's future depended. Thus the basic tenets of the 'Blood and Soil' school demanded a peasant base to society for ideological reasons whilst the failure of liberalism evident in the world economic crisis showed how dangerous were market forces to the very ideals which Darré and his cadre sought to uphold.

Quite explicit in this chain of reasoning was the emphasis, above all, on a peasant policy. Of course, the various other sections of agriculture, including estate-owners and agricultural labourers, were also important, as they all helped to produce food, without which there could be no independent foreign policy. The party had no objection either to small-holdings or to large estates as such, since varying climatic conditions in different districts imposed the need for a healthy mixture of farms.[27]

In itself this implied that not all food-producers would be embraced in the category 'peasant'. That the latter took ideological priority was, however, made very clear indeed by the 'Blood and Soil' enthusiasts, with their distinction between peasant (*Bauer*) and farmer (*Landwirt*).[28] The former represented the true Volk, the latter was the product of the French Revolution which had (allegedly) initiated the modern trends of selfish liberalism, which was anathema to the NSDAP.

For Darré then the point of departure was the need to save the peasantry by restructuring its administration and its place in the social order. The main plank in this platform was the Law of Hereditary Entail-ment (EHG). The law's stated object was to preserve the peasantry within the framework of old Germanic inheritance laws. In practice this meant quite simply that any holding large enough to provide adequately for an independent farm family (the upper size limit was normally 125 hectares) would become specially protected. Farms designated as heredi-tarily entailed (*Erbhöfe*) would remain in the same family line in perpe-tuity (hence 'Blood and Soil' as a description of the school which pro-duced the EHG). Only one child could inherit, to obviate any division of the farm among various heirs.[29] Like all entailed property the holding could not be sold, nor could it be used as collateral in a loan. In the future the owner would have to borrow money as an individual, and no entailed farm could have foreclosure applied to it. Thus at a stroke a substantial proportion of all food-producers in Germany had been saved from the results of speculation in land, in return for which they had been placed under a new form of neo-feudal obligation, where the medieval lord had been replaced by society in general. So clear was the link between rights and responsibilities that a guide for young citizens in 1938 could say of the *Erbhof* owner (*Bauer*), 'he has to carry out the work allotted to him by the state'.[30]

Almost no other piece of legislation in the Third Reich so enshrined basic National Socialist principles as the EHG, with its very clear emphasis on the overriding needs of the community, as opposed to the unfettered individual freedom which the NSDAP saw as the basic principle of liberalism. The peasant was freed from fear of foreclosure, but against this, severe testamentary restrictions were imposed upon him, as well as on the way in which he managed his farm. His ability to borrow money was now to some extent supervised, and he could be removed altogether for personal failings, summarized as inefficiency or lack of honour.[31] All this inevitably raises two related issues as to how the EHG was received in farming circles, and what effect it had on agrarian efficiency, which might be affected by a lowering of morale if the EHG was disliked.

There seems little doubt that the law was not generally popular, as witness the number of peasants who tried to prevent their holdings being enrolled on the official list.[32] Even semi-official circles spoke of 'opposition' and 'bitter resistance' to characterize peasant attitudes.[33] In the Saar, where a plebiscite was to be held in 1935 to determine whether the region was to rejoin the Reich, the NSDAP sought to influence the vote by promising that any hardship caused by the Act would be compensated for in other ways.[34] Almost as soon as the legislation came out von Papen told Darré that it was causing rural unrest. It soon became the focus of considerable criticism by conservatives such as Joachim von Rohr and Max Sering. The former concentrated particularly on the financial aspects and queried what the effect would be of the provisions against foreclosure. This point was grounded on the assumption that if a creditor could not foreclose to get his money back, he would be less willing to lend anything.[35] The whole matter was linked to monetary recompense for non-inheriting children (*Abfindung*), a description of which has to be offered to put the entire question into perspective.

Traditionally in those parts of Germany where one heir took over the farm undivided (*Anerbenrecht*), the remaining children received monetary compensation. Of course, the EHG's provision that only one could now inherit was no hardship in *Anerbenrecht* areas, but how were the others to be dealt with? The Act specifically stipulated that *Abfindung* could be paid henceforth from current receipts only. Theoretically, the anticipation of higher farm prices meant that this would be no problem. However, once the drive to maximize indigenous farm output began, peasants were obliged to invest current receipts in new equipment and buildings to the greatest extent possible. It was then that the battle between *Abfindung* and investment became really acute. This was one important reason why peasants were often reluctant to register their entire property as an *Erbhof*. They sought to keep a small piece outside the Act, which they could sell to raise funds for *Abfindung* for the disinherited.

Without question, it was at least in part due to the apprehension over possible peasant reaction to the EHG restrictions that it was in practice frequently applied less rigorously than its original form might suggest. The panels of judges (of whom two were peasants themselves) often showed understanding for individual cases. In the Hameln district the courts often allowed holdings to take up mortgages to finance *Abfindung*, although strictly this was against the Act. Moreover, the clause forbidding joint ownership of an *Erbhof* was modified in October 1933, and additional amendments with regard to the original disadvantages to the farmers' wives and daughters were largely lifted in 1936 and further modified during the war.

In several respects, therefore, it could plausibly be argued that pragmatism took precedence over ideology, at least sometimes. As the NSDAP needed the peasantry for practical reasons (that is, the *operative* goals) it could not afford to override its wishes too much and too often from ideological motives. To be sure, the party did not always meet the peasantry halfway: local attitude to the EHG was described as 'dissatisfied and critical' as late as 1938 in Hesse, principally due to *Abfindung*.[36] Additionally, there is little doubt that borrowing in general became harder for the peasant. Although the judgement of one writer that through the Act the *Erbhof* was cut off from capital sources may be an exaggeration, the EHG in this respect can hardly have made German farming more efficient.[37] Overall it cannot be said to have been either popular or effective, and no protests appear to have been raised in Germany when the occupying powers abolished it in 1947.

This does not imply that the law had no rationale but rather that peasants disliked the compulsion which accompanied it. Indeed, a strong movement for some reform of inheritance laws had existed since the 1920s, primarily to prevent any further fragmentation of farm property. In response to pressure from farm associations, several regions had already introduced legislation to this effect before 1933, but always based on a voluntary system.[38] The NSDAP diverged from these schemes by introducing one unified national policy, which took little account of regional variations, which had more severe testamentary and credit restrictions, and which included compulsory registration (although many smaller farms did evade enrolment).[39]

The National Socialist government also initiated a new, uniform marketing organization for agriculture in general (not just for peasants) which sprang from the co-ordinated body which Darré's cadre had installed in April 1933. Known as the *Reichsnährstand* (RNS), it embraced all facets of food production, distribution and processing, again based on the *Führerprinzip* and compulsory membership. Its origins can probably be traced to the long-standing desire of a socially and economically threatened sector, hostile to industrialization and seeking an alternative to parliamentary democracy. Equally important were the effects of the world economic crisis, which heightened the fear in agricultural circles of being permanently disadvantaged, and therefore increased agrarian readiness to present a uniform front to a hostile world.[40] Certainly one agrarian leader could call the programme of market regulation proposed in April 1933 the culmination of Rural League strivings. The unity of administration and the price control which the RNS brought to agriculture had long been demanded by right-wing agrarian interest groups in the 1920s. But its concept had in fact somewhat deeper roots.

Probably the most important attempt to work out a new form of market organization can be found in the writings of Gustav Ruhland, a pre-1914 publicist for the Agrarian League (which later became the Rural League). He was anti-Marxist and an advocate of both fixed prices for foodstuffs and some degree of state intervention and marketing control.[41] Darré was to base his concept for a new marketing system on Ruhland's ideas, a copy of which he gave to Dr. Reischle, the future Staff Office leader of the RNS, in 1931.[42] Ruhland himself has been seen in a larger perspective as belonging to the mercantilist tradition of Fichte, which implies both anti-liberalism and anti-marxism. How strong this school was in Germany in the 1920s and 1930s can be seen from the number of writers at the time who suggested a restructuring of agriculture along lines fairly similar to those of Ruhland and the future RNS. Among these were numbered non-Nazis such as von Rohr, whose memorandum of March–April 1933 advocated a very similar, but less authoritarian, version of the future RNS, and a book by the Osthilfe Commissar, Schlange-Schöningen in 1932 (*Acker und Arbeit*).[43] The RNS has to be seen in the context of a long-term trend of mercantilist thought in Germany, which still had many advocates.[44] Only in the use of the authoritarian *Führerprinzip* and compulsory membership did the RNS really differ from previous, or contemporary, neo-mercantilism. Decisive here in the last resort was the apparent failure of economic liberalism as demonstrated in the world depression.[45]

Planning for a future in which a fixed price policy would obviate 'liberal materialism', under which everyone allegedly 'prayed to one God, called the free play of market forces', began long before 1933.[46] A fair, stable price for his output would encourage the food-producer to steady production and would give him financial security. (In the case of *Erbhöfe* owners it should also obviate the need for outside credit facilities.) In this way farm production could be managed in the national interest, since a price mechanism could be employed to obtain from the land those products which consumers required. Financial leadership in this manner was perceived by Darré as far better than controlling sown areas by legal supervision, as von Rohr suggested.

The immediate background to this was the fall in dairy prices under the

Republic. Hugenberg (DNVP) had already suggested that this might lead to peasants switching to grain cultivation as a better alternative.[47] A bumper cereals harvest in 1933 made the danger of a surplus of grain greater still, and raised the spectre of high storage costs at public expense. A price mechanism to restore the equilibrium and induce producers to part with their produce when the public needed it, did not merely offer the security of fixed prices to farmers; it rationalized supply and distribution for the whole community, and obviated the need for legal restrictions on hectarage, as von Rohr wanted.

Moreover, the RNS should not merely be seen as a new organization for the farming sector; it was intended from the beginning to have a wider role, even in the area of foreign trade. One overriding problem here for the National Socialist regime was Germany's unfavourable trade balance, in which food represented half the country's imports. RNS regulations means that these no longer threatened to undercut prices for food-producers inside Germany, since producer–consumer prices could now be completely synchronized. This highlights the fact that although the RNS did represent the manifestation of long-held traditions in some German agrarian circles, the immediate context in which it came into being clearly also played an important part. How it operated after 1933 cannot be divorced from Germany's overall economic situation. Possibly both Marxist and bourgeois historians have been too prone to neglect this aspect of its origins and operations in their overall assessments.[48]

How effective was the policy of centrally directed food distribution? The organization tried to avoid a purely rigid, planned economy.[49] But it did get off to a very shaky start, and by mid-1934 so many complaints had been made in Prussia about the new corporation that Goering sent them to Darré for his comments.[50] The general tenor was that farmers had to sell to the RNS now instead of going directly to the consumer (if they could previously have done so). Milk had to be delivered increasingly to dairies, rather than being turned into butter on the farms, and administrative costs were too high in general. An early effort to correct deficiencies was made in November 1934,[51] above all, to smooth relations with local government officials. As a result, the corporation was simplified, but in November 1936 Darré admitted himself that distribution was the weak point of his organization.

However, there seems to be a broad historical consensus that teething troubles were eventually overcome.[52] In the final analysis the farmers themselves appear to have been quite well pleased with the arrangements. Peasants after the war asked if the RNS could be kept in existence, as 'it appears to have satisfied them and brought the food off the farms'.[53] Indeed the British seem to have decided to retain the organization as early as summer 1944 on the advice of agrarian experts studying the likely food problems of postwar Germany.[54] Clearly the RNS had achieved a genuine international reputation which cannot be overlooked as evidence in any assessment of its efficiency.

The question of guaranteed prices is more difficult to evaluate. After a long period of declining farm incomes, a measure of financial security was obviously welcome, and this is effectively what the RNS initially offered, especially for the more essential products. By 1936 Hitler's promise in the election campaign of March 1933 that profitability would be restored to agriculture within four years seemed to be well on its way to realization. If the agrarian price index for 1913 is taken as 100, it stood at 103·8 in 1931 and only 86·8 two years later: in 1936 the corresponding figure was 104·9.[55] Recovery had been sound if not dramatic, within what in effect had been a largely producer-oriented prices policy, so that the farming community actually did better than the population as a whole, especially over the period of 1933–5.[56]

By the latter year, however, the situation had already begun to change. There was a general economic recovery in Germany, with rapidly diminishing unemployment and growing consumption. By 1937 the German people were eating 25 per cent more white flour, 24 per cent more sugar, 23 per cent more butter and 11 per cent more meat than in 1932.[57] This would have enabled farmers to make a killing under the operations of the free market, which was exactly what the RNS had eliminated. Indeed, when in response to temporary shortages after a poor harvest in 1934 and the need to limit imports, food prices did start to go up, Hitler demanded the installation of a Price Commissioner to prevent this developing further.[58]

It was this decision which stopped the agrarian community from cashing in on shortages, and also unleashed a furious row between the Price Commissioner, Dr. Goerdeler, and Darré. Goerdeler believed that guaranteed prices merely protected the inefficient, in which he seems to have had the support of Schacht, himself no friend of the RNS. Darré could not accept this point for ideological reasons, since the elimination of the peasantry by the market forces of economic liberalism, and the threat which he perceived this as posing to Germany's racial future, was exactly what the EHG, RNS and its guaranteed prices had been installed to prevent. The crux of the matter here was 'Blood and Soil' and all it implied with respect to the peasantry. Schacht and Goerdeler were economic liberals and Darré was a racialist, for whom economics should, for political reasons, be in principle subordinated to the demands of racial ideology (that is, long-term *strategic* goals).

Darré's deputy in the RNS, Wilhelm Meinberg, was now obliged to make a virtue out of necessity and represent fixed prices as an aid to the consumer since without current farm price levels, the German public would be paying RM500 million more for its food every year.[59] This argument of 'equality of sacrifice' was based on the notion that whereas in 1933–4 the consumer had aided agriculture by paying for increased farm incomes, now the inability of the food-producers to cash in on supply and demand helped the whole community. Clearly this was perfectly correct, but it must have been a bitter pill for 'Blood and Soil' enthusiasts to swallow when they saw how increasing prosperity in general would not necessarily always be accompanied by any corresponding improvement in the farmers' financial well-being. Of course, the RNS still wished to retain guaranteed prices, largely for ideological reasons, but not always at the same level. By 1936 *guaranteed* prices had become *maximum* prices; the prices freeze of 26 November 1936 merely formalized this arrangement, although it is clear that the real decision to hold down prices, including those for foodstuffs, had been taken previously.

Fundamentally the decision to restrict price increases was due to the general fear of inflation which haunted Hitler. Partly this stemmed from his apprehension of the possible unrest which inflation might cause. In Cabinet discussions he continually voiced such fears, and they may well be related to the trauma of November 1918 for the NSDAP.[60] Having lived through one left-wing revolution and the German defeat which he believed it had brought, the *Führer* had no desire to see another. It was largely on these grounds that he refused an increase in the bread grain price in July 1934.[61] His conviction of the need to appease public opinion was by no means groundless; in August 1935 it was stated at a Trustee of Labour Conference that the working class expected Hitler to maintain his promise of preventing increases in the cost of living.[62]

Related to worries about political discontent was the problem of investment in the rearmament programme. If money lost its value inside Germany through inflation, these plans could be ruined. Here the ministerial discussion held in May 1935 was decisive, as the over-whelming majority of those present demanded a wage freeze. This reinforced the effects of Hitler's fear of inflation: wages, and conse-quently also prices, would not be allowed to go up. Effectively this sealed the financial fate of the farming population, as rearmament took priority. From now on only an increase in the volume of output could raise their incomes: the price mechanism was to be used in the Third Reich either to help consumers or, particularly after 1939, to steer pro-duction.

Up to 1933 the farming population believed it had been put behind export needs in order of governmental priority; after a brief interregnum between 1933 and 1935 when it really did seem to take first place, agri-culture was doomed to play second fiddle again, this time to rearmament. The RNS leaders resented this, and feared its consequences: diminishing production, largely caused by farmers' inability to invest, and rural migration to industry and construction, as these sectors boomed. Their demands for higher guaranteed prices were, however, rejected by the political leadership with monotonous regularity in 1938–9. The answer to one such request was a fair summary of Hitler's general attitude: 'The *Führer* has taken cognisance. He is in principle opposed to all price increases for agriculture.'[63]

A further task for the RNS was the maximization of indigenous agricultural production to save food imports. Consumption did rise after 1933. This did not facilitate the task of achieving a high degree of self-sufficiency in this campaign, called the *Erzeugungsschlacht* (Battle of Production). The aim here was never complete autarky, but simply the attainment of a scale of self-sufficiency which would permit an independent foreign policy.[64] This would be done by so limiting food imports that Germany could continue to fight even in the face of a blockade. Fewer imported foodstuffs would also permit the import of more raw materials from abroad for armaments. Basically the aims of the new agrarian campaign were to increase bread grain yields, produce more indigenous fodder (to help with the 'Fats Gap') and more fibre-bearing plants. 'Fats Gap' here meant the large difference between domestic supplies and consumption, which an emergency Weimar programme had in part tried to remedy in 1928. As this had not succeeded, Germany needed more home-grown feed-stuffs, which could support more pigs and larger dairy herds. In order to achieve this, Darré planned to appeal to the patriotic spirit of the farmers. He was convinced that controls and enforced direction would not work.[65] Thus, a combination of price-fixing and exhortation was to be employed.

Despite Darré's belief in the inefficacy of controls, however, there is no doubt that the Four-Year Plan of 1936 strengthened supervision in general on the land. Fodder distribution was more carefully controlled, and the provisions of the EHG which allowed inefficient peasants to be removed from management were now in effect made applicable to all farmers.[66] The year 1936 also saw the introduction of the *Hofkarte*, a card which gave the RNS full details of all holdings above 5 hectares. Compulsory delivery of all grain was ordered, but there was still no restriction on peasants to sow certain crops: a prices policy continued to steer them in this respect. Thus although the Four-Year Plan tightened up overall control on the land, it can hardly be said to have marked the introduction of terror methods to subdue the agrarian population. Apart from anything else, this would probably have been counter-productive, as Darré implied with his remark that no gendarme could teach a peasant how to run his farm. To upset the farmers by very close supervision would probably have meant less food for Germany.

To what extent the *Erzeugungsschlacht* did attain its goals is difficult to judge, as so many factors have to be taken into account. Poor weather ruined the harvests of 1934 and 1935; this meant less fodder, so Germany had fewer pigs and cattle in the latter year than in 1933.[67] An outbreak of foot and mouth disease in 1937 did not assist matters. Graver still for the *Erzeugungsschlacht*, however, was the running fight over currency allocations between Schacht and Darré. Funds were required by the RNS to finance the imports of fodder on which a solution to the fats problem depended. Beginning in April 1933, the Reichsbank was in constant communication with Darré over the question. The Agriculture Minister could not see how Germany's food problems could be solved unless some allocation was allowed to enable feed-stuffs to be bought abroad, whereas Schacht was loath to permit the use of foreign currency in a campaign aimed at *reducing* overall expenditure on outside food supplies. Ultimately, although Darré's appeal to the *Führer* for a bigger currency quota bore fruit, both Schacht and Darré were caught in a two-pronged trap.[68] One prong was Hitler's decision to rearm quickly, the other was the general economic position of Germany, and Germany's acute shortage of currency reserves. Logically the answer was a far slower rearmament programme. Schacht and Darré participated in the May 1935 ministerial discussion of rearmament and made no objection to granting it priority, although both no doubt would have preferred a less hectic tempo.

Ironically, Hitler's orders to speed up via the Four-Year Plan in themselves made it more difficult to reach a high degree of self-sufficiency. Labour left the land on an ever-increasing scale, lured by the construction and armament boom, whilst currency limitations, due to the need to purchase raw materials for arms, hit at the *Erzeugungsschlacht*.[69] In addition, the refusal to raise farm prices rendered agriculture less profitable (and therefore less attractive as a career) and curtailed investment. Indeed, by February 1938 Backe could admit publicly that profit margins were unsatisfactory; and the same point was made at the Peasants' Congress in October of the same year by an RNS spokesman. A long-term *strategic* goal designed to preserve the peasantry and the short-term *operative* aim of food production were both hit by rearmament and the priority it enjoyed. In other words, the whole issue of self-sufficiency was more than just a simple clash between ideology and pragmatism.

These considerations should not, however, conceal the fact that overall the *Erzeugungsschlacht* was a relative success, bearing in mind that it was carried out on a partly voluntary basis and under adverse conditions. Against a background of a quite considerable rise in consumption, Germany's degree of self-sufficiency went from 80 per cent across the board in 1933–4 to 83 per cent in 1938–9.[70] Two consequences resulted from this. First, the struggle to maximize indigenous output had saved foreign currency.[71] Secondly, the general state of food reserves in 1939 was satisfactory, enough to permit Germany to withstand a blockade at least for a year.[72] But the 'Fats Gap' still remained, and in January 1939 Darré described what the situation would be in the event of hostilities.[73] Germany would be well placed for supplies of essential foodstuffs such as bread, potatoes and sugar, but meat and fats were both to some degree dependent on fodder imports, which would be lost in a war. As he stressed, currency limitations would permit only half the oilseed imports he wanted for the first six months of 1939, and as a consequence reserves of margarine were going to have to be partly consumed. Two months later Backe was painting an even blacker picture and predicting potentially politically dangerous unrest in autumn, due to the impending fats shortage.[74]

Clearly, how effective the *Erzeugungsschlacht* had been can only really be judged by how well Germany was fed when war came. Such an evaluation lies outside the scope of this essay, but it should be pointed out that the question is more complicated than it appears. Germany did conquer half of Europe, but much of this consisted of food deficit regions. In May 1940 the RNS calculated the annual food deficit of then-occupied Europe at 25·7 million tons.[75] Only France and the Ukraine subsequently came to German assistance, but even food surplus areas, such as the Netherlands or Denmark, were hit by the loss of prewar fodder imports. Germany might actually have obtained more meat and fats from these countries if it had not occupied them.[76] The presence of POWs and foreign labour, plus extra rations for the enormous Wehrmacht, and the domestic demand, swelled by a small population growth, meant a staggering increase in demand in Germany. Flour consumption amounted to 8½ million tons in 1938–9 but by 1941–2 had risen to 10·22 million tons, even with rationing. By early 1942 the situation was so desperate that Backe had to persuade Hitler to cut rations.[77] This overrode Goering's order in September of the previous year that this was not to happen under any circumstances. Goering had maintained that such measures might hit civilian morale, which would afford the enemy his only chance of victory, as in 1918.[78]

Here we return exactly to the significance of November 1918 as the great National Socialist trauma. Such a recurrent theme in NSDAP thinking, based on the desire to make Germany immune to blockade in war in order to avoid the possible consequences of food shortages, raises an obvious question about the very nature of the RNS: was it ever intended to be a truly autonomous farming corporation, or was it merely a means of preparing Germany for war? Just after the outbreak in 1939 Darré asked for further finance for the RNS precisely on the grounds that it had made Germany free from the effects of potential blockade, and facilitated without friction the transfer to a wartime food economy.[79]

Not surprisingly, East German historians have suggested that this was its real raison d'être, although they do not always agree as to when war preparations began.[80] The difference here is only a question of timing, not intent:[81] Common in the East German literature is the description of the RNS as 'a typical example of the close collaboration between monopoly capital, landowners, state and party'.[82] What these analyses share is the belief that the RNS was not an autonomous agrarian body but one subordinate to political direction from the government.

On the other hand, some West Germans seem to accept that Darré's corporation was relatively independent until 1939 and point to hostility between the RNS and the NSDAP itself.[83] That such hostility existed is undeniable, and it was only when Backe dissolved Department I of the RNS in 1942, and left the political indoctrination of the peasantry to the party, that friction diminished.[84] As to relations with the German Labour Front (*Deutsche Arbeitsfront*), these were always poor, as the latter body was geared to agricultural labourers rather than to peasants. It is also true that at the regional level the RNS quarrelled with several Gauleiter, especially Koch of East Prussia; and its relations with local authorities were also frequently bad. Conflicts of this nature did arise from the pretensions of Darre's corporation, its readiness to circumvent existing administrative channels, and from the usual lack of clarity over areas of authority so typical of the Third Reich. Are they, however, sufficient to justify the thesis that of all the social sectors which originally supported the NSDAP the peasantry was the only one to get its own organization, which afforded political muscle to farmers?[85]

At a purely technical level it is true that the RNS always had the last word.[86] But politically it is doubtful if it ever carried much weight, and the abolition of its Department I by Backe has been seen as a clear victory for the main NSDAP headquarters.[87] Probably the most compelling evidence for the thesis that in practice the RNS was subordinated to higher political goals is the testimony of Darré himself. In an article in June 1933 he pointed to the fact that Hitler had accepted honorary guardianship of the new, unified farmers and marketing association (from which the RNS grew). Darré drew from this the principle that the corporation could not oppose state wishes in the future. Precisely this point, and the financial decline in relative terms of agriculture from 1936 onwards, make it hard to see in the RNS as anything more than an instrument for the implementation of political goals which it had not determined. The worst row inside the RNS arose partly due to the efforts of its deputy leader, Meinberg, to turn it into an autonomous corporation, against the opposition of Backe, at a time when Darré was on sick leave. That these efforts should have been largely responsible for Meinberg's dismissal must tell us something about the place of the RNS in German society.

Basically the autonomy of the RNS was limited in two ways: first, by the NSDAP's general principle of 'the common good before individual gain', which meant that all sectors of the economy had to be servants of national goals, which despite the 'peasant policy' of the RNS applied to food-producers as well as to everyone else. Secondly, Germany must be blockade-proof in any future conflict. There is no doubt that the poor agrarian and food-rationing administration of the First World War had made a deep impression, since it was held to be largely responsible for the events of November 1918. Such an experience was partly instrumental in producing the *Erzeugungsschlacht*, as well as in limiting the autonomy of the RNS. None of this implies that the leaders of the corporation planned for aggressive war; rather they hoped to avoid a collapse in civilian morale should conflict occur. It should be stressed that in this the RNS was successful, in that Germans were relatively well fed until 1944, which presumably contributed to keeping Germany in the struggle.[88]

Beside the RNS and the Hereditary Farm Act the third pillar of National Socialist policy on the land was a settlement programme, designed mainly to promote the growth of peasant farms in the eastern areas of the country, especially close to the Polish frontier. Again there was nothing original in this, as Bismarck had tried to bring more Germans into the eastern spaces in the 1880s, and in the 1920s the Weimar Republic had advanced a similar internal colonization as a defensive measure. What distinguished the NSDAP plans from those of their predecessors was a fundamental emphasis on the need for viable holdings, which would become new *Erbhöfe*. Guidelines for the new programmes were issued in July 1933, illustrating how eastern colonization was to be utilized to help to revive the German peasantry. Despite the enthusiasts of the RNS, however, little was achieved in the next six years. Fewer places were found for settlers than under the Republic, although in some cases the new farms were more viable.[89]

From the standpoint of 'Blood and Soil' these were disappointing results, and arose from several different factors. To begin with the demands of the motorway programme (*Autobahnen*) and the Wehrmacht restricted the amount of land available for farming.[90] The EHG had an even more disastrous effect, since it removed 55 per cent of all agricultural land from the normal market. These two factors in combination so undermined the settlement programme that the only remaining solution was either foreign conquest or the dissolution of the large estates east of the Elbe.

That Darré would have loved to destroy them is unquestionable.[91] His dislike of east Elbian landlords was socio-political in origin, and went back to the events of the nineteenth century, when landlords had taken over peasant holdings in the wake of the Stein-Hardenberg reforms.

Darré believed that landed estates in the eastern areas in question originated from political, not economic, determinants.[92] What he wanted in
1933, therefore, was to break them up for settlement purposes. Unfortunately, Germany's top leadership thwarted this desire, probably because
of the belief that large estates were needed to maximize indigenous
output.[93] This point was made by Hitler himself to a landowners'
deputation on 20 April 1933, although he did add that if large estates were
inefficient they should be dissolved for settlement 'on demographic
grounds'.[94] This latter observation may well be the crux of the matter:
since peasant farming was intensive, 1,000 hectares split into *Erbhöfe*
would ultimately sustain more people than ten 100-hectare estates. More
people equalled more political muscle for Germany in international
affairs, especially a bigger army.

For these reasons, Hitler ultimately favoured a peasant policy,
especially for eastern settlement, as he said during the war. Above all
then, despite Junker survival, it was the peasant who took ideological
priority, in Hitler's eyes as in Darré's. Since grain was also needed to make
Germany close to autarkic in wartime, self-sufficiency none the less took
immediate precedence, and pragmatism triumphed in the short term over
'Blood and Soil'.

However, although the Junkers' economic base was left intact, their
political influence diminished after 1933.[95] It is certainly difficult to see
how the foreign trade orientation towards the Balkans from 1934
onwards under the 'New Plan' represented the true interests of German
grain-producers and grain was one of the staples of east Elbian agriculture. Junkers had always campaigned against agrarian imports from
that area; indeed, the Rural League once called the furtherance of trade
with South-Eastern Europe 'a stab in the back for struggling farmers'.[96]

East German historians have refused to accept this line of argument,
preferring to see east Elbian interests linked closely with the NSDAP,
even after 1934.[97] The statement that in the RNS Junkers were given
authority over 'working peasants' is quite typical. Of course, Osthilfe did
continue to fill Junker coffers in the Third Reich. But inside the RNS,
most regional, district and local *Bauernführer* were peasants, and in this
respect the Third Reich saw a rather greater degree of social mobility on
the land, rather than a mere continuance of Junker dominance. It is
perfectly true that many landowners threw in their lot with the new
regime. On the other hand, there is plenty of evidence to support claims
of their opposition as well, long before July 1944. The fall of Hugenberg
as Minister of Agriculture in June 1933 provoked a lively reaction by
landowners against the RNS in East Prussia, which led to several
arrests.[98] On balance, therefore, the tendency in the G.D.R. to see the
sinister hand of the Junker behind every single agrarian policy move is

certainly overdone, as is the suggestion that the EHG served east Elbian interests.[99]

It is difficult to see how it did; many aristocratic landowners wished to be included in the act's provisions, and nearly all were disappointed. Indeed, in July 1938 the remaining entails on landed estates (*Fideikommisse*) were abolished by the National Socialist regime.[100] Effectively this left aristocratic holdings without any special legal protection, in sharp contrast to that recently afforded to peasants under the EHG. Here it must be borne in mind that Darré's criticism of Hugenberg was precisely that he was too 'capitalistic' in helping large landlords and failing to consider sufficiently the need of *völkisch* racial ideology. His fall surely represented, among other things, the end of a Junker-oriented agrarian policy, and the commencement of 'Blood and Soil' under Darré and his party associates.

Finally, it remains only to sum up the success or failure of Darré's policy. How well did the peasantry fare under National Socialism? There is no denying one merit of the NSDAP on the land: it did produce an overall programme, in contrast to previous governments, which had tackled agriculture problems in an unsystematic and uncoordinated fashion, and lost peasant support. The only real internal flaw in 'Blood and Soil' in the short term was the failure to produce an effective policy of land control, although Darré did attempt this, only to be rebuffed by other governmental agencies.[101] As a result of this omission, and the inability to break up east Elbian estates, no large settlement programme was possible in pre-1939 National Socialist Germany. By the eve of the war, the more sinister designs of Himmler and his idea of using the SS in frontier settlement (the so-called *Wehrbauern*) were beginning to supplant Darré's own plans.[102]

What really frustrated 'Blood and Soil' in the short term, however, was the priority given to rearmament. The boom which this engendered and the prices freeze linked to it restricted farm incomes increasingly whilst offering good job possibilities in industry and construction. This was a problem which the RNS never solved: the influx of wartime foreigners in the form of contract labour of POWs merely exacerbated a situation already developing through rural migration prior to 1939. By March 1944 one party agrarian journal could lament that the only German help left in villages were agricultural labour apprentices.[103] To see German rural areas packed with foreigners was hardly the goal of a racially oriented agrarian policy.

The impact of 'Blood and Soil' policy on the peasantry's material welfare is complicated, as shown in table 8.1. As can be seen, the agrarian price index overall had not recovered to the pre-depression level even after eleven years of National Socialist rule, but on the other hand, the

Table 8.1   *Agrarian Price Index and Indices for other Products/Materials Used by Farmers*[104]

Financial year	Agrarian prices Average 1909–1913 = 100	Calendar year 1913 = 100 in all cases	Fertilizer	Agricultural tools/machinery	Building costs
1928–9	132	1928	82	139	175
1931–2	89	1931	77	131	156
1934–5	94	1934	69	111	132
1938–9	104	1938	55	111	136
1943–4	121	1943	53	n.a.	163

costs to the food-producer of almost everything he required to assist him in production (except labour) was also down from 1928–9, in some cases quite sharply. The overall net effect on farm incomes was difficult to estimate, but farmers seem to have done better during the war than in 1936–9, in that their average financial surplus after debt payments, taxes and investments rose to an annual average of RM99 million for the war period, as compared to only RM18 million for 1936–9.[105]

The priority on rearmament accompanied the political downfall of Richard Darré and the corresponding rise of Herbert Backe. It should be stressed that this was largely due to the latter's superior administrative ability; in 1936 he was made head of the agricultural division of the Four-Year Plan. He had already begun to attack Darré for his alleged incapacity by suggesting to Goering that Darré was an object of ridicule to the lower ranks of the RNS.[106] In early 1941 there was a violent dispute between them over rationing, where Darré in effect accused Backe of going to the top political leadership behind his back.[107] When eventually Backe was given full control of the wartime food economy, his nominal superior was reported to be on sick leave, until 1944, when Darré was relieved even of his de jure position as Minister of Agriculture, having long since exercised no real de facto control. At his removal Backe attributed recent agricultural shortcomings to Hitler's loss of confidence in Darré.[108] It would be fallacious to see in this the end of a peasant policy or the substitution of a more efficient bureaucrat for an impractical ideologue. Backe was as much a National Socialist and a 'Blood and Soil' enthusiast as his predecessor, but in addition he was more able as an administrator.[109]

His appointment should not therefore be seen as an end to the 'Blood and Soil' policy executed since 1933, which must raise the question of this policy's long-term viability, as it would have continued had National Socialist Germany won the war. It is difficult to see how a real moderniz-ation programme could have been carried out under the terms of the EHG, which preserved the inefficient peasant for ideological reasons, by sheltering him from the results of genuine economic competition. On the other hand, despite Broszat's claim that the NSDAP never tackled land reform, a large consolidation programme did get under way in the late 1930s but was interrupted by the war.[110] The object of this was to bring scattered strips together for more efficient farming. In the long run this could have created more *Erbhöfe*, and so increased the amount of land embraced by the legislation, if the largely part-time owners of dwarf-holdings had been encouraged to sell out to peasants, or acquire enough property to become an *Erbhofbauer* in their own right.

Ultimately the arguments about whether the NSDAP was a moderniz-ing force or not must rest on a question of definitions. Even if it had been possible to bring agriculture up to date technically within the limits of the EHG, German society would have been left with a very large permanent peasant sector. Is it possible to describe such a rural social structure as 'modern'? It surely depends on what is meant by modernization and in particular what the links are between modernization in a technical, pro-fessional sense and socio-political organization.

English-speaking liberals are wont to assume that liberalism and mod-ernity are virtually synonymous. This is not a proposition that the German Right has necessarily accepted. Obviously what the NSDAP hoped was that the material benefits of German victory and a large-scale postwar investment programme in agriculture would have anchored many on the land permanently. Furthermore, through long-term indoc-trination with regard to the 'common good', economic progress would not have led to demands for individual freedom, normally seen in the West as the more or less inevitable concomitant to material advance and modernity in general. Would such a 'Bonapartist' society be viable in the long run? It does appear rather unlikely especially as the phenomenon of rural migration was of such long standing by 1933. The fruits of victory for industry in the shape of captive markets must surely have led to a postwar industrial boom had the National Socialists won the war, only further stimulating a rural migration to the cities.

In a real sense discussion of this topic, inevitably limited here by space, touches on the whole nature of the National Socialist ethos and goals. In the final analysis Hitler failed to stop the political clock which he believed the French Revolution had set in motion: economic and political liberal-ism, and their offshoot, Marxism, had then begun, as he saw it, to change the face of European society in a way repugnant to him. To counteract this trend, Hitler was convinced that a racial policy was the only solution, but obviously it would need to be accompanied by material improvement to become palatable to the twentieth-century masses. In other words, if the NSDAP could bring Germany the economic benefits of modern society it might have been possible to stave off the *political* liberalism which in the West had usually accompanied economic modernization. If National Socialist policy could not accomplish this objective on the land, there was little hope for realizing it in German society as a whole. It is certainly rather hard to imagine what a National Socialist regime would look like without a large-scale agrarian sector based on peasant holdings. In sum, it is difficult to avoid the conclusion that the 'Blood and Soil' dream came too late to be realized, and then even an essentially 'Bonapartist' government could not for ever have kept on the land millions for whom urban life had apparently more appeal. Moreover, the contradiction betwen 'Blood and Soil' policies and the demands of a forced rearmanent could ultimately not be reconciled. At least after 1935, when the necessities of Hitler's war machine clashed with the ideological commitment to a strong peasantry, it was the vision of 'Blood and Soil' that was sacrificed.

Notes: Chapter 8

ABBREVIATIONS

ADC	American Documents Centre, Berlin
BA	W. German National Archives
NB	Nachlass Backe
ND	Nachlass Darré
PRO	Public Record Office, London
VJH	*Vierteljahrshefte für Zeitgeschichte*

1 P. Villard, 'Antiquité et Weltanschauung hitlérienne', *Revue d'histoire de la deuxieme guerre mondiale* 88 (1972)· 18
2 See R. Koehl, *RKFDV: German Resettlement and Population Policy 1939–1945* (Cambridge, Mass., 1959) as an example of the treatment of some apsects of National Socialism as neo-feudal. See also 'The feudal aspects of National Socialism', *American Political Science Review*, 54 (1960): 921ff., by the same author.
3 H. A. Turner, *Faschismus und Modernismus in Deutschland* (Göttingen, 1972), 169ff.
4 Cited in J. Ackermann, *Heinrich Himmler als Ideologe* (Göttingen, 1970), 198. See also for this type of National Socialist thought, K. Bergmann, *Agrarromantik und Grossstadtfeindschaft* (Meisenheim/G., 1970).
5 NB, BA, file 5, no. 2, p. 7.
6 Quoted in M. Broszat, *The Hitler State* (London, 1981), 180.
7 For his general background, H. Haushofer, *Ideengeschichte der Agrarwirtschaft und Agrarpolitik*, Vol. 2 (Munich, 1958), 170ff., and H. Reischle, *Reichsbauernführer Darré, der Kämpfer um Blut und Boden, Eine Lebensbeschreibung* (Berlin, 1933). See for a more recent view of Darré, A. Bramwell, 'National Socialist agrarian theory and practice with special reference to Darré and the settlement movement' (Ph.D. thesis, Oxford, 1983).
8 See R. W. Darré, *Das Bauerntum als Lebensquell der nordischen Rasse* (Munich, 1928) and *Neuadel aus Blut und Boden* (Munich, 1929).

9   For example, Bergmann, *Agrarromantik*. 312.
10 See R. Breitling, *Die nationalsozialistische Rassenlehre. Entstehung, Ausbreitung, Nutzen und Schaden einer politischen Ideologie* (Meisenheim/G., 1971), 62.
11 At which Hindenburg, President of the Republic, and six Cabinet ministers were present. W. Clauss, *Erfahrungen aus 50 Jahren Agrarpolitik* (Rendsburg, 1979), 8–10.
12 See J. B. Holt, *German Agricultural Policy 1918–1934* (Chapel Hill, N.C., 1936), 163.
13 M. Tracy, *Agriculture in Western Europe* (New York, 1964), 198.
14 Clauss, *Erfahrungen aus 50 Jahren*, 8–10.
15 See R. Heberle, *Landbevölkerung und Nationalsozialismus* (Stuttgart, 1963).
16 The best account of how this was achieved is H. Gies, 'NSDAP und landwirtschaftliche Organisation in der Endphase der Weimarer Republik', *VJH* 15 (1967): 343ff.
17 'Bericht über die Tätigkeit der landwirtschaftlichen Abteilung der NSDAP im Gau Sachsen', ND, no. 140.
18 For an analysis of the uneven progress in Bavaria, E. Frölich and M. Broszat, 'Politische und soziale Macht auf dem Lande. Die Durchsetzung der NSDAP im Kreis Memmingen', *VJH*, 25 (1977): 546–72. Heberle, *Landbevölkerung und Nationalsozialismus*, has shown that peasants on the west coast of Schleswig-Holstein were more likely to vote NSDAP than those on the east coast.
19 Clauss, *Erfahrungen aus 50 Jahren*, 8–10.
20 Heberle, *Landbevölkerung und Nationalsozialismus*.
21 M. Vogt, 'Zur Finanzierung der NSDAP zwischen 1924 und 1928', *Zeitschrift für Geschichte und Wissenschaft* 4 (1970): 234ff. for a general account.
22 Reinhardt to Himmler, 5 March 1929, ADC, Himmler.
23 J. von Kruedener, 'Zielkonflikt in der nationalsozialistischen Agrarpolitik', *Zeitschrift für Wirtschaft und Sozialwissenschaften*, 94 (1974), 335ff. for a summary on these lines.
24 For the period from January to June 1933 on Hugenberg's ministry see J. Farquharson, *The Plough and the Swastika* (Beverly Hills, Calif., 1976), ch. 4.
25 See Darré's speech to the NSDAP Party Congress, Nuremberg, 2 September 1933, quoted in the *Völkischer Beobachter*, 3/4 September 1933.
26 F. Burgdörfer, *Der Geburtenrückgang und seine Bekämpfung* (Berlin, 1929).
27 cf. the 6 March 1930 programme in the *Völkischer Beobachter*.
28 See, for example, R. W. Darré, 'Bauer und Landwirt', in H. Reischle (ed.), *Deutsche Agrarpolitik* (Berlin, 1934), 46.
29 Fragmentation had long been a problem, especially in south and west Germany; of 3 million agricultural holdings in the country as a whole, well over 50 per cent were under 5 hectares in size, and a further 619,000 between 5 and 10 hectares. *Wirtschaft und Statistik*, 1934, 554.
30 See correspondence 7 May and 1 September 1938, Hauptstaatsarchiv, Nord Rhein-Westfalen, Kaiserswerth, 1012.
31 This process of removing him was known as *Abmeierung*, and in bad cases of failure could lead to the installation of a trustee. L. Weiss, *Die Abmeierung* (Leipzig, 1936).
32 In mid-1938 there were 684,997 *Erbhöfe* enrolled, out of a total number of 847,028 farms between 7½ and 125 hectares in size (7½ hectares was the usual lower limit criterion). *Vierteljahrsheft zur Statistik des Deutschen Reichs*, 1939, section II, p. 38.
33 Dr. Petersen, *Deutsche Zeitung*, 17 June 1934.
34 F. Grundmann, *Agrarpolitik im Dritten Reich; Anspruch und Wirklichkeit des Reichserbhofgesetzes* (Hamburg, 1979), 55.
35 Von Rohr's manuscript, 'Beitrag zur deutschen Agrarpolitik', BA-Kleine Erwerbung no. 4, 32ff.
36 Letter of 24 May 1938, ADC, Reichnährstand Wagner.
37 See Regierungspräsident Brandenburg report, July 1934, BA-R43/II 193.
38 Haushofer, *Ideengeschichte der Agrarwirtschaft und Agrarpolitik* 2:104, and Holt, *German Agricultural Policy*, 209. For agrarian pressure in this respect in the 1920s see correspondence in April 1925, Hauptstaatsarchiv, Baden-Württemberg, 343, E/130 IV.
39 As an example of how apparently arbitrary enrolment could be, a 20·33 hectare farm was rejected at an *Erbhof* court in Bamberg whereas in Hamburg a market garden of 5·5 hectares was taken in. W. Herferth, 'Der Reichsnährstand – ein Instrument der Krieg-

spolitik des faschistischen deutschen Imperialismus', *Wissenschaftliche Zeitschrift der Universität Rostock* 17 (1968): 231.

40 H. Haushofer, cited in Gies, 'Der Reichnährstand – Organ berufsständischer Selbst verwaltung oder Instrument staatlicher Wirtschaftslenkung?', *Zeitschrift für Agrargeschichte und Agrarsoziologie*, 21 (1973): 220.

41 Backe referred to Ruhland's book *Die internationale landwirtschaftliche Konkurrenz*, pub. 1901, in the 1920s. NB, file 5, no. 9.

42 According to Dr. Reischle, in an interview in February 1970.

43 Gies, 'Der Reichsnährstand', 223ff. for this section.

44 For NSDAP neo–mercantilism, G. Kroll, *Von der Weltwirtschaftskrise zur Staatskonjunktur* (Berlin, 1958), 456.

45 'The liberal economic motor has an empty tank.' H. Backe, 'Grundsätze einer lebensgesetzlichen Agrarpolitik', in Reischle (ed.), *Deutsche Agrarpolitik*, 71.

46 H. Reischle, *Die deutsche Ernährungswirtschaft* (Berlin, 1935), 5.

46 Cabinet minutes, February–March 1933, BA-R43/I 1460.

48 See L. Zumpe, *Wirtschaft und Staat in Deutschland 1933 bis 1945* (Berlin, 1980), 100ff.

49 cf. M. Broszat, *The Hitler State* (London, 1981). The best sources for the actual organization of the RNS are H. Reischle and W. Saure, *Der Reichsnährstand – Aufbau, Aufgaben und Bedeutung* (Berlin, 1936), and W. Meinhold, *Grundlagen der landwirtschaftlichen Marktordnung* (Berlin, 1937).

50 Correspondence, July 1934, BA-R43/II 193.

51 Conference minutes, 26 November 1934, Hauptstaatsarchiv, Niedersachsen, 122a XXXII 80, and Darré to Goering, 1 November 1936, ND, no. 146

52 Kroll, *op. cit.*, 539, citing C. W. Guillebaud and C. von Dietze. See also A. Hanau and R. Plate, *Die deutsche landwirtschaftliche Markt – und Preispolitik im Zweiten Weltkrieg* (Stuttgart, 1975), 32–3 for a similar assessment.

53 Visiting inspector of British Ministry of Agriculture and Fisheries Ministry, London, May 1945, PRO, F.O. 371/46884.

54 Minister of Agriculture and Fisheries to Attlee, Armistice and Postwar Committee of Cabinet, 20 July 1944, PRO, CAB 87/66.

55 *Statistisches Jahrbuch des Deutschen Reiches 1941–2*, (Berlin, 1942), p. 358.

56 W. Bauer and P. Dehen, 'Landwirtschaft und Volkseinkommen', *Vierteljahrsheft zur Wirtschaftsforschung* 4 (1938–9): 427.

57 W. Clauss, *Erfahrungen aus 50 Jahren*, 17.

58 Cabinet minutes, November 1934, BA-R43/I 1470.

59 See his article 'Diener des Volkes', *Völkischer Beobachter*, 1 January 1935.

60 See especially T. W. Mason, *Sozialpolitik im Dritten Reich* (Opladen, 1977), ch. 1.

61 Correspondence, July 1934, BA-R43/II 193. See his comments in Cabinet, November 1934, BA-R43/I 1470.

62 Report, August 1935, BA-R43/II 318.

63 Correspondence, May 1938, BA-R43/II 194.

64 The fact that Germany continued to buy foreign food does not mean that the *Erzeugungschlacht* was a failure. Darré was perfectly prepared to accept any treaty which entailed such purchases, as imports could no longer bring down prices in Germany. See his letter to Reich Chancellery, 13 January 1934, BA-R43/II 305c and further correspondence BA-R43/II 303b and 303c.

65 cf. his letter to Goering, 1 November 1936, ND, no. 146.

66 *Gesetz zur Sicherung der Landbewirtschaftung, Reichsgesetzblatt* (I) 1937, pp. 442ff. It is interesting to note that Darré asked that as little use be made of the legislation as possible, true to his idea of avoiding compulsion. Letter to the cabinet, 16 July 1937, BA-R2/18018.,

67 *Statistisches Jahrbuch*, 663.

68 Hitler awarded Darré a further RM60 million. D. Petzina, *Autarkiepolitik im Dritten Reich* (Stuttgart, 1968), 33ff.

69 At the RNS Congress in October 1938 Darré estimated that 800,000 people had left the land since 1933.

70 Petzina, *Autarkiepolitik*, 93–5. If all foodstuffs produced in Germany were reckoned in

grain equivalent, total indigenous production rose in four years from 34·7 million tons to 41·5, or by almost 20 per cent. Clauss, *Erfahrungen aus 50 Jahren*, 19.

71 Reischle put the savings for 1938 alone at RM2 billion. Cited in Herferth, 'Der Reichsnährstand', 226.

72 Grain reserves were 6½ million tons. H.-J. Riecke, 'Ernährung und Landwirtschaft im Zweiten Weltkrieg', in *Bilanz des Zweiten Weltkriegs* (Berlin, 1953), 333–4.

73 Memo to Hitler, 21 January 1939; a Chancellery reply, 5 February 1939, makes it clear that Hitler had seen this. BA-R43/II 213b.

74 Food Group Staff of Four-Year Plan conference, 29 March 1939, BA-R26/IV 12.

75 *Europas Nahrungsmittelversorgung*, 19 May 1940, BA-NS 10/107.

76 Undated memo of Food Group Staff of Four-Year Plan conference, 1942, p. 7, BA-R26/IV 51.

77 NB, BA, 'Grosser Bericht', 40.

78 Food Group Staff of Four-Year Plan conference, 18 September 1941, BA-R26/IV 51.

79 Letter to Ministry of Finance, 25 November 1939, BA-NS 10/107.

80 M. Ohlsen, 'Ständischer Aufbau und Monopole', *Zeitschrift für Geschichtswissenschaft* 1 (1974): 42–3 suggests from the foundation of the RNS.

81 Herferth, quoted in Zumpe, *Wirtschaft und Staat*, sees the *Erzeugungsschlacht* as the start of a war economy.

82 Zumpe, *Wirtschaft und Staat*, 121.

83 P. Hüttenberger, 'Nationalsozialistische Polykratie', *Geschichte und Gesellschaft*, 2 (1976): 430ff.

84 J. Lehmann, 'Zur Funktion des "Bäuerlichen Berufserziehungswerkes" in den Plänen der faschistischen Agrarführung während des Zweiten Weltkrieges', *Zeitschrift der Universität Rostock* 25 (1976): 800.

85 See H. Winkler, 'Faschismus als soziale Bewegung', in W. Schieder (ed.), *Deutschland und Italien im Vergleich* (Hamburg, 1979), 109.

86 As Gies points out, 'Der Reichsnährstand', 230. Against this, Herferth maintains that it was never more than a subordinate organ (*Unterbau*) of the Ministry of Food and Agriculture. Cited in Zumpe, *Wirtschaft und Staat*, 100ff.

87 Gies, 'Der Reichsnährstand', 232.

88 Riecke, 'Ernährung und Landwirtschaft', 340, gives the basic daily rations for normal consumers in Germany as 1,990 calories in 1941, 1,750 in 1942, then a rise to 1,980 and 1,930 in 1943 and 1944 respectively (in January of each of these years). Since some extra food was always available, daily consumption would be at least 300 calories in excess of these figures.

89 Under Weimar 57,457 new holdings were provided, in total over 600,000 hectares (average size 10·5 hectares): between 1933 and 1939 only 20,408 *Erbhöfe* were produced in the east, with 328,500 hectares (approximately 16 hectares in size on average). C. Horkenbach, *Das Deutsche Reich 1918–1933* (Berlin, 1935), 748 and F. Wunderlich, *Farm Labor in Germany 1810–1945* (Princeton, N.J., 1961), 179.

90 For the way in which defence took precedence, Dr. Vager, 'Gegenwartsprobleme der ländlichen Siedlung', *Deutsche Siedlung*, 5 March 1937.

91 G. H. Kleine, 'Adelsgenossenschaft und Nationalsozialismus', *VJH* 26 (1978); 113–14, citing a speech by Darré to peasants in 1934.

92 In any case, he disliked the existing German aristocrats as such; he accused them of grave incompetence in pre-1914 Germany. See his essay 'Adelserneuerung oder Neuadel?', 8 January 1931, cited in Kleine, 'Adelsgenossenschaft', 113.

93 This is the reason offered in K. Hildebrand, *The Third Reich* (London, 1984), 11.

94 Kleine, 'Adelsgenossenschaft', 133.

95 See R. Kühnl, 'Problem einer Theorie über den internationalen Faschismus', Part II, *Politische Vierteljahrsschrift* 1 (1975): 110.

96 J. Radkau, 'Entscheidungsprozesse und Entscheidungsdefizite in der deutschen Aussenwirtschaftspolitik 1933–1940', *Geschichte und Gesellschaft*, 2 (1976): 49–50; C. Bloch, *Die S.A. und die Krise des nationalsozialistischen Regimes*, 1934 (Frankfurt, 1970), 143ff. also maintains that from 1934 the Junkers lost influence to a real degree.

97   Herferth, 'Der Reichsnährstand', 226. He also makes the point that higher prices for agrarian products in east Germany assisted the Junkers financially. ibid., 227.

98   See correspondence, May–July 1933, Institut für Zeitgeschichte, Munich, Fa 508.

99   Zumpe, *Wirtschaft und Staat*, 110. She also alleges (p. 105), quite incorrectly, that Hugenberg and von Rohr were responsible for the introduction of the Prussian antecedent to the EHG, the *Bäuerliches Anerbenrecht*, in May 1933. In fact, the detailed planning of this was done by Willikens, Backe and Kerrl to keep it concealed from Hugenberg. See Backe to Darré, 15 April 1933, ADC, Reichsnährstand, Backe.

100 Kleine, 'Adelsgenossenschaft', 134.

101 Correspondence in October 1933, BA-R43/I 1301 and June–July 1934, BA-R43/II 207. For its effect on the settlement programme, Bramwell, 'National Socialist agrarian theory and practice'.

102 As a result Darré broke with Himmler in February 1938. For his rejection of the *Wehrbauern* scheme as 'impractical', Koehl, *RKFDV*, 44, 52.

103 *NS Landpost*, 2 March 1944, cited in Lehmann, 'Zur Funktion'.

104 Hanau and Plate, *Die deutsche landwirtschaftliche Markt*, 24.

105 ibid., 122–3.

106 According to his own account, 'Aufzeichnung HB über ein Gespräch mit Goering', NB, BA, file 5, no. 32.

107 Correspondence, January–February 1941, BA-R14/371.

108 Backe to Behrens, Deputy Head of RNS, 9 May 1944, NB II, no. 32.

109 For Backe's ideological background, his Nachlass is valuable testimony: the contributor wishes to thank his widow, Frau Backe of Hanover, for her kind permission to use this source.

110 For Broszat's point, *The Hitler State*, 176–8. The land consolidation (*Umlegung*) programme is detailed in *Reichsumlegungsgesetz*, 16 June 1937.

Notes on Contributors

J. E. FARQUHARSON is a Lecturer in Modern European History in the School of European Studies at Bradford University. He is the author of *Europe from Below* (with Stephen Holt) and *The Plough and the Swastika*, a study of National Socialist agrarian policy.

IAN FARR has been a lecturer in European History at the University of East Anglia since 1976. He is preparing a study of peasant society and politics in Bavaria before the First World War and has published articles on peasant organizations, anticlericalism and charivaris in nineteenth-century Bavaria.

LARRY EUGENE JONES teaches modern European and modern German history at Canisius College in Buffalo. He is preparing a study of political liberalism in the Weimar Republic and has published many articles on the social, economic and political history of Germany in the 1920s.

ROBERT G. MOELLER teaches modern European social history at Columbia University in New York. He has recently completed a study of the west German peasantry during the First World War and the postwar inflation, *German Peasants and Agrarian Politics, 1914–24: A Study of the Rhineland and Westphalia*, and has published articles on the peasantry in the Kaiserreich and Weimar.

JOSEF MOOSER teaches modern German social history at the University of Bielefeld. He is the author of *Arbeiterleben in Deutschland 1900–1970: Klassenlagen, Kultur und Politik*, and *Ländliche Klassengesellschaft 1770–1848: Bauern und Unterschichten, Landwirtschaft und Gewerbe im östlichen Westfalen*. He has also published many articles on nineteenth-century rural society and peasant protest in Germany.

JONATHAN OSMOND is a Lecturer in History at the University of Leicester. His research and publications have focused on the problems of the German peasantry in the post-First World War inflation. He is completing a doctoral dissertation at St. Antony's College, Oxford, on agrarian politics in the Bavarian Palatinate during the Weimar Republic, and is also preparing a book on modern Germany.

HANS-JÜRGEN PUHLE is Professor of History at the University of Bielefeld. He has published widely in the areas of comparative agrarian history, Latin American history and the history of the Kaiserreich. His most important publications include *Agrarische Interessen und preussischer Konservatismus im Wilhelminischen Reich (1893–1914)* and *Politische Agrarbewegungen in kapitalistischen Industriegesellschaften: Deutschland, USA und Frankreich im 20. Jahrhundert*.

HANNA SCHISSLER is a Research Associate at the Georg-Eckert-Institut für international Schulbuchforschung in Braunschweig. She is the author of *Preussische Agrargesellschaft im Wandel* and has written widely on agrarian reform, Prussian finance reform and economic development in the nineteenth century. She is currently completing a social history of the Junkers in modern Germany.

260

Index

Abel, Wilhelm 2, 45 n.9
Abfindung 240–1
Agrarian League (*Bund der Landwirte*): anti-
democratic stance 36, 106; anti-
modernization policy 112; attempted
coalitions 90; in Bavaria 130, 173, 175;
CDI relations 105; economic and political
role 89–90, 93, 96, 102, 113, 172; electoral
agreements with Centre 72; ethos 96–7;
expansion 92, 103, 131, 172, 175;
extremism 103; foundation (1893) 35, 87,
89, 121, 168; hegemony 102, 106;
ideology 93–5, 96–8, 103–5; imperialism
97; intermittent opposition to
government 103; Junker domination 8,
35, 36, 98, 112, 168; membership
statistics 187; merger with Rural League
199; Nazi infiltration 192; peasant protest
role 98; pressure from Council of
People's Commissars 176; Puhle's
research 2, 8–9; radicalism 103; Reichstag
activities 95; relations with DNVP and
DVP 199; social imperialism 96–8;
structure 188
agriculture (-cultural): Association(s) 117,
126, 132, 172, 187; capitalism 52–3;
Chamber for the Rhine Province 172;
Chambers 88, 89; crises (1820s) 56,
(1870s) 110–11; distress 198; East Elbian
43, 49 n.59, 81, 145; employers'
federations 188; employment 3–4, 83;
exports 101; imports 202; indebtedness
146; landholdings 84; modernization 56,
114, 172; policy 169; production 149–52,
156–9; Revolution 2; subsidies 89; tariff
200. *See also Reichsnährstand*
Allen, William Sheridan 16
anti-Semitism 93, 94–6, 98, 117–18, 130,
132, 174, 175
Autobahnen 250

Backe, Herbert 233–4, 236, 249, 253
Baden: confessional politics 190; early
peasant associations 90–1; economic
problems 189; Peasants' Association 174,
182–3; Protestant parties 190–1; Rural
League 183
barley 146
barter 160

Bauernführer 113
Bavaria(n): Agrarian League membership
122–3; Agricultural Association 117;
Agricultural Council 172; Allgäu politics
118; anticlericalism 9, 125, 126, 127; anti-
liberalism 116; Artamanen 233;
Bodenzinse campaign 124–5, 128, 130;
Catholic hierarchy 119, 121; Christian
Peasants' Association 91, 123, 128–31,
183; Church/government friction
118–19; credit co-operatives 117, 118;
defeat by Prussia 115; elections (1924)
201, (1932) 221; electoral reform 133;
entailed estates 191; Free Peasantry 185–6;
grain delivery strikes 186; grain
production 120, 189; indirect suffrage
119; *Landtag* 118, 119, 122, 185;
integration into Empire 118; Ministry of
Agriculture 189; owner-occupiers 115;
Patriotic peasant protest 11–12, 115–33;
Peasants' Associations 115–17; Peasants'
League (BBB) 9, 91, 122–3, 137 n.65,
184–5, 186, 190, 200–1, 203, 205, 207;
Prime Minister 184; property prices 121;
railways 124; Reichstag representation
121, 122, 222; revolution (1918–19) 184,
201; Rural League (BLB) 184; rural
taxation 120; secession threats 127, 184,
191; sovereignty 115. *See also* Political
Parties
BBB, *see* Bavarian Peasants' League
Beckh, Friedrich 116–17
Belgian occupation forces 176
Bendix, Reinhard 44
Berger, Suzanne 1
Berlin 86, 89
Bethge, Albert 207
bimetallism 95
birth-rate 238
Birkenfeld 173
Bismarck, Prince Otto Eduard von:
appointment as Minister President 81;
conservatism 1; internal colonization
policy 250; manipulative techniques 105;
support of Junkers 7; tariff policy 99,
116
Blackbourn, D. 123
Blasius, Dirk 54–5, 75–6
Bloch, Marc 54

261